THE EVOLUTION OF SEX

THE EVOLUTION OF SEX
An Examination of Current Ideas

Edited by Richard E. Michod
UNIVERSITY OF ARIZONA, TUCSON

and Bruce R. Levin
UNIVERSITY OF MASSACHUSETTS, AMHERST

SINAUER ASSOCIATES INC. • PUBLISHERS
SUNDERLAND, MASSACHUSETTS

THE COVER

"Yellow and Blue Iris," an oil painting by Lowell Nesbitt.
Courtesy of McNay Art Museum, San Antonio, Texas.

THE EVOLUTION OF SEX: AN EXAMINATION OF CURRENT IDEAS

Copyright © 1988 by Sinauer Associates Inc.

For information address Sinauer Associates Inc.,
Sunderland, Massachusetts 01375

Library of Congress Cataloging-in-Publication Data

The Evolution of sex: an examination of current ideas
    edited by Richard E. Michod and Bruce R. Levin.
            p.   cm.
    Bibliography: p.
    Includes index.
    ISBN 0-87893-458-8
    ISBN 0-87893-459-6 (pbk.)
    1. Genetic recombination.   2. Evolution.   I. Michod, Richard E.
II. Levin, Bruce R.
QH443.E96 1987
575'.9—dc19   87-22520
                                                                        CIP

This book is printed on paper that meets the guidelines
for permanence and durability of the Committee on
Production Guidelines for Book Longevity of the Council
on Library Resources.

Printed in U.S.A.

4   3   2   1

Contents

Preface

Problems do not exist in nature.
Nature only knows solutions.
A. Lwoff

Science is replete with small problems which are the objects of intense investigation. (Of course, those who work on these problems do not see them as anything other than profound—small problems are studied by other people.) The perception of the importance of a problem and how close we are to its solution are subjective matters and, within evolutionary biology, there is generally little agreement about this. The evolution of sex is one of the few exceptions to this rule. A survey of evolutionary biologists would doubtless come up with a consensus that the elucidation of the selective pressures responsible for the origin and maintenance of sex is a "big" (maybe the "biggest") unsolved problem in evolutionary biology. Or so it seems to us, who have worked on this problem and have now edited this collection.

While there may well be agreement about the importance of the problem of the evolution of sex, there is no consensus about where its solution lies. The present collection certainly reflects this—the authors of these chapters advocate a number of particular hypotheses. As with other recent works on the subject, the problem is aired, the controversy is sharpened, but no clear solution emerges. However, we believe this book differs from earlier treatises on this subject in at least two significant ways: (1) the scope is broader—more different kinds of hypotheses are examined, sex in prokaryotes is considered, and there is more extensive consideration of the molecular basis of recombination; and (2) there are signs that a pluralistic view of this problem is emerging, i.e., the possibility of multiple mechanisms contributing to the evolution of sex is becoming accepted. When we planned this collection, we wanted a comprehensive, up-to-date, and critical view of the problem of the evolution of sex. We believe we have achieved these goals and more.

We owe debts of gratitude to many people. First and foremost, we thank the contributors. As the reader will see, this is not just a collection of independent reviews. These chapters are syntheses of the subject at large and a forum for the presentation of new ideas as well as the critical reexamination of older ideas. The contributors served as reviewers of each others' chapters, a process that has enhanced the quality of this collection, made it more cohesive, and added elements of a debate.

Janet Wolkenstein constructed the bibliography from the individual lists of references provided by the authors. Joanne Fraser copy edited the chapters.

Carol Wigg coordinated the editorial activities involved in this endeavor. We greatly appreciate the quality of their efforts. We wish to acknowledge and express our appreciation to those who maintain and support BITnet, the inter-university computer communication network (a giant step towards the universal University), which greatly facilitated our editorial tasks. Finally and most importantly, we wish to thank Andy Sinauer for his moral, intellectual, and economic support of this project. We hope this volume will be as well received and as useful as the other books in evolutionary biology published by Sinauer Associates.

RICHARD E. MICHOD, *Tucson*
BRUCE R. LEVIN, *Amherst*
September, 1987

The Contributors

GRAHAM BELL, Department of Biology, McGill University, Montreal, PQ H3A 1B1, Canada

HARRIS BERNSTEIN, Department of Microbiology and Immunology, University of Arizona School of Medicine, Tucson, AZ 85721

LISA D. BROOKS, Biomedical Department, Brown University, Providence, RI 02912

JAMES F. CROW, Laboratory of Genetics, University of Wisconsin, Madison, WI 53706

RAYMOND DEVORET, GEMC Enzymology, CNRS, F-91190 Gif-sur-Yvette, France

JOSEPH FELSENSTEIN, Department of Genetics, University of Washington, Seattle, WA 98195

MICHAEL T. GHISELIN, California Academy of Sciences, San Francisco, CA 94119

WILLIAM D. HAMILTON, Department of Zoology, University of Oxford, Oxford OX1 3PS, England

DONAL A. HICKEY, Department of Biology, University of Ottawa, Ottawa, Ontario K1N 6N5, Canada

ROBIN HOLLIDAY, Genetics Division, National Institute for Medical Research, Mill Hill, London NW7 1AA, England

FREDERIC A. HOPF, Optical Sciences Center, University of Arizona, Tucson, AZ 85721

BRUCE R. LEVIN, Department of Zoology, University of Massachusetts, Amherst, MA 01003

DAVID G. LLOYD, Department of Plant and Microbial Sciences, University of Canterbury, Christchurch 1, New Zealand

J. MAYNARD SMITH, Population Biology Group, University of Sussex, Falmer, Brighton BN1 9QG, England

RICHARD E. MICHOD, Department of Ecology and Evolutionary Biology, University of Arizona, Tucson, AZ 85721

MICHAEL R. ROSE, Department of Ecology and Evolutionary Biology, University of California, Irvine, CA 92717

JON SEGER, Department of Biology, University of Utah, Salt Lake City, UT 84112

WILLIAM M. SHIELDS, Department of Environmental and Forest Biology, SUNY College of Environmental Science and Forestry, Syracuse, NY 13210

ROBERT TRIVERS, Department of Biology, University of California, Santa Cruz, CA 95064

MARCY K. UYENOYAMA, Department of Zoology, Duke University, Durham, NC 27706

GEORGE C. WILLIAMS, Department of Ecology and Evolution, State University of New York at Stony Brook, Stony Brook, NY 11794

INTRODUCTION

Richard E. Michod and Bruce R. Levin

A very obvious biological consequence of sex is the generation of new combinations of genes by mixing genomes, or portions thereof, from different individuals. This "mixis" has fundamental implications for both genetics and the evolutionary process. It makes the study of genetics by classical, in vivo, procedures possible—without mixis genes would be transmitted in large blocks and it would not be possible to "see" individual genes, much less determine their positions on chromosomes. Without the mixis generated by sex, adaptive evolution would simply consist of the sequential selection of mutations in genetically independent lineages. However, as a result of mixis, adaptive evolution becomes much more complicated and, at the same time, more interesting. With mixis the rate of increase of a particular genotype depends upon properties of other genotypes, and, as a result, phenotypic properties, and arguments which are based solely on them (such as optimization and ESS arguments), are not sufficient to predict evolution of a trait without knowledge of the underlying genetic system. Without the mixis produced by sex, there would not be species as we know them. Many other evolutionary consequences of mixis are discussed in the chapters that follow.

While biologists may agree that mixis is a fundamental consequence of sex, there is much less agreement concerning the mechanisms responsible for the origin and maintenance of sex. There is no doubt that heritable variation in fitness is the fuel of adaptive evolution and that sex can, although perhaps rarely, generate new combinations of alleles that are adaptive. However, it is not at all obvious whether the new adaptive combinations of alleles produced by sex are sufficient to confer a selective advantage on sexual individuals. There is considerable difference of opinion about whether, how and when mixis can be the proximal selective force responsible for the origin and maintenance of sex. As the reader will see, the chapters that follow illustrate this lack of consensus about the role of mixis in the evolution of sex. Some authors argue that there is a benefit per se for mixis, but these authors may differ in the postulated mechanisms by which this benefit is generated (Crow, Maynard

1

Smith, Bell, Ghiselin, Seger and Hamilton). Other authors view mixis as a coincidental effect of other more basic consequences of sex such as repair of errors in DNA (Bernstein et al., Shields, Holliday) or the transfer of infectious elements (Levin, Hickey and Rose). Some authors are more pluralistic and accept the DNA repair view for prokaryotes and the mixis view for eukaryotes (Crow, Maynard Smith, Brooks).

When Weismann (1889) realized that many of the variations which exist between individuals are not passed on through the germ line, he pointed to sex as the process which produces the needed new variation to fuel evolution. This view was further refined by Fisher (1930) and Muller (1932), who argued that the mixis generated by sex might benefit species by increasing their rate of evolution. However, it has proven difficult to produce explicit models that show that mixis accelerates adaptive evolution. The reasons are easy to see and are mentioned often in the chapters that follow. First, new combinations of alleles produced by sex may be either more fit or less fit than the parental combinations. Second, even if a new combination of alleles is more fit, it may be destroyed in subsequent generations by the very sexual process that created it. As Felsenstein (Chapter 5) discusses and Seger and Hamilton illustrate (Chapter 11), linkage disequilibrium must play a central role in clarifying both the individual level and the species level effects of mixis, since the primary effect of mixis in both cases is the reduction of linkage disequilibrium.

The effect of sex on the rate of evolution has frequently been addressed but never really resolved, as Williams (Chapter 17) points out. Nevertheless, several chapters concede (Crow, Maynard Smith, Williams), on the basis of the taxonomic distribution of sexual and asexual reproduction, that species-level benefits must have played a role in the evolution of sex. However, if the chapters that follow are an indication, the question of whether sex benefits a species by accelerating its evolution appears to have been sidestepped, rather than resolved, by the more pressing problem of short-term benefits to individuals. Hypotheses considering individual benefits form the basis of most of the chapters in this book.

The concern in the book with potential individual benefits of sex reflects the fact that the costs of sex to the individual are usually high (see chapters by Crow, Ghiselin, Seger and Hamilton, and Williams) and these costs are unlikely to be compensated for by benefits to the species. As Williams and others point out, the costs of sex are explicit and borne by individual organisms, while the postulated benefits of sex have been vague and not readily modeled. The crises involving the question of sex can be seen clearly in this contrast between the costs and benefits of sex. Are the postulated benefits of sex sufficient to overcome its costs?

As already mentioned, the chapters that argue that mixis has benefits at the individual level differ in the benefits that are emphasized. Most make reference to varying selection pressures, although, again, they differ in the precise details of how this comes about. Crow (Chapter 4), while accepting that mixis arose initially as a byproduct of DNA repair in prokaryotes, argues that in higher eukaryotes mixis itself is beneficial for adaptation to varying environments, for efficient removal of deleterious mutations, and for bringing together advantageous mutations. Similarly, Bell (Chapter 8) argues that mixis provides efficient elimination of deleterious mutations and variation for adaptation to heterogeneous environments. Maynard Smith (Chapter 7) also accepts the view that sex evolved initially in prokaryotes for DNA repair but is maintained in higher eukaryotes because of the benefits of mixis in adapting to varying selection pressures caused by a shifting optimum value of a polygenically determined trait. Seger and Hamilton (Chaper 11) argue that mixis is beneficial in adapting hosts to their parasites by allowing hosts to track the fluctuating linkage disequilibrium generated by the frequency-dependent selection pressures inherent in parasite/host coevolution.

Although genetic variation is a necessary condition for evolution and sex through mixis produces genetic variation, it does not necessarily follow that mixis is the reason sex evolved. The problems in determining the conditions under which mixis is advantageous have led to other hypotheses concerning the evolution of sex. In these alternative hypotheses, mixis is not the primary advantage of sex. Indeed, several of these alternative hypotheses take an approach that is almost opposite to many of the arguments that are based on mixis. Whereas the genetic variation produced by mixis is often seen as a progressive force leading to the adaptive diversification of life, these alternative theories postulate that the primary evolutionary function of sex is a conservative one, the correction of genetic errors. The errors postulated to be corrected by sex include nonheritable damages (Bernstein et al., Shields, Levin) and heritable epigenetic defects (Holliday).

There is an interesting historical point here. At the time when Weismann was forming his theory of the germ line and his views on the role of sex in evolution, one common view on the benefit of sexual reproduction was rejuvenation at each generation (see Weismann, 1889 for a discussion of this view). However, in the 1800s no mechanism was available for the rejuvenating effects of sex and recombination and so this view fell into disfavor. This rejuvenation view of the benefit of sex is itself being rejuvenated, but in more mechanistic ways, in the chapters that view sex as an error-correction system (Bernstein et al., Levin, Holliday, Shields). Bernstein et al. (Chapter 9) argue that repair of genetic damages and complementation of deleterious mutations are the dominant selective forces behind sex, and that mixis is a by-product of repair. Levin (Chapter 12) supports a DNA repair mechanism for the evolution and maintenance of transformation (recombination by picking up free DNA) in bacteria. Shields argues that damage repair and elimination of deleterious mutations are the dominant forces behind the evolution of sex. Holliday, while accepting a role for repair of nonheritable genetic damages, argues that the primary function of meiotic recombination is to repair heritable epigenetic defects, specifically the pattern of methylation, thereby allowing normal development. Devoret

(Chapter 2) discusses the molecular details underlying the best understood recombination system, that of the bacterium *E. coli*, from the point of view of its dual role in promoting homologous recombination and DNA repair.

As should be apparent by now, there is no consensus concerning the answer to the question of the adaptive significance of sex. Hickey and Rose (Chapter 10) take a different approach altogether and challenge whether sex is to the advantage of the individuals practicing it. They develop a multi-stage scenario for the evolution of sex in which parasitic gene transfer is the dominant factor. In their schema, mixis of host genes was originally a coincidental byproduct of parasite transfer. A coincidental evolution hypothesis for mixis is also favored by Levin (Chapter 12) and Maynard Smith (Chapter 7) for plasmid- and phage-mediated recombination. In these cases sex (the capacity for infectious transfer) is encoded by genes borne by the plasmid or phage, rather than by host genes, and the mixis of host genes is viewed as a coincidental byproduct of evolution of the plasmid or phage. Bernstein et al. see mixis as a byproduct of damage repair—whether this repair occurs in prokaryotes or during meiosis in eukaryotes.

As mentioned above, the genes involved in mixis come from different individuals. This outcrossing aspect of sex is fundamental to the sexual process and is often achieved by mating between separate individuals. Consequently, several chapters focus on the outcrossing and mating aspects of sex. Trivers (Chapter 16) argues that mated males are more fit than mated females since females choose more fit males to mate with. He further argues that since recombination breaks up selected parental combinations of genes and since males are more selected than females, recombination rates (i.e. rates of mixis) will tend to be lower in males than in females. Mating raises a host of issues concerning who and how-related the mates are (see chapters by Uyenoyama and Shields), how many of each kind of parent there are, or how much of each type of tissue there is in the case of hermaphrodites (Lloyd).

SOME TERMINOLOGICAL POINTS

Not only does this collection reflect the diversity of approaches to the problem of sex and recombination, it also mirrors some of the semantic variation, including the uses of even the most basic terms, such as the terms "sex" and "recombination" themselves.

The word "recombination" is used in a variety of ways. The commonly accepted usage, which has a long history dating back at least to the work of Bridges and Morgan (1923), is mixis, as considered above. Recombination as mixis may include the acquisition of new genes, as mentioned in the chapter by Levin, but, more commonly in the chapters that follow, it refers to the generation of new combinations of existing alleles at multiple, homologous loci (Brooks, Crow, Levin, Felsenstein, Trivers, Seger and Hamilton). New combinations of alleles at multiple loci can be produced or enhanced by a variety of processes. Physical recombination (see below) may produce new combinations of alleles but, as Crow points out, new combinations are more often produced, at least in organisms with meiosis, by independent assortment of non-homologous chromosomes. Outcrossing also increases the combinations of alleles which can be produced by either physical recombination or independent assortment.

Another usage of "recombination," which is common in molecular biology, is physical breakage and rejoining of DNA molecules (Bernstein et al., Devoret, Maynard Smith, Holliday, Hickey and Rose). The molecular details of physical recombination are fundamental to an understanding of the evolution of mixis and are extensively treated by Devoret and also by Bernstein et al. Physical recombination may or may not result in new combinations of alleles at loci that flank the site of physical recombination (i.e. may not result in mixis; see discussion by Bernstein et al.). Confusion is possible unless the different usages of "recombination" are kept clear. For example, Maynard Smith uses "recombination" to refer to physical recombination and "crossing over" to refer to the production of new combinations of alleles, whereas Crow uses "crossing over" to refer to the cytological effects of physical recombination.

As discussed by Ghiselin and by Felsenstein, the word "sex" has a variety of meanings and the problem of sex is viewed differently by different authors. In this book, "sex" is often used as synonymous with recombination in the sense of mixis (Levin, Crow, Shields, Felsenstein, Trivers). By viewing the problem of sex as involving one central issue, mixis, a common explanation is often sought for all contributing factors. Other workers emphasize the components of sex, such as outcrossing and physical recombination, and raise the possibility that these components have different evolutionary explanations (Bernstein et al., Holliday, Brooks, Hickey and Rose, Williams). Several authors raise the possibility that the origin of sex may have a different explanation than its maintenance (Brooks, Maynard Smith, Crow, Williams, Hickey and Rose, Bernstein et al., Levin). It is also important to keep in mind that in most higher eukaryotes, sex and reproduction are tied together. However, in prokaryotes and single-celled eukaryotes, sex and reproduction are independent processes.

A FINAL EDITORIAL REMARK

Although there may appear to be a bewildering diversity of approaches to the problem of sex in the chapters that follow, there are basically only three distinct classes of hypotheses considered for the evolution and maintenance of this character: (1) those in which mixis itself is the object of (individual or group) selection; (2) those in which error correction is the character under selection; and (3) hypotheses in which sex is an adaptation for the transfer of infectious (parasitic) genetic elements. In the hypotheses of the latter two classes, mixis is seen as a coincidental byproduct of this evolution. While there are other ideas in the literature that may not fit this three-class scheme, these three kinds of hypotheses are the dominant ones today. While most of the chapters favor one kind of hypothesis over the others, there are also signs that the subject is moving into a phase of integration and synthesis of the different views. This is an important advance, for these hypotheses are not mutually exclusive and they all may have played a role in the evolution of this ubiquitous and seemingly peculiar character.

CHAPTER 1

THE EVOLUTION OF SEX:
A HISTORY OF COMPETING
POINTS OF VIEW

Michael T. Ghiselin

INTRODUCTION

The perspective from which scientists view a problem determines both what questions get asked and what is considered a legitimate answer. The current debate concerning the reason or reasons why sex exists began in the 1960s. Prior to that time it was customary to approach problems of adaptive significance from the point of view of what benefits accrue to the species. Now we ask a very different kind of question, considering what gets optimized by natural selection, and doing so from the point view of what happens to the individuals of which those species are composed. Evolutionary theory as currently understood does not provide for adaptations at the species level.

One does not have to consider sex from an evolutionary point of view at all, and even within the evolutionary perspective there is much diversity in approach. We can ask about sex from the point of view of evolutionary history or from the point of view of evolutionary mechanisms. We can approach the topic from a theoretical point of view or from an empirical one. Or we can ask about molecules, genes, chromosomes, organisms, populations, environments, niches, and all sorts of other things. Ideally, the diverse viewpoints in evolutionary biology ought to lend each other mutual support, and they often do. But scientists working on a topic like sex are apt to come from very different backgrounds and to possess quite different skills, interests, and abilities. They may disagree on what constitutes a legitimate question or an appropriate answer, or even what the facts are.

This chapter attempts to present the issues and, more importantly, to clarify them by considering the history of the problem. But history likewise has to be presented from one point of view or another. Because the audience here is a scientific one, it seems appropriate to emphasize the intellectual aspects of the problem of the evolution of sex, even though the social ones are fascinating too. While trying to minimize the autobiographical point of view, I could not completely avoid it. In order to emphasize that very distinction, I use the third person when referring to myself in the historical narrative, but not in the commentary.

The approach here has been a kind of "economic" history that emphasizes tradeoffs and optimality of the sort familiar to contemporary biologists (Ghiselin, 1986). There are costs and benefits to all kinds of behavior—investigative as well as sexual. Scientists are viewed as hard-working and enterprising people who are trying to make as many discoveries as they can, and to get credit for doing so, with the least expenditure with respect to time and other resources. An obvious example would be the application of optimal foraging strategies to literature searches. Scientists obviously cannot hope to read everything that might be useful to them. Thus they will read until they have satisfied themselves that they probably have not overlooked anything important and can get their manuscripts past the reviewers. What they read will also be affected by their backgrounds and abilities. Interdisciplinary reading tends to be scant and inefficient. For example, zoologists tend to miss things published in botany journals. And it matters a great deal what languages one knows, how much mathematical ability one has, and whether one enjoys reading old books. The picture that emerges from the present study is that ideas diffuse very slowly through the intellectual community, often with considerable distortion, and that a great deal of valuable insight gets lost and has to be rediscovered.

A variation on the same theme is that scientists do not work with complete theories or with complete bodies of knowledge. How could they? Too much is known to master more than a small area. Therefore scientists work with simplified versions of theories that leave out a great deal of detail, sometimes with unfortunate results. Viewing evolution as "survival of the fittest" is perhaps the crudest example of this practice. In general it seems that biologists accept a version of evolutionary biology sophisticated enough to solve the problems that interest them and only proceed further when faced with serious difficulties in interpreting their data.

PRE-DARWINIAN VIEWS ON SEX

The history of our problem really begins in the nineteenth century, but its prehistory deserves a few comments. The scientific literature on sex goes back to antiquity, and such authors as Aristotle have continued to influence both popular and scholarly thinking to the present day. In such discussion the topics of gender and reproduction have been intricately mingled with that of sex.

Aristotle's notion that the mother provides the substance and the father the form reappeared in the eighteenth century, when preformationists debated whether the embryo preexisted in the egg or in the sperm, and this controversy did not altogether disappear with the triumph of epigenesis in the nineteenth century. Namely, was there any real difference between sexual and asexual reproduction? By the same token, there were traditional notions about masculinity and femininity that persisted in attempts to develop theories of active and passive forces entering into fertilization (Geddes and Thompson, 1901). Finally, the use of our own species as a standard of comparison led to the assumption that sex is the general rule, later giving way to the view that it is characteristic only of the higher organisms. This last controversy is still with us.

Still with us too is the confusion of terminology about reproduction and sex. The various authors in this book do not all use the word "sex" in the same way, and they have to explain what they mean in the different chapters (see especially Felsenstein). "Sex" has had three basic meanings: (1) genital union, (2) gender, and (3) mixis. Sex in the sense of *genital union*—whether of gametes or of copulating organisms—is only of peripheral interest in this book. Mainly it is treated as one of the costs that have to be paid if there is sex in another sense. *Gender* means the differentiation into males, females, and such alternatives as hermaphrodites. It also includes the differences between sperm and eggs. Such differences are important because they create the circumstances that make sex a puzzle. Otherwise we are not much concerned about gender either. *Mixis* means the mixing of hereditary material in a way that produces new genotypes. It is of two kinds. In automixis, or selfing, just one parent gives rise to offspring that are genetically different from itself and from each other. In amphimixis, or outcrossing sex, two parents combine to produce genetically divergent offspring. "Recombination" is generally used as a synonym for mixis, but some authors use recombination as a more general term that includes a taking apart and reunion of the genetic material without forming a new combination (see Bernstein et al., in this volume).

The nineteenth century was a period of immense change in biology. The rise of evolutionary biology was one of several developments that were by no means unrelated. Sex was one of the central topics of investigation (Churchill, 1979; Farley, 1982). The fact that sex is not altogether necessary for reproduction was known from the fact that domestic plants could be propagated by cuttings. That individual aphids could reproduce in isolation had been well established during the arguments about preformation. However, the difference between sexual and asexual reproduction was most obscure. The cell theory was not established until the late 1830s (Schwann, 1839), and the role of the chromosomes was understood only in the 1880s and later.

A crucial document was Steenstrup's book on alternation of generations (Steenstrup, 1845). This work made it clear that many animals reproduce both sexually and asexually on a regular basis. Steenstrup tried to relate this to the traditional notion of a natural hierarchy, with the less perfect organisms being able to dispense with sex. There was no evolutionary progression here, but a minor change would easily give us the notion that the lowest organisms have no sex. Richard Owen (1849) followed with a book on parthenogenesis, or reproduction without fertilization. He suggested that the alternation of generations and production of offspring from unfertilized eggs were really one and the same process. The male provided a "spermatic force" that had to be renewed from time to time, but in lower organisms it lasted for several generations. Owen's bitter rival, Huxley (1854), attacked this view as unscientific and argued that the fertilized egg together with its asexual progeny constituted an "individual." The same themes recur in the later literature. Physiologists would argue that the sperm provides a stimulus. The need for a renewal would endure as a tendency to senescence and the need for rejuvenation of the lineage. Treating clones as individuals would later play an important role in evolutionary theory. But it is hard to say how much of a real historical connection exists here. We can say that the issue of parthenogenesis was largely clarified by work on Hymenoptera, especially bees, in which the males are produced without fertilization (von Siebold, 1857).

While the history of how the relationship between sexual and asexual reproduction came to be understood is too complicated to treat in detail here (see Farley, 1982), two points need to be mentioned. First, evolution provided much of the stimulus for investigating sexual phenomena, especially in relation to embryology. Beginning with the notion of Haeckel (1866) that the hereditary apparatus is located in the nucleus, the focus was eventually narrowed down to the chromosomes. Not until the details of meiosis had been worked out was it clear that there is a fundamental difference between sexual and asexual reproduction. Second, Darwin developed his theory while such matters were being debated.

DARWIN ON SEX

Darwin's views on sex evolved. In his earliest work, prior to the time he read Malthus and discovered natural selection, Darwin theorized that sex generates differences between parent and offspring, and that this is an adaptation that makes it possible for species to evolve (Darwin, 1839, p. 262). This hypothesis had been proposed by an earlier evolutionary theorist, his grandfather Erasmus Darwin (1794, p. 519). Charles Darwin later rejected this and other "group selection" theories for the same reason many later workers have: it does not provide a tight adaptive fit with the environment. After reading Malthus, Darwin concluded that the "final cause of sex" is that it keeps the amount of variation within certain limits. Again, he was not the first person to have considered this possibility. In his later writings on sex (which include several books), Darwin was very circumspect. From his experimental work on inbreeding he concluded that sex brings together the sexual elements of organisms that have been exposed to different environments and that these are more vigorous (Darwin, 1876).

The problem of inbreeding is by no means the same as that of possible advantages to diversity. There was also the problem of blending inheritance—crosses supposedly led to uniformity. But if selection had been going on in diverse lineages, crossing would unlock a store of latent variability. Darwin (1868) modeled his theory of variation and selection upon artificial selection. Wright (1968–78) likewise concluded from the study of artificial selection that natural selection is most effective where the population is broken up into genetically homogeneous units.

Darwin was profoundly aware of the individualistic character of selection. Although he occasionally used such expressions as "the good of the species," he explicitly denied the possibility of such adaptations. This is clear from his discussions of the evolution of social behavior, especially the origin of the neuter castes of social insects. He treated families as "individuals" subject to selection and also recognized the existence of kin selection (Darwin, 1859, Chap. 7). That such matters were not properly understood by his contemporaries is clear from Darwin's having to explain them to Wallace in their correspondence. Much of the history of evolutionary biology has to be understood as a history of the failure to understand this most fundamental point (see Ghiselin, 1969a, 1974a). Darwin not only discovered natural selection, he also worked out its implications in minute detail and devised a comprehensive system based on it. In order to do this, he had to master the fundamental principles. If one is less ambitious, one can get away with a more superficial treatment and save a lot of work, but the results are not always satisfactory.

EARLY NEO-DARWINISM

To August Weismann must go the credit or the blame for treating sex as a means of providing the variability necessary if natural selection is to work (Weismann, 1891, 1892; Churchill, 1985; Mayr, 1985). Weismann explicitly stated that sex exists for the good of the species, and even though Lloyd Morgan (1890–91, pp. 184–186, 193) pointed out the fallacy, this view remained the dominant one for nearly 80 years. Why this should have happened is something of a puzzle. The view does have a certain intuitive appeal, but that does not explain why it was not subjected to more critical scrutiny.

Weismann's Neo-Darwinism and the views that accompanied it need to be understood as presented in opposition to such alternatives as Neo-Lamarckism and orthogenesis. If one accepts the continuity of the germ plasm, then one has to be a selectionist. For Lamarckians and mutationists, there is no problem of individualistic selection because selection is not the cause of adaptation at all. Only when selectionists got to arguing among themselves would the issue become crucial. In putting down the Lamarckians, Weismann opted for the positions that would best support his own position. Sex as an adaptation was just one of these. He also proposed that senescence is an adaptation for the good of the species; it gets rid of the older generation and makes room for the younger one. Theories of sex and theories of aging have been intimately connected, and not just in Weismann's day. There has been a long tradition of comparing the history of species to the life of the individual organism and of treating sexual generation as a kind of rejuvenation. The notion that somatic tissues wear out and have to be replaced had an obvious economic analog in machinery. Perhaps the most able advocate of a rejuvenation hypothesis was Maupas (1889), who studied the nuclear changes in Protozoa. Weismann countered that it seemed difficult to imagine how one could take two defective objects, put them together, and get a good one. To us the obvious answer is that one can take different parts from two defective automobiles, and get a car that works.

We are getting somewhat ahead of our story here, but it is interesting that those who have been advocating a repair hypothesis for senescence and sex alike have continued to argue their case from a bioeconomic point of view, while the opposition has argued for models based upon population genetics. Kirkwood and Holliday's (1979) notion of a "disposable phenotype" and Pearl and Miner's (1935) survival curves for motorcars are part of a long tradition that originated in the nineteenth century and has never lacked advocates. Quite recently Bernstein et al. (1985a) have used bioeconomic arguments to support the DNA repair hypothesis for the adaptive significance of sex.

INFLUENCE OF GENETICS

The emergence of modern genetics under the rubric of Mendelism occurred at the beginning of this century, but not until the 1930s was the new genetics seen as complementary to natural selection rather than opposed to it. Indeed, the immediate effect of the rediscovery of Mendel's laws was the emergence of mutationism. It is often said that genetics corrected the errors of Darwinism, but most of those errors turn out to be things like blending inheritance and hopeful monsters—matters of error with respect to genetics, rather than reflections of something basically wrong with the theory of selection. Be that as it may, many of the problems we moderns have had in dealing with the evolution of sex can be traced to the early history of genetics. Early work on genetics focused upon the larger, more conspicuous differences that arose by mutation. Such mutations, especially those induced by ionizing radiation, were almost always injurious. If such mutations are in fact the source of the variations that are selected, and if they are exposed to selection by recombination, then the effect of sex would mostly be to lower fitness. But if mutation is inevitable, then sex might be a way of getting rid of deleterious mutations. Thus, from regarding selection from this negative point of view we get two results: first, we have such notions as a "load of mutations," and a "cost of evolution," and second, we have Muller's ratchet, or the principle that without sex, deleterious mutations will accumulate (Muller, 1932, 1964). Muller's main contribution to biology was his work on mutation, and his concern for the radiation damage was well justified. The notion that mutations are mainly deleterious led people to look for other sources of variation, especially recombination. However, a theory that treats recombination as if it results primarily in the exposure of deleterious mutations to selection will give very different results from one that treats it as shifting frequencies from one advantageous condition to another.

It is very easy to oversimplify genetics, and good biologists of course are aware of the problems. Nonetheless it has been easy to forget that genes are pleiotropic, that the environment is heterogeneous, and so on. The version of evolutionary biology, grounded in population genetics, that emerged from the work of Chetverikov, Fisher, Haldane, Wright, and others provided a sound basis for investigation that led to the Synthetic Theory in the 1930s and 1940s. But it was not without its pitfalls. In dealing with selection theory, as with physics, one begins with certain simplifying assumptions, such as a system without friction. One then proceeds to modify the assumptions so as to make the model a more realistic approximation to nature. But there is always a problem with respect to the assumptions one makes, especially the ones that are not explicit, such as total panmixia, no assortative mating, or infinite population size. If the model generates false predictions, one knows that something is wrong. Reconsideration of the underlying assumptions may or may not lead to a recognition of what is wrong with the model.

The architects of the Synthetic Theory, including such luminaries as Dobzhansky, Mayr, Rensch, Simpson, and Huxley as well as many peripheral figures, were mainly interested in applying the genetic theory to various areas of evolutionary biology and not in developing an alternative. In this endeavor they were behaving like any reasonable entrepreneur. There were opportunities for explaining all sorts of things, and to question the basic premises would have been a waste of time. Because selection gives rise to adaptation, there was no particular reason to ask about the details. Therefore Weismann's notion that sex benefits the population was simply taken for granted, and nobody bothered to look at group selection very seriously. Furthermore, Fisher (1930) had clearly stated that sex was the one aspect of biology that had to be explained in terms of advantage to the species, not the individual. Hence, up to the mid-1960s, outstanding evolutionary biologists treated sex and other reproductive activities from a populational point of view (Stebbins, 1960; Mayr, 1963).

MODERN VIEWS

Matters changed in the 1960s, when, as the synthesis matured and was extended, certain anomalies became apparent. Some of these anomalies arose within the developing paradigm, others from outside it. These anomalies, to be explained as we proceed, consisted of (1) the paradox of recombination, (2) the paradox of meiosis, and (3) the paradox of variability. These anomalies seem paradoxical because from the point of view of certain versions of evolutionary theory, recombination, sex, and a high level of genetic variability ought not to occur.

But evidently they do, and this caused a crisis such that the theories in question have had to be replaced or at least modified in some important respect.

Group selection and populational consequences

The impetus for rethinking our views on sex came from outside evolutionary biology proper. Group selection was invoked by ecologists and students of animal behavior in a manner that did not seem reasonable to the more criticial evolutionary theorists. The main targets of criticism were the Chicago School of ecologists (Allee et al., 1949) and the animal sociologist Wynne-Edwards (1962). The Chicago School notions of Emerson on group selection among social insects were challenged in a seminal paper by Hamilton (1964), in which a rigorous theory of kin selection was formulated for the first time. Much of the credit for opposing group selection goes to Maynard Smith and Williams. It is not without significance that Maynard Smith (1959, 1962) and Williams (1957) both did early work on the evolution of senescence (see also Hamilton, 1966). A book by Williams (1966) made the problems surrounding group selection, including the notion that sex benefits the species, a major topic of discussion among biologists.

There was a transitional period, however, when researchers focused on the long-term consequences rather than the immediate advantages of sex. Apart from the question of how sex actually gets selected, one could merely ask how the recombination it produces might affect the rate of evolution, especially relative to the obvious alternative, namely, mutation. Traditionally it had been assumed that sex would indeed speed up evolution by bringing together a wider diversity of parentage.

The problem is that recombination not only produces favorable combinations of genes, it also breaks them up. One might think that stabilizing selection would militate against recombination, especially in a stable environment, and the main effect of sex would be to get rid of deleterious mutations, as suggested by Muller (1932) and others. This led to considerable work on the effects of linkage disequilibrium and epistasis. Crow and Kimura (1965) concluded that "sexual reproduction can be a distinct disadvantage if evolution progresses mainly by putting together groups of individually deleterious, but collectively beneficial mutations," and concluded that recombination had been produced by intergroup selection. This evoked a reply from Maynard Smith (1968), who rejected the group advantage hypothesis and suggested that "sexual processes are an advantage because they make it possible to bring together in an individual, not merely mutations which have occurred in different ancestors (because the same result can be achieved equally well by recurrent mutation), but different regions of DNA which have been programmed by natural selection in different environments" (see also Crow and Kimura, 1969). In effect, Maynard Smith was arguing for recombination among the elements of diverse subpopulations, in a manner suggestive of the views of Wright and others. He later developed this argument, adding that sex should be advantageous in variable environments and establishing the connection between Muller's ratchet and the DNA repair hypothesis (Maynard Smith, 1971a, 1971b).

The question asked by Turner (1967), "Why does the genotype not congeal?" suggests that under stabilizing selection the most advantageous genotype ought to become fixed and invariable (see Brooks, in this volume). This in turn suggests that sexual populations are constantly changing, even in the case of apparent stasis. One solution is to propose that the environment is changing all the time. Another is that the population is changing. Real populations are finite in size: hence genetic drift would tend to erode the fitness of their members. Likewise, mutations would accumulate by virtue of Muller's ratchet. Felsenstein (1985, and in this volume) examined such possibilities. A paper presupposing group selection (Felsenstein, 1974) was followed by one giving similar results with organismal selection (Felsenstein and Yokoyama, 1976). Strobeck, Maynard Smith, and Charlesworth (1976) argued that linkage would allow genes for recombination to accumulate through a kind of "hitchhiking" effect. Although the paradox of recombination is not quite the same thing as the paradox of meiosis, the two are of course related.

Theories of individual advantage

Williams (1966) discussed the adaptive significance of sex as part of his critique of group selection. He mentioned a paper by Dougherty (1955) that treated sex as a mechanism of DNA repair, but did not discuss that hypothesis. Instead, he suggested that adaptations to changing environments might be treated from an organismal, rather than a populational, view and adumbrated his notions about environmental uncertainty that he would develop in much greater detail later.

Ghiselin's views owed a great deal to Williams, but had a different historical origin. Ghiselin did his early research on the comparative anatomy of reproductive systems. Subsequently he produced an analysis of Darwin's works, including those on sex (Ghiselin, 1969a). Ghiselin was working on his book when Williams's critique of group selection appeared, and it could hardly have come at a more appropriate time. Darwin understood the importance of individualistic selection remarkably well. A shift from thinking about groups to thinking about individual organisms was the crucial insight that Darwin had derived from Malthus. Darwin's theory of sexual selection could not be understood unless it was treated as a critical test of selection theory in general; for sexual selection is "pure" reproductive competition and can lead to maladapted species rather than adapted ones.

Williams looked upon sex as an important problem largely because it was hard to explain without invoking group selection, and hence viewed it as a threat to the Neo-Darwinian position. Ghiselin, on the other hand, was attracted by the opportunity for devising individualistic theories for sexual and reproductive phenomena. The first of these was a "size advantage model" for sequential hermaphroditism (sex switches). It was a straightforward but unexpected application of Darwin's theory of sexual selection and plays a significant role in sex allocation theory (Charnov, 1982).

In his paper on hermaphroditism, Ghiselin (1969b) suggested one way in which sex might benefit a sexual organism. Suppose there was a family with parental care and offspring that differed with respect to disease resistance. Let some of the offspring die from a plague. The parent could then allocate future resources to surviving offspring. Williams, who reviewed the paper for the journal in which it appeared, responded by drawing attention to a point that both of them had overlooked, but that had come to his attention from a book by Maynard Smith (1966): that mictic females pass on half as many genes to the next generation as parthenogenetic females do. Ghiselin was not very impressed, suggesting, among other things, that parthenogenetic clones are not parts of sexual populations. This of course was the "paradox of meiosis," which suggested that any proper theory of sex would have to give not just a competitive edge, but a twofold competitive edge, to organisms that reproduce sexually.

Ghiselin (1974a) treated various aspects of organic diversity from the point of view of individual advantage and economic principles. Ghiselin's explanation for sex has been called the "Tangled Bank" theory by Bell (1982). Briefly summarized, it asserts that in a saturated economy, it pays to diversify. When it is a seller's market for, say, automobiles, manufacturers should produce just one kind of good. But in a buyer's market, the manufacturers should produce a variety of automobiles of different sizes and costs. When they do, the market for such goods will actually increase; for example, some people will do without a car if only expensive ones are available. Translated into ecological jargon, diversity raises environmental carrying capacity by increasing the number of niches.

Like some other "ecological" theories, Tangled Bank invokes adaptation to environmental heterogeneity, but Bell (1982) suggested that what matters is "spatial" rather than "temporal" heterogeneity. Actually, what is heterogeneous is economic opportunity—"empty niches," in one sense. Therefore Bell's version of Tangled Bank would seem to be a restricted version of a more general hypothesis. The initial statement of the theory did consider competition within families to be a relevant consideration, but only because some group selectionists had explained sexual dimorphism as a means of reducing competition within the species. Equating Tangled Bank with competition reduction results from treating competition from a purely negative point of view (see Young, 1981); physicians do not become neurologists in order to avoid competition with ophthalmologists. Finally it should be emphasized that the Tangled Bank theory invokes frequency-dependent selection (Hutson and Law, 1981). In the classical version of the synthetic theory it was presupposed that polymorphism is unusual, the main reason for it being heterozygote advantage. The kind of balanced polymorphism we find among Batesian mimics was deemed unusual. The use of allozyme techniques led to the discovery of unexpectedly high levels of variation within natural populations—in other words, the "paradox of variation." The balance view, which invokes frequency-dependent selection, is one way of resolving the paradox (Lewontin, 1974). Frequency-dependent selection and the equilibria that result from it are straightforward implications of the well-known principle of diminishing marginal return upon investment.

Tangled Bank predicts that there will be more parthenogenesis and other forms of asexual reproduction in undersaturated environments, including those subject to unpredictable conditions and density-independent mortality. Environmental uncertainty hypotheses predict the opposite. Group selection hypotheses predict discontinuous distributions of sexuality, rather than clines and precise adjustment to environmental influences. Ghiselin (1974a) argued that the empirical data fitted the Tangled Bank theory better than the alternatives. Furthermore, it made sense as a more particular case of the global pattern of organic diversity in space and time. Bell (1982) elaborated the theory and went through an even more extensive review of the data and, taking more recent theoretical developments into consideration, again concluded that the Tangled Bank theory best fit the facts. Subsequently he has added some further evidence (Bell, 1985), as has Ghiselin (in press). Similar notions involving frequency-dependent selection have been discussed by Case and Taper (1986), whose model gives somewhat different results from that of Bell. Frequency-dependent selection has also been invoked by Antonovics and Ellstrand (1984; see also Ellstrand and Antonovics, 1985; and Seger and Hamilton, in this volume).

A somewhat analogous theory was proposed by Hamilton and May (1977) to account for dispersal, which Ghiselin (1974a) had treated as "an alternative to sex." Their model, which is counterintuitive, predicts substantial dispersal even in saturated and uniform habitats. As they stated, "the evolutionary pressure that commits at least half the offspring to migration, no matter how risky migration is, results from an advantage in arranging competitive interactions as far as possible with unlike genotypes."

Maynard Smith (1975) reviewed Ghiselin's book and with good reasons called it "infuriating." Williams and he had cast the problem of sexuality in terms of the twofold cost of meiosis, and Ghiselin had chosen to evade it by a kind of intellectual gerrymandering—asking why sex exists, not what was wrong with a theory that made it seem paradoxical. Maynard Smith (1978) later evened the score by ignoring the Tangled Bank theory altogether (but see Maynard Smith, in this volume).

Whatever the adaptive significance of sex may be, the paradox itself has evoked a great deal of commentary (Manning, 1976; Charlesworth, 1980a,b; Uyenoyama, 1984, 1985, 1986, 1987). One wonders if some underlying assumption is not false—much as were the notions about blending inheritance that plagued Darwin. For example, Steven C. Stearns has drawn my attention to the very common assumption that fitness can be measured by single-generation reproductive output. Analysis has clarified the distinction between an ecological cost of sex and a genetic cost of sex (Williams, 1980). A group of lineages in which half the organisms are male, and in which the males do not care for the young, should have half the reproductive output of a purely asexual assemblage. There are other costs to sexuality, such as those associated with finding a mate (Gerritsen, 1980; Lloyd, 1980; Lewis, 1983). None of this is to be equated with the genetic cost, which derives from the fact that meiosis means a parent contributes just half of the offspring's genome.

Efforts to resolve the paradox have sometimes attempted to show that it does not exist, as, for example, by arguing that it makes no difference from the point of view of the gene (Barash, 1976; Treisman and Dawkins, 1976). The empirical assumptions can also be challenged. For example, the notion that partheno-genetic females are as fecund as their mictic relatives has been rejected by some authors (Lamb and Willey, 1979; Lynch, 1984). Another effort attempts to show that the genetic assumptions are not realistic. Where there is inbreeding, for example, the cost of meiosis is considerably lower (Uyenoyama, 1985, 1986a). Shields (1982a,b, and in this volume) has developed this notion and, combining it with DNA repair, has constructed an elaborate theory. Another alternative is to try to find a model in which there is in fact a twofold advantage to sex.

Williams (1975; Williams and Mitton, 1973) attempted to find ecological conditions under which fitness would be high enough to pay the cost of meiosis. These were "lottery-ticket models" in which a small minority of recombinants would have unusually high fitness (sisyphean recombinants). With a very high reproductive rate in a saturated environment, a sisyphean recombinant might win out over all the others (elm–oyster model). Or a group of organisms might invade a patch but, even though the asexual ones might reproduce faster, they might nonetheless lose out in competition with sisyphean recombinants (aphid–rotifer model). These theories invoke sibling competition among rather unusual conditions, and neither Williams (1975) nor Maynard Smith (1976, 1978) considered them general enough to explain the prevalence of sex in nature. Stearns (1985) treated Williams's models as particular forms of Ghiselin's. Glesener and Tilman (1978), on the contrary, made Ghiselin's the more par-ticular, and Felsenstein (1985) tried to make them all an instance of his own! From Felsenstein's remarks in this volume, it would seem that he treats theories as alike if they can be interpreted from the same genetic point of view. All the theories appeal to recombination as a means of coming up with variants. To me it seems both obvious and trivial that an organism is so constrained by its genetics that it cannot have the best of all possible phenotypes in every possible world.

According to what Bell calls the "Red Queen" hypothesis, sex is necessary because the environment is always changing, and organisms must evolve simply to keep up with it. The environment changes because of biotic interactions, especially those between host and parasite. Although it definitely has precursors, this view was first enunciated in the modern context by Levin (1975), and has been further developed by Clarke (1976), Jaenike (1978), Glesener and Tilman

(1978), Glesener (1979), Bremermann (1980, 1985), Hamilton (1980, 1982), Rice (1983), and others.

Williams (1975) concluded that his models would not apply to such animals as vertebrates, in which sex occurs but fecundity is low. Therefore he proposed the ad hoc hypothesis that much of sexual reproduction is due to historical accident; that is, sex is no longer useful but there is no way to get rid of it. The data of ecology and systematics do not support this hypothesis, but historical constraints are plausible and may be significant. There is no reason why features cannot change functions.

Dougherty (1955) suggested that sex originally functioned as a mechanism of DNA repair. Ghiselin (1974a) and Bell (1982) did not reject this hypothesis, but concluded that in and of itself it does not explain the ecological and phylogenetic data. Other authors have endorsed the hypothesis almost as an act of desperation, having felt that the alternatives have been excluded. Current interest stems from the work of Harris Bernstein (1977) and collaborators (C. Bernstein, 1979, 1981; H. Bernstein, 1983; Bernstein et al., 1981, 1985a–c; Gensler and Bernstein, 1981). Bernstein's investigations began with the molecular aspects of aging. It was clear that various recombinatory processes in microorganisms did in fact repair damage to DNA, and it was a straightforward matter to extend the hypothesis to other organisms (see other chapters in this volume). As a molecular biologist who was not in the habit of reading such journals as Systematic Zoology, Bernstein was for some time unaware of Dougherty's contribution and was therefore disappointed, upon reading the book by Bell (1982), to find out that somebody had thought of the hypothesis before. However, Dougherty's work was not altogether original either, and not just because early molecular biologists had thought along the same lines. Dougherty was a nematode nutritionist, and the link to his predecessors is obvious to those who know the arcane literature (Maupas, 1889, 1900). It is important to remember, however, that it makes a real difference when our modern understanding of the genetic material gets added to the discussion.

It seems to me that Bernstein, Hopf, and Michod, like other authors in this book, take a position too close to old-fashioned mutationism. Perhaps the best example is the treatment of diploidy, which is thought to exist because it masks deleterious genes in the recessive state (see also Maynard Smith, in this volume). If this is so, then it becomes difficult to explain the conditions that exist in the many organisms that undergo a regular alternation of haploid and diploid generations. The notion that the haploid stages are physiologically inferior to the diploid stages does not hold up under critical examination. Indeed, the data on algae have been used to support the Tangled Bank hypothesis (Ghiselin, 1974a, pp. 68–72; Bell, 1982, pp. 442–80). The life histories are set up in a way that assures the release of variability at the appropriate place and time. In general I would argue that the question is not "Is meiosis an adaptation for repairing DNA, producing genetic variation, or both?" Rather, the question ought to be "What selective influences are responsible for the various kinds of life cycles?" or, more generally still, "How can we account for the phenomena of organic diversity?"

It may seem an act of desperation to solve the problem of the adaptive significance of sex by proposing that really there is not any. It might be the product of selfish DNA—a kind of nuclear parasite as suggested by Hickey (1982) and Rose (1983) (see Hickey and Rose, in this volume). The main evidence against this hypothesis is the sort amassed by Brooks (in this volume). The eukaryote genome turns out to be very highly organized, and the whole apparatus shows every indication that the amount, kind, and timing of recombination, and also the release of variability, are adaptive. Similar objections can be raised to any effort to make DNA repair more important than the ecological consequences. Both the parasitic DNA hypothesis and the DNA repair hypothesis suggest that there should be little correlation between what goes on and when and where it happens. Such a correlation definitely does exist. If the so-called parasitic DNA does little harm, creating only a weak selection pressure to get rid of it, then it is virtually commensal. If it has some function, such as producing advantageous position effects, it is mutualistic, not parasitic.

SOME WIDER ISSUES

The debate about sex has stimulated much important research in areas only peripherally related to its adaptive significance. For example, there are historical problems. How, in fact, have reproductive features such as the meiotic apparatus (Margulis and Sagan, 1986) evolved? Work on recombination has led to a renewed interest in the problem of how the genome is organized (Brooks, in this volume).

Population biologists are now armed with a new range of hypotheses that suggest what may be going on in nature. The differences between species and mere clones, and between sexual and asexual phases of a given life cycle, present many opportunities. Weismann (1892) suggested that parthenogenetic animals have a greater reproductive potential than mictic ones; but he was not the first to make this suggestion, and he did not conceptualize the problem in terms of a disadvantage to sex. Seasonal parthenogenesis seems to occur during times when the environment is economically undersaturated, and this provides an obvious advantage to it (Clark, 1973; Ghiselin, 1974a; Bell, 1982). Furthermore, the traditional notion that parthenogenesis is an evolutionary dead end is currently much less popular than it was 20 years ago (Asher, 1970; Suomalainen et al., 1976; Lynch and Gabriel, 1983).

Increasing attention has been focused upon the problem of how clones interact with species and with each other (King, 1972; Cuellar, 1977, 1979; Snell, 1979; Browne, 1980; Loaring and Herbert, 1981; Bullmer, 1982). Calow et al. (1979) found it difficult to apply Williams's models to freshwater flatworms. Vrijenhoek (1984) applied the Tangled Bank hypothesis to freshwater fishes (see also Vrijenhoek, 1979; Parker, 1979; Angus, 1980). Lynch (1984) suggests that parthenogens have general-purpose genotypes, which seems reasonable, but it does not seem to me that the facts agree with this version of the environmental uncertainty hypothesis. Nor can I accept the notion of Glesener and Tilman (1978) that phenotypic plasticity would provide for all the advantages hypothesized by the Tangled Bank theory. Their economics is flawed. Universities do not produce uniform graduates, all equally competent in every subject.

If there were no sex, then species, by definition, would not exist. Species are reproductive communities. This makes them concrete, functional wholes, or "individuals" at a supraorganismal level. They have been compared to "firms" in economic theory (Ghiselin, 1974b, 1981). This suggests that species might "do something" apart from the separate activities of their component organisms. Eldredge (1985) has devoted an entire book to this topic. It would seem that species are not ecological units, in the sense that cells are components of organisms. Species speciate, become transformed, and go extinct, but otherwise they seem to do very little. On the other hand, they may be said to provide their component organisms with a certain kind of resource: access to a store of potential variability. They can shift gene frequencies as environmental conditions vary from time to time and place to place. According to the theory of punctuated equilibria (Eldredge, 1971; Eldredge and Gould, 1972), major evolutionary change occurs at the time of speciation. According to the theory of species selection, change results from the activities of species, especially differential speciation and differential extinction (Stanley, 1975). There is, of course, some kinship here with group selection. Stanley (1976, 1978) maintains that sex exists because of species selection, with clades being more persistent than clones. Ghiselin (1974a) rejected this kind of explanation for sex on the basis of clinal and other distribution patterns. Nonetheless, it does seem that clones rapidly become extinct, and only persist in places very favorable to them. The punctuational model, invoking speciation at the periphery of the range of the species, accompanied by a genetic revolution, makes a great deal of sense. Closely related species often differ substantially in their chromosomes. Mictic populations often give rise to parthenogenetic lineages that diffuse outward beyond the species border, often into climatically unstable habitats of the sort in which "weeds" flourish.

Bernstein et al. (1985b) propose that parthenogens flourish at low densities, because the cost of mating is inversely proportional to the effective population density. This reduces the number of species, because of the diminishing returns of any specialization that reduces population density. Clearly this does help to explain why there is a lower limit to species diversity (Ghiselin, 1974a) and why parthenogens can coexist in the face of competition with species. The exigencies of reproduction reduce the amount of diversity in many other ways. Nonetheless, sexual organisms do remarkably well in those environments where population densities are low. Such places as rain forests, coral reefs, and the deep sea do not seem to be populated by many parthenogens, and it is here that maximal genetic diversity occurs. In many cases the cost of mating is paid out of the male half of the budget, as in the dwarf males of deep-sea fishes. Thus one might want also to invoke the advantage to having the components of a sexual population sufficiently homogeneous to interact efficiently and function as integrated wholes, as well as other limitations to diversity within species.

Williams (1975) suggested that what species really do is avoid becoming extinct. In his view, sex reduces the closeness of adaptation, preventing over-specialization. From the perspective of Tangled Bank theory one might argue instead that by diversifying in a manner that gives closer adaptation, the species manages to persist in a more diverse niche. In either case, this would tend to imply that extinction occurs not when adaptation fails, but when niches disappear. Minor adjustments occur through changes in the relative proportion of the organisms within a species that collectively occupy the total spectrum of the niche. Anagenesis may occur, but new species appear within the biota as a result of new and divergent ecological opportunity, perhaps through structural and functional innovation or perhaps as a result of changes extrinsic to the organisms (Wright, 1982). Rather than niches being "partitioned," as the usual metaphor has it, they are opened up or expanded. Adaptive radiation would then be viewed as a process of addition, rather than division, of places in the natural economy (Darwin, 1859, Chap. 4). If so, what species do is merely persevere, outlasting their competitors until the requisite economic opportunities present themselves.

If we look upon genes, not as material for the sake of which organisms exist (Dawkins, 1976, 1982), but as resources (Ghiselin, 1987), then it is clear that the gene pools that exist because there are species serve as repositories of capital goods. Sex creates a kind of market, as a consequence of which such goods are made available to organisms and allocated efficiently in the analog of a free market. If this is so, then the cost of meiosis is puzzling for the same reasons that many critics of capitalism have looked upon middlemen as economic parasites. We would be dealing with the well-known phenomenon of an "unintended order." As Adam Smith (1776, vol. 1, p. 17) remarked, "It is not from the benevolence of the butcher, the brewer, or the baker, that we expect our dinner, but from their regard to their own interest." The sexual organisms would then act in their own interests, creating an entity from which they derive advantage, but one that has no interests of its own. Perhaps the appropriate point of view is not the species, nor the gene, nor the organism, but the economy that keeps them all going in the first place.

WHAT POINTS OF VIEW ARE APPROPRIATE?

The various points of view presented in this book are not always mutually exclusive. One can consider the selective advantage of sex from the point of view of strictly short-term, individualistic selection and nonetheless recognize that it may affect the long-term survival of the species. Most of us would agree that the DNA repair hypothesis can coexist quite happily with the ecological ones. Perhaps we shall have to accept a pluralistic assemblage of explanations. From the point of view of testing hypotheses, life is simpler if we can refute at least some of them. From the point of view of having an adequate explanation for all the data, we may have to accept more than one hypothesis. From a purely theoretical point of view, we may find certain models intuitively satisfying. From an empirical point of view, what really matters is how well the hypotheses agree with the facts.

CHAPTER 2

MOLECULAR ASPECTS OF GENETIC RECOMBINATION

Raymond Devoret

INTRODUCTION

One of the aims of molecular biology is to reconstruct in a test tube (in vitro) the processes that operate in a living organism (in vivo). The reader may consider that, because genetic recombination is being used daily as a tool by the pharmaceutical industry (under the guise of biotechnology), we know a great deal about its molecular aspects. This is not the case. Even though genetic engineers can cut DNA pieces and recombine them artfully, we know relatively little about the mechanisms of genetic recombination in a living organism.

This chapter deals with recombination of DNA, which is the most prevalent hereditary material. Recombination of RNA will not be dealt with here (for references, see Bujarski and Kaesberg, 1986; Green, 1986).

Recombination has been defined by geneticists as "an arrangement, a combination of genes in a progeny DNA molecule that is different from that observed in the parental molecules" (see Maynard Smith, in this volume). Geneticists have characterized the rearrangement of genetic markers in many species, from prokaryotes to higher eukaryotes. They have drawn maps establishing the order of genetic markers on various chromosomes. From the rearrangements observed in fungi and other species, geneticists were able to put forward hypotheses explaining the way "natural" recombination proceeds. Theoretical models, one of the first of which was proposed by Holliday (1964), have guided biochemists in their attempt to reconstruct in vitro the steps leading to recombination. Now we can redefine recombination (in molecular terms) as resulting from the exchange of DNA segments between two DNA molecules.

Biochemists have extracted and purified enzymes from various organisms. Enzymes that act on DNA are plentiful. Among them are ligases that weld DNA fragments, and restriction enzymes that cut DNA at specific sites. The availability of numerous restriction enzymes has fostered genetic engineering. But the way recombinant DNA is produced in a test tube does not necessarily mimic the way recombination proceeds in living organisms. For instance, restriction enzymes are not used in the natural process of genetic recombination. Restriction enzymes, as their name suggests, restrict the entry of foreign genetic material into a cell.

DNA is generally found in replicons—that is, in DNA replicating units. Recombination in a living organism results from the exchange of DNA segments between replicating units, or between DNA molecules, at least one of which is replicating. One well-studied replicon is the chromosome of *Escherichia coli*— one millimeter long, packed into a cell a thousand times shorter. The DNA of a replicon is not naked. A multitude of enzymes as well as nonenzymatic proteins cover the chromosome to promote its replication as well as its transcription, two key processes that permit the cells to reproduce and survive.

Recently biochemists have made great progress in mimicking in vitro the first stages of the recombination process. This accomplishment has mainly resulted from the use of *E. coli* as the host for the smallest existing replicons. *E. coli* has been, and still is, the organism of choice for the molecular study of recombination. Indeed, *E. coli* offers: (1) well-characterized proteins that are known to promote recombination; (2) small replicons that can be manipulated at the biochemical as well as at the genetic level; and (3) a recipient for foreign DNA that can be introduced by various means: transformation, transfection, transduction, and conjugation (see Levin, in this volume). Proteins that may be involved in recombination in mammalian cells have been recognized but not fully characterized (Rauth et al., 1986; Hsieh et al., 1986).

Recombination occurs between DNAs that share homology, in other words, that share a long stretch of identical bases. Two questions then follow: (1) is homology always required for recombination? (2) and if so, why is homology required?

Let us consider the first question. Recombination can occur between DNAs with very limited homology. For instance, phage lambda can insert into the chromosome of *Escherichia coli* to become a prophage. This type of recombination, designated site-specific recombination, requires: (1) some specific sequences, called *att* sites, that must be present on the phage DNA as well as on the chromosome (*att* sites have only 15 identical bases in common); (2) proteins coded by the phage that stitch together the cleaved recognition sites; and (3) host proteins that facilitate integrative recombination (for review, see Weisberg and Landy, 1983).

In contrast to homologous recombination, which preserves the original gene order of the DNA, insertion of DNA into the chromosome modifies the linkage between chromosomal genes. Such a modification can have functional consequences. For instance, a provirus carrying a potent promoter may rule over a chromosomal gene located downstream, changing gene expression of the host cell (Levine et al., 1978). Transposons may act likewise (Shapiro et al., 1977).

This chapter deals with *homologous* recombination that operates on DNAs sharing homology over distances of a few hundred or thousand bases. A second question, as to why homology of two DNAs is a prerequisite for their recombination, is examined in the following section.

STRUCTURAL PROPERTIES OF DNA THAT SUPPORT HOMOLOGOUS RECOMBINATION

Genetic engineering can exist because DNA and RNA replicons are resilient molecules. The bases that are the building blocks of nucleotide chains are stable compounds. The DNA double helix is built with two single-stranded polynucleotides held together by hydrogen bonds between complementary bases, guanine (G) pairing with cytosine (C) and adenine (A) with thymine (T). Hydrophobic interactions between these bases result in their stacking, thus contributing to the stability of the double helix (Kornberg, 1980).

Destabilization of the double helix can be achieved at elevated temperatures. More than half of the hydrogen bonds are broken when the temperature in solution of a DNA with a 50% G + C content reaches 90°C. If the DNA sample is then submitted to fast cooling the two strands fall apart, whereas if the DNA cools down slowly to room temperature the strands spontaneously reform a double helix. Renaturation does not need energy; the separated strands have a "natural tendency" to zip back. This corresponds to what the second law of thermodynamics tells us in a more elaborate way: there is a decrease of free energy (ΔG is negative) in spontaneous reactions.

The strength of hydrogen bonding between two complementary single strands can be illustrated by the attraction observed between the so-called cohesive sites of phage lambda DNA. When phage lambda DNA is in a linear form, two complementary 12-base single-strand pieces protrude at each extremity. These pieces pair so easily that lambda DNA molecules can concatenate, thus producing an artifact when separating DNA molecules according to their size. In vivo, the affinity between cohesive sites is advantageous for the phage, since it entails its recircularization in the host cell after infection.

Two DNA molecules must pair if they are to recombine. Pairing can occur in vitro if: (1) a DNA molecule A undergoes some local melting (called here "breathing"); (2) a single-stranded DNA fragment B is displaced from a *homologous* DNA molecule close to the first DNA molecule A; and (3) single-stranded B will intrude into the breathing DNA A, thus forming a joint molecule (Holloman et al., 1975). Hydrogen bonding between the paired single strands plays a major role in producing a stable attachment. The affinity between single strands increases as a function of the number of complementary bases that bind together. Pairing is associated with strand exchange.

When two DNA molecules having imperfect homology exchange strands, if the homologous pieces extend over a long stretch, a binding force is generated that is strong enough to hold the two DNA molecules together, allowing the formation of heteroduplex DNA. Two genes that differ by a single base (such as wild-type and mutant genes) will pair as if they were identical. Consequently, recombination can occur between similar molecules whose gene products are functionally different.

The physical forces inherent in the structure of DNA can promote the first step in the recombination process—pairing and strand exchange—even when the DNA is naked (that is, devoid of enzymes facilitating the reaction). Now, if RecA protein, which will be considered in detail in a subsequent section, is present on single-stranded DNA, pairing with duplex DNA is highly efficient. The rate of the reaction is one or two orders of magnitude faster than the spontaneous renaturation of single-stranded DNA (Honigberg et al., 1986). Before examining the enzymatic processes involved in recombination, it will be useful to study a few accepted models of this process that will serve as guidelines in further sections of this review.

MODELS OF RECOMBINATION

A few models have been proposed to explain the mechanism of homologous recombination. Most models account for the data observed in fungi whose life cycle, including tetrad formation, permits a detailed quantitative analysis of recombination (for review, see Orr-Weaver and Szostak, 1985).

Holliday (1964) proposed a model that introduced the idea that heteroduplex DNA might be generated during the breakage and rejoining of chromatids during the meiotic process. First, two homologous chromatids are nicked at the same position on strands with the same polarity, and then the strands of each chromatid are exchanged to produce symmetrical heteroduplex DNA (Figure 1). It is obvious that the structure formed by the crossed strands—"the Holliday junction"—has to be cut (resolved) in order to restore two separate DNA molecules. Depending on the position of the cut, the two DNAs will produce either patch recombinants that differ by a short length of single-stranded DNA, or full-fledged recombinant chromosomes in which there is exchange of flanking markers (Figure 1). Holliday's model provided a conceptual advance, since it accounted for the recombination and segregation patterns observed in fungi.

A variation of the Holliday model was proposed later by Meselson and Radding (1975) to accommodate some recombination data, also observed in fungi, suggesting that heteroduplex DNA may sometimes be formed on only one duplex, not on both as in the Holliday model (Figure 2). In addition, Meselson and Radding proposed an enzymatic basis for strand transfer. DNA polymerase initiates synthesis at a nick on one duplex, with the displacement (not degradation) of one strand. This strand pairs with the other duplex, one strand of which is degraded by DNA polymerase. Following this asymmetrical phase of strand transfer, symmetrical (i.e., reciprocal) transfer is initiated by the joining of the 3' end of the newly-synthesized strand to the 5' end of the strand being degraded on the other duplex. The resulting crossed-strand structure, a

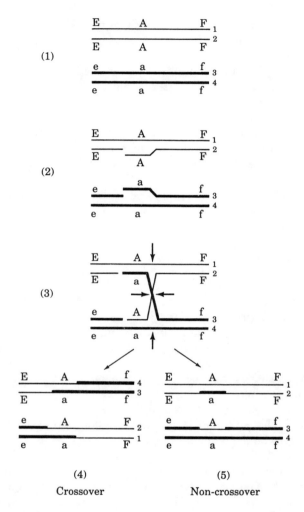

FIGURE 1. The Holliday model for recombination. Strands of the same polarity (1) are nicked at homologous sites (2) and are then exchanged to produce symmetrical heteroduplex DNA (3). The crossed strand, or Holliday junction, can be resolved either with or without the exchange of flanking markers. A cut (indicated by vertical or horizontal arrows) leads to either (4) or (5).

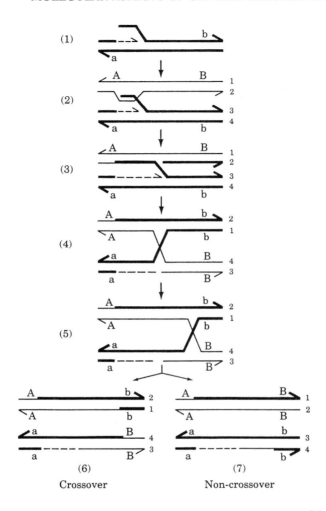

FIGURE 2. The Meselson-Radding model. Recombination is initiated by a single-strand nick, which serves as a primer for DNA repair synthesis (1). This displaces a single strand that can then pair with a homologous region on the other chromatid (2). The resulting joint molecule is degraded, and the asymmetrical heteroduplex DNA is enlarged by DNA synthesis on the donor chromatid coupled with degradation on the recipient duplex (3). Branch migration and ligation of the nicks produces a Holliday junction, which can be isomerized (4). Symmetrical heteroduplex DNA can be formed by branch migration of the Holliday junction (5). Resolution can yield either the crossover (6) or the non-crossover (7) configuration.

Holliday junction, can thereafter move along the chromosome by branch migration. Resolution of the junction occurs as in the previous model.

A third model, the double-strand break repair model (Figure 3), has been recently proposed (Szostak et al., 1983). Recombination is initiated by a double-strand break in one chromatid A which is enlarged by exonucleases so as to form a gap with 3' single-stranded ends. One of the free 3' ends then invades a homologous region on the other intact chromatid B, forming a small joint molecule. This joint molecule will be enlarged by repair synthesis primed by the invading 3' end; it may then reach a length larger than the size of the gap. This process partially regenerates chromatid A as a single strand at the gap site. Repair synthesis can now fill the gap using the 3' end as a primer. Thus, a double-stranded gap is repaired by two rounds of repair synthesis.

The model differs from the Meselson-Radding model in four ways (Szostak et al., 1983): (1) recombination is initiated by a double-strand break; (2) the

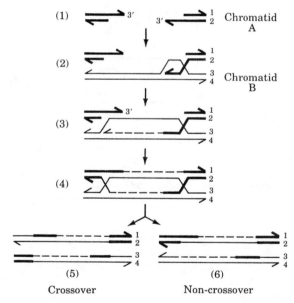

FIGURE 3. The double-strand break repair model. Recombination is initiated by a double-strand break in one chromatid, called A, which is enlarged by exonucleases so as to form a gap with 3' single-stranded ends (1). One of the free 3' ends then invades a homologous region on the other intact chromatid, called B, forming a small joint molecule (2). This joint molecule will be enlarged by repair synthesis (dashed lines) primed by the invading 3' end; it may then reach a length larger than the size of the gap (3). This process partially regenerates chromatid A as a single strand at the gap site (4). Repair synthesis can now fill the gap, using the 3' end as a primer. Thus, a double-stranded gap can be repaired by two rounds of repair synthesis. (After Szostak et al., 1983)

initiation chromatid is the recipient rather than the donor of information; (3) gene conversion results from the process that transfers two newly synthesized strands to fill a gap in a chromatid. There is no heteroduplex intermediate and no mismatch repair in the heteroduplex DNA adjacent to the region of gap repair; and (4) the recombination mechanism produces a region of gene conversion flanked by two Holliday junctions.

Clearly, all the models involve three main steps (Figure 4):

1. The formation of single-stranded DNA regions.
2. The formation of hybrid (heteroduplex) DNA, with the generation of a cross-strand structure (the Holliday junction).
3. The resolution of this crossed-strand structure by cutting and ligation of exchanged ends.

Molecular biologists have been able to reconstruct in vitro the formation of heteroduplex DNA (Radding et al., 1983a,b; Howard-Flanders et al., 1984a), the generation of a Holliday junction, and even its resolution (Mizuuchi et al., 1982; Lilley and Kemper, 1984; West and Körner, 1985; Symington and Kolodner, 1985). This biochemical analysis of recombination has been accomplished following a period of fruitful genetic investigation that led to the identification of recombination genes and their products.

PROTEINS REQUIRED FOR RECOMBINATION

This discussion is documented with what we have learned from the study of *Escherichia coli* and two of its phages, lambda (for review, see Smith, 1983b) and T4 (Alberts and Frey, 1970). Our knowledge has evolved according to a classical pattern. Genes governing recombination were identified first. Gene-encoded proteins were characterized subsequently, followed by the more recent determination of their enzymatic activities. Attempts have been made to demonstrate that extracts from mammalian cells promote strand exchange between two DNA molecules (Rauth et al., 1986; Hsieh et al., 1986), but the genes and gene products involved in recombination in mammalian cells have not yet been fully characterized.

Identification of genes and gene-encoded proteins

Clark and Margulies (1965) isolated in *Escherichia coli* the first mutant deficient in recombination, thus demonstrating that lack of recombination was not lethal. This discovery opened a new field of research. Soon other recombination-deficient mutants were identified. Two classes were defined: *recA* (Clark, 1973) and *recB* (Emmerson and Howard-Flanders, 1967; Low, 1968; Willetts et al., 1969; Willetts and Mount, 1969).

There is a hundred-fold difference in the recombination ability of the two mutants. Compared to a wild-type $recA^+$ recipient, a $recB^-$ recipient crossed with an Hfr donor yields 10^{-2} recombinants; but a $recA^-$ recipient is even more

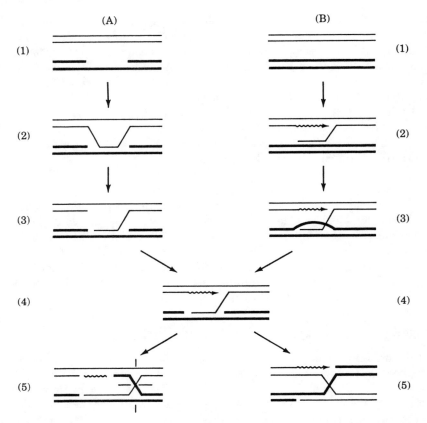

FIGURE 4. Current models for the mechanism of general recombination. (A) (1) Recombination initiated by a single-stranded gap. (2) Unwinding and pairing. (3) Paired strand is cut. (4) Repair synthesis. (5) Isomerization and resolution of one crossover to

affected, yielding less than 10^{-4} recombinants. Transduction of the mutants by phage P1 gives similar yields.

We now know that the *recA* gene codes for a 37.8-kD polypeptide whose synthesis is increased more than ten times after DNA damage (Gudas and Pardee, 1976; McEntee, 1977). The sequence of the *recA* gene has been determined (Horii et al., 1980; Sancar et al., 1980). The polypeptide—RecA protein—is essential to the cell for two functions: (1) it acts as a recombinase, promoting pairing and strand exchange, a basic first step in homologous recombination, and (2) it acts as a specific protease, cleaving a protein that normally represses the induction of an error-prone repair pathway (SOS pathway). This dual involvement of RecA protein points to a close relationship between homologous recombination and DNA repair (see next sections, and discussions by Bernstein et al. and by Maynard Smith, in this volume).

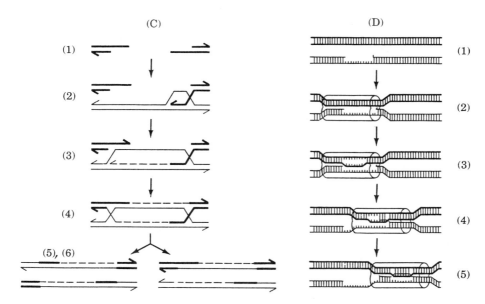

form recombinants. (B) (1) Recombination initiated by a nick. (2) DNA synthesis at nick displaces strand. (3) Homologous pairing. (4) Intact duplex is cut in response to pairing. (5) Isomerization and resolution of one crossover to form recombinants. (C) (1) Recombination initiated by a two-strand break in one duplex. (2) Pairing by 3′ end. (3) Repair synthesis from 3′ end, second 3′ end pairs. (4) Repair synthesis from second 3′ end completes gap repair and formation of two crossovers. (5,6) Resolution of two crossovers to form recombinants. (D) (1) Recombination initiated by a single-strand gap. (2) RecA protein condenses on gap and promotes homologous pairing. (3) Strand exchange to form heteroduplex at gap. (4) Branch migration to the right allows end of strand to interwind with duplex. (5) Strand crosses back. The gap is repaired and the two crossovers are resolved to form recombinants. The intact homologue is cut only at the resolution of the crossovers. (After Howard-Flanders et al., 1983)

The complexity of the *rec*B gene has just been resolved and its full sequence established (Amundsen et al., 1986; Finch et al., 1986b,c,d). The gene has just been renamed *rec*BCD since it codes for three polypeptides that make up exonuclease V. The recently found third polypeptide confers a DNA-unwinding activity to exonuclease V, which is an ATP-dependent exonuclease, a DNA-dependent ATPase, and an ATP-stimulated endonuclease (Wright et al., 1971; Lieberman and Oishi, 1974; Chaudhury and Smith, 1985). Lack of exonuclease V strongly affects the viability of *Escherichia coli* bacteria (Capaldo and Barbour, 1975).

As seen above, the *rec*BCD mutant displays some residual recombination activity. This was interpreted by Clark (1973) as resulting from the action of proteins coded by genes other than *rec*A and *rec*BCD. To test this assumption, Clark and associates set about to isolate mutations that would restore recombination in recBCD-deficient bacteria. They succeeded in isolating two new genes—sbcA and sbcB.

The sbcA gene codes for exonuclease VIII. This normally cryptic enzyme, when induced, substitutes for exonuclease V (Kushner et al., 1974). In contrast, in the case of gene sbcB, which codes for exonuclease I, it is the *disappearance* of this enzyme that makes the lack of exonuclease V tolerable (Kushner et al., 1971). The latter situation, in which the loss of two enzymes restores a wild-type phenotype, is intriguing. Clark (1973) has postulated that in the absence of exonuclease V, a lethal recombination intermediate is formed that is scavenged by exonuclease I.

If mutants lacking both exonucleases V and I can recombine, it is clear that there are other proteins that are functional substitutes. Such proteins are many, and are the products of genes recF, recJ, recN, recQ, and ruv (Horii and Clark, 1973; Lovett and Clark, 1984; Picksley et al., 1985; Nakayama et al., 1984; Attfield et al., 1985). The sequences of recF and recQ are known (Blanar et al., 1984; Irino et al., 1986). recN codes for one major inducible protein belonging to the SOS pathway that repairs double-strand breaks (Finch et al., 1985; Picksley et al., 1984).

Clark (1980) has proposed that all the known rec gene-encoded proteins belong to either of two recombination pathways, called RecBCD and RecF, each requiring the RecA protein function (Lovett and Clark, 1983). Contrasting with the proteins of the RecBCD pathway, some proteins of the RecF pathway also belong to the SOS pathway. The RecF pathway may constitute primarily an inducible recombination pathway involved in repair of DNA damage.

Role of RecA protein

Among the many enzymatic activities of RecA protein, two of them contribute to make it a recombinase. RecA protein binds cooperatively to single-stranded DNA and has a single-strand, DNA-dependent ATPase activity (Ogawa et al., 1978; Roberts et al., 1979; Craig and Roberts, 1980, 1981; McEntee and Weinstock, 1981). These two activities of RecA protein account for both its extensive polymerization on single-stranded DNA (RecA-protein coating of DNA), and its property to endow the RecA-protein coated single strand to search for a homologous single strand.

Apart from a recombinase action, RecA protein, when bound to single-stranded DNA, also has a protease activity that results in the cleavage of specific repressors required for the induction of the SOS pathway (for reviews, see Little and Mount, 1982; Roberts and Devoret, 1983).

Earlier in this chapter I described a synopsis of how pairing and strand exchange between two naked DNAs occur by formation of a joint molecule. In the presence of RecA protein, the synopsis turns into a substantiated scenario. The RecA protein-coated single-stranded DNA can invade intact duplex DNA, causing its complementary strands to separate. The RecA protein-coated single strand probes the duplex DNA until it finds a homologous sequence of nucleotides (Howard-Flanders et al., 1984a,b). It then forms a new duplex with the complementary strand, which abandons its previous companion. The resulting structure is a complex spiral filament (Howard-Flanders et al., 1984a). The formation of long filaments by RecA protein along single-stranded and double-stranded DNA has been observed by electron microscopy (Stasiak et al., 1984; Egelman and Stasiak, 1986).

The switch of RecA protein from a recombinase to a protease is discussed at the end of this chapter.

Chi sites and exonuclease V

Stahl and associates found that recombination is increased in phage lambda when some recognition sites called Chi are present in a given orientation with respect to *cos*, the cohesive end site of mature lambda DNA (Lam et al., 1974; Stahl et al., 1980; Faulds et al., 1979; Kobayashi et al., 1984; Smith, 1983a; for review, see Smith, 1983b).

Chi sites are also present in the chromosome of *Escherichia coli* at an average of 1 per 5 kB (about 10^3 sites per chromosome) (for review, see Smith et al., 1984). The sequence of Chi is 5'G–C–T–G–G–T–G–G3' and operates as a recognition site even when some single base-pairs are substituted (Smith et al., 1984; Schultz et al., 1981; Cheng and Smith, 1984).

Smith et al. (1981) have proposed a model for the involvement of Chi sites and exonuclease V in homologous recombination in *Escherichia coli*. Exonuclease V would unwind DNA from right to left starting at a blunt end, then cut the DNA at a Chi sequence about 5 nucleotides to the 3' end of Chi (Ponticelli et al., 1985; Taylor et al., 1985; Taylor and Smith, 1980). Mutations of either exonuclease V or of the Chi sequence affect both recombination stimulation and cutting (Schultz et al., 1981; Ponticelli et al., 1985; Taylor et al., 1985).

After cutting DNA at a Chi site, exonuclease V continues unwinding DNA, with the production of an elongating, single-strand tail. This tail synapses with a homologous duplex DNA molecule through the action of RecA protein. Annealing of the displaced strand of the second parental DNA forms a Holliday junction, which is cleaved to form a recombinant molecule (Smith et al., 1984) (Figure 5).

Role of proteins involved in DNA replication

Under natural conditions, recombination occurs mostly between two replicons and far much less between a replicon and a non-replicating DNA fragment. The latter case is found most often in "laboratory" recombination, such as Hfr $\times$ F$^-$ crosses or phage P1 transduction (for review, see Levin, in this

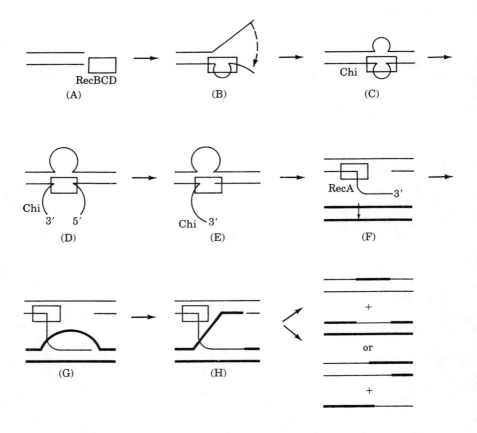

FIGURE 5. Role of exonuclease V in recombination. Exonuclease V (rectangular box) produces twin loops (C) and nicks one strand when a Chi site is encountered (D). The displaced strand forms a joint molecule (G), through the action of RecA protein. Branch migration (H) is postulated to be driven by exonuclease V and RecA protein (see Smith et al., 1981).

volume). If replicons engage in recombination, then replication proteins participate in recombination.

The *E. coli ssb* gene codes for a 18.5 kD polypeptide that in a tetrameric form binds single-stranded DNA. The SSB protein is essential for bacterial DNA replication. In the *ssb*-1 mutant, homologous recombination tested by P1-mediated transduction is reduced about five-fold (Glassberg et al., 1979). In vitro, SSB facilitates the formation of a joint molecule as well as repressor cleavage by RecA protein (McEntee et al., 1980; Resnick and Sussman, 1982;

West et al., 1982; Moreau and Roberts, 1984). SSB influences the balance between the protease and the recombinase activities of RecA protein (Moreau, 1987).

The *pol*A gene codes for DNA polymerse I (for review, see Kornberg, 1980). Possible roles for this enzyme in recombination are (1) the displacement, during DNA synthesis, of one DNA strand that could be used by *rec*A protein to form a joint molecule (Figure 2) and (2) the filling in of the gaps remaining after strand exchange (Figure 4C).

The *lig* gene encodes DNA ligase, which seals nicks in DNA (Gellert et al., 1968; Gottesman et al., 1973). It is likely that this enzymatic activity is essential for a terminal step in recombination. *E. coli* bacteria mutated in either *pol*A or *lig* gene recombine at increased frequency (Konrad and Lehman, 1975; Konrad, 1977). A hyper-recombination phenotype is observed that may stem from the increased frequency of unrepaired nicks, which entail the formation of single-stranded regions.

Two genes, *gyr*A and *gyr*B, formerly designated *nal* and *cou*, respectively, code for the two subunits of DNA gyrase, which introduces negative supercoils into DNA; DNA is then underwound (Gellert et al., 1976; Gellert, 1981). Site-specific recombination promoted by the integrase of phage lambda proceeds best with negatively supercoiled DNA (Mizuuchi et al., 1978; for review, see Weisberg and Landy, 1983). An involvement of DNA gyrase in recombination is inferred from the observation that coumermycin, an inhibitor of DNA gyrase, inhibits lambda recombination (Hays and Boehmer, 1978).

That many enzymes take part in recombination is not surprising in view of the successive biochemical reactions involved in the process. It is also not unexpected, from an evolutionary viewpoint, that some DNA sites may have become hot spots for homologous recombination. This has been observed in diverse organisms from prokaryotes to mammals (Schultz and Smith, 1986; Steinmetz et al., 1987; for reviews, see Catcheside, 1977; Stahl, 1979; Whitehouse, 1982).

One may also wonder whether some other sites might be "cold" spots for recombination. No experimental evidence has been provided yet for a well characterized anti-recombination mechanism although there is some evidence for a plasmid-coded anti-RecA protein that prevents intrachromosomal recombination (Bagdasarian et al., 1986; Bailone et al., in preparation).

VALIDITY OF THE MODELS

Now that we have reviewed the molecular components involved in homologous recombination, we can come back to the models and question their validity. All the models for recombination postulate three successive steps in the recombination process. What is the experimental evidence for the existence of these successive steps in a living organism?

Formation of single-stranded DNA

The replication fork is a major source of single-stranded DNA under physiological conditions. DNA has an asymmetric replication, one strand is replicated continuously (leading strand), the other discontinuously (lagging strand). The synthesis of single-strand replicative fragments on the lagging strand (Okazaki fragments) leaves single-stranded DNA between the already replicated fragments.

In bacteria diploid for the *lac* region, the intrachromosomal recombination between the two *lac*$^+$ genes (Konrad, 1977) might be accounted for by the following mechanism. During replication of one *lac* gene, single-stranded DNA formed on the lagging strand will search for a homologous sequence (the other *lac* gene) and exchange strands. This hypothesis is supported by the observed increase in Lac$^+$ recombinants when there are mutations in polymerase I or in dUTPase (affecting DNA replication) or mutations in the *dam* methylase or in the *uvr*D helicase (preventing the repair of mismatches in heteroduplex DNA) (Konrad, 1977).

Let us now summarize some results concerning recombination between two *lacZ* genes, located one on the F plasmid, the other on the chromosome (Porter et al., 1979). There is a fifty-fold increase in recombinants as compared to those arising from recombination between two *lacZ* genes on the chromosome. Seifert and Porter have demonstrated that nicks are produced at *oriT*, the site at which conjugative transfer of plasmid F is initiated (Seifert and Porter, 1984a,b). The nicks are constantly produced and repaired by a nicking-closing enzyme coded by a *tra* gene present on F plasmid. Nicking of the DNA increases the availability of single-stranded DNA, thus triggering homologous recombination (Figure 5).

Single-stranded regions can also be formed by (1) DNA unwinding by the RecBCD enzyme (Chaudhury and Smith, 1984; Bailone et al., 1985), (2) transfer of DNA upon Hfr $\times$ F$^-$ conjugation (Lloyd and Thomas, 1984; Sommer et al., in preparation), (3) formation of long and persistent single-stranded regions flanked by double-stranded regions (gaps) arising at high frequency during repair of UV-damage (Figure 6) (Rupp and Howard-Flanders, 1968; Rupp et al., 1971).

Formation of heteroduplex DNA

What permits a double helix to accommodate an intruding third strand? Normally, the circular DNA found in most replicons displays negative supercoiling, in other words, DNA is mostly in an underwound state. Supercoiled DNA has greater free energy than relaxed DNA: supercoiling is spontaneously lost whenever a nick occurs in the DNA. In a sense, supercoiled DNA is under strain and it stores mechanical energy. Processes which unwind DNA (DNA replication and transcription) are expected to be energetically favored in negative supercoiled DNA molecules relative to linear or relaxed DNA because processes relieve negative superhelical strain (Drlica, 1984).

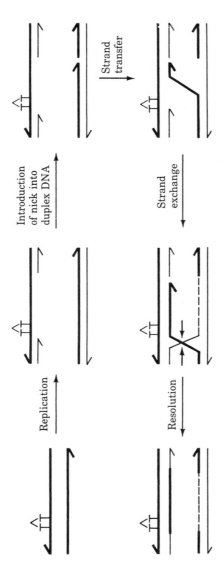

FIGURE 6. A model for daughter-strand gap repair. The figure outlines the succession of some of the events that are thought to occur during daughter strand gap repair. The nicking of the duplex DNA does not necessarily precede strand invasion. (After Rupp et al., 1971)

As was reviewed before, a short, single-stranded DNA fragment can associate with supercoiled DNA to form a joint molecule (Holloman et al., 1975) (Figures 2 and 4b). The addition of RecA protein accelerates the reaction. At present, there is so much information accumulated on the activities of RecA protein that it is firmly admitted that the initiation of heteroduplex formation is catalyzed by RecA protein (for review, see Kowalczykowski, 1987)

Resolution of cross-stranded structures

There are two problems here: the cutting of the junction between the recombining DNAs and the fate of the heteroduplex DNA produced.

In vitro, it has been demonstrated that endonuclease VII of phage T4 cleaves Holliday junctions by introducing a pair of nicks at the junction, and DNA ligase can seal these nicks to produce linear duplex DNA (Mizuuchi et al., 1982; Lilley and Kemper, 1984).

The fate of heteroduplex DNA has long been the object of various studies concerning meiotic gene conversion or the peculiar pattern of transformation in *Diplococcus pneumoniae* (for review, see Radding, 1978). The action of mismatch repair on recombination has benefited from recent investigations on phage lambda recombination (Lieb, 1983, 1985; for review, see Radman and Wagner, 1986)

RECOMBINATION AND REPAIR

In the preceding sections, recombination was viewed as taking place under physiological conditions—that is, in a cell growing in rich medium at 37°C in an incubator. But *Escherichia coli*, during its natural cycle, is sometimes exposed to deleterious conditions, among which is irradiation by ultraviolet light that damages the cell's chromosome. It was discovered early that a large part of damage to phage DNA is repaired by recombination (Luria and Dulbecco, 1948). DNA damage also induces recombination (for review, see Devoret el al., 1975). The importance of recombination in repair is illustrated by the fact that mutations affecting homologous recombination render the cells highly sensitive to physical (ultraviolet light, X-rays) or chemical carcinogens (benzopyrene, etc.). Among the repair systems, one called the SOS repair pathway deserves particular attention, since one of its key elements is RecA protein.

The SOS pathway

The SOS pathway is induced by the very DNA lesions it should remove. Its effect is to increase *cell survival* and also provide a mechanism for *mutagenesis* after DNA damage (for review, see Radman, 1975; Witkin, 1976; Devoret, 1981; Walker, 1985). The SOS pathway is expressed by almost a score of cellular genes (called SOS genes) that are normally repressed by LexA protein.

The SOS pathway provides an interesting example of regulatory loops. Two genes, recA and lexA, controlling the SOS pathway are themselves SOS genes (Little and Harper, 1979). Under physiological conditions, more than ten thousand RecA protein molecules are synthesized in an *E. coli* cell (Moreau, 1987). But efficient repair of chromosomal DNA demands ten times more RecA protein (Quillardet et al., 1982). Normally, LexA repressor locks up the recA gene; more RecA protein can only be produced if RecA protein synthesis escapes repression (for review, see Little and Mount, 1982). This vicious circle can be broken if RecA protein is transmogrified into a "protease"[1] that will get rid of LexA repressor by proteolysis.

In vitro, RecA protein is "activated" into a protease by the formation of a ternary complex with single-stranded DNA and dATP, which cleaves LexA repressor (Craig and Roberts, 1980, 1981). Recent evidence in vivo indicates that the formation of long, persistent stretches of single-stranded DNA constitutes the SOS signal—the structure that activates RecA protein (Bailone et al., 1985; Chaudhury and Smith, 1985; for review, see Roberts and Devoret, 1983). The activation of RecA protein entails the derepression of many SOS genes. Ultimately, when repair has removed DNA lesions, RecA protein ceases to be activated, LexA repressor is no longer inactivated, and SOS genes are turned off again (Little and Mount, 1982).

Many prophages are induced by chromosomal damage because their repressors are cleaved by activated RecA protein. This phenomenon (lysogenic induction) exemplifies the adaptation of temperate phages, which have evolved a mechanism that senses when their host is doomed to die. Indeed, the kinetics of lambda phage repressor cleavage is about ten times slower than that of LexA repressor, allowing ample time for cellular SOS functions to restore cell survival before prophage develops into vegetative phage—a process lethal to the cell (Bailone et al., 1979). In other words, when the SOS functions fail to restore DNA damage, for as long as single-stranded DNA persists, RecA protein remains activated as a protease able to cleave phage lambda repressor completely. Then a previously dormant virus will burst out of the cell, killing its host (for review, see Roberts and Devoret, 1983).

Recombination and repair functions

Lack of data does not forbid speculation. A few questions can be raised: Is it biologically necessary that a small protein like RecA be a recombinase as well as a protease? Can repair and mutagenesis be functionally separated from homologous recombination? Are the two activities maintained on the same molecule along the evolution of living organisms? The functions of RecA protein can be dissociated artificially by mutations in the recA gene (Devoret et al.,

---

[1]The recent results of Slilaty and Little (1987) indicate that cleavage of LexA repressor is caused by the repressor itself (autocleavage), RecA protein acting as coprotease.

1983; Dutreix et al., in preparation). One mutant of interest is RecA430 protein, which can effect homologous recombination but no visible SOS induction. Other *recA* mutants sport a converse phenotype: they are deficient in recombination, but constitutive for the induction of SOS functions (RecA protease action) (Tessman and Peterson, 1985; Wang and Tessman, 1986).

To exert its functions as a recombinase or as a protease, RecA protein must bind to single-stranded DNA. This requirement by RecA protein for a common substrate provides the molecular connection between recombination and repair. What tips the balance in favor of one process relative to the other? What makes RecA protein engage in SOS induction or in homologous recombination?

The following scenario has been recently proposed by Moreau (1987). If replication is hampered by DNA lesions, the amount of single-stranded DNA present in the cell increases. For instance, single-stranded gaps appear opposite the lesions (replication gaps; Figure 6) (Rupp and Howard-Flanders, 1968). Along with SSB, RecA protein molecules will bind to single-stranded DNA. Then the bound RecA molecules will initially be activated to support cleavage of repressors such as LexA protein. Thus, the amount of RecA protein produced can increase as much as ten-fold by derepression of the *recA* gene. If the induction of SOS functions leads to efficient repair, gaps will disappear and single-stranded DNA will be reduced in number and size. RecA protein will then polymerize extensively on the remaining single-stranded DNA pieces displacing SSB. This process will favor single-strand exchange, the first step of homologous recombination. From this scheme, one can deduce that, after DNA damage, the SOS pathway is induced first, followed by homologous recombination.

Another aspect of the relation between recombination and repair is dealt with and discussed elsewhere (Bernstein et al., in this volume; Maynard Smith, in this volume).

Rec-like proteins in bacteria and lower eukaryotes

Until now, this review of the molecular aspects of recombination has been based on what we have learned from *Escherichia coli* and its phages. Since the functions of recombination and repair are highly conserved during evolution, do we find among other proteins analogs of RecA protein and exonuclease V?

RecA-like proteins The strand exchange activity of RecA protein is unique in nucleic acid enzymology. It is thought to play an important role in the recombination process. Proteins with strand exchange activity have now been identified in organisms as diverse as bacteriophage T4 (Yonesaki et al., 1985), bacteria (for references, see below), lower eukaryotes (for references, see below) and human cells (Hsieh et al., 1986). This implies that DNA strand exchange activity is a property of a class of ubiquitous proteins that can be referred to as recombinases.

Let us first look at a list of RecA-like proteins involved in recombination and inducible repair in diverse Gram-negative and Gram-positive bacteria (as of June 1987): *Bacillus subtilis* (Lovett and Roberts, 1985; Love and Yasbin, 1986); *Caulobacter crescentus* (Bender, 1984); *Erwinia carotovora* (Zink et al., 1985); *Methylophilus methylotrophus* (Finch et al., 1986a); *Proteus mirabilis* (Eitner et al., 1981, 1982); *Pseudomonas aeruginosa* (Kokjohn and Miller, 1985); *Rhizobium meliloti* (Better and Helinski, 1983); *Salmonella typhimurium* (Sedgwick and Goodwin, 1985); *Shigella flexneri* (Keener et al., 1984); *Streptococcus faecalis* (Yagi and Clewell, 1980); and *Vibrio cholerae* (Ghosh et al., 1985; Hamood et al., 1986).

Proteus mirabilis RecA protein (West and Little, 1984) manifests interspecies complementation, as do other RecA-like proteins; that of *Bacillus subtilis* (Love and Yasbin, 1986) and *Proteus mirabilis* cleaves *Escherichia coli* LexA repressor. Interspecific complementation is now studied in many laboratories, and the resulting picture will provide a better view of evolution among microorganisms.

A RecA-like enzyme involved in homologous recombination has been characterized in a eukaryote, *Ustilago maydis* (Kmiec and Holloman, 1982). The so-called *rec*1 protein is an ATPase that catalyzes homologous strand transfer. Although ATP is required for synapsis, its hydrolysis is needed only for strand transfer (Kmiec and Holloman, 1983). The *rec*1 protein, like the RecA protein, shows a polarity in the direction of strand transfer. The *rec*1 protein catalyzes a reaction in which a single-strand circle pairs with the 5' end of a linear duplex, and strand transfer displaces the 3' end of the duplex. Thus *rec*1-driven strand transfer has a directionality opposite to that catalyzed by the RecA protein (Kmiec and Holloman, 1983).

The *rec*1 activity is absent in *U. maydis rec*1⁻ mutants, which lack both induced DNA repair and recombination (Holliday et al., 1976; Kmiec and Holloman, 1984).

RecBCD-like proteins and Chi sites DNA unwinding and hydrolysis by enzymes similar to exonuclease V of *Escherichia coli* may be common features in recombination in many bacterial species (Telander-Muskavitch and Linn, 1981; Doly et al., 1981). Chi sites that provide a substrate for the action of the RecBCD enzyme have been found in marine bacteria related to Enterobacteriacae (Schultz and Smith, 1986). Chi-like hot spots of recombination have been observed in the major histocompatibility complex of the mouse (Steinmetz et al., 1987).

DNA REPLICATION AND RECOMBINATION

The normal replication fork, namely the lagging strand, is a source of single-stranded DNA, which may trigger recombination. One can speculate that when life originated on Earth, recombination arose initially as part of a sloppy replication process with too much DNA unwound in advance of the replication fork.

Conversely, DNA replication in phage T4 can be dependent on homologous recombination, as inferred from in vitro data (Formosa and Alberts, 1986).

How nature manages replication as compared to homologous recombination is of great interest. Nature takes great care in reproducing DNA with maximal accuracy. Change in base composition is carefully controlled, and the mutation rate is maintained at a low level by a succession of repair processes, the last of which is mismatch repair (Radman and Wagner, 1986). In contrast, long single-stranded DNA stretches can be swapped frequently and easily.

SUMMARY

The elucidation of the process of homologous recombination remains a difficult challenge since it cannot be resolved alone. It seems likely that this elucidation will obtain as we learn more about the processes of DNA replication and repair.

CHAPTER 3

A POSSIBLE ROLE FOR MEIOTIC RECOMBINATION IN GERM LINE REPROGRAMMING AND MAINTENANCE

Robin Holliday

INTRODUCTION

Cells in higher eukaryotic organisms are partitioned into the soma and the germ line. Somatic cells can form complex differentiated structures that very often have a finite life span. The mortality of the soma is in striking contrast to the potential immortality of the germ line, a fundamental distinction that was first clearly recognized by Weismann (see Kirkwood and Cremer, 1982). The biological function of the soma is to transmit totipotent germ cells to the next and subsequent generations; and for all extant species, continuity of the germ line has been maintained through the period of their own evolution and that of their ancestors.

These major features of the biological organization of many higher organisms have been incorporated into the "disposable soma" theory of the evolution of aging (Kirkwood, 1977, 1981; Kirkwood and Holliday, 1979, 1986). It is proposed that for each organism there is a tradeoff between investment of resources in the development and maintenance of the soma and investment in the production of germ cells and other components of the reproductive system. This division of resources must optimize the survival of the germ cells, but it becomes counterproductive to ensure the continual survival of the soma. The aging process is therefore the result of a limitation of all those mechanisms that

45

might maintain a soma indefinitely. These would include repair of damage in DNA; accuracy in the synthesis of DNA, RNA, and proteins; removal of abnormal or denatured proteins; scavenging of harmful free radicals; elimination and replacement of nonfunctional or inviable cells; wound healing; and defense against invading organisms by the immune system. According to the hypothesis, aging is due to the gradual accumulation of defective macromolecules and cells as an inevitable result of the limitation of maintenance. The germ cells remain in a rejuvenated state, because appropriate maintenance mechanisms are effectively used by the organism to ensure that the germ line does not age or die out. This argument accounts for the fundamental partition between soma and germ line cells in sexually reproducing animals and many plants, but it does not explain the existence of sex itself. For reasons discussed elsewhere in this volume (see especially the chapters by Crow and by Shields), it is far from obvious why organisms do not invest their resources in producing totipotent asexual eggs, which develop normally without fertilization.

In this chapter, I propose that the problem of the development of higher organisms cannot be separated from the problem of producing normal totipotent germ cells. The production of a normal adult organism depends on the formation in the first place of a normal egg, and the normal program for development cannot proceed unless the initial information is correct. Since the genetic material is DNA, it is clear that the information it encodes must be free from errors or defects. The argument can therefore be made that meiosis, recombination, and sexual reproduction are the additional essential mechanisms that ensure that the continuity of the DNA in the germ line is maintained (Bernstein et al., 1981, 1984, 1985a,b, and in this volume; Medvedev, 1981). Damage to DNA is not itself heritable, but it can give rise to mutations that are fixed as changes in DNA sequence. We know that mutations occur in the germ line and are transmitted to subsequent offspring, so a crucial problem is the distinction between defects that can be recognized and removed (for example, by recombination repair involving homologous chromosomes at meiosis) and those that are passively transmitted to eggs and sperm. I argue that there are indeed two types of defect that arise in the germ line. One is the classical mutation established as a change in DNA base sequence and that cannot be removed at meiosis. The other is an epigenetic defect that changes the structure of DNA and is heritable, but does not change base sequence. The methylation of cytosine in specific base sequences provides a possible basis for the epigenetic control of gene activity during development. Defects in the normal pattern of methylation may arise in the germ line, and these defects may be recognized at meiosis and repaired by recombination (Holliday, 1984, 1986a). Since the repair depends on the existence of normal epigenetic information on one homologue, the hypothesis therefore provides a possible explanation for the importance of sexual reproduction and outbreeding and the short-term harmful effects of asexual reproduction and inbreeding.

THE EPIGENETIC CONTROL OF GENE EXPRESSION

The unfolding of the genetic program depends on two fundamental events: one is the ordered segregation of gene activities during development, and the other is the maintenance through cell division of a determined or differentiated phenotype. At many points in development a given cell gives rise to one daughter that differs in phenotype from itself or to two daughters, each of which differs from their parent and, in some cases, differ from each other. Innumerable examples show that these phenotypic differences are often heritable. In the case of a stem cell, the heritable phenotype is its ability to produce a differentiated daughter cell that subsequently maintains its own phenotype either with or without division. The end product of differentiation is a set of specialized gene functions that are quite distinct from the specialized functions of cells in another tissue. The intrinsic stability of the epigenetic control of gene activity at the DNA level is exemplified by the existence of active and inactive X chromosomes in a common nucleoplasm and cytoplasm.

It was proposed that segregation and maintenance of gene activities could be based on the methylation of cytosine in DNA at specific sequences and the maintenance of that methylation through cell divisions (Holliday and Pugh, 1975; Riggs, 1975). Cytosine methylation is a postsynthetic modification of DNA, and different patterns of methylation could arise through the activity of enzymic switch mechanisms, which methylate cytosine in the DNA of only one daughter cell. Alternatively, DNA methylation could be removed by the action of specific DNA binding proteins that block normal postsynthetic modification. Cooperative binding of such a protein could lead to a loss of methylation in only one of the two daughter chromatids. Once established, the pattern of methylation would be inherited through the activity of one or more maintenance enzymes, which recognize hemimethylated DNA after replication and methylate the nascent strand. Nonmethylated DNA would not be a substrate for a maintenance enzyme. This is illustrated in Figure 1 (top right).

Evidence for the importance of DNA methylation in the control of gene activity in higher organisms has come from many sources and a number of reviews have been published (Doerfler, 1983; Riggs and Jones, 1983; Razin and Cedar, 1984; Razin et al., 1984; Adams and Burdon, 1985). There are many examples of gene expression being correlated with the absence of methylation at particular sites, and when these sites are methylated, transcription is shut off. There is also evidence for the heritability of the pattern of methylation through cell division. The cytosine analogue 5-azacytidine is known to be a potent inhibitor of DNA methylation, and it has been shown to activate silent genes in a variety of contexts (Jones, 1985; Jeggo and Holliday, 1986).

The general hypothesis for the epigenetic control of gene expression depends on the specificity of DNA–protein interactions. Since most CpG doublets in the DNA of higher organisms are methylated and a doublet does not provide

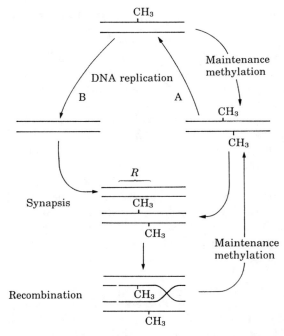

FIGURE 1. Maintenance of methylation at critical sites in the germ line. Normal DNA replication (A) gives rise to hemimethylated DNA, which is a substrate for a maintenance methylase. Failure of maintenance, or DNA damage (see Holliday, 1979), followed by a second round of replication (B) produces an aberrant nonmethylated site that is not a substrate for the maintenance methylase. Nonmethylated sites adjacent to structural genes (R) can be recognized as recombinator sequences (Holliday, 1968), which initiate recombination between homologues. The formation of hybrid DNA allows remethylation of the previously nonmethylated sequence. Hybrid DNA can be formed as illustrated or by other means (see Meselson and Radding, 1975; Szostak et al., 1983).

specificity, it is likely that the vast bulk of methylated cytosines have nothing to do with the control of gene expression and have some other function. In this connection it may be significant that certain insects, including Drosophila (Achwal et al., 1984), have very low levels of DNA methylation. RNA polymerases are known not to distinguish between methylated or nonmethylated promotors. Instead, it is supposed that there are specific protein transcription factors that do recognize methylated or nonmethylated sequences and interact with the polymerases. Until recently, little has been known about methylation switch mechanisms, which may bring about differences in methylation pattern in different cell types. However, recent studies have shown that muscle cells can specifically remove methyl groups from transfected actin genes and thereby activate them (Yisraeli et al., 1986). Also, vitellogenin synthesis induced by estradiol is specifically associated with the removal of methyl groups at the estradiol-receptor binding site at the 5' end of the vitellogenin gene (Saluz et al., 1986).

Meiocytes are specialized cells with their own pattern of gene functions, and it is obvious that innumerable genes expressed in somatic tissues are shut off. According to the methylation hypothesis, a meiotic cell would have its own distinct pattern of DNA methylation in critical sites and the same would be true for premeiotic germ cells and postmeiotic gametes. Monk et al. (1987) have recently shown that premeiotic germ cells in both males and females have very under-methylated DNA compared to somatic cells or sperm. However, these studies are largely concerned with nonspecific global methylation, and it cannot be assumed that such major differences exist for methylation sites that are essential for the control of gene expression.

It is a reasonable possibility that one function of meiosis is to reprogram the DNA prior to the formation of germ cells and the fertilized egg. Although specific de novo methylation and demethylation may occur, it seems very unlikely that the total specific pattern of methylation could be imposed on the DNA by a large series of sequence-specific methylases or demethylases in a single cell. It is much more likely that the continuity of the germ plasm is maintained not only by the DNA sequence, but also by the continuity of the pattern of DNA methylation due to the fidelity of maintenance methylases. If a large proportion of the control methylation sites are maintained in this way, it is possible that errors or mistakes in methylation could arise. There are several ways that this could happen, including occasional failure of the maintenance DNA transmethylase reaction, DNA damage followed by excision repair immediately before or after the replication fork (Holliday, 1979), or DNA damage that inhibits maintenance methylation. All these epigenetic errors would be heritable and therefore transmitted to the next generation, unless a specific mechanism exists to detect and remove them.

INITIATION OF RECOMBINATION

It has been known for many years that recombination is not initiated at random sites in DNA. Early evidence came from studies of gene conversion and fine-structure mapping in fungi. It was evident that conversion and recombination events were more common at the ends rather than the middle of the gene (Whitehouse and Hastings, 1965). This is referred to as polarized recombination, and it was initially best explained by supposing that there were discrete initiation sites for recombination, sometimes referred to as recombinators (Holliday, 1968), that were located to one side of a gene. Later, direct evidence for recombination hot spots (chi sites) was obtained in bacteriophage lambda (for reviews, see Stahl, 1979; Smith, 1983), and there have also been strong indications that recombination hot spots exist in mammalian DNA (Steinmetz et al., 1982, 1986; Treco et al., 1985; Kobori et al., 1986; Lafuse et al., 1986).

Other evidence that recombination is not random comes from a consideration of overall recombination frequency in meiosis and recombination in individual genes (Thuriaux, 1977). It has long been evident that the number of recombination events at meiosis is totally unrelated to the DNA content of the genome. Thus, there is more recombination in meiosis in yeast than in maize or humans, in spite of the enormous difference in DNA content. This means that recombination per unit of DNA is much greater in yeast than in maize or humans. However, when recombination within individual genes is examined, the frequencies in different species are broadly similar. Most genetic markers occur in structural genes, so these observations mean that the frequency of recombination per unit of unique-sequence DNA is also roughly similar. Thuriaux (1977) draws the almost inescapable conclusion that most recombination in eukaryotic organisms occurs within or near structural genes. It follows that initiation sites or hot spots for recombination must also be confined to the vicinity of structural genes. This strongly suggests that recombination may have a specific function relative to the locus where it can be initiated, rather than the more general function of redistributing homologous maternal and paternal DNA into new combinations.

From the discussion in this and the previous section, it can be concluded, first, that methylation sites important for the control of gene expression occur in or near promoter sequences and, second, that recombinator sequences are also adjacent or close to structural genes. I suggest these features of DNA structure are not coincidental and that important methylation sites occur in the same sequences as recombinators or in overlapping sequences. If methylation is normal, then the sequence does not initiate recombination, but if methylation is abnormal—that is, a critical cytosine has become demethylated—then recombination is initiated. Subsequently, hybrid or heteroduplex DNA is formed and this will produce hemimethylated DNA (see Figure 1). The ubiquitous maintenance methylase now inserts the missing methyl group and the epigenetic defect is repaired.

It could be argued that a simpler mechanism would be to put right the defect through the activity of a de novo methylase without resource to a recombination repair pathway. However, such a de novo methylase would have to be either highly sequence specific, in which case it could not recognize all possible demethylated sites, or nonspecific, in which case it would methylate a large number of sites that must not be methylated in meiosis. The point is the same as that made previously, namely, that the complete information required for reprogramming the pattern of methylation is very unlikely to reside in a single cell. It is much more feasible that reprogramming occurs in sequential steps in germ line cells or very early in development. The meiocyte has partial rather than total specifity: it recognizes defects due to the heritable loss of methylation sites that are an important component of the epigenetic program.

In the ascomycete *Neurospora crassa* a number of genes or mutants have been identified that control recombination. One of the mutants designated *cog,* strongly influences recombination in its immediate vicinity. Of two alleles, *cog* and *cog*[+], only the latter stimulates recombination. It has been proposed that the difference between *cog* and *cog*[+] is due to DNA methylation and that this in turn is controlled by another gene, *rec2*, located on another chromosome (Catcheside, 1986). The nonmethylated DNA in *cog*[+] is a substrate for a type 1 restriction enzyme that initiates recombination. The interpretation of these experiments therefore leads to a conclusion identical with that suggested here, although the evidence and lines of reasoning are totally dissimilar.

The proposal that recombination is initiated at nonmethylated sites is broadly compatible with the known contribution of recombination events of meiosis. For any short chromosomal region, such as a single gene, recombination is a rare event, but for paired homologues there is one or a small number of recombination events, the distribution of which appears to be fairly random. This would be expected if there were many potential sites where recombination could be initiated, but a rather low probability of any of these sites becoming a recombinator through loss of methylation.

HERITABLE EPIMUTATIONS

Molecular studies of classical mutations have shown that each is due to a change in base sequence. This can either be a base substitution, insertion or deletion of one base, a sequence of bases, or some other rearrangement of DNA. On the other hand, the known heritability of the pattern of methylation raises a new possibility in which heritable changes affecting gene expression are not due to alterations in nucleotide sequences. It has been proposed that such changes should be designated *epimutations* (Jeggo and Holliday, 1986). Rules for the induction and reversion of epimutations will be very different from those of classical mutations. For example, many inactive genes are methylated, but they can be reactivated at a very high frequency by the demethylating agent azacytidine (Jones, 1985). There is strong evidence that many permanent cell lines spontaneously inactivate genes by de novo methylation (Clough et al., 1982; Gasson et al., 1983; Flatau et al., 1984). In contrast, diploid somatic cells with a finite life span in culture progressively lose DNA methylation, perhaps from inefficient maintenance (Wilson and Jones, 1983; Holliday, 1985, 1986b; Fairweather et al., 1987). This might lead to the activation of genes that are not normally expressed. There is also evidence that one or more of the steps in carcinogenesis may be due to abnormal epigenetic changes in gene expression (Jones, 1986; Holliday and Jeggo, 1985).

So far, almost all studies on gene expression and methylation have been carried out with somatic cells, but recently evidence for transmission of epimutations through the germ line has been obtained. Controlling elements in maize are a subject of methylation control. An inactive form of the element Ac has been shown to be methylated in CAG, CTG, and CCGG sequences, and these can be inherited through normal sexual crosses. Reversion to the active state is associated with demethylation that can occur either in the germ line or in somatic tissue (Schwartz and Dennis, 1986; Chomet et al., 1987). Other examples of sexual transmission of heritable changes in DNA modification in maize are also known (Chandler and Walbot, 1986; Lillis and Freeling, 1986).

Imprinting is due to heritable differences between maternal and paternal chromosomes (see Cattanach, 1986). This phenomenon contravenes the normal rules of Mendelian inheritance and cannot be due to gene mutation, since the chromosomal condition is reversible. Changes in DNA methylation provide a possible basis for chromosome imprinting. The variability of inbred lines of mice is very much higher than that expected from normal mutation frequencies (Gruneberg, 1979; Festing, 1973; Fitch and Atchley, 1985). In other experiments with mice it has been shown that X-ray or urethene treatments of parents can predispose offspring to carcinogenesis (Nomura, 1982). The frequency of alteration of offspring is so high that on a classical induced mutation interpretation, there would have to be at least 400 loci involved in delayed carcinogenesis. Other examples of germ line inheritance that do not follow the normal rules of Mendelian genetics include the environmental induction of genotrophs in flax (for review, see Cullis, 1977), the transmission of fragile chromosome sites in humans (Sutherland, 1985), and paramutation in maize. Paramutation occurs in heterozygotes and is defined by Brink (1973) as "an interaction between alleles that leads to directed, heritable changes at the locus with high frequency, within the timespan of a generation." It could be the same as the removal of epimutations.

In summary, there are many examples of variability inherited through the germ line that cannot be attributed to normal gene mutation or to maternal cytoplasmic effects. It is suggested that some of these could be due to changes in DNA modification that could sometimes arise with high frequency and might also be reversible. It may well be that many heritable phenotypes that are at present attributed to classical mutation may also be due to DNA modification.

IMMORTALITY OF THE GERM LINE

In the introduction to this chapter, I outlined a possible explanation for the basic difference in the survival of somatic and germ line cells. The theory proposes that whereas somatic cells are only maintained for a finite length of time, metabolic resources are invested in maintaining germ line cells indefinitely through successive generations. There are several ways in which maintenance mechanisms may operate in the germ line, but a crucial question is whether recombination and sexual reproduction constitute one of them. It could be argued that organisms that reproduce only by asexual means are unable to maintain the continued survival of germ line cells; in other words, such cells age through successive generations and finally die out. Obviously, evidence relating to this is very hard to obtain because any species in which this occurred would be extinct. Suggestions that successive generations of asexually reproducing metazoans eventually lose vigor appear to be mainly anecdotal. However, well-documented cases exist for protozoa and fungi that alternate vegetative cell division with sexual reproduction. Clones of *Paramecium aurelia* have finite division potential and are rejuvented by meiosis and conjugation (Siegel, 1967). Similarly, vegetative cells of the ascomycete *Podospora ansinera* invariably become senescent and die out, and sexual reproduction is essential for survival (Marcou, 1961). There appear to be no comparable studies of more advanced eukaryotic organisms, such as rotifers, aphids, and many plants, which can reproduce both sexually and asexually. In these species it is a major problem to explain the persistence of sexual reproduction, since asexual forms have a twofold selective advantage. A possible explanation is that indefinite asexual reproduction would lead to extinction, whereas sexual reproduction rejuvenates the germ line. Thus, these species have the best of both worlds: the maximum rate of clonal proliferation without sex for a fairly brief period under favorable environmental conditions, alternating with sexual reproduction that ensures maintenance of the germ line. The existence of some species that reproduce only by asexual means does not necessarily counter the argument if most attempts to bypass normal mechanisms of sexual reproduction have rapidly led to extinction. This is a complex issue discussed much more fully elsewhere in this volume.

Possible mechanisms of rejuvenation must depend either on the elimination of heritable defects or on a reprogramming process that ensures that fertilized eggs in each generation are equivalent to those in the preceding generation. In this chapter, I have suggested that both of these mechanisms are important and that they are closely interrelated: the normal program for development depends on the correct pattern of epigenetic controls and on the fact that defects in such controls are recognizable and repairable by recombination at meiosis. In contrast to germ line cells, somatic cells may have no means of recognizing epigenetic defects, and these would then contribute to the overall process of aging (Holliday, 1985, 1986b). It has been shown that the rate of loss of 5-methylcytosine correlates directly with the longevity of somatic cells in culture (Wilson and Jones, 1983), and there is also evidence that methylation declines with aging in vivo (Mays Hoopes et al., 1983).

EPIGENETIC DEFECTS AND INBREEDING

Although it has been proposed that a function of recombination is to remove epigenetic defects at meiosis, the possible efficiency of this process is a matter for speculation. Results previously mentioned suggest that epimutations may be transmitted from generation to generation and that some of these may be due to a loss of DNA methylation. When a normal mutation is heterozygous, half the offspring inherit the mutant allele and half the wild type. However, when an epigenetic defect is heterozygous, there will be a given probability of its removal or conversion to wild type by recombination at meiosis. This provides a possible basis for the importance of sexual reproduction and outbreeding.

Let it be assumed that epigenetic defects arise in a germ line at a constant frequency at any of a large number of sites in a genome. According to the hypothesis, there is a given probability that each will be removed at meiosis, but a proportion may be transmitted to the next generation. With outbreeding there will be essentially the same probability that each defect will be eliminated at the subsequent meiosis. Thus, epigenetic defects will be continually arising and continually being removed. Leaving aside selection, the end result will be a steady-state level of defects. This situation is in sharp contrast to inbreeding, which will produce fertilized eggs that are often homozygous for the defect, nonrepairable, and therefore transmitted to all subsequent offspring. Inbreeding thus leads to an accumulation of deleterious epigenetic defects, and the short-term effect of this might be severe enough to explain inbreeding depression. Similarly, hybrid vigor resulting from crosses between inbred lines may be due not only to complementation of defects, but also to the subsequent elimination of many of these at meiosis. Methods of asexual reproduction that incorporate meiosis (see Maynard Smith, 1986) may permit removal of epigenetic effects in the generation in which they arise, but the final outcome may be similar to inbreeding.

The general argument is in many ways similar to that presented by Bernstein et al. (1981, 1984, 1985a,b, and in this volume), but the basic difference is in the *recognition* of DNA abnormalities of meiosis. DNA damage may be repaired by a variety of pathways, but once it is fixed as a true mutation (i.e., a change in DNA sequence), it can no longer be a target for repair. Thus, most mutations are passively transmitted through meiosis. DNA damage or failure of maintenance methylase can also lead to heritable loss of DNA methylation. This may in some cases be made good by de novo methylase activity, but the demethylated sites are also targets for repair and meiosis. In other words, the substitution of epimutations for classical mutations makes the arguments of Bernstein and colleagues much more compelling.

SUMMARY

It has been proposed that the control of gene activity during the development of higher organisms depends in part on the presence or absence of 5-methylcytosine in specific controlling DNA sequences. The methylation of cytosine is heritable through the activity of a maintenance DNA transmethylase. There are ordered changes in the pattern of methylation during the unfolding of the genetic program for development, but a constant pattern must be transmitted through the germ line. Maintenance of the pattern is essential for normal development from the fertilized egg. It is suggested that DNA defects can arise in both somatic and germ line cells. The former can contribute to the aging of the soma; the latter can be transmitted to the next generation, and this would be deleterious. This event would be avoided if the loss of methylation in important controlling sequences produced a signal for recombination (a recombinator). The subsequent formation of heteroduplex DNA and the activity of maintenance methylase would allow repair of the demethylated site, i.e., restoration of methylation. this could only otherwise be achieved by a battery of highly specific de novo methylase activities, which are unlikely to exist in a single cell. Sexual reproduction and outbreeding maximize the opportunities for the removal of heterozygous epigenetic defects. Asexual reproduction and inbreeding will often result in the accumulation of epigenetic defects as homozygotes that can no longer be removed at meiosis.

CHAPTER 4

THE IMPORTANCE OF RECOMBINATION

James F. Crow

INTRODUCTION

H. J. Muller, Indiana University. How much is evolution accelerated by sexual reproduction? (15 min.)
So reads the questioning title of Muller's talk given at the 1958 Meeting of the Genetics Society of America, with its answer inadvertently supplied by the program arranger. This talk is memorable in being, I believe, the first attempt to treat the advantage of sexual reproduction quantitatively. The argument was published in full the same year (Muller, 1958).

The classical arguments for the evolutionary advantages of sexual reproduction are three: (1) adjusting to temporal or spatial environmental changes, (2) facilitating the incorporation of beneficial mutations, and (3) facilitating the removal of deleterious ones. Arguments (2) and (3) might well be regarded as two sides of the same coin, but it is convenient to discuss them separately. Most of the discussion, pro and con, for the past three decades has involved variations on these themes. At the same time, several authors have been at pains to point out that recombination is not always advantageous and natural selection may sometimes reduce it.

For the most part I shall be going over familiar ground, although I hope to add a few new twists. Let me record at the outset my indebtedness to and general agreement with Maynard Smith and Felsenstein. I shall often be repeating what they have said in earlier writings and in this volume.

Felsenstein (1974) was the first to cut through the fog in the early literature and see a major regularity: Those authors who found recombination to be advantageous implicitly regarded the population as finite and assumed gametic ("linkage") disequilibrium, whereas those who found it to be disadvantageous regarded the population as infinite. In this volume he continues his campaign to uphold and enhance the already considerable fame of Hill and Robertson (1966, 1968), who were the first to show that gametic disequilibrium is generated by the interaction of selection and random drift in finite populations.

Felsenstein wonders why the subject of the evolutionary importance of sexual reproduction has again come up, despite the absence of new information that would justify a reassessment at this time. To be sure, most recent ideas are variations on familiar themes, and I agree that the old ideas still seem best. Nevertheless, there are some important advances. For the most part these have been greater specification of details within the existing framework. One example is the discovery of segmental replication of RNA viruses, which presumably mitigates the effects of a high mutation rate (Pressing and Reanney, 1984; L. Chao, personal communication). Another is Hamilton's (1980) treatment of parasites as a particularly unpredictable and malevolent environmental variable. Parthenogenesis has undergone renewed study (Maynard Smith, 1986). In another direction, there have been a number of mathematical papers dealing with various specific models (reviewed by Brooks in this volume; see also Sasaki and Iwasa, 1987). In my view none of these alters the central ideas in a fundamental way, but they enrich the theory by adding detail and rigor.

With East, Muller, Fisher, Wright, Sturtevant, Mather, Williams, Maynard Smith, Felsenstein, Bell, and many others, I assume that the evolutionary value of sex is the promotion of recombination, brought about in eukaryotes by meiosis and syngamy. Weinshall (1986) has cleverly contrived a single-locus example where segregation is advantageous. Yet, in general, recombination is far more important evolutionarily (except for segregation's ordinarily being a requisite for recombination). In Muller's (1932) words: "The essence of sexuality, then, is Mendelian recombination."

There are other important related issues: those of isogamy versus anisogamy, hermaphroditism versus separate sexes, inbreeding versus panmixia, and regular sexual reproduction versus alternation of generations. My concern, however, is the underlying issue—the advantages and disadvantages of recombination.

Recombination includes both Mendelian assortment and exchange between homologous chromosomes. Although their mechanisms are quite different, and they may have had different historical origins, their evolutionary consequences are the same. Quantitatively, Mendelian assortment is more important than crossing over in any organism with a haploid chromosome number greater than two. Considering only pairwise combinations of genes among chromosomes of equal size, the probability that two random loci are syntenic is $1/n$. There are $n-1$ times as many interchromosome as intrachromosome gene pairs. Since I shall be discussing mainly multicellular eukaryotes with several chromosomes, my emphasis will be more on the free recombination of independent pairs than on recombination of linked pairs; that is, on the evolutionary merits of free recombination versus none rather than on the adjustment of the amount of recombination between linked loci.

Definitions

There is such diversity in the use of words that I had best make my meanings clear from the outset. In classical genetics *recombination* means the production of gametes with other than the parental combination of alleles, and I shall continue this time-honored usage. Recombination thus includes both *independent assortment* of whole chromosomes and *crossing over* between homologous pairs. When the emphasis is on molecular events in DNA that may or may not lead to exchange of outside markers, I shall use *molecular recombination* to stand for mismatch repair, heteroduplex resolution, and other localized DNA processes.

SOME DISADVANTAGES OF RECOMBINATION

Before discussing the evolutionary advantages of sexual reproduction, I shall first note that sexuality is not always advantageous. It can be disadvantageous in many important ways.

1. Sexual reproduction is not very efficient qua reproduction. The time and energy required for meiosis and syngamy are substantial. As a means of multiplication, many asexual systems are more effective and less error-prone; for example, meiotic nondisjunction rates are considerably higher than mitotic. Many plants that have bypassed meiosis and adopted an asexual mode of seed production—dandelions, for example—are remarkably prolific.
2. With anisogamy and separate sexes there is the cost of males. A female that could produce female progeny asexually with the same efficiency as by fertilization would have a twofold advantage.
3. With sexual reproduction selection acts on the genic or additive component of the genetic variance (Fisher, 1930), whereas selection among asexual individuals acts on the genotypic or total genetic variance. If the genetic variances are the same, an asexual species can respond more rapidly to selection—at least for a limited time.
4. If dominance and epistasis are present, there may be segregation and recombination loads (Crow, 1958). If there is overdominance, there is reduced fitness caused by segregation from favored heterozygotes. If there is epistasis, there is reduced fitness caused by recombinational breakup of favorable gene combinations. Under this circumstance, as first noted by Fisher (1930), selection would favor modifiers that reduce the amount of recombination, making the system more like that of an asexual species. For the first explicit formulation of this process, see Kimura (1956).
5. Free recombination does not provide a way for two or more rare genes that are individually deleterious, but collectively beneficial, to spread through a population. Extending this idea, Wright (1932 and since; see 1982 for a recent review and references to earlier work) has continually emphasized

that with free recombination, selection cannot carry a large panmictic population from one favorable combination of allele frequencies to a better one if populations with intermediate values are less fit. In Wright's familiar metaphor, the population cannot pass from one adaptive peak to a higher one. Wright's emphasis on random drift and interdemic selection in a structured population could be described as providing some of the advantages of asexuality in a sexual population. Of course, the favorable combinations may have arisen in the first place by a sexual process within a deme.

6. There are well-established examples of situations in which there is a clear advantage in holding certain genes together. Linked groups of coordinately expressed genes in bacteria allow for rapid turning on or off of sets of genes appropriate to a particular environment. Some inversion polymorphisms in Drosophila that respond rapidly to seasonal changes may have a similar function of locking together genes with interrelated functions. Mimetic polymorphisms in Lepidoptera provide another example. More could be cited.

WHAT REASON IS THERE TO THINK THAT SEXUAL REPRODUCTION IS ADVANTAGEOUS?

With all these disadvantages, one might expect there to be no Mendelian heredity. Yet it is ubiquitous. There must be some reason for this. One clue is offered by the evolutionary patterns. There are many asexual species, but they tend to be related to each other through sexual ancestors. Asexual species are the twigs on the phylogenetic tree, not the main stems and branches. Although some asexual species have apparently survived for very long times, this is not the rule. Thus we arrive at the standard conclusion that asexual species may well have immediate evolutionary advantages, but are less successful in the long run. (For a discussion of the evidence, see Stebbins, 1950; Darlington, 1939; White, 1973, and, explicitly, Maynard Smith, 1978, pp. 51–57.) The prevailing view is that asexual species are less able to keep up with environmental changes than are sexual ones.

Before continuing, I shall note a few dissenting views. Thompson (1976) makes the curious suggestion that sexual reproduction is advantageous by slowing the evolutionary response to a changing environment, thus acting as a rein to prevent the species from chasing after transitory environmental changes. But the historical record argues that asexual species change more slowly in evolutionary time. Hickey and Rose argue in this volume that biparental inheritance exists to make transposition easier. This is an obvious advantage to the transposon, but is it to the host? Margulis and Sagan (1986) argue that Mendelian inheritance is a historical accident. They say that it exists "not because sexual species are better equipped to handle the contingencies of a dynamically changing environment but because of a series of historical accidents that took place in and permitted the survival of ancestral protists. . . . Not only is the question of maintenance of sex as stated a nonscientific one, but the very construction of the problem in this way leads to intellectual mischief and confusion." But sexual reproduction seems like a lot of excess baggage to carry along if it is functionless. Evolutionary conservatism perpetuates relics, but does it do so on such a grand scale as this?

Bernstein et al. in this volume (and earlier) take a different tack. In their view, recombination is evolutionarily disadvantageous. They state that (Bernstein et al., 1985) "The traditional view of the consequence of sex for evolution is that sex speeds up adaptation by promoting the spread of favorable mutants and elimination of deleterious mutations. However we argue here that the opposite is true; that sex acts as a constraint on adaptation." They argue that meiosis does indeed have a function, but that the function is repair of DNA damage. Bengtsson (1985) argues that biased conversion is the primary function of recombination between homologous chromosomes. However, I prefer to think that there are evolutionary advantages of recombination and that these are because of recombination per se. It is difficult to see how a process as elaborate, ubiquitous, and expensive as sexual reproduction has been maintained without serving some important purpose of its own, not one that is secondary to another adaptive function that could probably be accomplished without the complications of Mendelism. Yet, although I think the primary reason for recombination and outcrossing is their evolutionary advantage, this does not preclude there being other reasons.

The unique accomplishment of recombination is that without changing allele frequencies, it does change genotype frequencies and, in a finite population, generates new ones. This view was vigorously argued by East (1918), but has antecedents extending to pre-Mendelian writers, including two Darwins, Erasmus and Charles, and especially Weismann (see Ghiselin, in this volume).

THREE MAJOR ADVANTAGES OF RECOMBINATION

Simply showing that a property has evolutionary advantages does not itself mean that this property will increase under natural selection. But for the moment I want to consider only the question of whether sexuality is evolutionarily advantageous, and to defer until later the more difficult question of how such a property has evolved and is being maintained. The three arguments for the evolutionary advantages of sexual reproduction, as mentioned at the beginning of this chapter are: (1) adjusting to a changing environment, (2) incorporating beneficial mutations, and (3) getting rid of deleterious mutations. These basic ideas have been restated, clarified, exemplified, and enriched by many workers in the past 25 years.

Adjusting to a changing environment

Muller (1932), in his original paper, noted that an advantage of sexual reproduction is "the providing of an opportunity for continual shifting and readjustment of the relative abundance of different types as external conditions vary." In a similar vein, Wright (1932) said:

> The observed properties of gene mutation—fortuitous in origin, infrequent in oc- currence and deleterious when not negligible in effect—seem about as unfavorable as possible for an evolutionary process. Under biparental reproduction, however, a limited number of mutations which are not too injurious to be carried by the species furnish an almost infinite field of possible variations through which the species may work its way under natural selection.

The changing external environment may be physical or, surely more often, biotic.

A simple example was given by Sturtevant and Mather (1938). They pos- tulated a species that is subjected frequently to two environments, one in which *Ab* is favored and one in which *aB* is favored. In this situation, gametic (linkage) disequilibrium is generated and recombination would be unfavorable. However, if a third environment occurs such that *AB* is favored, then recombination can be beneficial.

It seems likely that most evolutionarily important traits are polygenic. The neutral theory (Kimura, 1983) has added to the evidence for Darwinian grad- ualism; if there are neutral alleles, there must also be very nearly neutral ones. For most traits the optimum fitness is associated with an intermediate value of the phenotype (e.g., size). By supplying a virtually continous range of quanti- tative variability, polygenic inheritance offers the opportunity for fine-tuning so that the optimum phenotype can be most closely approximated. If the fitness function is rounded and almost flat near the optimum (e.g., quadratic or normal) and the population is reasonably large, a very small mutation rate is sufficient to maintain a substantial genetic variance on the phenotypic scale. Selection toward the intermediate optimum leads to a balanced combination of + alleles, increasing the value of the trait, and − alleles, decreasing it. Selection will therefore generate gametic disequilibrium. As long as the environment is un- changing, recombination will be harmful, since it produces gametes with an excess of + alleles or of − alleles. However, if the optimum changes, such combinations will be favored. Therefore, if there is continuous selection for an optimum phenotype and the optimum keeps changing, recombination can be advantageous. Maynard Smith (in this volume) stresses this argument, and I agree.

The ineffectiveness of selection within inbred lines, where recombination cannot generate the variability to meet the changed environment imposed by the selection regime, has been recognized since the "pure lines" of Johannsen and has been amply documented by many experiments dating from the early days of Mendelism. New mutations are therefore not likely to supply much of the standing variation on which selection acts (although mutations in the past are the ultimate source of the standing variation). Thus the relevant comparison is between a sexual population and a set of asexual strains having the same initial amount of genetic variance rather than a single asexual clone. However, selection among such strains reduces the variance much more rapidly than does selection in a sexual population.

Polygenic Mendelian inheritance offers the advantage of a large potential variance with a small standing variance. If the environmental change is small enough that the new optimum is within the range of existing variants, an asexual strain will usually be advantageous, since it can respond more rapidly to selection. But if the new optimum is outside the existing range, new combinations are needed. Numerous laboratory and field experiments have demonstrated that a few generations of selection can produce individuals far outside the range of the original population, something that would not happen in an asexual system.

It could be argued that natural environments do not change rapidly enough for this consideration to be important. But while not likely to select as intensively and consistently as the breeder, nature is also less single-minded. An environmental change will affect many different, more or less independent traits, each with an intermediate optimum. It is then likely that no individual exists that is near the optimum for *all* traits in the new environment, but such could easily arise by recombination. It is not necessary that the environmental change be sudden. For recombination to be advantageous, it is only necessary that the change be rapid enough that new mutations cannot supply sufficient variability to track it.

Finally, many—probably most—polygenic traits with an intermediate optimum show rather little dominance and epistasis. When this is the case, the segregation and recombination loads are minimal, the genic and genotypic variance are equal, and sexual and asexual populations respond to weak, short-term selection at the same rate. But to the extent that an asexual system cannot supply appropriate variants at a sufficient rate for fine-tuning and to keep up with environmental whims, the sexual system is better.

In recent years, a number of variations on the general theme of keeping up with environmental changes have been proposed. Several have been summarized by Maynard Smith (1978) and Ghiselin (in this volume). One aspect of the environment that is liable to sudden, large, unpredictable changes is infectious disease. This has been emphasized especially by Hamilton (1980).

Combining Beneficial Mutations from Different Lineages

To Fisher (1930) and Muller (1932, 1958) this was the major advantage of recombination. With asexual reproduction, two or more favorable mutations can be combined in the same individual only if the second and subsequent ones occur in a descendant of the individual in which the first occurred. On the contrary, with recombination mutations that occur in separate individuals can be combined into the same lineage. The first attempt to quantify this argument was made by Muller (1958). Muller's calculations were subsequently improved (Crow and Kimura, 1965, 1969), but the essential argument remained unchanged. The maximum relative advantage of sexual reproduction is the number of separate mutations that occur in the population during the time required for the descendants of a favorable mutant individual to multiply to the point where there is a 50:50 chance of a new favorable mutation occurring among them. If the population is large or the favorable mutation rate high, this advantage can be manyfold.

Maynard Smith (1968) pointed out that Muller's argument requires a finite population; in an infinite population with linkage equilibrium, sexual and asexual evolution occur at the same rate. I had also realized this and discussed it with Muller, who had planned to write an article on the subject, but his death intervened. I was also bothered by the fact that in our 1965 model sexual reproduction is most advantageous as the selective advantage of the mutant gene gets smaller; yet in the limit as the advantage approaches zero there is surely no advantage in recombination. The paradox was cleared up by Felsenstein (1974), who showed our result to be an artifact caused by treating deterministically a problem that is essentially stochastic.

An important point is that this argument remains valid only if individual mutations, as well as combinations, are beneficial. In particular, if two deleterious mutations occur, whether in the same or in separate lineages, they will not increase unless there is close linkage or extreme selective advantage in combination (Crow and Kimura, 1965). This point was confirmed and developed more completely by Eshel and Feldman (1970). Recombination does not facilitate the evolution of favorable combinations of individually deleterious components.

Getting rid of deleterious mutations

The majority of mutations, if they have a fitness effect at all, are deleterious. The Haldane (1937) principle states that the reduction in fitness of a population because of recurrent mutation is proportional to the mutation rate and not the deleteriousness of the individual mutant genes. With no dominance or epistasis, the fitness reduction (load, L) is equal to twice the (haploid) genomic mutation rate, $2\Sigma\mu$ (more accurately, $L = 1 - e^{-2\Sigma\mu}$). However, with allelic interactions, especially interlocus interactions, it is possible for several mutant genes to be picked off by a single "genetic death" (Muller, 1950).

A useful statement of the principle, due to King (1966), is that the mutation load is twice the genomic mutation rate divided by the difference in the number of mutants in those individuals eliminated by selection and those not eliminated. It has long been realized that truncation, or rank-order, selection is the most efficient form of selection for a quantitative trait. Nature is not likely to truncate exactly in the manner of an animal or plant breeder, but something approximating this probably occurs in limited-density populations. A quite wide departure from strict truncation still permits a close approximation to the genetic consequences of rank-order selection (Kimura and Crow, 1978). Furthermore, deleterious polygenic mutations affecting viability in Drosophila interact synergistically (Mukai, 1969; Crow, 1970). With multiple mutations producing individually small effects, one can construct realistic quasitruncation models in which the mutation load is reduced to ⅕ or less of what it would be if the mutants were eliminated independently (Crow and Kimura, 1979).

This load reduction does not happen with asexual reproduction, however. Without recombination, mutant genes must be eliminated in the same combinations in which they occur. The mutation load in an asexual population was first formulated by Kimura and Maruyama (1966). I later gave a simple derivation (Crow, 1970), as follows. Let P be the frequency of the most common type, A, with fitness w, and U be the frequency of asexual progeny with one or more *new* mutant genes. Then the frequency of A next generation is given by

$$P' = P(1 - U)w/\overline{w}$$

where $\overline{w}$ is the mean fitness. At equilibrium, $P' = P$, and the mutation load is

$$L \equiv (w - \overline{w})/w = U$$

If mutations occur independently, which is reasonable at least to a first approximation, $L = U = 1 - e^{-2\Sigma\mu}$ for a diploid where, as before, $\Sigma\mu$ is the mutation rate per haploid genome.

This is the same as in a sexual population with deleterious mutations acting independently. So it has seemed to me that mutation load reduction is an important advantage of sexual reproduction. This argument has been subsequently developed more fully by Kondrashov (1982, 1984). This is one argument for sexual reproduction that does not depend on a finite population size. It depends on epistasis, but epistasis in the direction that seems to be the rule because of the general occurrence of the synergistic effects of deleterious mutations and quasitruncation selection.

A related argument was given earlier by Muller (1964) and is now widely known as Muller's ratchet, being so designated by Felsenstein (1974). In a finite asexual population there is always a nonzero probability that no individual in the population will be free of deleterious mutations at all loci. In a sexual population, the mutant-free type can be reconstituted by recombination. In an asexual population, it can be obtained only by back mutation. This problem has been treated mathematically by several people (Haigh, 1978; Maynard Smith, 1978, and this volume). The ratchet may well play a role in limiting the genome size in asexual organisms, especially in small or moderate-sized populations.

Arguments for getting rid of deleterious mutations efficiently are especially clear and convincing for RNA viruses, where the mutation rate is very high. This viewpoint has been used by Pressing and Reanney (1984) and by L. Chao (personal communication) to account for replication of some RNA viruses in segments that are later joined into a single virus. Suppose, for simplicity, that we consider only two subunits and only lethal mutations, each occurring at a rate μ per nucleotide per infectious generation. If the length of the RNA genome is n nucleotides, the probability of a lethal-free virus is $e^{-n\mu}$. If the RNA were divided into two equal segments, the probability of a segment being lethal free is $e^{-n\mu/2}$. If $n\mu$ is large, the probability of survival of a segment can be much higher than that of the full RNA molecule. With k virus genomes entering the cell, the probability of at least one being mutant free is $1 - (1 - e^{-n\mu})^k$. If $k/2$ of each segment enter, the probability of at least one of each kind being mutant free is $1 - [(1 - e^{-n\mu/2})^{k/2}]^2$. For example, if $n\mu = 2$ and $k = 10$, the two probabilities are 0.766 and 0.990, respectively. The mutation load is $(1 - 0.766)/(1 - 0.990)$, or 23 times as large in the unsegmented system. Unless the cost of segmentation is large, it produces a real advantage. Although this calculation is simplified, it illustrates the advantage of complementing segments. As the number of segments increases, the advantage increases until something else (e.g., difficulties of assembly) becomes limiting.

When the mutations are lethal, as in this example, the argument is essentially Muller's ratchet. In the more general case, however, L. Chao's argument is one of load reduction.

WHICH OF THE HISTORICAL ADVANTAGES OF RECOMBINATION IS MOST IMPORTANT?

Is (1) adjusting to environmental differences, (2) incorporating favorable mutations, or (3) getting rid of deleterious mutations the most important reason for the ubiquity of Mendelism?

I believe that, at least in multicellular eukaryotes, evolutionary progress depends more on the changing frequencies of existing alleles than on new mutations. The standing population of alleles contains many that have arisen by mutation in the past and are now held near some sort of equilibrium frequency. Many of these are only mildly harmful and are at comparatively high frequencies; the worst ones have been eliminated by selection. Any sexual population has a large reservoir of such mutations that have been tested and found to be not too bad. They are the most likely candidates for being advantageous after an environmental shift, much more so than newly occurring mutations.

If this is true, then argument 1 is more important than argument 2. The Fisher–Muller argument (2) might perhaps play a role in prokaryotes, where drastic population changes can follow environmental shifts. One experimental test for evolution of polygenic drug resistance in T4 viruses (Malmberg, 1977) did indeed show a more rapid change with higher recombination. The Fisher–Muller argument may also apply to the early history of life on earth. But I doubt its current importance in multicellular eukaryotes.

Argument 3, either the load or the ratchet argument, is the only one that applies to a constant environment. I think the load argument deserves more attention than it has had, although perhaps the papers of Kondrashov (1982, 1984) have rectified this. I prefer argument 3 to argument 2 for the additional reason that harmful mutations are much more common than beneficial ones. I find no compelling reason to prefer argument 1 over argument 3. Which is more important would depend on the relative importance of keeping up with environmental changes versus reducing the mutation load.

IS IT NECESSARY TO INVOKE GROUP SELECTION?

The discussion thus far has asked: Is recombination good for the evolution of a population? Stated this way, it is a group selection argument. Although such optimizing arguments usually lead to a correct conclusion, there are pitfalls for the unwary. Nature does not always optimize. Recently there has been a great deal of interest in devising models for the evolution of recombination that depend on individual selection.

One form of mathematical analysis asks whether a neutral modifier of recombination frequency would increase if introduced into the population. Modifiers of recombination rates that have no other observable effects are common, and several experimenters have changed recombination rates by selection (see Brooks, in this volume). Mathematical arguments for the evolution of recombination rates are individual, not group selection, models. Charlesworth (1976) showed in detail that the Sturtevant–Mather argument would work without invoking group selection. Felsenstein and Yokoyama (1976) produced a specific model of individual selection for recombination. Thus there is plenty of evidence, both experimental and mathematical, for situations in which individual selection can affect recombination.

The distinction between individual and group selection gets to be fuzzy in some instances. A recessive mutant genotype changing an individual from asexual to sexual is immediately isolated. Likewise, if a dominant asexual mutant genotype arises in a sexual population, it is forever isolated from its former sexual partners. In either case the sexual and asexual moieties no longer exchange genes. Thus the selection is between one population and another, and not individual selection in which the gene (or the linked cluster) is the unit of selection.

Because of such considerations, I think it likely that the kind of arguments that I have been using in this chapter are valid. I am sufficiently confident of the eventual success of efforts to produce individual selection models to think it appropriate to consider arguments based on the group advantages of sexual reproduction. But, as Felsenstein says in this volume, it is being "intellectually lazy" not to work out the detailed models. The formulation of realistic individual selection models is a challenge that I hope will continue to be accepted by mathematical biologists.

ADVANTAGES OF DIPLOIDY

Segregation and recombination do not require an extended diploid phase; meiosis can follow fertilization immediately, and it does in many species. Yet there has been an evolution toward an extended diploid phase in most large, highly differentiated organisms. In attempting to answer why, I shall mostly repeat earlier arguments (Crow and Kimura, 1965).

One obvious advantage of diploidization is that, by providing a complementing chromosome, it can conceal recessive and partially recessive deleterious mutations. But this is clearly only a transitory advantage. The population will soon reach a new equilibrium with a higher frequency of deleterious alleles than before. The fitness will then be about what it was before diploidy; if recessiveness is not complete, as is almost always the case, the load will be increased because there are now twice as many genes to mutate. So it may well be that diploidy is not permanently advantageous, but has only an immediate advantage, and the population cannot return to haploidy without having all the undesirable consequences of inbreeding.

A second advantage of diploidy is that it permits the exploitation of loci that are overdominant for fitness. To the extent that such loci are important, diploidy is advantageous. I might note, though, that asexual diploidy is still better, for it abolishes the segregation load. An overdominant locus might produce permanent "heterozygosity" with no segregation load by unequal crossing over, leading to homozygotes that have both alleles, as suggested several times by Haldane and developed by Spofford (1969).

A third possible advantage of extended diploidy is protection against somatic mutation. To the extent that aging, malignancy, and other kinds of damage are due to recessive or nearly recessive mutations, diploidy provides protection. This idea receives some support from the observation that organisms with the most elaborate and highly differentiated soma (e.g., most animals) are usually diploid.

A fourth possible advantage, related to the arguments of Bernstein et al. (this volume and earlier), is that diploidy provides a normal template for double-strand repair and in this way provides further protection from somatic mutation.

These are arguments for increased fitness, but they are not arguments for the facilitation of evolution. An extended diploid phase, in contrast to meiosis and syngamy, is probably a survival strategy, not an evolutionary strategy.

This discussion prompts the question of why polyploidy is not more common. The most obvious answer is that the ploidy level is a compromise between such benefits as I have been discussing and problems with the sex-determining system and the disadvantages of having to manage too many chromosomes. For example, nondisjunction increases as the ploidy increases, especially in auto-polyploids.

IS PASSING THROUGH A SINGLE-CELL STAGE ITSELF ADVANTAGEOUS?

Asexual species sometimes reproduce by twinning or budding in such a way that the two new organisms both start out with a large number of often-differentiated cells. In other cases asexual species bypass meiosis to produce mitotically derived eggs, seeds, or spores from which another generation develops. Are there advantages to doing this?

It may be that this is simply a reproductive strategy for producing a large number of progeny; apogamous dandelions are conspicuously successful in this regard. Yet I think there may also be an evolutionary advantage.

Starting with a single cell, sexual or asexual, permits each generation to begin with a tabula rasa largely unencumbered by the somatic mutations from previous generations. If a population produces single-celled, diploid seeds, these will be of many genotypes, and selection acts on the genotypic variance among them as they develop. Those individuals with the largest number of harmful mutations are efficiently eliminated. In contrast, suppose that the organism produces multicelled buds or cuttings. Each bud or cutting has a variety of mutant genotypes among its differentiating cells. Selection operates on some sort of weighted average of the effects of these mutant cells. There will be relatively little variation in fitness among the different individuals, on the general principle that the variance of a mean is less than the variance of the individual values. With less genetic variance, selection is less effective. Thus, producing asexual seeds or spores would seem to be evolutionarily advantageous.

Furthermore, with budding, Muller's ratchet should become important. It becomes less and less likely that there is an individual free of mutant genes in all its cells. A key question is how many generations back one has to go to reach the ancestral cell. Going through a single-cell stage with an enormous number of genotypes represented among such cells reduces the effectiveness of the ratchet. Moreover, if the species produces a large number of asexual eggs or seeds, the population is at that stage very large. This too reduces the effectiveness of the ratchet, which is less important as the population size increases. Perhaps this fact explains why asexual budding is rare in higher animals, where somatic tissues are so varied. The ratchet principle predicts that among asexual plants, those with the longest evolutionary history are those that reproduce by seeds rather than cuttings. This might provide a test of the ratchet idea.

I have never heard the importance of going through a single-cell stage expressed before, and would welcome comments both as to its possible merits and as to whether it has been proposed somewhere in the enormous literature on the subject. A rather similar point has been made by Dawkins (1982, Chapter 14). There may be others.

A FEW SPECIAL TOPICS

Anisogamy

I share the commonly held view that the original development of meiosis and fertilization involved isogamous fusions. In that case there would be no twofold cost of males. The evolutionary advantages and disadvantages of recombination are the same whether the gametes are isogamous or anisogamous. It is reasonable, therefore, that the development of anisogamy and separate sexes was a reproductive and not an evolutionary strategy. Division of labor and allocation of parental expenditure are presumably determined to maximize the effectiveness of reproduction, not the amount of recombination.

The other side of this coin is that in dioecious, anisogamous plants and animals, there is an immediate twofold advantage of parthenogenetic females. Thus, one is not surprised at occasional asexual offshoots of anisogamous sexual species in the course of evolution.

Frequency and distribution of chiasmata

If you ask a cytologist for the function of chiasmata, the likely reply is that they regularize meiosis and minimize the deleterious effects of nondisjunction. If you ask an evolutionist, the answer is that the function is an evolutionary strategy to bring about gene recombination. Which explanation is right?

I think that both are. With Maynard Smith, I note that since organisms such as male Drosophila go through meiosis very well, there is no absolute mechanical necessity for chiasmata. Yet it is well established that nondisjunctional eggs in Drosophila contain a disproportionate number of non-crossover chromosomes. I therefore believe that interference and chiasma localization, by assuring at least one chiasma in each chromosome arm, *do* have a meiotic function.

Whatever the evolutionary advantages of recombination, they will be maximized if there are many chromosomes and high, interferenceless recombination on each (ideally, a separate chromosome for each gene). Actual meioses are, I believe, a compromise between the evolutionary advantages of completely free recombination and the requirements of an orderly meiosis. At the same time there may well be selection for reduced recombination in chromosome areas where there are linked alleles with specific, epistatic coadaptations. The actual distribution of chiasmata presumably represents the result of all these, and doubtless other, forces.

Transposons

Almost immediately after the general realization that transposons were widely distributed among higher eukaryotes, and were not simply an eccentricity of cultivated maize, it was noted that they constituted a paradigm for "selfish DNA" (Doolittle and Sapienza, 1980; Orgel and Crick, 1980). It was also quickly noted by several people (e.g., Hickey, 1982; Crow, 1984) that transposons, such as P factors in Drosophila, spread much more effectively in populations with biparental inheritance.

Hickey and Rose (in this volume) go much further and suggest that the function of sexual reproduction is to facilitate transposition. Surely this is putting the cart before the horse. To be sure, transposons take advantage of the sexual mechanism. But they are almost always harmful rather than beneficial and are much better regarded as parasites than as potentially valuable symbionts. It is hardly in the interest of the host to facilitate the spread of harmful parasites.

The P factor in Drosophila causes chromosome breakage, mutation, segregation distortion, and sterility (Kidwell et al., 1977; Engels, 1983). I think that, on the principle that the successful parasite does not kill its host, the harmful effects of this entity are confined to the germ cells, where, although they cause some sterility, they are nonetheless in a location where they can be transmitted to other flies and spread through the population. That this property is the result of natural selection is supported by the finding that splicing out of a specific intron in the transposon is required to confine the effects to the germ line (Laski et al., 1986). When this intron is missing, the P factor can produce lethality (W. R. Engels and A. Robertson, personal communication).

I think it much more likely that in the contest between host and parasite, the parasite is taking advantage of whatever host properties are useful to it. The number of instances in which parasitic DNA has been taken over by the host and put to good use is so small compared to the number of times in which the parasitic DNA has been harmful that I cannot imagine a species evolving a specific strategy to take advantage of such very rare opportunities.

MENDELISM AS A "PERFECT" SYSTEM OF HEREDITY

Mendelian inheritance with free recombination is something like a factorial experiment (Fisher, 1960). Each allele is tested in combination with many others, every zygote in every generation having a different combination. In this way, those alleles that confer the highest average fitness in the largest number of combinations—those that are "good mixers" to use Ernst Mayr's apt expression—increase in frequency. In Fisher's terms, alleles are selected on the basis of their additive effects on fitness. The precision of the meiotic process guarantees that the test is scrupulously fair. If the number of genes involved in a trait is large and the alleles act cumulatively (i.e., with little or no dominance or epistasis), selection is as efficient as an asexual system.

That the Mendelian system has such optimum properties is clear. However, more work is needed to clarify the detailed selection processes that brought it about.

The problem of segregation distortion

The Mendelian system works best if the testing of each allele is done fairly. Ultraselfish genes may beat the system by cheating, but the system is weakened. There are examples of distorted segregation ratios in several species. Generally such genes are kept in check by being intrinsically harmful or by alleles that resist the effect. In the *Segregation distorter* system in Drosophila, for example, there is an important selective advantage—for the drive system, not for the species—in holding the different components of the system together. But there is also selection for alleles on the homologous chromosome that reduce the distortion (Charlesworth and Hartl, 1978; Crow, 1979).

The welfare of the species depends on keeping meiotic drive systems out of the population, for they only reduce the fairness and therefore the efficiency of the Mendelian mechanism. Eshel (1985) has recently made an important contribution to this subject by showing that, in the presence of a locus with a distorted segregation ratio, a rare neutral, independent modifier that changes the ratio in the direction of 1:1 will always increase. Surprisingly, and strikingly, this principle always works only for independent modifier loci; there is almost a qualitative difference between independent assortment and loose linkage. As mentioned earlier, in a species with several chromosomes, most pairs of loci are independent. The efficiency of a Mendelian system in maintaining its fairness to all loci against the threat of cheaters is greatest when the number of chromosomes is large.

This is one more argument in favor of free recombination as an evolutionarily advantageous mechanism. It offers another reason for thinking that Mendelian independent assortment is evolutionarily more important than crossing over. How important the meiotic drive argument is, relative to the others mentioned earlier, remains to be seen, as does the question of whether group selection is required.

HISTORICAL VERSUS PRESENT MECHANISMS

The discovery, some years ago, that mutants deficient in enzymatic repair of DNA lesions also were deficient in crossing over immediately suggested that crossing over had its origins in repair mechanisms. Repair mechanisms must be very old, going back to a time when ultraviolet radiation was a major threat. They almost certainly antedate mechanisms for molecular recombination.

Dougherty (1955) was, I believe, the first to suggest the evolutionary connection between recombination and DNA repair, although the possibility must have occurred to many. As Bernstein (1977 and later) argues, it is very likely that recombination arose as a by-product of repair mechanisms, and this interpretation has been very favorably received.

Bernstein et al. (in this volume and earlier) go further, however. They hypothesize that repair of DNA damage is the major reason for the evolution and persistence of recombination in higher eukaryotes. It is true that repair of double-strand breaks requires information from another DNA molecule (Szostak et al., 1983; for a recent review, see Radman and Wagner, 1986). Bernstein and colleagues argue that outcrossing is a consequence of the necessity for recombinational repair of DNA damage. They present a scenario in which Mendelian inheritance evolved from the need for outside chromosomes to replace those in which deleterious recessives were made homozygous as a by-product of the repair process. To me it seems that if Mendelian assortment and crossing over are as evolutionarily harmful as these workers believe, surely there would be some other less expensive way found to carry out the repair function. Thus, I find this argument interesting, but unconvincing.

I note, with Maynard Smith, that the evolution of recombination in pro-karyotes, the origin of meiosis and syngamy in early eukaryotes, and the maintenance of these processes in multicellular eukaryotes very likely have different answers. The literature on the evolution of sex has dealt almost entirely with the third, the maintenance, as does this article. Recombination in prokaryotes may well be a consequence of DNA repair. The origins of meiosis and syngamy and the selective forces that brought these about remain a mystery.

SUMMARY

It is likely that recombination between DNA strands arose as a by-product of DNA repair mechanisms. The reasons for maintenance of recombination in prokaryotes, with their many mechanisms of DNA exchange, may well be different from those in higher eukaryotes, with their chromosomes, orderly meiosis, and syngamy.

In higher eukaryotes, the advantages of recombination (crossing over and independent assortment) are of three basic types: (1) adjusting to temporally or spatially varying environments, (2) combining in a single lineage favorable mutations that occur in different individuals, and (3) more efficient elimination of deleterious mutations. It is emphasized that independent assortment is more important than crossing over as a recombination mechanism in any species with a haploid chromosome number larger than two.

Because deleterious mutations are much more common than beneficial ones, the third argument is probably more important than the second. For the first argument, recombination appears to be most important for quantitative, polygenic traits with an intermediate optimum. This generates gametic disequilibrium, and recombination is required to produce new gametic types when the environment changes. For the third argument, there are two advantages of recombination. One is Muller's ratchet, which may limit the size of the genome in asexual species, especially when the population size is small or moderate. The other is the lower mutation load in a sexual population, which by recombination can eliminate deleterious mutations in bunches. I share Maynard Smith's (1986) view that for multicellular eukaryotes "the main theoretical explanations have already been formulated, and our task is to decide their relative importance."

It is probably not necessary to invoke group selection for the evolution of recombination. Examples where individual selection suffices have been produced and, most likely, more will follow as more realistic mathematical models are examined. The problem in trying to achieve a detailed understanding of the evolution and maintenance of sex is that "what's good for the population" arguments are fuzzy, while specific individual selection models are oversimplified. The issues are so broad and general that no individual experiment or observation can be definitive. Deeper understanding will require broad syntheses, together with mathematical modeling.

CHAPTER 5

SEX AND THE EVOLUTION OF

RECOMBINATION

Joseph Felsenstein

INTRODUCTION

Over a decade ago, I wrote two papers (Felsenstein, 1974; Felsenstein and Yokoyama, 1976) on models for the evolution of recombination. The central concern of those papers was to demonstrate the relationship between various models that had previously been proposed for the evolution of recombination and to present some simulation and theoretical results. The problem has continued to be of interest to evolutionary biologists, although they seem particularly entranced by it when it is called "the evolution of sex" rather than, more accurately, "the evolution of recombination." When books are written on the subject, the noun in their title is inevitably "sex" rather than "recombination." One wonders how many fewer people would buy a book on this subject if the word "sex" were not in the title.

ˈ Recently, interest in the subject seems to be increasing. In his monograph, Williams (1975, p. v) has declared that "I hope at least to convince [readers] that there is a kind of crisis at hand in evolutionary biology, and that my suggestions are plausible enough to warrant serious consideration." Crises in evolutionary biology have been declared quite frequently recently, although it has been noticeable that the biologist declaring one usually just happens to have completed a piece of work that is thought to solve it. These crises seem comparable in importance to the "constitutional crises" that used to be declared daily by the press during the Watergate hearings of 1973. After a time, it became clear that a constitutional crisis was somewhat less serious than a flat tire on your car.

This year, the sex crisis seems to have returned. Shortly after I finished a short review on this subject for a volume in honor of John Maynard Smith

74

(Felsenstein, 1985), I was asked by two different editors to write similar articles for volumes on the evolution of sex, and there is talk of at least one conference as well. What has happened? Has a new source of data or a new kind of experiment been discovered that will help us resolve the controversies? Has the failure to arrive at a consensus here become a barrier to further progress in some other area?

There is a continuing flow of new theories and variants of existing theories, but there seems to be no major new source of data, no illuminating new experiment, no barrier to progress in other fields. The problem has simply flared up again and will probably gutter out after a while. Biologists will once again all become convinced that they know the answer, but once again there will be no unanimity as to what the answer turned out to be.

TWO DISTINCTIONS

The issue of "the evolution of sex" covers at least four distinguishable phenomena: differentiation of the sexes, anisogamy, outcrossing, and recombination. Most of the work under that heading is actually on the last two phenomena. In this chapter, I provide an overview of the main categories of theories for the evolution of outcrossing and recombination. Note that for haploid organisms the absence of recombination has in effect the same consequences as the absence of outcrossing.

Explanations for the origin and maintenance of recombination are of two kinds. The crucial difference between them is whether or not they argue that recombination exists because of its action in reducing the extent of linkage disequilibrium. For example, Bernstein, Hopf, and Michod (in this volume) argue that recombination acts as a repair mechanism near the site of the chiasma. In that argument, the recombination between outside markers does not play an important role. Models in which the proper functioning of the chromosomes in meiosis depend on the presence of recombinations fall into the same class. By contrast, in the classical models of Fisher (1930) and Muller (1932), the essential function of recombination is to remove nonrandom associations between genotypes at different loci, or linkage disequilibrium. Unfortunately, the distinction I am making is not quite the same as that made by Maynard Smith (1978, p. 73), between "physiological" and "genetic" theories of the evolution of recombination. Maynard Smith defined the physiological theories as those in which recombination is maintained to ensure "the proper functioning of meiosis." The repair theory and the classical theory would both have been called "genetic" by Maynard Smith, although one involves local effects and the other outside markers.

My intention here is to comment on the theories that invoke linkage disequilibrium, leaving it to others to cover the other theories.

IS LINKAGE DISEQUILIBRIUM A BAD THING?

It is worth repeating here some of the fundamental properties of linkage dise-
quibrium in the presence of selection, since it is one of the most abstruse
population genetic phenomena and many evolutionists have little feel for it.
Imagine first that we have a diploid population with two loci (a haploid version
of the argument is easily constructed as well). At locus A there are two alleles,
A and a, and at locus B there are two alleles, B and b. Now suppose that the
population is in linkage equilibrium, meaning that there is no association
between the presence of any genotype at the A locus and the presence of any
genotype at the B locus. Then the fraction of BB genotypes among individuals
who are AA is the same as the overall fraction of BB genotypes. Thus if $P(AA)$
is the overall fraction of AA genotypes in the population, and $P(BB)$ the fraction
of BB genotypes,

$$P(AA\ BB) = P(AA)\ P(BB) \tag{1}$$

At the gametic or haplotype level, too, the presence of an A allele is independent
of the presence of a B allele if there is linkage equilibrium:

$$g(AB) = p(A)\ p(B) \tag{2}$$

Natural selection acting on only one of these loci (say, the B locus) will not
change the gene or genotype frequencies at the other. If, say, half of the bb and
one-eighth of the Bb individuals die, irrespective of their genotypes at the A
locus, then we can see that the chance that an individual dies is independent
of its genotype at the A locus, and hence that the gene and genotype frequencies
at the A locus are unchanged. Furthermore, after those deaths, the A locus
and the B locus continue to be in linkage equilibrium.

   Now suppose that a similar mortality occurs at the A locus, irrespective of
the genotype at the B locus. It does not change the gene or genotype frequencies
at the B locus, and it too leaves the population still in linkage equilibrium.
Thus the effect of linkage equilibrium is that natural selection can go on
independently at each locus, without affecting the rate or outcome at the other.

   If in a generation we impose viability selection first at the A locus and then
at the B locus, the effect will be the same as if a selection regime were imposed
according to which the fitness of each genotype is the product of fitnesses at
the A locus and at the B locus. Thus if the fitnesses of AA, Aa, and aa are
1:0.9:0.7, and fitnesses of BB, Bb, and bb are 1:0.8:0.4, then a multiplicative
fitness scheme in which the fitness of AaBb is $0.9 \times 0.8 = 0.72$ will have
exactly the same effect as two successive bouts of selection, one at each locus.
This follows because the chance of surviving both rounds of selection is the
product 0.9×0.8 of the chances of surviving each of them. If fitnesses are
multiplicative, then linkage disequilibrium will be preserved and selection at
each locus will not affect selection at the other. Even if the fitnesses are fertilities

rather than viabilities, multiplicative determination of the multilocus fitnesses is the relevant condition.

I showed (Felsenstein, 1965) that, with multiplicative selection, linkage disequilibrium (departure from linkage equilibrium) will not arise if it does not already exist. In fact, the effect of recombination, at least at the population genetic level, is to reduce linkage disequilibrium towards zero by creating gametes that contain genes randomly assembled from different gametes of the previous generation. If the population is already in linkage equilibrium, then it does not matter whether recombination occurs or not—the genetic composition of the population is unaffected by it. Individuals are affected, but the numbers of various kinds of genotypes and gametes created and eliminated exactly cancel out as long as there is linkage equilibrium.

If there is linkage disequilibrium, then this affects the rate of response of each locus to natural selection. For instance, if a population has alleles A and B associated with each other, then a and b will also be nonrandomly associated. By virtue of the association, natural selection eliminating a alleles will also concurrently tend to eliminate b alleles as well. Thus natural selection at each locus will change gene frequencies at the other. If the favored alleles A and B are associated (in "coupling" linkage disequilibrium), then selection on each speeds the change of gene frequencies at the other. Coupling linkage disequilibrium increases the rate at which the population responds to natural selection. Association between A and b alleles (and correspondingly between a and B alleles) causes selection at the two loci to conflict. Of course, the terms "coupling" and "repulsion" require us to specify which alleles at each locus are to be regarded as comparable: in the present case, the favored alleles are those denoted by capital letters.

The easiest way to see the effect of disequilibrium is to consider haploids where the fitnesses at the loci are multiplicative, so that the fitnesses of AB, Ab, aB, and ab are in the ratios $(1+s)^2:1+s:1+s:1$. This is the situation in which at each locus the capital letter allele is favored with a selection coefficient of s, and the loci do not interact. If the gene frequencies happen to be identical at the two loci, then the most extreme coupling disequilibrium that could exist would be for the population to consist entirely of AB and ab gametes. Their fitnesses are in the ratio $(1+s)^2:1$. The coupling disequilibrium means that A-bearing gametes and a-bearing gametes differ more strongly in fitness than $1+s:1$, and that will speed the change of the A locus by natural selection. The most extreme repulsion disequilibrium would be to have all aB and Ab gametes. Both of these types have the same fitness, $1+s$, so that the repulsion disequilibrium results in selection being completely stalled: selection favoring A exactly counterbalances selection favoring B.

Maynard Smith (1968) drew from these facts the implication for theories of the evolution of recombination. If a population starts in linkage equilibrium and undergoes natural selection with multiplicative fitnesses, then it will remain in linkage equilibrium at all times. The rate of change at each locus will be the same regardless of the amount of recombination, since all that recombination could do would be to restore linkage equilibrium, and that already exists. One can go farther than Maynard Smith and show that a modifier gene affecting the rate of recombination will not undergo any change of gene frequencies in this situation.

The broader implication of the argument is that if we are to see any effect of recombination on the rate of evolution or the genetic equilibria in a population, we must have either nonmultiplicative fitnesses or some other force creating linkage disequilibrium. From the point of view of natural selection, it is departure from multiplicative combination of fitnesses that constitutes "interaction," although this conflicts with a statistical tradition that associates interaction with departure from additivity. The way to reconcile these two views seems to be to think not of the fitness of a genotype, but of the logarithm of its fitness. Additivity on a logarithmic scale is multiplicative interaction on the original fitness scale. Provided that we are talking of the logarithm of fitness, "interaction" in the (log) fitnesses is the condition for selection to cause departure from linkage equilibrium.

It is worth noting that Maynard Smith's argument invalidates the earliest genetic argument for the evolution of recombination, that advanced by East (1918). That argument is also the one commonly found in textbooks, which tend to be a bit out of date (in this case, by over 50 years). East argued that recombination creates new genotypes. So it does. An AB/ab parent will have among its gametes not only the two types that formed it, AB and ab, but also Ab and aB if there is recombination between the two loci. But if the population is in linkage equilibrium, then somewhere else an Ab/aB parent will be undergoing recombination, which will remove Ab and aB gametes and replace them by AB and ab. These two processes will exactly cancel each other if the two types of double heterozygote, coupling (AB/ab) and repulsion (Ab/aB) are equally frequent. This will happen precisely when the population is in linkage equilibrium. In that case no new genotypes arise by recombination.

In some cases, of course, new genotypes are disadvantageous. This will happen, for example, when natural selection favors particular multilocus genotypes. For example, suppose that natural selection favored genotypes that had as many capital letters (A and B) as lowercase letters (a and b). If we have a population consisting only of the genotypes Ab/Ab, Ab/aB, and aB/aB, then recombination will be deleterious to the population. It will produce AB and ab gametes from the heterozygotes. Except for the rare case of these two combining with each other, all other genotypes resulting from this recombination will have too many or too few capital letters.

Thus when the population comes to equilibrium under selection regimes involving multilocus interaction, there will be linkage disequilibrium. This disequilibrium increases the fitness, and its disruption by recombination will be deleterious. Such an argument was made by Lewontin (1971). But it is by no means obvious that an argument based on mean population fitness will convince a modifier gene altering recombination frequency to be a good sport and change its frequency. Nei (1967) made an approximate argument and Feldman (1972) a more exact argument that the modifiers would usually do the honorable thing. Many references to work since then can be found in the interesting recent paper by Feldman and Libermann (1986) and in the chapter by Brooks in this volume. I have assumed and will assume throughout this chapter that the modifiers will behave themselves and be selected in the direction that improves the fitness of the population. But this is not invariably so; I am being intellectually lazy, and there is no substitute for a genuine analysis of a model having modifier loci.

We have the anomalous situation that a detailed population genetic analysis reveals not only that the standard explanation for the evolution of recombination will not work, but also that there is a good evolutionary reason for believing that modifiers will be selected to eliminate recombination.

TWO THEORIES OF THE EVOLUTION OF RECOMBINATION

To have a theory that predicts that recombination will be favored, or at least not eliminated from a population, a necessary part of that theory will be a source of linkage disequilibrium. Without it, recombination will have no effect on the genetic composition of the population, and modifiers increasing or decreasing its frequency will not be selected.

Two major classes of theory have been proposed, differing in the evolutionary source of the disequilibrium. For each of these, a variety of biological mechanisms have been suggested. When people talk of "a theory" for the evolution of recombination they usually are referring to the biological scenario rather than to the combination of evolutionary forces. I have been concerned with understanding the theories in the latter sense. Once we ask what forces are at work, it turns out that there are only these two distinguishable theories.

We may call these the Fisher–Muller theory and the varying selection theory. Fisher (1930) and Muller (1932) argued, in very similar terms, that recombination was advantageous to a population because it enabled favorable mutations that occurred in different individuals in the population to be fixed in the same gene pool. Without recombination the two favorable mutations could at best compete with each other and could not both be incorporated into the same genome.

How can we understand Fisher and Muller's theory in terms of linkage disequilibrium? I have argued (Felsenstein, 1974, 1985) that in their theory the source of linkage disequilibrium is genetic drift. For example, if two favorable mutants happen to occur in the same generation in a diploid population of size N, one at the A locus and one at the B locus, then the chance that these will occur in different gametes is $1 - 1/(2N)$. They will occur in the same gamete $1/(2N)$ of the time. Either way the population will be in linkage disequilibrium. The disequilibrium is random and a result of the finiteness of the population size. If the population were of infinite size, each mutant would recur many times and would arise at a frequency μ. A fraction μ^2 of the gametes would be double mutants, so that the population would be at linkage equilibrium.

The varying selection theory is the work of Sturtevant and Mather (1938). They imagined natural selection that favored in some generations coupling gametes (AB and ab) and, not long after, repulsion gametes (aB and Ab). If natural selection has favored the coupling types for some time, then the only way of generating repulsion gametes will be to have them produced by recombination. A population having recombination could come up with the appropriate recombinant types, while one that had no recombination might have lost them.

One can immediately see the similarity of the two theories—they both appeal to recombination as a means of coming up with absent gamete types. Both thus envisage linkage disequilibrium, but have different forces producing the disequilibrium. The two theories are one of the dimensions—the horizontal—of the classification used by Maynard Smith in this volume.

VARIANTS OF THE FISHER–MULLER THEORY

A number of other theories have been proposed that turn out to be variants of one or the other of these two. Muller (1964, p.8) pointed out "that an asexual population incorporates a kind of ratchet mechanism, such that it can never get to contain, in any of its lines, a load of mutations smaller than that already existing in its at presently least-loaded lines." Once every asexual genome contains deleterious mutants, one can never get back to a genome that has no deleterious mutants, except by back-mutation. With recombination, however, a mutant-free gamete can be produced from two parental gametes having different mutants. The asexual lineages will thus accumulate deleterious mutants at a higher rate than sexual ones. This seems at first to be a theory wholly different from the two I have just cited. In fact, it involves linkage disequilibrium randomly generated by genetic drift, as I have pointed out (Felsenstein, 1974). If the population contains mutants at a large number of loci, if it is finite, every gamete is likely to contain at least one mutant. But if it were infinite, then all possible gametic types would exist in their linkage equilibrium proportions, including the gamete that lacks all these deleterious mutants.

Muller's ratchet is thus a variant of the Fisher–Muller theory. It assumes that the favorable alleles being substituted start out at very high frequencies, instead of at very low frequencies, for the simple reason that the favorable alleles are the preexisting "wild-type" alleles rather than new advantageous mutations. The ratchet mechanism is a particularly plausible biological scenario, although Haigh (1978) has shown that the ratchet will be a fairly weak force favoring recombination under many of the possible combinations of parameters. Nevertheless, the universality of occurrence of deleterious mutations makes it an appealing explanation. Charlesworth (1978) has made a particularly interesting application of it to explain the genetic inactivation of Y chromosomes. Heller and Maynard Smith (1978) have argued that it would also operate in selfing species.

Another theory that turns out to be identical to the Fisher–Muller theory is that of Williams (1975; Williams and Mitton, 1973). I have argued elsewhere (Felsenstein and Yokoyama, 1976; Felsenstein, 1985) that Williams's "short-term" theory of selection in patches presents another biological scenario for the classical Fisher–Muller theory. The theory of Ghiselin (1974, p. 57) seems to be closely related to Williams's theory. Strobeck, Maynard Smith, and Charlesworth (1976) have put forward "hitchhiking" as a force acting to favor modifiers promoting recombination. I have argued (Felsenstein and Yokoyama, 1976) that this too is equivalent to the Fisher–Muller theory. Manning (1983) has emphasized the potential importance of hitchhiking effects.

VARIANTS OF THE VARYING SELECTION THEORY

A number of interesting biological scenarios have been proposed that would lead to the kinds of patterns of natural selection envisaged by Sturtevant and Mather (1938). One class of these is the parasite–host models, in which, if the loci A and B interact, a predominance of coupling hosts could select for a mixture of parasites adapted to those hosts. In the next few generations this might make repulsion genotypes favorable. This negative correlation between the disequilibrium favored in one generation with that favored in the next seems to require selection strong enough to cause rapid change of the parasite mix, as well as interactions between the loci so that coupling and repulsion gametes have significantly different parasite resistances. Theories of this sort have been put forward by Bremermann (1979), Glesener (1979), Hamilton (1980), and Price and Waser (1982).

Another situation that could lead to an appropriate conflict between selection for coupling and repulsion gamete types is Maynard Smith's (1980) optimum selection scheme. He supposes that natural selection is selecting for an intermediate optimum value of a phenotype, one controlled additively by a number of loci. This is likely to be a quite common pattern of selection. One of its normal effects is to create negative (repulsion) linkage disequilibrium, so that if A and B are alleles that increase the phenotype, Ab and aB gametes will be favored. Maynard Smith also assumes that the position of the optimum continually shifts back and forth. As we have already seen, when A and B are both being favored, the response to selection is fastest, and the fitness of the population highest when A and B are in coupling disequilibrium. Maynard Smith suggests, and shows by simulation, that this pattern of selection does in fact select for modifiers that increase the frequency of recombination. The generality of the pattern of selection makes this hypothesis particularly attractive, even if the strength of selection on the modifiers seems to be rather weak.

For some other biological scenarios, particularly Bell's (1982) "tangled bank" theory, I cannot easily tell whether they are versions of the Fisher–Muller theory or the varying selection theory, or whether they represent some completely new theory. The matter is worth investigation. This can be done most efficiently by the author of each scenario before its publication.

THE COST OF MEIOSIS

Maynard Smith (1971) argued that there was a "cost of meiosis" amounting to one-half. Fisher's (1930) theory of sex ratios showed that outcrossing sexual hermaphrodites would be selected to devote as much reproductive effort to male as to female gametes, even though this would amount to a great overproduction of sperm. If these same individuals were, say, to self-fertilize, they could produce just a few sperm and about twice as many eggs. Competition between the outcrossers and the selfers would favor the selfers by a large margin.

Maynard Smith's argument has attracted much attention, because it is correct, and seems to prove that there is an enormous barrier to the origin of outcrossing and a great benefit to be reaped from its elimination. That in turn seems to put a premium on theories of the evolution of recombination that can show it to be favored by at least a factor of two. I think that the matter is not so simple. As the exchange between Barash (1976) and Maynard Smith and Williams (1976) shows, the argument for the cost of meiosis depends on anisogamy. If sperm are as large and costly as eggs, there will be no cost of meiosis. In an isogamous organism like Chalmydomonas, outcrossing could arise without suffering a factor of two disadvantage.

Once recombination and outcrossing exist, total elimination of the outcrossing will not have any immediate advantage, unless the investment in male gametes is simultaneously reduced. Furthermore, reduction of the amount of recombination will have no advantage; it is outcrossing, not recombination, that incurs the cost. The Maynard Smith argument is an important one, but it would be a mistake to take its implications as being simple. In particular, it would be interesting to have a theory that reworked Parker, Baker, and Smith's (1972) theory of the evolution of anisogamy while at the same time allowing outcrossing and investment in eggs and sperm to be under genetic control. The model of Harper (1982) would provide one possible starting point.

THE HILL–ROBERTSON EFFECT

The hardest part to understand in the major theories is the role of the linkage disequilibrium in the Fisher–Muller theory. Thus it seems worthwhile to devote some attention to explaining its paradoxical nature. After all, the disequilibrium between two loci is generated by genetic drift. On average it is zero, being sometimes positive and sometimes negative. When it is positive, selection at each locus increases the rate of adaptation at the other. When it is negative, selection at the two loci conflicts. Doesn't this lead to the two effects canceling each other out on average? If so, then we would not expect there to be any natural selection favoring modifiers increasing the rate of recombination.

The two effects do not cancel. Let me try to explain this in two ways. The first is a heuristic argument, the second a (nearly) exact calculation. The heuristic argument involves seeing each locus as a source of random variation of background fitnesses for the other. Suppose first that we consider what happens when two loci are not linked and are substituting in the same population. A basic background fact is that variation from individual to individual in the number of offspring, even when uncorrelated with the genotype at a locus, reduces the effective population size. The extreme case of this is when in each generation one individual is chosen at random to do all the reproducing. It should be obvious in such a case that the effective population size is one rather than the nominal size. When the variation of fitness among individuals is less extreme, the effect is still qualitatively the same: a reduction of effective population size. This in turn means that the probability of fixation of a gene that is being selected is reduced, since that depends on the product $N_e s$ of effective population size and selection coefficient.

When the source of the random variation in fitnesses is the fitness of the genotypes at the other locus, the variation is not quite independent from one generation to another. If a gamete is A and the background locus is B, in the next generation the background locus will not be drawn completely independently. It will be unaltered 50% of the time, so that associations between the two loci persist for an average of two generations. This means that the effect of a random association between the two loci will be slightly larger if it gets to act for two generations before being re-formed at random.

When the loci are tightly linked, the effect should be much more dramatic. Random associations (random linkage disequilibria) will persist much longer and have a much larger effect. The tighter the linkage, the more strongly each locus acts to create large and long-lasting variations of fitness, thereby randomly perturbing gene frequencies at the other locus. The tighter the linkage, the more each locus creates a form of noise that reduces the effectiveness of selection at the other.

This phenomenon was first described by Hill and Robertson (1966), who were studying the effect of linkage on selection limits. They found, quite generally, that loci that did not interact nevertheless interfered with each other's response to selection as a net effect of random linkage disequilibria. They found that the size of this disequilibrium would be relatively small if $4N_e c$ was large, where c is the recombination fraction. Hill and Robertson discuss the phenomenon in a variety of ways and show by computer simulation how its strength depends on population sizes, selection coefficients, recombination fractions, and gene frequencies. Although their argument is unfortunately not well known, they have identified the common phenomenon underlying all forms of the Fisher–Muller theory.

There is one case in which we can provide a reasonably exact calculation (I am indebted to W.G. Hill for suggesting the approach). Consider a situation where the same selection coefficient s is at the two loci, and where initially the population has one mutant allele at each locus, so that there is exactly one A and one B. If these are placed at random in a diploid population of size N without recombination, then with probability $1/(2N)$ they will occur in the same gamete and with probability $1 - 1/(2N)$ they will occur in different gametes. In both of these cases we can calculate the probability of each locus fixing. In the first case, one gamete is AB and the rest ab. The selective advantage of the AB gamete will be $(1+s)^2 - 1 = 2s - s^2$. In the second case, there are two new gametes, one Ab and one aB, each with a selective advantage of s over the ab gametes. The probability that one or the other of these will fix is simply the probability that a single allele, present in two copies and having a selective advantage of s, will fix. Given that, there is obviously a 50% chance that it is the Ab gamete that ends up fixing.

Kimura (1962) gave an extremely accurate approximation for the probability of fixation in a two-allele case with constant fitnesses. For initial gene frequency p it is:

$$U(p) = \frac{1 - e^{-4Nsp}}{1 - e^{-4Ns}} \qquad (3)$$

Moran (1962) has shown that the true fixation probability lies between this value and the value obtained from Equation 3 when s is replaced by $s/(1+s)$. These are very tight bounds in most cases. We can use Equation 3 to give the fixation probabilities in the two cases above. When the selective advantage is $2s-s^2$, the fixation probability of A is the probability of fixation of the AB gametes, whose initial frequency is $1/(2N)$, or

$$U_C = \frac{1 - e^{-2(2s-s^2)}}{1 - e^{-4N(2s-s^2)}} \qquad (4)$$

When the two genes are in repulsion, the fixation probability is half the probability of fixing an allele with selective advantage s and initial frequency $2/(2N)$, or

$$U_R = (\tfrac{1}{2}) \frac{1 - e^{-4s}}{1 - e^{-4Ns}} \qquad (5)$$

The overall probability that A will fix in the absence of recombination is then

$$U_O = [1/(2N)]U_C + [1 - 1/(2N)]U_R \qquad (6)$$

This could be compared with the probability in the presence of free recombination. Unfortunately, we have no formula for that. The best we can do is to pretend that the rather small and fleeting linkage disequilibria formed under free recombination do not exist at all and to compute the probability of fixation of A as if B were not present at all. This is simply Equation 3 with an initial frequency of $p = 1/(2N)$.

Figure 1 shows the ratio between the fixation probability of A without recombination and with recombination (or at least without any background genetic variation). The ratio drops as s increases. For large N it approaches 0.5 as s increases. This is reasonable: If s is very large and N is large, almost all cases will be of repulsion, in which case even if the favored gametes are certain to fix, only half of those have the A allele. Figure 1 may be compared to the curve for no recombination in Figure 10 of Hill and Robertson (1966). The two differ in that here s is the selection coefficient at both loci, whereas the strength of selection is being varied at only one locus in Hill and Robertson's figure.

The calculations show the reality of the Hill–Robertson effect and also show that it requires relatively strong selection at one locus for it to interfere substantially with selection at another. What cannot be seen from this case is that when many loci are simultaneously under selection, interference between the selection processes at different loci can be substantial. In the simulation results I published (Felsenstein, 1974), fixation probabilities of favorable mutants were noticeably lower when there was complete linkage, with selection coefficients as small as $s = 0.01$, provided that the rate of occurrence of favorable mutants was high enough that several of them would typically be segregating in the same population.

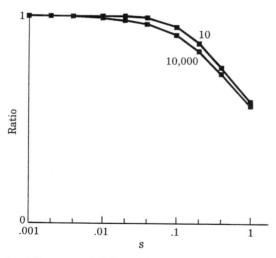

FIGURE 1. Ratio of fixation probability of the favored allele at a locus with complete linkage to that with free recombination, where both loci have the same selection coefficient s and both are present initially as single copies. The horizontal scale is logarithmic. Next to each curve is shown the value of N.

SUMMARY

At the population genetic level, the effect of recombination and outcrossing is to remove linkage disequilibrium (association between genotypes at different loci) from the population. A number of theories have been proposed under which this disequilibrium is deleterious, and modifier loci affecting recombination rates are selected to favor nonzero levels of recombination. These theories fall naturally into two groups, according to whether the linkage disequilibrium is originally produced by natural selection or by random genetic drift. Within these two theories, the detailed proposals of different authors amount to different biological scenarios enabling the action of the same evolutionary forces. In the absence of a comprehensive picture of the evolutionary forces affecting a population, and the genetic variability available, it is unlikely that we can make an informed decision as to which of these theories, if any, is important for the original evolution and subsequent maintenance of outcrossing and recombination. Progress in resolving these questions is likely to continue to be slow. Fortunately, the failure to resolve them does not constitute a crisis in evolutionary biology.

CHAPTER 6

THE EVOLUTION OF

RECOMBINATION RATES

Lisa D. Brooks

INTRODUCTION

Recombination is one part of the sexual system. Organisms differ in whether they reproduce asexually or sexually, and how much they outcross. This book contains discussions about the advantages and disadvantages of various aspects of sexual systems. In this chapter I discuss models of how selection acts on recombination, showing what factors are important and over how much of the genome they act. I then discuss evidence about the form of genetic variation for recombination in order to understand how populations can respond to the various types of selection on recombination.

The cost of meiosis argument (Maynard Smith, 1971, 1978; Williams, 1975) shows an advantage for asexual over sexual reproduction. Asexual females produce asexual female offspring. Sexual females produce the same number of offspring as do the asexual females, everything else being equal, but only half of them are female. This results in almost a doubling in frequency of asexual females every generation, a strong selective advantage. A problem for this argument is that many sexual organisms seem to be unaware of the conclusion. One explanation is simply that genetic variation for being asexual may not exist (Williams, 1975), since within most species there is little variation in the mode of reproduction. A stronger test occurs when there is variation for mode of reproduction within a population; that both modes of reproduction are maintained implies there are compensating advantages for sexual reproduction.

Zero recombination over the genome is equivalent to being asexual, with respect to the preservation of gene associations. When outcrossing occurs, though, zero recombination is not the same as being asexual, with respect to mating. Thus, the cost of meiosis argument does not apply to differences in recombination rates. Recombination is relevant to the cost of meiosis argument, however, when advantages are found for nonzero recombination rates over zero rates, and hence over asexual reproduction as well. Recombination provides an excellent opportunity to study some of these questions, because individual variation for recombination commonly exists within species.

How selection acts on recombination is not the same question as the origin of recombination. Recombination may well have originated as part of the DNA repair mechanism (see Bernstein et al., in this volume). The term "recombination" as used in this chapter means allelic recombination: the exchange of alleles at loci flanking the point of recombination, changing the combinations of alleles on chromosomes. Physical recombination, the breaking and rejoining of DNA strands, is necessary for allelic recombination. The mechanism of DNA repair results in recombination of flanking genes about 30 to 50% of the time. Many types of DNA damage are fatal to cells unless repaired, so that repair of DNA is still a major function of meiosis. DNA repair could act as a constraint against low levels of recombination if there were no other genetic variation reducing recombination. Another constraint against low recombination rates in most eukaryotes is the role of recombination in the proper segregation of chromosomes during meiosis.

Bernstein, Hopf, and Michod argue that meiosis is not "designed" for the production of variation. They argue that some complex steps in meiosis are there to reduce allelic recombination, because a simpler process would increase it. However, many processes in development are more complicated than they "need" to be. Selection acts on the variation that actually exists, rather than on what might exist. Once recombination arose and became genetically variable, there was opportunity for forms of selection other than DNA repair to act on the variation.

The loci involved in DNA repair are not the only ones affecting recombination, as discussed in a later section ("Genetic Variation for Recombination"). Structural variants such as inversions suppress recombination. The amount of recombination per physical length of DNA varies along chromosomes. For example, in *Drosophila melanogaster*, recombination rates are lowest near the centromeres. In *Neurospora crassa*, *con* sites act as operators for the local action of recombination suppressors. In many organisms, recombination rates differ between the sexes. Most Drosophila species are extreme cases, with no recombination occurring in males. In mammals, females generally have higher rates than males do, although in some chromosome regions males may have higher rates (for humans, see Meyers and Beatty, 1986). Variation in heterochromatin among individuals causes variation in recombination. Thus modifier loci not directly involved in DNA repair may be available for responding to selection on recombination.

In the first part of this chapter I discuss various selection forces on recombination. I do not try to find "the" force that provides the advantage for sexual over asexual recombination, but rather point out that there are many forces. Their effects depend on the population structure and the linkage and fitness interactions among the loci. Some of these selective pressures act over the entire genome; others act in small regions. For any particular region, several of these forces may be acting at once. Different regions of the genome may be selected in different directions for recombination.

With all these forces, what is a genome to do? The armchair organism should respond to all general selective forces and in specific regions to the net effect of the forces there. Real organisms respond with what variation is available. The form of this variation is important for understanding how populations can respond to selection on recombination. In the second part of this chapter I discuss evidence about the regional specificity of modifiers of recombination. This regional specificity allows regions to respond to selection, but the coarse-scale variation that also contributes to response will result in correlated effects in other regions.

THEORETICAL STUDIES OF SELECTION ON RECOMBINATION

Studying how selection acts on recombination is similar to studying how various forces influence genetic diversity. No model includes all of mutation, mating system, various forms of selection, migration, and drift. However, the models provide a great deal of insight about how those forces, alone or in combinations, affect genetic diversity. Similarly, each model of selection on recombination includes only one or two factors at a time, and indicates the selective forces on recombination rates due to those factors. Natural recombination rates will be responding to the net effect of all of the forces.

Discussions about how selection acts on recombination are asymmetric regarding lower or higher rates. There are clear selective forces that eliminate or reduce recombination. The twofold cost of meiosis (Maynard Smith, 1978) is an argument that outcrossing and thus effective recombination should be eliminated from a population polymorphic for sexual systems. Fisher (1930) states and Feldman et al. (1980) show for general fitnesses that at equilibrium, interacting polymorphic loci select for decreased recombination. The emphasis, then, has been to find sets of forces that result in selection for increased recombination.

Table 1 shows a classification of these models that can be compared with classifications of Felsenstein (in this volume) and Maynard Smith (in this volume). Models with interacting polymorphic loci at equilibrium are explicitly included as a class. I also include models that are more restricted in scope than they do. The purpose of their classifications is to understand the basic forces selecting for recombination, of sufficient generality to balance the forces selecting against recombination. My purpose is different; I am reveling in the diversity of forces that affect recombination.

For selection on recombination to occur between two loci, the linkage disequilibrium, D, between them must not be zero. Felsenstein (in this volume)

TABLE 1. A classification of how selection acts on recombination in various models

Type of model	Selection on recombination	Authors of models
Interacting polymorphic loci (random mating; constant selection in time, space, and gene frequency)	Down	Fisher (1930), Kimura (1956), Nei (1967), Turner (1967a), Teague (1976), Feldman et al. (1980)
Directional selection		
General	Up if $D < 0$ Down if $D > 0$	Felsenstein (1965), Turner (1967b), Eshel and Feldman (1970)
Always or on average $D < 0$	Up (since $D < 0$)	Fisher (1930), Muller (1932, 1964), Crow and Kimura (1965), Hill and Robertson (1966)
Fluctuating environment	Up if much fluctuation, thus like directional selection with $D < 0$ Down if not much fluctuation and like interacting loci Down or up if not much fluctuation and like directional selection	Charlesworth (1976), Maynard Smith (1980), Sturtevant and Mather (1938), Jaenike (1978)
Frequency-dependent selection (e.g., parasites)	Depends on the fitnesses and the virulence and transmissibility of the parasite; up promoted by strong selection	Hamilton (1980), May and Anderson (1983), Bremermann (1985)
Mutation–selection balance	Up if $D < 0$ Down if $D > 0$ } and modifier closely linked to major loci Possibly reversed if modifier loosely linked	Feldman et al. (1980)
Nonrandom mating		
Selfing	Down	Feldman and Balkau (1972)
Mixed random mating and selfing	Depends on the amount of selfing, the type of epistasis, the amount of recombination, and which initial equilibrium was used	Holden (1979), Charlesworth et al. (1979), Holsinger and Feldman (1983)
Selection in clines	Depends on the strength of selection and the amount of migration	Slatkin (1975), Maynard Smith (1977), Charlesworth and Charlesworth (1979b)

discusses how linkage disequilibrium affects response to selection. If the linkage disequilibrium is zero, then alleles at the two loci are randomly associated with each other. The gene combinations formed by recombination will exactly balance the ones broken down. Different recombination rates will not change chromosome distributions, so there can be no selective force on recombination.

The equilibrium value of linkage disequilibrium is zero when fitnesses are additive across loci and also when fitnesses are multiplicative across loci and the recombination rate is above a critical value (Lewontin and Kojima, 1960; Bodmer and Felsenstein, 1967). These are special cases without epistasis. Epistasis occurs when fitnesses cannot be described as independent contributions from each locus; the loci interact so that fitnesses have to be specified for genotypes, rather than just for alleles or loci. In general, without special relationships among the fitnesses, the linkage disequilibrium is not zero at equilibrium (Karlin, 1975).

Selection on modifiers of recombination will occur when major loci are selected on and linkage disequilibrium is not zero. This selection on recombination rates is a by-product of the selection at the major loci. Just as the chromosome frequencies of the major loci change under selection, the frequencies of alleles that affect the distribution of chromosomes will also change under selection. The linkage disequilibrium can arise from selection, since general fitnesses do not produce zero linkage disequilibrium. The linkage disequilibrium can also arise randomly in finite populations (Hill and Robertson, 1966). Even if selection on the major loci is not epistatic, the randomly generated linkage disequilibrium results in selection on recombination (for example, see Charlesworth and Charlesworth, 1979a with respect to multiplicative fitnesses). Selection on modifiers of recombination will occur to the extent that loci are selected on and linkage disequilibrium exists. Modifiers that affect several regions of the genome are affected by selection in any of those regions.

Models with interacting polymorphic loci at equilibrium

When loci are polymorphic at equilibrium, with nonzero linkage disequilibrium, selection reduces the recombination rate between them (Fisher, 1930; Kimura, 1956; Nei, 1967; Turner, 1967a; Teague, 1976). Nei introduced a modifier model in which selection reduces the recombination rate between two major loci by changing the frequency of alleles at a modifier locus that controls the recombination rates between the major loci. This result holds for general fitness schemes (Feldman et al., 1980).

The result that selection favors reduced recombination is general in terms of fitnesses. No particular fitness relationships are assumed. In particular, additive fitnesses and multiplicative fitnesses with zero linkage disequilibrium do not fit the conditions. The loci must interact for fitness to generate the nonzero linkage disequilibrium. Any loci that are polymorphic at equilibrium with nonzero linkage disequilibrium will be under selective pressure for tighter linkage. This result is not general in some other respects. Random mating and constant fitnesses are assumed. The fitnesses must maintain polymorphism at both loci at equilibrium. If alleles are directionally selected so that they would fix at equilibrium, or if the system is far from equilibrium, then this result does not apply.

Models with directional selection

When alleles are on their way to fixation under directional selection, different recombination rates will hasten or slow the process. The effect of recombination depends on the sign of the linkage disequilibrium (Felsenstein, 1965, and in this volume; Turner, 1967b). When advantageous alleles are associated on chromosomes, the linkage disequilibrium is positive. This association means that an advantageous allele at one locus more frequently than randomly is associated with an advantageous allele at the other locus. Thus response to selection at one locus is enhanced by the association between the alleles at two loci. This association increases the effective selective force. Low recombination rates, by breaking down this association slowly, result in the fastest response to selection. Similarly, negative linkage disequilibrium occurs when advantageous alleles are associated with disadvantageous alleles, which lessens the effective selective force on the alleles. High recombination rates, by breaking down this association quickly, result in the fastest response. The selective effect on recombination depends on the particular loci involved. Their fitness relationships will influence the sign of the linkage disequilibrium.

Felsenstein (1974 and in this volume) points out how three arguments for the advantage of recombination are related to negative linkage disequilibrium in populations. The loci do not interact for fitness; alleles are selected for or against, regardless of the rest of the genotype. Muller's ratchet states that populations without recombination will accumulate deleterious mutations, whereas populations with recombination will be able to regenerate mutation-free chromosomes (Muller, 1964). The Fisher–Muller argument posits that recombination allows all good mutations to be incorporated into the population (Fisher, 1930; Muller, 1932; Crow and Kimura, 1965). In both of these cases the loci are in negative linkage disequilibrium, because the chromosome with the multiple mutations has not been formed. Thus, higher recombination rates prevent the accumulation of deleterious mutations and allow the accumulation of advantageous ones. Hill and Robertson (1966) found that under directional multiplicative selection, which in an infinite population would preserve initial zero linkage disequilibrium, the average value of randomly generated linkage disequilibrium is negative. Thus, linked loci slow each other's response to selection. These arguments apply over the entire genome.

Felsenstein defines this category on the basis that the linkage disequilibrium is generated randomly, because of finite population size. I feel that the crucial distinction is that the selection is directional and the linkage disequilibrium negative. Thus, I also include in it the deterministic model by Eshel and Feldman (1970), which has recurrent mutation at two loci, with the double mutant the most fit; the effect of recombination is determined by the sign of the linkage disequilibrium in the same way as above.

Maynard Smith distinguishes between models with deleterious and favorable genes, splitting this group into two. I find Felsenstein's argument persuasive that the advantage of recombination in the Fisher–Muller model for combining favorable mutations is equivalent to that in the Muller's ratchet model for generating chromosomes free of deleterious mutations.

Fluctuating environment models

The second set of models that Felsenstein discusses involves selection that fluctuates in time. These include models of fluctuating environments (Sturtevant and Mather, 1938; Charlesworth, 1976; Jaenike, 1978), and normalizing selection around a fluctuating optimum (Maynard Smith, 1980, and in this volume). Felsenstein defines this category on the basis that the linkage disequilibrium is generated by selection. I agree with the sets of models included, but do not agree with the origin of the linkage disequilibrium. Loci with fitness interactions that are polymorphic at equilibrium also have linkage disequilibrium generated by selection; these are the previously discussed models in which selection is for reduced recombination. If fitnesses were constant, these fluctuating environment models would either have directional selection, with the effect of recombination depending on the sign of the linkage disequilibrium, or they would have interacting fitnesses at equilibrium and recombination would be selected against. However, with the fluctuating selection, the population is always away from an equilibrium.

This fluctuating selection results in negative linkage disequilibrium. In Maynard Smith's model with normalizing selection around a fluctuating optimum, some alleles are + and others are −. The loci are additive on the phenotypic scale; individuals with more pluses have larger phenotypic values. The fitnesses are normalizing, though, so that the most fit genotype has some + and some − alleles. This leads to much epistatic interaction for fitness among the loci: a + allele adds to the fitness of genotypes with many − alleles, but subtracts from the fitness of genotypes with many + alleles (Wright, 1935). There are usually an excess of balanced gametes, so that linkage disequilibrium is negative. The negative linkage disequilibrium is generated explicitly.

In the other models the linkage disequilibrium fluctuates in sign. It is a subtle point that this is essentially negative linkage disequilibrium. The fluctuating D arises because the fitnesses fluctuate. The alleles are labeled so that D is positive when AB and ab chromosomes are in excess and Ab and aB chromosomes are deficient, and D is negative when those abundances are reversed. Initially, AB and ab are selected for, and Ab and aB are selected against. These fitnesses lead to positive D. When the environment switches, Ab and aB are selected for, but these chromosomes are deficient. Based on the constant labels, D is positive. However, based on how selection is now occurring, D is essentially negative. Higher recombination rates speed the response to selection. When the selection results in an excess of the selected chromosomes, D becomes essentially positive. When the environment switches again, the chromosomes selected for are deficient, D again is essentially negative, and so on.

Just as with directional selection, higher recombination rates are advantageous when the linkage disequilibrium is negative. In these models there is a balance between the interacting loci selecting for decreased recombination and the negative linkage disequilibrium away from equilibrium, causing selection for increased recombination. Maynard Smith (1980) finds that modifiers increasing recombination are selected for if the directional component of selection is large enough relative to the stabilizing component. In the other models, too, the selection is for higher recombination when the fluctuations keep the system sufficiently away from equilibrium.

Models with more complexity that have selection for increased recombination

In models with interacting polymorphic loci at equilibrium, selection is always for decreased recombination. When more complexity is included, though, selection can be for increased recombination. An example occurs when interacting polymorphic loci are away from equilibrium and the linkage disequilibrium is negative, as discussed above. Other assumptions of constancy may be dropped. Because they are special cases, these models are not included in Felsenstein's or Maynard Smith's classifications. While all populations are finite and any set of loci can be away from a selective equilibrium, not all populations self-fertilize nor does selection on all loci occur in a cline. These are examples of how the direction of selection on recombination may depend on population properties such as mating system, on genome properties such as the linkage relationships, and on how the organisms interact with the environment, which shows up in fitnesses. Thus, selection may be for increased or decreased recombination in different regions, depending on how those factors interact for different sets of loci.

Polymorphism can be maintained when mutation to deleterious alleles is balanced by selection against them. How selection acts on recombination depends on the sign of the linkage disequilibrium, which depends on the fitnesses (Feldman et al., 1980). If the fitness of the double mutant is more than the product of the fitnesses of the single mutants, then D is positive; if less, then D is negative. A positive D results in selection for lower recombination, a negative D results in selection for higher recombination. If the modifier locus is loosely linked to the major loci, then these selective effects may be reversed.

Here again, the sign of the linkage disequilibrium is important, as well as the linkage of the modifier with the region it affects.

The pattern of mating in a population influences how selection acts on recombination. Under random mating (Feldman et al., 1980) and under complete selfing (Feldman and Balkau, 1972), when starting from a polymorphic equilibrium at the major loci, selection on a modifier locus reduces recombination. In a population with mixed random mating and selfing, however, there are cases when selection on a modifier locus increases recombination (Holden, 1979; Charlesworth et al., 1979; Holsinger and Feldman, 1983).

Polymorphisms may be maintained by spatial differences in selection along clines (Slatkin, 1975; Maynard Smith, 1977; Charlesworth and Charlesworth, 1979b). Selection at a locus is for one allele in part of the cline and for the other allele in the rest of the cline. With two loci, a region of overlap occurs where the selection values have switched for one locus but not the other. Charlesworth and Charlesworth find that how selection acts on a modifier depends on the length of the overlap, the strength of selection on the major loci, and the amount of migration along the cline. Selection for increased recombination can occur, although it is generally weaker than the selection for decreased recombination.

In models with frequency-dependent selection, caused, for example, by parasites (Hamilton, 1980; May and Anderson, 1983; Bremermann, 1985), higher recombination rates sometimes have the advantage over lower and zero rates. These models are related to the fluctuating environment models discussed above, such as the ones by Charlesworth (1976) and Jaenike (1978). In both sets of models, the sign of the linkage disequilibrium fluctuates. This essentially negative linkage disequilibrium causes the selection for higher recombination rates. The difference is that in these models the fluctuating linkage disequilibrium arises from the dynamics included in the model, rather than having the environmental fluctuations imposed from outside.

Simulations show that multiple loci enhance the effects of recombination that occur in two-locus models. Martin and Cockerham (1960) find, for the same total amount of selection, that differences in recombination have larger effects on selection response as the number of loci increases from 5 to 20. In numerical analyses of heterotic models, the magnitude of linkage disequilibrium is larger with 5 loci than expected under two-locus theory (Lewontin, 1964a). The linkage disequilibrium is even larger with 36 loci (Franklin and Lewontin, 1970), because of higher-order interactions among the loci. Lewontin and Hull (1967) simulate two blocks of genes. When loci in one block are tightly linked and loci in the other block are loosely linked, the joint selection exaggerates the response to selection that occurs for each block alone. The loosely linked loci fix more quickly, and the tightly linked loci have more intermediate frequencies. Thus, how gene frequencies change under selection can be different in different blocks of genes, depending on the linkage relationships.

The linkage relationships of modifiers with the regions they affect are important for selection on the modifiers and the modified regions. Nei (1969) finds that the closer the linkage of the modifier locus to the major loci, the faster the increase in frequency of the modifier allele. Strobeck et al. (1976) have studied a model in which a modifier allele that allows recombination will cause a new advantageous gene combination to form. As this chromosome increases in frequency, so will the linked modifier allele. The closer the modifier locus to the loci it affects, the stronger the hitchhiking effect. Therefore they predict that modifiers will always modify recombination in their own chromosome region.

Several ecological explanations have been proposed for the advantage of sexual over asexual reproduction (Ghiselin, 1974). Recombination produces a much more diverse progeny, as discussed in the lottery-ticket model (Williams, 1975), the sibling-competition model (Maynard Smith, 1978) and the tangled bank model (Bell, 1982). This argument is generally discussed in terms of some recombination versus none. The argument still applies, although not as strongly, to higher versus lower recombination rates. The higher the recombination rate, up to its biological maximum of 0.5, the more diverse the progeny. Asexual species are mainly at the tips of phylogenetic trees (Maynard Smith, 1978); recombination may allow a long-term evolutionary flexibility.

Some of these factors always select for decreased recombination; others always select for increased recombination. For some factors, the direction of selection depends on the sign of the linkage disequilibrium, which is affected by relations among the fitnesses. The strength of selection, and sometimes the direction, may depend on how closely linked a modifier locus is to the region it affects. For models in which the direction of selection depends on the form of the fitnesses, some sets of loci may select for decreased recombination and some for increased recombination. Several of these factors may be occurring in the population at the same time.

Criteria for evaluating recombination rates

Several criteria have been used to evaluate how selection acts on recombination. In modifier models, the effect of selection is clearly shown by the fate of the modifier alleles. The results fall out of the model, and no external criteria have to be invoked. In other cases the analysis either cannot or has not been done with modifiers. Criteria are needed to decide when higher or lower recombination rates are better and, implicitly, would be selected for.

For directional selection, a direct criterion is the rate of response to selection (Felsenstein, 1965, and this volume; Turner, 1967a). As discussed previously, the sign of the linkage disequilibrium determines whether recombination speeds or slows response to selection. With recurrent mutation to alleles that have high fitness together, a criterion is the proportion of chromosomes that have both of these alleles (Eshel and Feldman, 1970). For a flux of good mutations, as under the Fisher–Muller argument, or a flux of bad mutations, as under the Muller's ratchet argument, a criterion is the expected time of formation of the first multiple good allele chromosome. Karlin (1973) shows that this time is faster, the higher the recombination rate. However, he also shows that when the initial linkage disequilibrium is zero or positive, the time to fixation of the multiple good allele chromosome is slower, the higher the recombination rate. Thus high recombination initially speeds evolution but eventually slows it down.

Another criterion is the mean fitness of the population under various recombination rates. For constant fitnesses, Lewontin (1971) shows that the mean fitness is maximum when recombination is zero. However, the population mean fitness does not necessarily decrease continuously as the recombination rate increases from zero to 0.5. Kalin and Carmelli (1975) show examples of constant two-locus fitnesses in which, as the recombination rate increases from zero, the equilibrium mean fitness decreases initially and then rises and plateaus at a lower level than it had with zero recombination (Figure 1). In Figure 1, both loci are polymorphic at equilibrium, the linkage disequilibrium is negative, and mean fitness increases as the recombination rate increases, for recombination rates in the range of about 0.08 to 0.105. Selection would reduce recombination

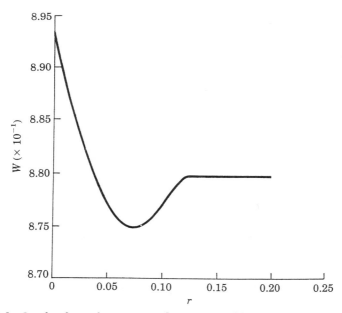

FIGURE 1. Graph of population mean fitness at equilibrium, W, as a function of recombination rate, r. The model is of two loci with constant fitnesses. The fitness matrix is

$$\begin{pmatrix} 0.300695 & 0.397564 & 0.233345 \\ 0.016887 & 0.988557 & 0.141322 \\ 0.879733 & 0.460876 & 0.969690 \end{pmatrix}$$

(From Karlin, 1975.)

(Feldman et al., 1980), even though decreasing recombination would lower the mean fitness. Charlesworth et al. (1979) discuss an example in a partially self-fertilizing population where the mean fitness as a function of recombination rate has a similar nonmonotonic shape. A modifier increasing the recombination rate from zero to 0.5 is selected for, even though mean fitness decreases. Thus, recombination modification does not necessarily increase mean fitness.

Another criterion reverses the conclusions based on the previous criteria for deciding which recombination rates are better under directional selection. Populations that respond quickly to directional selection will fix alleles quickly. They will therefore lose variability faster than if they respond slowly (Lewontin, 1964b; Levins, 1965; Eshel and Feldman, 1970). Consequently, they may not have the variation to respond well to later selection.

When populations with different recombination rates are compared by criteria such as the rate of response to selection, then the form of selection on recombination is implicitly group selection (Felsenstein, 1974). The population with the "better" recombination rate would do better than the one with the "worse" rate. Some of these arguments could be recast in individual selection terms. In the Fisher–Muller and Muller's ratchet models, for example, the lineages with the high-fitness chromosomes are those with recombination. With modifier models, the dynamics of the system result in selection on recombination rates within a population, without invoking outside criteria for "better" or "worse."

GENETIC VARIATION FOR RECOMBINATION

As discussed above, there may be many selective forces acting on recombination over the genome. Some may affect particular regions; others may affect the entire genome. The direction of selection may be different in different regions. The response to these various selection pressures will depend on how recombination is controlled. The type of variation for recombination in the population will determine what sort of selective responses are possible. The variation for recombination that is coarse-scale will result in correlated responses over large parts of the genome; that which is fine-scale will allow response within particular regions. In this way, different regions can respond to different selection pressures.

The nature of genetic variation for recombination can distinguish among some of the theoretical models. If modifiers affect regions to which they are only loosely linked, then hitchhiking cannot explain their presence in the population. Interacting genes are most effective at changing the frequency of modifiers that are closely linked. If loosely linked modifiers are common, then more theoretical work is needed to understand them. Part of the explanation may lie in genome-wide effects such as contained in the Muller's ratchet argument. Muller's argument does not depend on loci that specifically interact, but on mutations arising anywhere on the same chromosome.

There have been many studies showing genetic variation for recombination rates or chiasma frequency. Studies comparing laboratory stocks or different populations are useful for showing that the variation exists. Once that is established, studies within natural populations show the magnitude and form of the variation. This is basic information for understanding how selection could act in nature.

Recombination rates have been found to differ among various laboratory stocks of *Drosophila melanogaster* (Lawrence, 1958, 1963; Green, 1959; Kidwell 1972a; Broadhead et al., 1977; Clegg et al., 1979) and within stocks (Broadhead and Kidwell, 1975; Tracey and Dempsey, 1981). Levine and Levine (1954, 1955) found that lines from a natural population of *D. pseudoobscura* differ in both the amount and distribution of crossovers. Gale and Rees (1970) found that subspecies of barley differ in chiasma frequency, partly due to chromosome two. De Boer and van der Hoeven (1977) found that chiasma frequencies vary in mice.

From the viewpont of the evolution of sex, the genetic system regulating recombination is important. Inversions have well-understood effects on recombination (Schultz and Redfield, 1951; Lucchesi, 1976); the modifiers of recombination discussed here are more genic than structural. Meiosis is understood fairly well in eukaryotes (Catcheside, 1977; Whitehouse, 1982), but individual variation in recombination rates and its genetic basis have not been studied as much.

Recombination rates are not uniform along the length of chromosomes. In *D. melanogaster* (Lindsley and Sandler, 1977), recombination is reduced in the centromere and distal regions of chromosomes. In some organisms, such as rye (Jones, 1967) and grasshoppers (White, 1973), most chiasmata are localized to parts of chromosomes.

Meiotic mutants affect the number of crossovers, their distribution along chromosomes, or both (in *D. melanogaster*, see Sandler et al., 1968; in *Caenorhabditis elegans*, Rose and Baillie, 1979; in rye, Jones, 1967; review by Baker et al., 1976). These mutants affect recombination over large parts of the genome and have large effects; some reduce recombination by one-half or even stop it completely in all chromosomes. Sandler et al. found evidence that many genes affecting recombination rates are segregating in the populations; only mutants with large, clear effects were isolated for further analysis of how meiosis occurs. Genes with small effects, though, could be an important part of the natural variation for recombination. These could be either loci not involved in meiosis or alleles at meiotic loci that have less drastic effects.

In most sexual species, recombination is necessary for the proper pairing and disjunction of homologous chromosomes during meiosis. Meiotic mutants that reduce recombination increase the amount of nondisjunction. Charlesworth et al. (1985) found that a high recombination line has less nondisjunction, but the selective effect of this reduction is extremely small. Nondisjunction may have little selective effect among different intermediate-to-high recombination rates; it may cause a strong mechanistic selective force against genome-wide low recombination rates.

The fungus *Neurospora crassa* has genes that control recombination at specific chromosome sites (Figure 2) (Catcheside, 1977). A *rec* locus affects recombination at several specific sites, which may be on the same or different

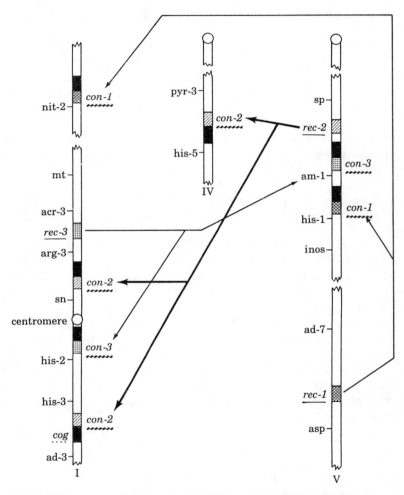

FIGURE 2 *Neurospora crassa* linkage maps of groups I, IV, and V to show the locations of known repressors (or regulators, symbols underlined) of local recombination (*rec-1*, *rec-2*, and *rec-3*) and a known promoter (*cog*, dotted underline) as well as the probable locations of inferred *control* (*con*) genes (analogous to operators, symbols with wavy underline). The *con* genes are shaded the same way as their corresponding *rec* genes. (From Catcheside, 1977.)

chromosomes. These sites have recognition loci, *con* sites. Each *rec* locus is associated with particular *con* sites; other *rec* loci recognize other *con* sites. The *rec* loci are polymorphic, with some alleles reducing recombination by factors of 2 to 25. It is unknown whether other eukaryotes have this regulatory system; anything similar would provide a mechanism for fine-scale control of recombination at linked and unlinked loci.

Heterochromatin affects recombination on the same chromosome (Miklos and Nankivell, 1976) and on other chromosomes (Yamamoto, 1979). In *D. melanogaster*, the centromere inhibits recombination in nearby euchromatin; the centromeric heterochromatin reduces this effect by acting as a spacer (Yamamoto and Miklos, 1978; Szauter, 1984). By affecting how strongly the euchromatin is exposed to the inhibitory effect of the centromere, differences in the amount of heterochromatin result in differences in recombination rates.

There is considerable genetic variation for heterochromatin within populations. Craig-Holmes et al. (1973) found at least 30 variants for amount of constitutive heterochromatin in 20 normal people; Forejt (1973) found 35 variants for centromeric heterochromatin in 5 Bohemian wild mice. With this much variation, as many as several chromosome pairs within an individual had variants. In these studies the differences are for large blocks of heterochromatin. Studies are needed of the sizes, distribution, and effects on recombination of small variants. Since heterochromatin affects both the amount and distribution of crossing over (review in John, 1973), differences in the distribution of heterochromatin contribute to variation in recombination rates.

To understand the evolution of modifiers, the extent of their effects in natural populations must be studied. Wild strains of the fungus *Schizophyllum commune* show large variation in recombination rates. They vary from 0.1% to 8% in the B incompatibility region (Koltin et al., 1967), from 3.8% to 34.9% in the *nic2–ura*1 region (Simchen and Samberg, 1969), and from 3.3% to 22.8% as well as 0% in the A incompatibility region (Raper et al., 1960). This A region variation is not due to alleles in the region itself, but to the genetic background. Simchen and Stamberg (1969) find that more than one locus affects recombination in each of these three unlinked regions. The effects of some recombination-modifying loci are specific to short regions. Some loci affect recombination in more than one region, giving rise to positive or negative correlations among the recombination rates in separate regions.

Brooks and Marks (1986) studied how six second chromosomes and Brooks (1985) studied how seven third chromosomes from natural populations of *D. melanogaster* vary for recombination. Since the genetic background is uniform, the variation in a chromosome is due to modifiers on that chromosome. The total amount of crossing over varies by 13% for the second chromosome and 14% for the third chromosome; regions vary by 15% to 38%, and even by 220% in a small region. The effects of these second chromosomes on recombination in the X and third chromosomes were also studied. Modifiers on the second chromosome cause the amount of crossing over to vary by 14% on the X and

12% on the third chromosome. They do not cause variation in the distribution of crossing over in the third chromosome, but do cause such variation in the X chromosome, where regions vary by 22% to 38%. These experiments show that there is region-specific, fine-scale variation for recombination. There is also coarse-scale variation, causing positive correlations in the amount of crossing over for regions on chromosomes and for all three major chromosomes.

The above experiments show how modifiers on one chromosome affect recombination on that and on the other chromosomes. To look more specifically at where modifiers act in relation to where they are located, regions smaller than chromosomes must be studied. In a laboratory stock of D. *melanogaster*, Law (1961) found that the proximal region of the X affects recombination in the distal region of the X, but not the reverse. Brooks (1985) studied how the centromere and right distal regions of chromosome three affected recombination in the rest of the chromosome in two natural populations of D. *melanogaster*. Modifiers in the centromere region change recombination rates from 20% below to 15% above the wild line values; modifiers in the distal region change recombination rates from 41% below to 14% above the wild line values. Modifiers frequently affect the region where they are located, adjacent regions, or far regions. None of the modifiers affect all the regions of a chromosome; they affect one or a few regions, which are sometimes adjacent to each other or to the modifier region.

Selection experiments on recombination

Selection experiments concentrate modifiers into separate up or down lines. They show that the variation is of a form that can respond to selection, and the accumulated modifiers can be studied for the specificity of their effects. Several experiments show that genetic variation for recombination exists by changing recombination rates (in D. *melanogaster*, see Kidwell, 1972a,b; Chinnici, 1971a,b; Charlesworth and Charlesworth, 1985a,b; Detlefsen and Roberts, 1921; Parsons, 1958; Valentin, 1973; Abdullah and Charlesworth, 1974; in the silkmoth, Hasimoto, reference in Turner, 1979; in the desert locust, Shaw, 1972; in *Tribolium castaneum*, Dewees, 1975; in the lima bean, Allard, 1963).

In these experiments, lines from a base population are selected up or down for recombination rate in a region. One type of selection is on chromosomes; individuals from gametes with recombinant chromosomes are kept for the high lines and ones from gametes with nonrecombinant chromosomes are kept for the low lines. Another type of selection is on families; many individuals are scored for recombination rate, and the progeny of those with the most extreme rates are kept. Family selection allows the accumulation of recombination modifiers that are loosely linked to the region of interest; these modifiers may easily recombine away with chromosome selection.

Hasimoto succeeded in selecting both up and down on recombination in the second chromosome of the silkmoth *Bombyx mori*. He changed the recombination rate from 26% to 38% and 5%. The variation for recombination was polygenic. Recombination in chromosome two was affected by modifiers in chromosome two, in the X chromosome, and in the other chromosomes (Turner, 1979; Ebinuma and Yoshitake, 1981). These modifiers of recombination in chromosome two did not affect recombination in chromosome five (Ebinuma and Yoshitake, 1981). The selected lines contained modifiers that did affect recombination in chromosome three (H. Ebinuma, unpublished data).

In *D. melanogaster*, Kidwell (1972a,b), Chinnici (1971a,b), and Charlesworth and Charlesworth (1985a,b) selected up and down on recombination. Chinnici's lines responded in both directions; Kidwell's lines responded up and some lines down; and one of the Charlesworths' lines responded up. Kidwell and Chinnici used mixtures of laboratory stocks; Charlesworth and Charlesworth used flies from a natural population. At the end of the selection experiments, the selected lines were tested for the chromosomal distribution and specificity of recombination modifiers. Chinnici and the Charlesworths found that the X, second, and third chromosomes all affected recombination in the selected region. The Charlesworths mapped two modifiers to the selected third chromosome.

Kidwell (1972a) found the largest differences between the high and low lines in the selected region. Chinnici, too, found the largest effects in the selected region, for all three of the chromosomes. Charlesworth et al. (1985) found that the high line third chromosome increased recombination most in the selected region of the third chromosome; the X increased recombination in the selected region but also at the ends. Although the selected regions, not surprisingly, had the largest response to selection, the other regions on the same chromosome also responded (Kidwell, 1972a; Charlesworth et al., 1985). This response was in the same direction as for the selected region.

Chromosomes from the selected lines affected recombination in the chromosomes that had not contained the selected region. Kidwell found a modifier on chromosome two that increased recombination not only in the selected centromere region of chromosome three, but also in the centromere region of chromosome two. Chinnici found that chromosomes two and three from the selected lines each affected recombination in both chromosomes two and three, but uncorrelated with their effect on the selected X. Charlesworth et al. (1985) found that the high line chromosome three increased recombination in some regions of the unselected X, but decreased recombination in the centromere region of chromosome two. Thus, how modifiers affected recombination in one chromosome did not indicate how they affected it in other chromosomes.

Chinnici found that the X did not differ from the other chromosomes in its effect on recombination in the selected region of the X. The joint effect of the X, second and third chromosomes was larger than the individual effects. Charlesworth et al. (1985) found a strong interaction among the modifiers in the high line. The high line second chromosome increased recombination in the selected third chromosome region when it was in a background of high line X and third chromosomes, but otherwise it reduced recombination.

Conclusions about recombination modifiers

The studies of S. *commune*, B. *mori*, and D. *melanogaster* lead to similar results. The recombination rate in a region is affected by multiple loci, which may be linked or unlinked to that region. Linked modifiers are not particularly different from unlinked ones. Conversely, some modifiers and some chromosomes or chromosome regions affect recombination in multiple regions of the genome. The studies are not detailed enough to reveal whether the effects of a chromosome region are due to one or to several closely linked loci. While for short-term evolution that makes no difference, for understanding how modifiers work more detailed studies are needed.

There is coarse-scale control that increases or decreases recombination over large parts of the genome. There is also variation specific to particular regions. Response to selection uses both types of variations. Selection on one region, therefore, may result in correlated changes in other regions. Still, the region-specific variation means that different regions can respond to different selective pressures.

The large proportion of modifiers affecting regions close to their location is evidence that hitchhiking (Strobeck et al., 1976) could be occurring in natural populations. Hitchhiking cannot explain the presence of modifiers that affect regions to which they are only loosely linked or unlinked, such as other chromosomes, unless they affect their own region as well as other regions. Modifiers of recombination that are closely linked to the region they affect can have stronger effects than if they are loosely linked. That modifiers affect the region they are in, and most effectively their own region, means that much of response to selection on recombination in a particular region could be due to modifiers within that region.

The dynamics of selection on modifier alleles with multiple effects is complex, depending on selection occurring in several regions. Modifiers may have direct effects of their own on fitness, in addition to affecting recombination. Then selection on a modifier allele depends on both its direct selective effect and its effect on recombination.

Studies of modifiers of recombination provide some solution to the question, "Why does the genotype not congeal?" (Turner, 1967b). Studying many models of how selection acts on recombination shows that the genome is not always expected to congeal. Variation in particular regions or small overall variation is a different matter than general loss of recombination over the whole genome. Although in some sexual organisms one sex has no recombination, other organisms cannot necessarily easily change meiosis like that, even if selective forces were in that direction. Meiotic mutants that severely reduce recombination are rare in natural populations; they have large effects on fecundity because of nondisjunction. The coarse-scale variation and modifiers with effects on multiple regions mean that selection on recombination in one region affects recombination in other regions as well. Selection in those regions may or may not correspond to the selective effect in the first region.

SUMMARY

There are many selective forces on recombination. In some situations there is genome-wide selection for reduced recombination. The cost of meiosis argument shows an advantage for asexual reproduction, which essentially eliminates recombination, in populations polymorphic for sexual system. When loci are polymorphic at equilibrium, with random mating and constant fitnesses, selection is for decreased recombination. In models of several other situations, however, selection is for increased recombination. These include models with directional selection, fluctuating environments, and frequency-dependent selection. In these models, the selection on recombination occurs because higher recombination rates speed response to selection when linkage disequilibrium is negative and selection on the major loci is directional. In still other situations, selection may be for increased or decreased recombination, depending on the mating system, linkage relationships, and the form of the fitnesses. These include models with mutation-selection balance, mixed random mating and selfing, or selection in clines.

Several of these factors may be acting at once, selecting for increased recombination in some regions of the genome and for decreased recombination in others. Modifiers of recombination are selected on most strongly if they are closely linked to the regions they affect.

The form of the genetic variation for recombination determines how fine the scale of the response to selection can be. Natural populations contain much variation for recombination. Multiple loci affect recombination rates within regions. Modifiers frequently affect the region they are in; they may affect other regions, including unlinked ones. Some modifiers of recombination affect the amount of crossing over, the distribution, or both. Some affect large parts of the genome; others are region-specific. Thus, regions of the genome can respond to differing selection pressures. Part of the response includes closely linked modifiers, and part includes modifiers that will also change recombination rates in other regions.

CHAPTER 7

THE EVOLUTION OF

RECOMBINATION

J. Maynard Smith

INTRODUCTION

Recombination depends on the presence of a number of enzymes, and hence a number of genes. What selective processes have been responsible for the evolution of these genes? Typically, population geneticists explain the evolution of a gene by showing that the phenotypic effects of that gene, in the individual that carries it, increase the fitness (survival and fecundity) of that individual. Can the evolution of recombination genes be explained in this way? Most models of the evolution of recombination (reviewed in Maynard Smith, 1978) have assumed that the relevant genes have no effects at all on the fitness of their carrier. Instead, recombination genes spread because, by causing recombination, they alter the constellation of genes at other loci with which they will be associated in future generations. Specifically, a recombination gene becomes linked in coupling with other genes that do increase fitness. I will call such models "hitchhiking" models, because the recombination gene gets a lift in frequency from the high-fitness genes to which it is linked.

But is it true that recombination genes have no immediate effect on the fitness of their carriers? Bacterial geneticists have long been aware that *rec*⁻ mutants are of low viability, basically because they cannot repair damaged DNA. They therefore tend to assume that recombination has evolved because it is necessary for repair. Bernstein et al. (1985a,b) have elaborated this idea into a detailed theory of the evolution of sex and recombination in prokaryotes and eukaryotes. Similar ideas have been proposed by Holliday (1984) and Bengtsson (1985).

One aim of this chapter is to discuss how far the evolution of recombination is to be explained by its immediate role in repair and how far by longer-term hitchhiking effects. First, there is a terminological point to make. For classical genetics, "recombination" meant the process whereby genes inherited from different parents were brought together in a single offspring, either by the free assortment of genes on different chromosomes or by crossing over between genes on the same chromosome. To molecular geneticists, recombination has come to mean the breaking and rejoining of nucleic acid molecules. This dual usage can lead to confusion. For genes on the same chromosome, recombination in the classical sense requires molecular recombination, but the reverse is not true: the breaking and rejoining of strands may or may not result in crossing over between genes away from the point of breakage. I shall use recombination in the molecular sense and shall employ crossing over to refer to the process of creating and breaking combinations of genes. I think this usage is in some ways unfortunate, but the present predominance of molecular genetics makes it necessary if confusion is to be avoided.

I do not doubt that most, if not all, of the enzymes involved in molecular recombination evolved initially because of their role in DNA repair. The debate, if there is one, is over the evolution of meiosis and syngamy in eukaryotes, and that of conjugation and other processes in prokaryotes, which provide the contexts in which molecular recombination can, through crossing over, give rise to new constellations of linked genes. Are these processes a mere unselected consequence of repair, or has selection for crossing over been essential? In this chapter I discuss the idea (Holliday, 1984; Bernstein et al., 1985a,b; Bengtsson, 1985) that meiosis occurs in eukaryotes because of the role it plays in error correction. Although stimulating, I think these ideas are mistaken.

At least in eukaryotes, I argue that crossing over has been an essential selective force in the evolution of sex and recombination. Accordingly, I review hitchhiking models for the evolution of recombination, mainly with eukaryotes in mind. I then briefly consider recombination in the prokaryotes, suggesting that recombination genes originated, and are maintained, primarily because of their role in DNA repair. The crossovers that they cause may occasionally have important evolutionary consequences, but are probably irrelevant to the selective forces maintaining recombination. Finally, I discuss the role of recombination in the predictable and adaptive rearrangement of the genetic material.

REPAIR, RECOMBINATION AND SEX

Bernstein et al. (1985a) distinguish three kinds of change that can happen to DNA:

1. Mutation: the replacement of one base, or group of bases, by another. In general, a mutation cannot be recognized, and so cannot be repaired, unless it is recognized as a mismatch between bases immediately after replication, when new and old strands can be distinguished. In any case, correction of mismatches does not involve recombination. They distinguish mutation from

damage, which can be recognized at any time, and they also distinguish two kinds of damage.

2. Single-strand damage (e.g., thymine dimers). Such damage is often corrected by "recombinational repair." Two points, however, are crucial:
   a. Repair of single-strand damage does *not* require the presence of a homologous DNA molecule. Hence, an asexual haploid organism can repair single-strand damage.
   b. Although crossing over may occur between sites on either side of the point of damage, this is typically between "sister strands"—that is, two DNA molecules that have just arisen by replication of a single molecule. Hence recombinational repair usually has no genetic consequences away from the point of damage.

3. Double-strand damage (e.g., cross-links; double-strand breaks). Such damage can only be repaired in the presence of a homologous molecule, since only then is the necessary sequence information available. Repair typically involves crossing over between outside markers (either always or, more plausibly, in 50% of cases; see Figure 1). An example is the production of twin-spot mosaics in Drosophila by X-irradiation (Figure 2). It is this type of repair that Bernstein et al. (1985a, and in this volume) argue is central to the evolution of recombination, diploidy and sex.

Clearly, double-strand repair does require diploidy, because a homologous molecule is needed to provide information. If the only selective force was the need for double-strand repair, diploidy could be achieved by chromosome doubling in a single haploid cell. However, I suspect (Maynard Smith, 1978) that diploidy, perhaps with an intermediate stage of heterokaryosis, originated because of the complementation of different deleterious recessive mutations in

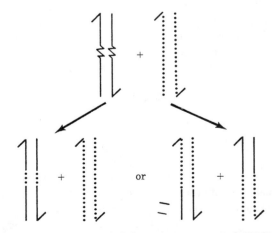

FIGURE 1. Double-strand repair. Each line represents a single DNA strand.

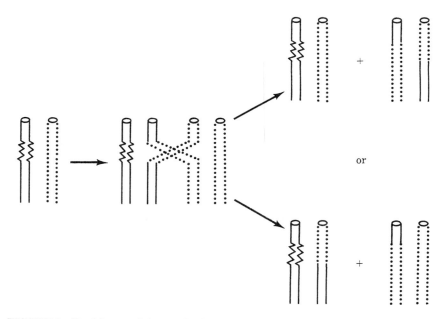

FIGURE 2. Double-strand damage leading to a twin-spot mosaic. Repair of the damage during replication causes a somatic crossover. Depending on how the centromeres disjoin, this can lead to two clones of cells, each homozygous for one of the two chromosome regions distal to the point of damage.

the two fusing cells; that is, diploidy confers hybrid vigor through genetic complementation of harmful mutations. This provides an explanation of diploidy, but not of sex. To explain sex, Bernstein et al. argue as follows: Since double-strand repair involves crossing over between outside markers, its consequence is to produce homozygosity for genes distal to the crossover (as in twin-spot mosaics; see Figure 2). Homozygotes will, among other things, be homozygous for deleterious mutations. Gamete production and syngamy will then be favored, because they will restore heterozygosity—each parent will complement the deficiency of the other. Thus, the argument is that repair requires diploidy and that sex (meiosis and syngamy) evolves not to make crossing over possible, but to restore the heterozygosity destroyed by repair. An asexual diploid that does not undergo meiosis cannot repair double-strand damage: if it does repair damage by recombination, it becomes homozygous for harmful recessives.

I find it hard to accept this argument, for two reasons. First, I cannot see why double-strand repair should *necessarily* require crossing over between outside markers. There is certainly no logical necessity for crossing over (as there is for the presence of a homologue). In at least one case—mating-type change in yeast—a process equivalent to double-strand repair occurs without crossing over, which would be lethal if it did happen. It seems more plausible that the production of inviable homozygotes would be avoided by the evolution of repair not involving crossing over rather than by sex. Second, there are at least some cases in higher eukaryotes in which double-strand repair leading to homozygosity does *not* happen in the germ line. Thus, if it happened in the germ line of male Drosophila, it would result in recombinant gametes, which are in fact absent (although, interestingly, they can be induced by X-rays [Hanna-Alava, 1965]). Yet in many crosses, well over 90% of eggs hatch, indicating that unrepaired damage cannot be all that important. More decisive still, many parthenogens retain heterozygosity indefinitely. In some cases, such as clado-cerans and aphids, and in many plants, meiosis is suppressed. In others, such as the lizard *Cnemidophorus uniparens*, there is a doubling of the chromosome number (endomitosis), followed by a meiosis in which sister chromosomes pair; thus there is no opportunity to repair double-strand damage that occurred before the last premeiotic division, and offspring are genetically identical to their parent.

How are male Drosophila and heterozygous parthenogens to be explained? There are various possibilities:

1. Double-strand damage does occur in the germ line and is repaired, but by a process not causing crossing over.
2. Double-strand damage occurs, but is not repaired. Cells suffering such damage cannot divide and are selectively eliminated.
3. Double-strand damage in the germ line is very rare.

Whichever of these explanations is correct, the argument that meiosis and syngamy evolved to restore heterozygosity lost through double-strand repair fails.

Before leaving this topic, it is worth emphasizing that many parthenogens have nonadaptive features that are best thought of as sexual hang-ups (Maynard Smith, 1986) present only because of recent descent from a sexual ancestor. The most obvious is pseudogamy—the need for egg development to be stimulated by sperm from a sexual relative. Another example is the heavy egg mortality in automictic parthenogens (that is, those that undergo a normal meiosis and then restore diploidy by fusion of two haploid products of meiosis, or of two identical haploid cleavage nuclei), because of homozygosity for deleterious genes (Templeton, 1983). The retention of meiosis in species such as Cnemidophorus probably belongs in this category. As Bernstein et al. (1985a,b, and in this volume) correctly point out, it cannot be explained by a "generation of variability" hypothesis, because offspring are identical to their parent. Nor can it serve the function of double-strand repair, except for damage that has occurred since the last round of DNA replication.

There are, however, many organisms that appear to have escaped such sexual hang-ups, in particular the ameiotic parthenogens such as aphids, cladocerans, and many plants. If Bernstein et al. are correct, all these should suffer heavy egg mortality caused by unrepaired double-strand damage. It is difficult to find published evidence on the hatchability of ameiotically produced eggs. In dandelions, over 90% of seed may germinate (M. Mogie, personal communication; Van Loenhoud and Duyts, 1981); obligatory parthenogenetic Daphnia do not produce noticeable levels of inviable eggs (M. Lynch, personal communication). It would be valuable to have further data on this point. For the present, I can only say that there is no evidence for excessive mortality caused by the absence of double-strand repair and some evidence (male Drosophila, dandelions, and some Daphnia) that such mortality does not occur.

Holliday (1984) also supposes that the function of meiosis is to correct errors, but those of a different kind. He points out that cell differentiation involves changes in the pattern of DNA methylation. If a specific methylation is lost in the germ line, this represents a potential genetic defect. Typically, the loss will affect only one of two homologous chromosomes. Pairing of the relevant chromosome regions, and the formation of hybrid DNA, would then provide an opportunity for correction of the error, when half-methylated sequences become fully methylated. If, as Holliday suggests, nonmethylated sequences act as promoters of recombination, this could be a very efficient way of "repairing" errors in methylation, provided, of course, that in the germ line demethylation is always the "error" and methylation the correct state.

Holliday gives two interesting arguments in support of his view. First, it does seem that, at least in higher animals, meiosis is typically needed to "reset" the developmental program. Even in parthenogens, meiosis is usually present. It is particularly persuasive that many parthenogens undergo "endomitosis," a form of meiosis producing offspring genetically identical to the parent; why bother, unless meiosis is needed to reset the cell to a totipotent state? The difficulty, of course, is that higher plants, in which single somatic cells can give rise to a new plant, also undergo meiosis, although they do not seem to need it for epigenetic reasons.

Holliday's second argument rests on the work of Thuriaux (1977), who showed, first, that the map length of eukaryotic chromosomes is independent of DNA content (over a 1000-fold range, from yeast to maize) and, second, that the map length of individual genes is also similar in all eukaryotes. This strongly suggests that recombination is confined to the vicinity of structural genes. This argument would make sense if the function of recombination is to correct the state of gene differentiation.

Bengtsson (1985) proposes a third repair function for meiosis, through gene conversion. Suppose that some kinds of mutations occur more often than their opposites, for example, that deletion of a base is more common than insertion. Since most mutations are harmful, selection would favor an opposite bias in gene conversion: that is, when two homologous genes differ by the presence of one base, it should be more common to correct the mismatch by adding a base to the deficient gene than by removing a base from the other allele. Further, once biased gene conversion was a fact, there would be selection favoring chromosome pairing in meiosis, to provide an opportunity for conversion.

Both Holliday's and Bengtsson's ideas are ingenious and are not without empirical support. But both seem to me to suffer from the same crucial difficulty faced by the Bernstein et al. model (1985a,b, and in this volume) based on double-strand repair: They can explain diploidy, but not meiosis and syngamy.

One other immediate advantage for recombination that has often been proposed is that chiasmata are needed to ensure proper disjunction in meiosis. This seems implausible, for several reasons. First, efficient disjunction without chiasmata has evolved several times, as in male Diptera and in female Lepidoptera. Second, if the genetic consequences of recombination were selected against, we would expect chiasmata to be localized. Third, genetic variance for recombination rate, unassociated with infertility, has been found in eukaryotes almost whenever it has been looked for. Finally, and decisively, if you do not want the genetic effects of recombination, why have sex and meiosis at all?

I conclude that, at least in eukaryotes, the evolution of recombination cannot be explained by the immediate requirements of DNA repair, of methylation, of gene conversion, or of disjunction in meiosis. We must therefore seek a hitchhiking type of explanation.

THE SELECTIVE ADVANTAGES OF CROSSING OVER

Before discussing the various types of hitchhiking models that have been proposed, two general points should be made. First, both the frequency and location of crossovers vary within populations (Maynard Smith, 1978; Brooks, in this volume). Second, in an unchanging environment, and in the absence of mutation, it is a theoretical prediction that selection will reduce crossing over (for a discussion of this point, see Feldman et al., 1980; Felsenstein, in this volume), and there is some evidence that such selection does occur (Charlesworth and Charlesworth, 1975). It follows that crossing over would be reduced to low levels (by localization of chiasmata or other means) were it not for the presence of counteracting selection for higher recombination rates. This section discusses how such selection might arise. My treatment is complementary to that of Felsenstein (in this volume). He is primarily concerned with showing that all models of the evolution of crossing over fall into two main categories, according to whether linkage disequilibrium was generated by selection or by chance. I have accepted this distinction below, but have been more concerned with identifying the biological and environmental circumstances in which different models might apply.

As a start, consider an explanation that does have a "damage-repair" theme, although it involves crossing over between nonallelic genes (Figure 3). Suppose that a gene R mediates crossing over between two chromosomes, each carrying a lethal mutation. Depending on gene order, R has a 50% chance of emerging

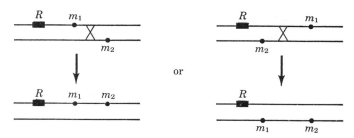

FIGURE 3. The "engine and gear box" model of the evolution of recombination. R represents a gene mediating recombination; m_1 and m_2 represent lethal mutations.

linked to two lethals and a 50% chance of being on a chromosome free of lethals. Since two lethals are no worse than one, the gene R has improved its chance of a future by mediating recombination.

This model is attractive. Recombination is favored because it produces one good chromosome out of two bad ones. By analogy, one can make one functional car by combining the engine from one broken-down car and the gear box from another. But, while attractive, the model is—at least in this simple form—false, basically because it assumes that R is always linked to the lethal. The correct picture is shown in Figure 4. Suppose that the cycle of events is Replication + Recombination → Selection → Mutation → Replication + Recombination →. Immediately after selection, there is a population of "perfect" chromosomes. Mutation, as a random process, produces chromosomes with 0, 1, 2 . . . mutations in a Poisson distribution. All that recombination can do is to produce a more random distribution from a less random one; technically, it produces "linkage equilibrium" from "linkage disequilibrium." If the chromosomes are initially in linkage equilibrium, it does nothing. In Figure 4, gene R is neither more nor less likely to be on a chromosome free of lethals after recombination than before. This point is made particularly clearly by Felsenstein in this volume.

Although false, the model does tell us what *kinds* of explanations of recombination are possible. In fact, explanations can be classified according to two criteria, as follows:

1. What is the origin of the linkage disequilibrium? In particular, is it stochastic or deterministic? Felsenstein (1985) has suggested that all models fall into one of these two classes.
2. Are we concerned with harmful mutations or beneficial ones? In Figure 3, gene R is favored because recombination disconnects it from harmful mutations. There are alternative models in which recombination brings R into coupling with favorable mutations. Another way of seeing this distinction is as follows. Models such as that in Figure 3 will operate in a constant environment, since harmful mutations are always with us. Models requiring

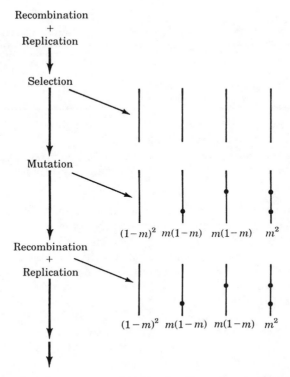

FIGURE 4. A correct model of mutation and recombination. Each line represents a chromosome. The black circles represent deleterious mutations; m is the mutation rate per replication.

favorable mutations typically require an environment that changes, either in space or in time.

Applying these criteria simultaneously gives us the classification of models shown in Table 1 and discussed below.

Muller's ratchet

Muller (1964) imagined an asexual haploid population in which deleterious mutations are occurring and are being eliminated by selection. We can classify individuals according to whether they have 0, 1, 2 . . . mutations. At equilibrium between mutation and selection, the number of individuals in the optimal (no mutations) class may be quite small. If so, in one generation all those individuals may, by chance, fail to reproduce. There is then no way in which the zero-mutation class could be reconstituted (except by the rare event of a back mutation): the "ratchet" has clicked round one notch (Figure 5). There is

TABLE 1. A classification of models

	Origin of Linkage Disequilibrium	
Effects of Recombination	Chance	Selection
Avoids deleterious genes	Muller's ratchet (Muller, 1964)	Eliminating mutants (Feldman et al., 1980; Kondrashov, 1982)
Combines favorable genes	Faster evolution (Fisher, 1930; Muller, 1932)	Shifting optimum (Maynard Smith, 1980) Parasitism (Jaenike, 1978; Hamilton, 1980)

now a new optimal class, with one harmful mutation. In time, this class too will, by chance, be lost. Thus, harmful mutations will gradually accumulate in the population. But in a sexual population the zero-mutation class can be regenerated by recombination: the ratchet will not operate.

Imagine a recessive gene R that makes recombination possible. As Felsenstein and Yokoyama (1976) have pointed out, a population in which such a

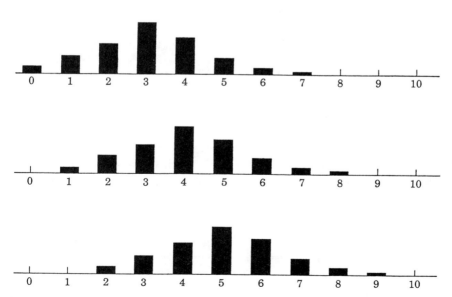

FIGURE 5. Muller's ratchet. Frequency in a population of individuals with different numbers of slightly deleterious mutations, after successive steps of the ratchet.

gene is segregating would, in effect, consist of two genetically isolated populations, one with and one without recombination. The ratchet would operate in the latter, but not the former. Hence the mean fitness of the subpopulation with R would be higher, and R would spread.

There is an odd feature of this model: the fittest class is eliminated. How can this be? The number n_0 in the optimal class has an expected value, $E(n_0)$, under mutation and selection. If n_0 rises above $E(n_0)$, it is driven down (by mutation); if it falls below, it is driven up (by selection). But there is an asymmetry, because below there is an "absorbing boundary": if ever the optimal class falls to zero, it is lost forever.

This model can be made quantitative (Haigh, 1978). Consider a population of size N, with a per genome, per generation mutation rate U, and a selective disadvantage of s per mutation. If fitnesses are multiplicative, so that an individual with i mutations has fitness $(1 - s)^i$, then in an infinite population, the proportions of individuals with 0, 1, 2 . . . i . . . mutations are distributed as a Poisson random variable with mean U/s. Hence in a finite population, the expected number in the optimal class is

$$E(n_0) = N \, e^{-U/s}$$

If $E(n_0)$ is large—say, greater than 1000—the ratchet will not operate; if $E(n_0) < 10$, the ratchet proceeds quite rapidly. An analytical value for the speed of the ratchet has not been obtained, but Haigh (1978) gives some approximate estimates.

The ratchet operates if U/s is large; thus it is important only for slightly deleterious mutations, not for lethals. With, say, $U = 0.4$ and $s = 0.01$, $e^{-U/s} = 10^{-17}$, so that the ratchet will operate even in a very large population. However, the mean fitness $\overline{W}$ of a sexual population is e^{-U}, so with $U = 0.4$, $\overline{W} = 0.67$, which is quite compatible with population survival.

One last theoretical point: the ratchet operates in a population with 100% selfing as it does in an asexual haploid population (Heller and Maynard Smith, 1979). The reason is easy to see. Every deleterious mutation in a selfing population either becomes fixed ($p = \frac{1}{2}$) or is eliminated; if it is fixed, it is equivalent to a mutation in an asexual haploid.

What is the practical significance of the ratchet? Clearly, it sets an upper limit on genome size in asexual organisms, because the relevant mutation rate, U, is the per genome rate, which will increase as the genome size increases. This limit may be small compared to the limit set by $W = e^{-U}$. In bacteria, I suspect that effective recombination is so rare that the genome size is indeed set by the ratchet, as it must be in any primitively asexual eukaryote (if there are any). What of eukaryotes? In higher eukaryotes, the genome size has probably increased to a level above that which could be maintained without recombination. If so, secondarily asexual eukaryotes are condemned to extinction by the ratchet, if for no other reason. What, then, are the oldest eukaryotic clones? It is difficult to say. There have been dandelions since the Cretaceous, and most of them were probably asexual. But each clone may be relatively short-lived, because new ones are regularly being produced from sexual parents. The whiptail lizard *Cnemidophorus uniparens* is a single clone, as proved by the compatibility of scale grafts. But how old is it? The patchy taxonomic distribution of parthenogens certainly suggests that few eukaryotic parthenogens are very ancient. The major exception is the bdelloid rotifers—a whole order without males. Do they have particularly small genomes? Or a very low mutation rate? Or some secret substitute for sex? We badly need to know.

The ratchet will operate in any DNA segment that does not recombine, and not only in whole genomes. Charlesworth (1978) has suggested it may be responsible for the genetic decay of Y chromosomes. Mitochondria are probably saved from the ratchet by their small genome size (approximately 16,000 base pairs in mammals); this small genome size, and the transfer of genetic information to the nucleus, may be an evolutionary response to the ratchet.

There are unsolved theoretical questions. I have already mentioned that we have no analytical solution for its rate of movement. A second question is how much recombination is needed to arrest the ratchet? Equivalently, how much outcrossing is needed to arrest the ratchet in selfing species? A third question is what is N? How much dispersal is needed to ensure that the effective N is the size of the whole species?

Mutation in an infinite population

Muller's ratchet is confined to finite populations. Kondrashov (1982) pointed out that recombination would confer an advantage even in an infinite population if the effect of harmful mutations is not multiplicative but synergistic, so that two mutations have a more severe effect than would be predicted if they acted independently. To see this, consider the extreme case of "truncation selection," in which n mutations together are lethal, but $(n - 1)$ have no effect. At equilibrium, the number of new mutations arising per generation (which is the same for sexual and asexual populations) is exactly balanced by the number of mutations removed by selection. But (mutations removed) = (selective deaths) × (mutations per dead individual). As Figure 6 shows, the number of mutations per dead individual is greater in the sexual population, so the selective deaths are fewer. Thus, as in Muller's ratchet, selection would favor a recessive gene for recombination.

Feldman et al. (1980) analyzed selection on a gene for recombination in an infinite sexual population in which deleterious mutations with synergistic effects are occurring. They calculated that the gene for recombination would increase in frequency. Kondrashov's (1982) model can be seen as providing an intuitive explanation for this result.

The practical significance of this argument is hard to evaluate, although there is some evidence (Mukai, 1969) that deleterious mutations do have synergistic effects on fitness.

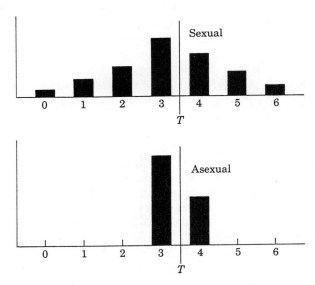

FIGURE 6. Kondrashov's (1982) model. The frequencies of individuals with different numbers of deleterious mutations in a sexual and an asexual population, before selection. T is the threshold, above which mutations are lethal.

Favorable genes in a finite population

I turn now to the suggestion that recombination genes spread because they get a hitchhike from favorable combinations of genes (Figure 7). The idea originates with Fisher (1930) and Muller (1932). Imagine that the environment has recently changed, so that several mutations, A, B, C, and so on, would be favored if they occurred. Suppose that A occurs and increases to fixation. In an asexual population, B can only be fixed if it occurs in an individual that is already A, and C can only be fixed if it occurs in an individual that is already AB, and so on. (Of course, the sequence of establishment could vary, but favorable mutations are wasted unless they occur in individuals that have the highest number of previous favorable mutations.) In contrast, in a sexual population, if A, B, and C occur in different individuals, they can be combined in a single descendant. Note that the initial linkage disequilibrium arises by chance; in an infinite population, AB genotypes would be generated by mutation in the frequency expected from linkage equilibrium.

It is not always true that recombination accelerates the accumulation of favorable mutations. Wright (1931) argued that evolutionary progress may depend on the transition from *ab* to *AB*, when the single substitutions, *Ab* and *aB*, are unfavorable. He suggested that such "valleys" can be crossed by a species divided into many demes. It is worth noting that it would be crossed most easily

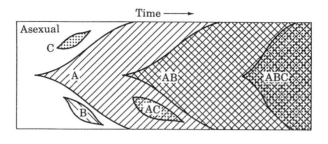

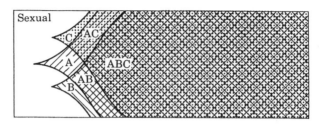

FIGURE 7. The rate of evolution in sexual and asexual populations. (After Muller, 1932.)

by an asexual population, in which *AB* genotypes, once they arise by mutation, are not broken up by recombination. This accords with the conclusion of Eshel and Feldman (1970) that recombination can slow down evolution when there are nonadditive fitness interactions between loci.

Selection for recombination in an infinite population

The essential feature of the Fisher–Muller model is that two favorable alleles, *A* and *B*, arise by mutation in different individuals. Thus the linkage disequilibrium arises because populations are finite and mutation is a rare event.

The final corner of our table contains models in which *R* gets a hitchhike from high-fitness gene combinations that are spreading in a changing environment, but in which the initial linkage disequilibrium arises from selection and not from chance. Sturtevant and Mather (1938) pointed out that if the environment changes in such a way that for some period genotypes *AB* and *ab* are favored, and *Ab* and *aB* are selected against, whereas at other times the fitness differences are reversed, then genes for recombination will be favored. Charlesworth (1976) showed in a detailed model that this is indeed so.

There is, at least at first sight, a serious difficulty with such models. I have pointed out (1978) that these models require the environment to behave in a very odd way. Suppose that allele *A* adapts the organism to hot places and *a* to cold, and that allele *B* adapts the organism to wet places and *b* to dry. Then the model supposes that in the first period, hot places tend to be wet and cold ones dry, whereas the opposite is true in the second period. Not only do environmental features change, correlations between features change. It is difficult to believe that God is as bloody-minded as that.

However, two very different ways of overcoming this difficulty have recently been suggested. The first (Maynard Smith, 1980) concerns normalizing selection for a quantitative trait. Normalizing selection *does* generate linkage disequilibrium. To see this, consider the two-locus, two-allele model in Figure 8. Clearly, gametes *Ab* and *aB* tend to occur in high-fitness genotypes, and *AB* and *ab* in low-fitness ones. Hence there is selection for repulsion linkages.

Continued normalizing selection for a fixed optimum leads first to linkage disequilibrium and ultimately to genetic homozygosity. However, normalizing selection for an optimum that is changing—either unidirectionally or in a

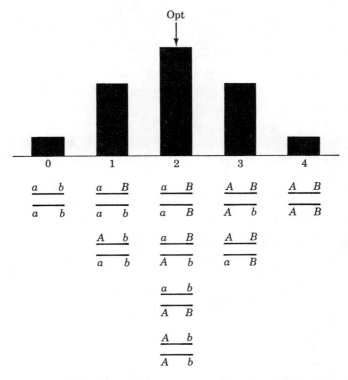

FIGURE 8. Normalizing selection and linkage disequilibrium. A phenotypic trait is determined additively by two alleles at each of two loci. The phenotypic distribution, when alleles have a frequency of 0.5, is shown, together with the genotypes. If selection favors the intermediate phenotype, chromosomes *aB* and *Ab* tend to occur in fit genotypes, and *ab* and *AB* in unfit genotypes. Hence there is selection for linkage disequilibrium. Opt = optimal.

fluctuating fashion—can select for increased recombination (Maynard Smith, 1980). Simulation of a multilocus model showed that alleles for high recombination increase quite rapidly when there is normalizing selection for a changing optimum. I think this is a major reason for the maintenance of crossing over. Normalizing selection for quantitative traits is almost universal, but optima vary. However, we have at present no analytical insight into the process.

A second situation in which selection may favor a change in the sign of linkage disequilibrium has been suggested by Jaenike (1978) and Hamilton (1980). Suppose that alleles at two linked loci are concerned with resistance to a parasite, which has a corresponding pair of virulence loci. This can give rise to cyclical changes in genotype frequency and to changing linkage disequilibria. It is not God, but a parasite, that is being bloody-minded.

In the shifting optimum and host–parasite models, the environment changes between generations, but in any one generation all individuals are exposed to the same selective forces. In Bell's (1985) expressive terminology, they are Red Queen rather than tangled bank models. In the tangled bank model, the relevant environmental variation is spatial rather than temporal: the environment varies between patches, but the range and frequency of patch types is constant from generation to generation. Williams' (1975) aphid–rotifer and elm–oyster models are of this kind. He argued that a sexual parent has an advantage over an asexual one because it produces a genetically variable progeny and hence is more likely to have at least one offspring of particularly high fitness in the local patch; in his analogy, an asexual parent resembles a man who buys 100 tickets for a raffle with only one prize, and finds that they all have the same number.

I have argued (1976) that in this type of model, sex and crossing over are favored only if there is competition between close relatives within a patch. If the offspring of a single parent are sufficiently widely dispersed, an asexual parent resembles a man who buys 100 raffle tickets with the same number, but in 100 different raffles: sex would confer no advantage. Given competition between siblings, I showed that selection could favor crossing over. The model has, however, two significant limitations:

1. It requires a particular pattern of dispersal, in which sibs compete with each other, but in a patch different from that of their parents.
2. If a set of linked genes are concerned with adaptation to the same environmental feature (or to features that are themselves correlated), selection will favor reduced crossing over between them.

Because of these limitations, I think that Red Queen models are a better explanation for the maintenance of crossing over.

It is clear that for each of the four categories there are plausible models for the selection of higher rates of crossing over. It is hard to estimate their relative importance. My impression is that Muller's ratchet is important in limiting genome size in primitively asexual organisms and perhaps in eliminating secondarily asexual ones. But the process is slow to take effect. There is some evidence (Charlesworth and Charlesworth, 1975) of selection against recombination in sexual populations. The process most likely to counterbalance this in the short term is normalizing selection for a shifting optimum.

RECOMBINATION IN PROKARYOTES

What of recombination in prokaryotes? I think that the genes responsible for recombination in prokaryotes are present because of their role in recombinational repair of single-strand damage and not because of any effects on outside markers. Thus, recombinational repair typically involves sister strands and has no genetic consequences except at the site of damage. In *Escherichia coli*, two homologous nonsister chromosomes are rarely present in a single cell; in fact, they are present only immediately after conjugation is induced. This happens too rarely to have any measurable effect on the genetic structure of *E. coli* populations. Thus Selander and Whittam (1983) conclude that "natural populations consist of mixtures of numerous, more or less independently evolving, clones."

This does not alter the fact that, very occasionally, a recombinational event brings together genes from different ancestors—sometimes very distantly related ancestors—and by so doing produces a new genotype that inherits the earth. But this should be seen as a consequence, not a cause, of genetic recombination. This is most obvious when the genes mediating the recombination are unlinked to the new, successful genotype (Figure 9). A new, successful phage is generated by recombination, but the recombination genes are on the host chromosome and thus get no benefit. There are, of course, cases in which the recombination genes are linked to the new genotype—for example, when a new *E. coli* clone is produced after conjugation. Such events are important in evolution, but I do not think they provide the selective advantage responsible for the origin or maintenance of recombination genes. They are consequences rather than causes of the evolution of recombination. I am encouraged that Levin and Lenski (1983) have reached the same conclusion on the basis of a much greater familiarity with bacterial genetics; also see Levin (this volume).

RECOMBINATION AND THE ADAPTIVE REARRANGEMENT OF THE GENETIC MATERIAL

There is a third context in which recombination may be favored by selection. In addition to the repair of local damage, and the production of new groups of linked genes by crossing over, recombination may cause a rearrangement of the genetic material that has repeatable and adaptive consequences. Some examples will help to make this clear. In the phage μ there is a length of DNA, the G-loop, that can be inverted by a recombinational event mediated by one of the phage genes. The effect of the inversion is to alter the host range of the phage.

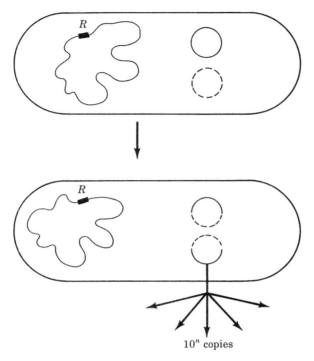

FIGURE 9. Phage recombination. It is supposed, in the upper diagram, that a bacterium is infected by two phage particles. A recombination between these phages is mediated by a gene, R, of the bacterial chromosome. One of the recombinant phages is an evolutionary success. This does not increase the frequency of gene R.

To give a eukaryotic example, there are a number of genes responsible for the antigenic properties of trypanosomes. These genes are activated in turn, thus enabling the parasites to escape the immunological response of their hosts. This gene switching depends on recombination. Other examples include mating-type changes in yeasts and the generation of immunological diversity in verte-brates.

What is common to these examples, and thus distinguishes them from typical crossing over, is that recombination takes place repeatedly and at specific sites, and has predictable and adaptive consequences. It seems likely that many more examples of this type of process remain to be discovered.

SUMMARY

Two different kinds of explanations for the evolution of recombination have been discussed. The first is that the relevant genes are needed to repair DNA.

They may also produce new genetic variability that is important in evolution, but this should be seen as an unselected consequence, rather than the cause, of the evolution of recombination. The alternative view is that the role of recombination genes in producing new gene combinations by crossing over has itself been an important selective force in their evolution.

In the case of prokaryotes, I think the first kind of explanation may well be correct. Almost certainly, recombination genes arose in the first instance because of their role in repair, and this has remained their major function. But what of the proposal that, in eukaryotes, sex, meiosis, and crossing over originated and are maintained because of their role in repair? That many of the relevant enzymes originated as repair enzymes and continue to play a role in repair is almost certainly true. But I have difficulty accepting the full thesis. Clearly, some types of repair (double-strand repair) require the presence of a homologous chromosome, without which there is no source of the necessary information. Hence such repair requires diploidy, or at least a diploid phase in the life cycle. However, the origin of diploidy can be more plausibly explained by genetic complementation. A more fundamental difficulty is that although double-strand repair requires diploidy, it does not require meiosis and syngamy. The explanation of sex as a way of restoring genetic heterozygosity is unsatisfactory, basically because the existence of ameiotic parthenogens demonstrates that any selection pressure arising from this cause must operate over a very long time scale.

I conclude that the production of crossovers is a relevant function in maintaining recombination in eukaryotes. This implies that genes are maintained not because of any effect they have on the fitness of the individual in which they find themselves, but because, by causing crossovers, they are associated in future generations with gene combinations of high fitness. I have reviewed a range of models of this kind. They can be classified according to two orthogonal criteria. First, are the recombination genes associated with gene combinations that are increasing under selection, or do they avoid association with recurrent deleterious mutations? Second, since crossing over is relevant only in populations that are initially in linkage disequilibrium, does that disequilibrium originate because of selection on alleles with epistatic fitness effects or because of chance events in finite populations? This two-way classification indicates four classes of process, all of which may be relevant.

My present view (which differs from that expressed in *The Evolution of Sex*, 1978) is as follows. Muller's ratchet (the accumulation of deleterious mutations that is inevitable in a finite population if the per-genome mutation rate is too high) is relevant mainly in limiting the genome size in primitively asexual organisms and perhaps in causing the extinction of secondarily asexual eukaryotes. The main short-term selection pressure that maintains crossing over in sexual eukaryotes arises because, in a changing environment, there will be changes in the favored value of the linkage disequilibrium for fitness loci. This will happen if there is selection for a shifting optimum value of a polygenically determined trait. Cyclical coevolution of hosts and their parasites may have a similar effect.

Another function of recombination genes is to bring about specific rearrangements of the genetic material, repeatedly and with predictable adaptive consequences. Several examples of this phenomenon are known, and more will doubtless be discovered. Although important, such functions are almost certainly secondary in an evolutionary sense.

Note added in proof

I have recently re-analyzed the effects of selection in a polygenic model on the frequency of a gene for high recombination. Such a gene will increase in frequency under directional selection, and will decrease in frequency if selection is normalizing (provided that the optimum is close to the population mean) or if the direction of selection changes frequently. The reason for the increase under directional selection is as follows. Directional selection generates negative $(+ - + -)$ linkage disequilibrium, which is greater for rec$^-$ chromosomes (that is, chromosomes not carrying the high recombination allele) than for rec$^+$ chromosomes. Hence, the phenotypic variance contributed by rec$^+$ chromosomes is greater. Therefore rec$^+$ chromosomes respond more to selection: that is, they accumulate favored alleles. Therefore the high recombination allele increases in frequency. Thus my earlier conclusion that selection for a shifting optimum can lead to an increase in the frequency of a gene for recombination was correct, but I did not understand the reason for the increase. Essentially, it is continued directional selection that causes the increase.

CHAPTER 8

UNIFORMITY AND DIVERSITY IN THE EVOLUTION OF SEX

Graham Bell

INTRODUCTION

When many minds combine to pronounce on so knotty a problem as the evolution of sex, there is a danger that the diversity of opinion may bewilder rather than enlighten. For this reason, it is important to be clear at the outset what is to be explained, and what sort of explanation will be accepted. Three items will figure prominently in any short list of what is to be explained.

1. The very general and widespread occurrence of a process involving meiosis and fertilization, despite the greater efficiency of mitotic replication. This is the primary observation responsible for the present interest in the topic.
2. The taxonomic distribution of sexual and asexual modes. Obligate parthenogenesis occurs very sporadically among metazoans and metaphytes; with few exceptions, asexual forms occur as small, taxonomically isolated groups whose nearest relatives are all sexual. Among protists, and still more among prokaryotes, this pattern breaks down, and sex is often absent, or at least extremely scarce, throughout large taxa.
3. The ecological correlates of sexuality. Although the distribution of parthenogenesis among metazoans is sporadic, it is by no means random. For example, parthenogenetic animals tend to occupy recent, novel, or disturbed environments.

Our first requirement is a theory that will cover all of these generalizations. But it is also essential that any such theory refer to processes that are presently in operation, so that we can study them in the laboratory or the field. No one will put much faith in a theory that explains comparative observations but cannot make experimental predictions.

This essay is a digest of conclusions set out in much more detail in three recent publications: a large-scale comparative survey of sexual systems in metazoans (Bell, 1982), a brief review of relevant experiments (Bell, 1985), and an extensive treatment of the fate of asexual lines cultured in isolation (G. Bell, in preparation). I shall argue that to account for the principal features of sexuality we need two hypotheses: (1) that sex prevents the irreversible accumulation of mutational damage by combining deleterious mutations that have arisen independently into the same line of descent, which can then be eliminated by selection, and (2) that the genetic variance created as a by-product of this process is adaptive in heterogeneous environments.

SEX MAINTAINS THE UNIFORMITY OF THE GENOME

Individuals are mortal; they must die either by accident or as the result of senescent decline, which has evolved because genes that increase reproductive success early in life will be favored even though they have crippling effects later on (Williams, 1957). Only lines of descent have appreciable longevity on a geological scale. The genome must therefore be replicated very many times; contemporary eukaryotic protists are separated from their common ancestor by more than 10^{10} successive replications. Any lack of precision in gene replication will therefore quickly be magnified to levels at which continued existence is impossible. However desirable, complete precision is unattainable. Information cannot be transmitted with 100% precision, any more than energy can be transformed with 100% efficiency. A fundamental requirement for any replicating system is therefore a means of correcting errors.

There are two ways of checking and repairing a series of artifacts. The first is to compare them one by one with a master copy that is known or assumed to be free of errors. I shall call this "endogenous" repair, since the rules used for repairing are a part of the system of fabrication; no external process is involved. In this way, genetic damage that prevents replication, such as cross-linking, can be repaired by patching in the corresponding sequence from an homologous DNA molecule. Bernstein et al. (1985a, b, and this volume) have argued that such endogenous repair represents the original function for which the molecular machinery of recombination was designed, and their argument is very plausible. However, it will not work for replicable damage, such as base substitutions, for the reasons given by Maynard Smith in this volume. Such errors cannot be corrected by endogenous systems, but cannot be allowed to accumulate; they require a quite different method of repair.

The second way of repairing a series of artifacts is to subject each to a stringent test of performance. Those performing within the limits of tolerance are accepted, while those that fail are rejected. I shall call this "exogenous" repair, since it requires an operation that is outside the system of fabrication. For living organisms, the testing procedure is represented by natural selection. Because endogenous repair cannot deal with all categories of error, an efficient system of exogenous repair is essential for the indefinite persistence of a line of descent. By making the limits of tolerance arbitrarily narrow, it might be thought that exogenous repair could always be made adequate. This is false. Exogenous repair can be perfected only in sexual organisms.

Imagine an infinite population of haploid organisms inhabiting a uniform and unchanging environment. To begin with, the genome is so well adapted to the environment that there is an unambiguous advantage in preserving it intact. Nevertheless, mutations cannot be detected and corrected by endogenous repair systems, and as time goes on mutational load will increase. This increase will tend to be checked by the poor performance of heavily loaded individuals, so that the population will eventually reach an equilibrium when the opposed forces of mutation and selection are just balanced. The equilibrium population has a frequency distribution of deleterious mutations per genome, and this distribution will thereafter remain the same from generation to generation. A small proportion of the population has no deleterious mutations; a correspondingly small proportion is very heavily loaded; and most individuals have intermediate loads. The distribution is the same, whether the population is sexual or not.

This simple analysis breaks down if the population is finite. In a finite asexual population, at equilibrium only a small absolute number of individuals bears no mutations. Since they are asexual, these unloaded individuals constitute a small isolated population whose number will fluctuate stochastically through time because of sampling error. Eventually, the number of individuals in the unloaded class is nearly certain to fluctuate to zero, so that the best-adapted individuals in the population are now those bearing a single deleterious mutation. The crucial point is that this process is essentially irreversible; back-mutation cannot restore the unloaded class because it occurs so infrequently that the single-mutant class will itself have disappeared long before the appropriate back-mutation has arisen. This is the basis of Muller's contention that asexual populations exhibit a sort of ratchet mechanism, such that the population can never come to contain fewer mutations than are currently borne by its least-loaded line (Muller, 1964). There is no such ratchet in a sexual population, since, while the unloaded class may still disappear from time to time, it will eventually be restored by recombination between loaded gametes. Asexual populations will thus inevitably decay through geological time, at last becoming extinct; sex provides an exogenous repair device essential for indefinite persistence. As Felsenstein (1974) has pointed out, Muller's ratchet is simply the obverse of the more popular theory, now in eclipse, that views the function of sex as being to bring together favorable mutations arising independently into the same line of descent, thus increasing the rate of evolution (Weismann, 1889). The ratchet is likely to be more important because deleterious mutations are vastly more numerous than favorable ones.

Just how important the ratchet is depends on how fast it will turn. This depends primarily on the number of individuals in the least-loaded class at equilibrium. The frequency distribution of load at equilibrium is a Poisson distribution with parameter U/s, where U is the mutation rate per genome, per generation, and s is the selection coefficient associated with the mutations; the number of individuals in the least-loaded class at equilibrium in a population of total size N is thus $n_0 = N \exp(-U/s)$ (Haigh, 1978). A series of numerical experiments (described in Bell, in press) has suggested that the ratchet turns once in about $10n_0$ generations, reducing viability by 1% as it does so. We know very little about the rate at which mildly deleterious mutations arise, but the most accurate and extensive work (Mukai, 1964; Mukai et al., 1972) suggests that, at least in Drosophila, about one such mutation per genome will arise every three or four generations. Since reducing viability to levels that will cause rapid extinction will require 100 or so turns of the ratchet, it is easy to calculate that asexual populations of fewer than 10^{10} individuals will not last long in geological time. Conversely, populations of 10^{12} or more individuals will suffer relatively little. Since the ratchet will turn more slowly when the genome is smaller—and the total rate of deleterious mutation correspondingly lower— these numbers will be smaller for organisms that have fewer genes than Drosophila. The ratchet will therefore bear most heavily on large organisms that have large genomes and relatively small populations; sex is probably indispensable for the long-term persistence of organisms of more than 1 g in mass. It will be of much less consequence to smaller and simpler organisms forming enormous populations, for whom sex may often be unnecessary.

Since the ratchet turns once every $10n_0$ generations or so, it can be halted by the production of $K = 0 \cdot 1$ unloaded recombinant genomes per generation, irrespective of total population size. Obviously, rather low rates of recombination may be enough to halt the ratchet in large populations. The critical rate of recombination r^* just sufficient to prevent irreversible decay is related to population size in the following way (Bell, in press):

$$r^* \sim -2 \log_e (1 - K/n_0)$$

Very infrequent sex, giving average rates of recombination of the order of 10^{-4}, will do the job in populations of 10^{10} individuals, while obligate sexuality will be required in populations with 10^7 or fewer members. Even maximal rates of recombination will not be enough to prevent the deterioration of populations below some critical value, of around 10^5 individuals. Thus, sex is unnecessary in very large ($N > 10^{10}$) populations and ineffective in very small ($N < 10^5$) populations; but for very many organisms, with populations falling between these extremes, it represents an exogenous repair system essential to their long-term persistence.

Muller's ratchet very neatly explains two of the three generalizations about sex with which I began this chapter. Sex is very generally distributed because of its role in exogenous genome repair. Asexuality has a patchy taxonomic distribution because asexual metazoans are the short-lived offshoots of sexual lineages, doomed to early extinction. It is much more frequent among smaller organisms because of their simpler genomes and larger populations. The first two-thirds of the history of life was occupied exclusively by small unicells; I would attribute this not to the difficulty of evolving large multicellular forms, but to the very brief geological life span of large and complex creatures until sex became available as an efficient means of exogenous repair.

Because deleterious mutation is a very frequent and general event, it should be possible to study the ratchet routinely in laboratory systems. One way of speeding up the ratchet is to reduce the population size, in the limit to a single organism, replaced at intervals by one of its own offspring. Such isolate cultures of short-lived organisms should deteriorate rather rapidly. I have reviewed the extensive literature on isolate cultures, which shows that vitality almost always declines through time, that this decline can best be interpreted in terms of the irreversible accumulation of mildly deleterious mutations, and that it is effectively arrested by occasional sexual episodes (G. Bell, in preparation). The history of isolate cultures thus provides a verification of Muller's ratchet, in the same way that artificial selection verifies the operation of natural selection. Another opportunity to study the ratchet is provided by mitochondria, which can be viewed as asexual organisms living in small, closed populations. The extensive variation of mitochondrial genomes between individuals can be interpreted as a consequence of the ratchet, and they are presumably protected from a fatal loss of function only by virtue of their very small genomes. Where mitochondria are very few and have relatively large genomes, they would have to recombine in order to maintain the integrity of their genomes, as seems to be the case in yeast and Chlamydomonas. Nonrecombining segments of the nuclear genome, such as inversions and Y chromosomes, should also accumulate more deleterious mutations than comparable recombining segments (see Charlesworth, 1978).

In short, the ratchet suggests that sex, acting as an exogenous repair system, is an essential condition for the persistence of relatively large and complex organisms, at least, through geological time. It provides a plausible interpretation of the major features of the taxonomic distribution of sexuality and can be studied routinely in the laboratory. It cannot be the whole story, since it fails to explain the major ecological correlates of sex among metazoans and metaphytes. This is presumably because it is a relatively weak evolutionary force, acting in the long term through the differential survival of sexual and asexual populations.

SEX EXPLOITS THE DIVERSITY OF THE ENVIRONMENT

In the uniform environment postulated by Muller's ratchet, the vast majority of mutations will be deleterious; it is extremely improbable that a random change in an enzyme, selected over long ages for its particular role and locked into a functional relationship with many other such enzymes, should result in an improvement. But environments are unlikely to be uniform, and it is my guess that most are highly heterogeneous; unfortunately, ecologists have so far failed to provide a good description of the scaling of environmental variance (see Tilman, 1982). In a heterogeneous environment most mutations, no doubt, will still be deleterious, under all conditions where the organism can survive at all. But other mutations, while deleterious under some conditions, may actually be beneficial in other circumstances. Sexuality halts the ratchet by creating variance with respect to deleterious genes; as an inescapable by-product, it also creates variance with respect to genes whose effect on fitness varies with conditions.

To explain how environmental diversity and genetic diversification are related, I shall begin with the simplest possible representation of the relationship between genotype and environment, and then ask how it must be elaborated in order to make sex comprehensible.

Imagine a field in which a number of plants are growing. There are only two types of site, one having a high level and the other having a low level of nitrogen in the soil (having physically discrete sites is not essential to the argument, but makes the outcome easier to visualize). Likewise, there are two types of plant: N^+ plants require a high level of nitrogen and have very high fecundity if they grow in a high-N site, whereas N^0 plants can do reasonably well even in low-N sites. The overall fitness of either type is then determined by the four quantities describing the performance of each type of plant in each type of site:

a. Performance of N^+ in high-N sites
b. Performance of N^+ in low-N sites
c. Performance of N^0 in high-N sites
d. Performance of N^0 in low-N sites

The outcome of selection depends in part on these performances and in part on the way in which they determine the size of the next generation. If the population is regulated at the level of the entire field, then one of the two genotypes will have the greater mean fitness and will eliminate its competitor. On the other hand, if density regulation occurs on the level of the site, both types may coexist at equilibrium (Levene, 1953). For example, suppose that the high-N sites between them contribute a fixed fraction Z of all zygotes, which are subsequently scattered at random onto the field. If either genotype is rare, its fitness will be high, since most of the sites to which it is well adapted, with their guaranteed contribution to the seed pool of the population, are currently occupied by an inferior competitor. As the genotype spreads, its fitness will fall, since individuals germinating in a site to which they are well adapted are increasingly likely to be competing with others having the same superior genotype. In a phrase, fitnesses will be frequency dependent in heterogeneous environments as the consequence of local population regulation. This does not by any means guarantee the preservation of genetic variation; for example, if Z is large and the relative fitness of N^+ much greater in high-N sites than that of

N^0 in low-N sites, the N^+ type will be fixed (see Maynard Smith and Hoekstra, 1980). But if both Z and the differences in performance are moderate, then the two types will coexist, the frequency of the N^+ individuals being

$$\hat{p} = \frac{Z(ad - bc) - c(b - d)}{(a - c)\,(b - d)}$$

The denominator of this expression is a genetic variance; the right-hand term in the numerator merely identifies the frequency as being that of N^+ rather than N^0. The point of writing out the equation is to draw attention to the remaining term, involving the expression $(ad - bc)$. This is the difference between the two diagonals of the performance matrix. What does it mean?

Suppose that a, b, c, and d represent the actual outcome of an experiment in which two varieties of, say, barley were sown into each of two types of plot. We could then use the analysis of variance to identify the effects of genotype and environment on yield. This leads to an estimation of the various components of the overall variance; thus, a quantity $\frac{1}{2}\,(a - c)\,(b - d)$ is attributable to the difference between varieties, and a quantity $\frac{1}{2}\,(a - b)\,(c - d)$ to the difference between plot types. But these genetic and environmental components do not necessarily add up to 100%, even if we continue to pretend that there is no error variance. Indeed, it is easy to imagine a situation in which the genetic, environmental, and error components are all zero, despite the fact that the data have an arbitrarily large variance; for instance, $a = d = 10$ and $b = c = 1$. The missing component is the genotype-by-environment interaction, which reflects the extent to which genotypes differ in their response to environmental change. In this particular example, the interaction component is equal to $\frac{1}{4}\,[(a + d) - (b + c)]^2$. Notice that this again involves the difference between the diagonals of the performance matrix. (It is a difference between sums rather than between products merely because it comes from an additive rather than a multiplicative model.) We can therefore relate the population–genetic model analyzed first to the biometrical model: the outcome of selection depends on the magnitude of the genotype-by-environment interaction. This is not to say that this interaction, however great, will inevitably lead to frequency-dependent selection, since this also requires local population regulation. What we can say is that selection will be frequency dependent whenever there is genotype-by-environment interaction on the environmental scale at which population growth is density dependent.

The importance of this statement lies wholly in the extent to which it allows a fresh empirical attack on the problem of genetic variation. The concept of frequency dependence is familiar from its application to particular situations, such as the sex ratio or the choice of food items. Precisely because its use has been restricted to a series of special cases, it has been marginalized in population genetics texts, with many of the standard references ignoring it completely. This situation is unlikely to be changed through direct measurement of fitness as a function of frequency, because of the great labor involved in making such measurements. There is, however, a large agronomic literature specifically concerned with the contribution of genotype-by-environment interaction to characters (such as yield) closely related to fitness. If it were to turn out that this contribution is usually on a par with the main effect of genotype, it would become difficult to deny the near-universality of frequency dependence.

One way of expressing the frequency dependence generated in heterogeneous environments is to say that like genotypes will compete more intensely than unlike genotypes, by virtue of their more similar ecological requirements. It follows that a mixture of genotypes, such as a sexual sibship, will outyield a pure line, such as the uniform progeny of an asexual female. This is the hypothesis that I have previously referred to as the Tangled Bank (Bell, 1982; Ghiselin, 1974, and in this volume). Any such effect can be detected directly by comparing the yield of a genotypic mixture with that of its component pure lines; it is a commonplace of the agronomic literature that mixtures frequently yield more than the average of their components (for references, see Bell, 1985). More generally, the Tangled Bank requires that the interaction variance should be substantial relative to the genetic variance. This effect can be quantified by calculating the ratio of the genetic variance to the sum of the genetic and interaction variances, a sort of intraclass correlation coefficient expressing the similarity between individuals with the same genotype raised in different environments. A low value of this coefficient is good evidence that diversification of progeny may be favored. If the N^+ and N^0 genotypes represented different combinations of genes, this might provide us with the basis of a general theory of sex and recombination.

The great drawback of the Tangled Bank is a theoretical one: like Muller's ratchet, it will operate only between reproductively isolated populations. If an obligately sexual population and an obligately asexual population compete, the sexual population may prevail because of its greater ecological range. But suppose that the asexual individuals occasionally produce fertilizable eggs. Then a gene causing asexuality that is initially restricted to a multilocus N^+ genotype will eventually be combined with the N^0 genotype also. The greater efficiency of asexual reproduction will then ensure that the two clones eliminate the sexual population. The same argument applies to more complex environments: selection will always favor a reduction in sexuality, so that at equilibrium the environment will be occupied by a large number of specialized clones without adding further assumptions to the model; environmental heterogeneity will favor sex only when a gene causing sexuality is completely recessive to an allele causing the complete suppression of sex.

I think that this difficulty can be resolved in the following way. Imagine that the field, having been harvested, is sown again in the following year with a mixture of N^+ and N^0. With its high requirement for nitrogen, the effect of the N^+ genotype is to deplete soil nitrogen levels over the course of the growing season. If resources can be depleted faster than they can be renewed, the success of an N^+ plant will depend on the previous occupancy of the site in which it is growing: it will be more successful than N^0 if its site was previously occupied by N^0, but less successful if its site was previously occupied by N^+. Conversely, N^0 will do better in a site presently occupied by N^+ than in one previously occupied by N^0. This illustrates how we can express the environment in terms of the previous activity of nitrogen-using genotypes, rather than in terms of nitrogen. More generally, it will be possible to reformulate any genotype-by-environment interaction in terms of a genotype-by-genotype interaction, provided that the resources involved can be depleted faster than they can be renewed.

This new way of expressing the interaction does not immediately produce any surprises. Either one type eliminates the other or both continue to persist at stable intermediate frequencies. But let us pursue the experiment one stage further, by sowing the plants for a third year. We have already seen how the effect of environmental heterogeneity may extend through time, with the activity of an individual reducing the fitness of similar individuals in the next generation. There is no good reason to suppose that this effect must be confined to a single season; it might extend over several subsequent seasons, although naturally it will weaken with time. Once we admit this extension the behavior of the model changes radically. If the mutual facilitation of the genotypes—the extent to which the growth of one is favored by the previous presence of the other—is sufficiently marked, and if this effect persists for sufficiently long, then the stable point of the single-generation model is replaced by a cycle. The genetic equilibrium has been destabilized by the lag between the growth of a genotype and its effect on the future success of similar individuals. We can express this by saying that there is an interaction between the relative fitness of a genotype and its frequency in previous generations. Just as genotype-by-genotype interactions generate frequency-dependent selection, so genotype-by-genotype interactions that are lagged in time generate time-lagged frequency-dependent selection, which tends to produce oscillations rather than stable genetic equilibria.

The relevance of this argument to the evolution of sex is that it applies to combinations of characters as well as to single characters. I have used N^+ and N^0 to represent genotypes differing in nitrogen requirements; let P^+ and P^0 be genotypes, determined at a different locus or set of loci, which differ analogously in phosphorus requirements. In a two-locus model of this sort, gene frequencies may oscillate at both the N and the P loci. Even more importantly, the correlation between the two loci will oscillate as the result of selection sometimes favoring the coupling genotypes $N^+ P^+$ and $N^0 P^0$ when the repulsion genotypes $N^+ P^0$ and $N^0 P^+$ are common in the population, and at other times favoring the repulsion genotypes when the coupling genotypes are common. Selection that frequently favors a change in the sign of linkage disequilibrium will indirectly favor genes that cause recombination, since these genes will hitch a ride on the high-fitness recombinant chromosomes that they create (see Maynard Smith, 1971; Charlesworth, 1978).

A scheme of this sort was first suggested by Jaenike (1978). Hutson and Law (1981) and Bell (1982) subsequently proved that nonzero rates of recombination will evolve in explicit genetic models under time-lagged frequency dependence. The remaining problem is to find a source of time-lagged frequency dependence sufficiently general in its operation to account for the very general maintenance of sex in natural populations. I have argued that selection of the appropriate sort will arise whenever the rate of renewal of resources is low relative to the rate at which they can be depleted. The renewal of resources such as nitrogen and phosphorus will normally depend on the activities of populations of micro-organisms and detritivores, whose population dynamics influence the population genetics of the plants. It is not necessary to suppose that genetic changes in the plant population will affect the decomposer community, but in some circumstances this would be a very reasonable assumption. For example, if the N and P loci controlled the production of secondary components rather than controlling resource utilization, genetic changes among the plants might easily influence the population dynamics of their herbivores. This is, in fact, the sort of situation envisaged by Jaenike, with the evolution of some target species causing a shift in the composition of the community of species that exploit it, and then in turn being redirected by this shift. However, perhaps the most plausible candidate for a source of powerful time-lagged frequency dependence is the coevolution of two mutually antagonistic species (Bremermann, 1980; Bell, 1982; Tooby, 1982), especially parasites and hosts (Hamilton, 1980). This is the hypothesis that I have previously called the Red Queen, by analogy with L. Van Valen's well-known speculation that the rate at which species become extinct is more or less constant because their environment is continually changing; recombination is selected because the coevolution of antagonists continually reverses the direction of selection acting on combinations of genes.

Suppose that resistance in the host and virulence in the parasite are both controlled by alleles at two loci, A and B. A parasite is most successful if its genotype matches that of the host that it infects, so the A1B1 parasites, for example, have high fitness when infecting A1B1 hosts; among hosts, the converse applies, so that A1B1 hosts are most successful in resisting the attack of A2B2 parasites. There are two ways of representing the phenotype of A1B2 and A2B1 individuals. If resistance and virulence are properties of particular alleles, so that A1 in the parasite specifically antagonizes A1 in the host, and B1 similarly antagonizes B1, then A1B2 and A2B1 have opposite phenotypes; this is a "gene-for-gene" model (Flor, 1955). On the other hand, the response of parasite to host, and vice versa, might depend only on the sum of effects at the two loci, in which case A1B2 and A2B1 have identical phenotypes; this is a "polygenic" model. Both possibilities are realized in nature. The evolution of such coupled systems has recently been investigated (Bell and Maynard Smith, 1987). The most important result is that genes causing recombination between the A and the B loci will always spread in a nonrecombining population, provided that the A and B genes have additive effects on phenotype. (The nonadditive case is more complex, with recombination sometimes spreading and sometimes not.) The coevolution of mutual antagonists thus provides the general source of powerful short-term selection for recombination that we have been seeking.

The argument that I have developed in this section can be summarized as follows:

1. A genotype that is well adapted to one set of circumstances is likely to be less well adapted in others—otherwise, organisms would be perfect. Environmental heterogeneity therefore leads to genotype-by-environment interaction.
2. Genotype-by-environment interaction, combined with local population regulation, creates frequency-dependent selection. One consequence of this is that mixtures will commonly outperform pure lines.
3. When the resources being competed for are renewable, but can be depleted faster than they can be renewed, genotype-by-environment interaction leads to genotype-by-genotype interaction.
4. Genotype-by-genotype interaction may extend over several generations. Interactions that are lagged in time give rise to time-lagged frequency-dependent selection.
5. Time-lagged frequency dependence tends to destabilize genetic equilibria; not only gene frequencies, but also linkage disequilibria oscillate through time. This is precisely the situation in which recombination will be favored.
6. Mutually antagonistic species represent a special case in which the "renewable resource" is the genotype of the antagonist and the lag involved is the time required for selection to produce evolutionary change. They are likely to be the most important source of short-term selection for recombination.

The great attraction of this scheme is its extreme vulnerability to both comparative and experimental analyses, and the fertility with which it suggests observations and manipulations. I have already dealt with the comparative evidence at some length (Bell, 1982) and have shown that sex is associated with old, stable, complex environments. These are the circumstances in which environmental heterogeneity (and thus genotype-by-environment interaction) and mutually antagonistic relationships between species (and thus genotype-by-genotype interactions) are likely to be the most pronounced. We still know very little about the precise quantitative correlates of recombination, but the scheme above points very clearly to the genetic control of biotic interactions as the most promising area in which to search. I anticipate that the amount of recombination, as expressed by variables such as chromosome number and chiasma frequency, will turn out to be correlated both with direct measures of biotic influences, such as pathogen load, and with indirect measures reflecting the intensity of selection or the time lag involved in its operation, such as the specificity of the host–parasite relationship or the disparity in generation times between the antagonists. What I wish to emphasize here, however, is the wealth of experimental work that can be brought to bear on the issue. The interpretation of the short-term maintenance of sex and recombination that I have advanced above is based on a general view of the relationship between genotype and environment that lies at the heart of population genetics. This answers Felsenstein's question (in this volume) of why we should be so interested in the evolution of sex: it is because the problem exposes so clearly the inadequacy of current models of the environment in population genetics, with the consequent marginalization of frequency dependence. I suggest three areas in which some information is already available, but where it should be possible to make rapid progress. While I discuss these areas as though plants were the experimental organisms, the same principles apply to animals or algae.

First, we know rather little about the spatial heterogeneity of the environment. According to the Tangled Bank, the environment varies widely from point to point on scales within the typical dispersal distance of the propagules. The appropriate measure of environmental heterogeneity is the variance in fitness of a genetically uniform stock. When samples of the environment (e.g., soil cores) are collected in a nested fashion at a series of levels, a large fraction of the variance (of the fitness of plants grown in the soil cores) should occur between samples at a scale corresponding to the typical distance of dispersal of propagules.

Second, we know even less about the relationship between genotype and environment. The appropriate measure of this relationship is the variance in fitness between environments of a genetically diverse stock. More specifically, the Tangled Bank predicts that when both environments and genotypes are randomly sampled from natural populations, the genotype-by-environment interaction will constitute a large fraction of the overall genotypic variance. It is a withering comment on the ecological naivety of current population genetics that no such measurement is available from an undisturbed natural population, though large genotype-by-environment effects have often been reported in the agronomic literature. The best information that we have comes from studies of the genotype–environment covariance that is the consequence of genotype-by-environment interaction. For example, reciprocal transplantation experiments usually show that moving a plant to a random nearby site causes a reduction in fitness (see Bell, 1985).

Finally, the study of genotype-by-genotype interaction has scarcely begun, except in applied fields such as the genetics of the parasite–host interaction or the yield of varietal mixtures of cereals. There is no shortage of experimental designs: we can predict that sexual sibships will be more productive than clones, that culture medium that has been exhausted by the growth of one genotype will still permit the further growth of other genotypes, that the growth of a plant will be suppressed more severely by relatives than by unrelated individuals, and so forth. What we lack is a determined application of these designs to the range of genotypes and environments found in natural populations.

SUMMARY

I advocate a dual view of sexuality and recombination. Because sex acts as an exogenous repair mechanism, it is an essential prerequisite for the long-term persistence of many organisms, and in particular those large and complex organisms in which the near-universality of sex constitutes such an absorbing puzzle. According to this view, sex creates variance with respect to the load of mildly deleterious mutations, allowing them to be eliminated by selection and evading the irreversible deterioration of asexual populations under Muller's ratchet. In doing so, it must unavoidably create variance with respect to mutations that are deleterious in some conditions but beneficial in others. This genotype–environment interaction implies that sexual populations can exploit heterogeneous environments more effectively. When the resources in question are renewable, there can be straightforward individual selection for nonzero rates of sex and recombination as the result of genetic instability caused by time-lagged frequency dependence; this process may be most potent when there are antagonistic interactions between species. Taken together, these two theories account for the major taxonomic and ecological patterns shown by sexual systems. Even more importantly, they lead to explicit protocols for feasible laboratory and field experiments and are, in general, supported by such experiments as have been reported. If not the final word on the matter, they at least provide us with a firm foundation for future work.

CHAPTER 9

IS MEIOTIC RECOMBINATION AN ADAPTATION FOR REPAIRING DNA, PRODUCING GENETIC VARIATION, OR BOTH?

Harris Bernstein*, Frederic A. Hopf and Richard E. Michod

INTRODUCTION

Sex involves two basic processes: (1) recombination, in the sense of the breakage and reunion of two different DNA molecules (i.e., physical recombination) and (2) outcrossing, in the sense that the two DNA molecules involved in recombination come from different individuals. Of the two, recombination is clearly the more basic aspect of reproduction, as evidenced by the variety of reproductive systems, such as selfing, automixis, and endomitosis, that have abandoned outcrossing yet maintain recombination. In contrast, there are relatively few reproductive systems in which outcrossing occurs without recombination.

Sex is often defined as a process that produces new combinations of alleles from different individuals. This usually involves the processes of physical recombination and outcrossing. However, the converse is not true: physical recombination and outcrossing may occur with no effect on the combination of alleles at linked loci. In addition, there are other consequences of physical recombination and outcrossing other than new combinations of alleles. We

---

*The order of authors is strictly alphabetical and is not intended to imply seniority.

believe that the evidence discussed below shows that repair is more intimately associated with recombination than are new allelic combinations. Consequently, if we were to follow the precedent set by the variation school of defining a process in terms of its hypothesized function, we might define sex as a process that produces repair. However, we feel it is better to define a process in terms of its components and not to prejudice an evolutionary explanation of it by defining it in terms of a hypothesized function.

Recombination and exchange of alleles

Sex (i.e., recombination with outcrossing) is often explained by assuming that its advantage lies in the genetic variation (new combination of alleles) it produces (see chapters by Bell, Felsenstein, Maynard Smith, Brooks, Ghiselin, and Crow, in this volume). Indeed, in modeling recombination, evolutionary theorists have interpreted the evolution of recombination as synonymous with the evolution of increased rates of allelic exchange. In this theory, a locus encoding a recombination enzyme is assumed to be a neutral modifier of linkage relationships. In other words, the recombination locus has no direct effect on fitness but functions only to influence the exchange of alleles at other loci that have direct effects on fitness (see Brooks, in this volume). Such a modifier of recombination presumably affects the induction of chromosome breaks (i.e., damages), leading to the repair of these breaks by rejoining the broken chromosome with its homologue. In contrast, the repair hypothesis emphasizes repair of naturally and spontaneously occurring damages rather than actively induced damages.

There are several problems with the neutral modifier approach to recombination. First, genes encoding recombination are not neutral as assumed. They have direct effects on fitness insofar as they are employed in a major form of DNA repair (see the next section). Second, as discussed in more detail below, allelic exchange is an occasional but by no means universal consequence of physical recombination. Third, to select for allelic recombination, neutral modifier models depend on special conditions that are not broadly applicable. The generality of sex in the biota suggests that the benefits of sex should be general, yet the modifier models depend on relatively restrictive conditions to work.

Since physical recombination may or may not result in allelic recombination (i.e., exchange of alleles at flanking loci), we do not use the word recombination as synonymous with the exchange of alleles, although we realize it is common to do so (for example, see chapters by Crow, Brooks, and Felsenstein, in this volume). To avoid ambiguity, we use the phrase "physical recombination" to mean breakage and reunion of two DNA molecules and "allelic recombination" to mean physical recombination that results in exchange of alleles at flanking loci. Physical recombination that does not result in allelic recombination is "cryptic" from the traditional point of view of evolutionary biology, which identifies recombination with exchange of alleles.

Recombination and DNA damage

Four broad generalizations, based on numerous studies, support the hypothesis that repair is a direct consequence of recombination (for reviews, see Bernstein, 1983; Bernstein et al., 1987). First, survival after treatment with a DNA damaging agent is substantially enhanced when two or more chromosomes are present in a cell, rather than one, and when normal recombination functions are present. Second, mutations in genes known to be responsible for genetic recombination increase sensitivity to DNA damaging agents. Third, DNA damaging agents generally increase levels of recombination. Fourth, mutations blocking other nonrecombinational repair pathways increase levels of damage-induced recombination. All four lines of evidence are found in viruses, bacteria, and yeast. In Drosophila and other multicellular organisms, such as mammals and plants, only some of these kinds of evidence have been obtained. Evidence from yeast and Drosophila is particularly relevant here because these organisms undergo meiosis. Work with these organisms indicates that recombinational repair is a significant process in eukaryotic organisms.

Studies in bacteriophages T4 and λ, *Escherichia coli*, yeast, and Drosophila indicate that recombinational repair acts against many different types of DNA lesions and is often highly efficient. There is also substantial evidence that DNA damage in general and double-strand damages in particular constitute an important problem in nature (for review and discussion, see Bernstein et al., 1985b,c, and in press).

Recently we have proposed that both the recombinational and the outcrossing aspects of sex arose early in evolution because of the direct advantage of recombinational repair of genetic damage (Bernstein et al., 1984; 1985a,c). In addition, we have argued that recombination is maintained by the advantage of repair and that outcrossing in diploid organisms is maintained by the masking of deleterious mutations in reproductive systems that have recombination (Bernstein et al., 1985a–c). We call this set of ideas the repair hypothesis to distinguish it from the traditional explanation for sex, which we refer to as the variation hypothesis.

Rationale of chapter

There are two fundamental aspects of meiosis that distinguish it from mitosis. The first is the much higher rates of recombination that occur during meiosis than during mitosis. The second concerns the ploidy of the cells produced by these processes. Diploid mitosis produces diploid daughter cells, whereas diploid meiosis produces haploid daughter cells (gametes). The reduction in ploidy occurring as a result of meiosis prepares the gametes for fusion (fertilization), which restores the diploid state. The evolution of reduction division with subsequent fertilization concerns the evolution of outcrossing. Our basic view concerning the evolution of outcrossing in diploids is as follows. Physical recombination produces allelic recombination and, hence, produces homozygosity at heterozygous loci. Thus recombinational repair, which requires physical recombination, tends to express deleterious recessive alleles at heterozygous loci. Outcrossing functions to mask the expression of these deleterious recessives. In Maynard Smith's words (in this volume) used to describe our hypothesis, outcrossing "evolves to restore the heterozygosity destroyed by repair." We will not address the issue of outcrossing here, having considered it elsewhere (Bernstein et al., 1985b, 1987; Hopf et al., in press), but instead will primarily concern ourselves with explaining the first basic aspect of meiosis, recombination.

Generally, the questions asked in evolutionary discussions of recombination concern when, where, and under what conditions it occurs. The approach taken here, however, to testing the variation and repair hypotheses is to focus on the mechanics of meiotic recombination. In other words, we focus on *how* recombination is accomplished in eukaryotes. We take the general perspective that by analyzing a structure something can be inferred about its function. While we do not believe that a biological structure need be optimally designed for its function, we nevertheless feel it is appropriate, given alternative functional hypotheses, to ask whether the structure in question has evolved such that it is designed to better carry out one function than another. Thus we focus on meiotic recombination as the key stage of the sexual cycle and ask whether, on the basis of its mechanical design, it is an adaptation for DNA repair or allelic recombination or both. Interpreting the detailed mechanical, cellular, and molecular events of sexual systems in terms of the various evolutionary hypotheses for sex complements the more common approaches based on ecological conditions. As knowledge accumulates concerning natural levels of damage, an analysis of the ecological conditions favoring repair should prove possible.

We ask specifically whether the mechanical features of meiosis promote either allelic recombination or cryptic recombination. We first consider premeiotic replication, which is a general feature of meiosis. We then consider the association between recombination, as detected by gene conversion, and allelic exchange at flanking loci. Finally, we ask the question, if recombination is often initiated by repair of DNA damage, does this repair occur in such a way as to generate high rates of allelic recombination? Our general conclusion is that meiotic recombination is designed to promote efficient and versatile recombinational repair while keeping allelic exchange of loci flanking the site of recombination at a low level.

PREMEIOTIC REPLICATION

Premeiotic replication is a general feature of meiosis producing four homologous chromatids that are then able to recombine in pairs. In this section, we argue that premeiotic replication is better explained as an adaptation for DNA repair than as an adaptation for allelic recombination.

Repair hypothesis

In the repair hypothesis a definite function can be attributed to premeiotic replication: the formation of a gap in the newly replicated complementary strand, which can then act as a general signal for recombinational repair.

Studies in *E. coli* show that replication of DNA with single-strand damages leads to gaps in the new strand opposite the damages (Rupp and Howard-Flanders, 1968) and that these gaps promote recombinational repair (West et al., 1982). Such gaps have a molecular structure independent of the structure of the original damage and can serve as a universal initiator of recombinational repair. Excision of the damage opposite the single-strand gap (by an enzyme such as the nuclease controlled by RAD52 in yeast [Resnick et al., 1984]) would result in a double-strand gap. A recent authoritative model for meiotic recombination (Szostak et al., 1983; Orr-Weaver and Szostak, 1985; see Appendix) argues that double-strand gaps initiate recombination.

Naturally occurring damages are probably a mixture of many types with a large proportion of types represented in low frequency. This alone makes it unlikely that enzymes will evolve to recognize each specific type of DNA damage, especially those types represented in low frequency. In addition, DNA undergoes transient structural variations associated with normal gene expression, and these variations are also probably of many types. These structural variations would make damages difficult to detect. However, as the DNA polymerase passes along the DNA and the duplex unwinds, such functional variations should be released and damages should become readily distinguishable. The various single-strand damages could be translated into a "common currrency" by the polymerase, leaving a gap opposite the damage in the new strand. This gap could then initiate recombinational repair via the mechanism of Szostak et al. (1983).

Such a mechanism of converting single-strand damages into a common currency would avoid the alternative of evolving excision repair enzymes to distinguish the wide variety of DNA damages from the normal variations in DNA structure. For these reasons we do not expect excision repair to be 100% efficient in repairing single-strand damages. Support for this view can be found in bacteria and phages. One of the most well-studied excision repair systems, pyrimidine-dimer excision repair in phage T4, is only 45% to 60% efficient (Pawl et al., 1976). Also, experimental evidence in *E. coli* (DeFlora et al., 1984) and evidence reviewed by Bernstein (1983) show that recombinational repair is able to overcome a wide variety of lethal damages to DNA, as is expected by this view.

Variation hypothesis

We can see no advantage to premeiotic replication in the variation hypothesis. Instead, premeiotic replication is wasteful from the perspective of the variation hypothesis, because cryptic recombination in the form of sister chromatid exchanges (SCEs) becomes possible. If it could be shown that allelic recombination is promoted by suppressing SCE and favoring non-SCE, then it could be argued that variation is being selected for in spite of an apparently pointless premeiotic replication. By comparing in males the levels of SCE for the X chromosome and the autosomes one can ascertain if there is a preference for non-SCE when both types of recombination are possible (the X chromosome has only a sister homologue, whereas autosomes have both sister and nonsister homologues). According to Peacock (1970), there is no such preference, since SCEs occur "in the X chromosome, where they are as frequent per unit chromosome length, as in the autosomes." This implies that the autosomes used SCE even when the variation-generating non-SCE could have been used instead. Consequently, SCE is not suppressed when a nonsister chromosome is present and could serve as a partner for allelic recombination.

Our main point in this section is that a very general feature of meiosis, premeiotic replication, is unlikely to be an adaptation for recombinational variation but is explained by the hypothesis that meiotic recombination is an adaptation for DNA repair. Premeiotic replication serves no apparent purpose on the variation hypothesis. In addition, its direct consequence—cryptic recombination in the form of SCE—appears to be wasteful and should be suppressed in favor of non-SCE. However, this prediction is refuted by available evidence. In the next section, we consider evidence that most meiotic recombination is cryptic.

PHYSICAL RECOMBINATION IS USUALLY CRYPTIC

Data

Many studies have been carried out in fungi where meiotic recombination was detected by aberrant segregation at a genetically marked site, and allelic markers at flanking loci were scored as to whether they were exchanged or not. In most of these studies, the flanking alleles were exchanged less than 50% of the time (Whitehouse, 1982, p. 321). In ten separate studies involving five different species, the ratio of nonexchanged to exchanged flanking alleles was on average 66:34 (for summaries of these data, see Whitehouse, 1982, Tables 19 and 38). The average frequency for a species of exchange of flanking alleles varied from about 20% in *Sordaria brevicollis* to about 50% in *Saccharomyces cerevisiae*. Within the genome of a species, the percentage could vary from region to region. In addition to the fungal data, data from half-tetrad analyses using compound autosomes in *Drosophila melanogaster* showed that only one-third of recombination events at the rosy cistron resulted in allelic recombination of flanking loci (Chovnick et al., 1970).

Why is most recombination cryptic?

The predominance of cryptic recombination can be explained either as an unavoidable consequence of the basic mechanism of recombination or as a result of an adaptation. In the variation hypothesis, cryptic recombination is disadvantageous and thus should be eliminated by natural selection unless it is unavoidable. In the Appendix, we show that cryptic recombination could easily be avoided by eliminating a complex and costly step in meiotic recombination. This step is the formation of the second Holliday junction (see Figure 2, step F on page 159). Without this step, physical recombination would produce allelic exchange all the time (see Figure 2). Consequently, we believe that the function of this step is to reduce exchange of alleles at loci outside the small region of physical recombination.

The basic conclusion of this section is that in most cases physical recombination does not produce allelic recombination. In other words, recombination is usually cryptic. This fact suggests that the common approach in evolutionary biology of modeling recombination in terms of the modification of the linkage relationship of genes (for review, see Brooks, in this volume), is, at best, an incomplete description of the phenomenon to be explained and, at worst, misleading with respect to the evolutionary forces operating on recombination. The fact that physical recombination does not result in allelic recombination in about 66% of the cases is inconsistent with the variation hypothesis unless it is a necessary consequence of the mechanism of recombination. As argued in the Appendix, it appears that this is not the case and that the mechanism of recombination is actually more complex than need be, so as to reduce the level of allelic recombination. We argue later that it may not be cost effective in most situations to reduce the level of allelic recombination much below the level set by the equilibrium chemistry. It may be argued from the variation point of view that it is not cost effective to raise it much above 34%. However, as illustrated by the pathway in Figure 2 of the Appendix, 100% allelic recombination could be accomplished easily with no cost. In general, we feel that the reduction of allelic recombination from 100% to a level below 50% is the first-order effect, but that the specific level attained below 50% depends on a variety of second-order factors.

INDEPENDENT ASSORTMENT

The physical linkage of genes on chromosomes is an almost universal feature of life. Many organisms have multiple chromosomes, and during meiosis loci on separate chromosomes assort independently of one another. Crow (in this volume) has stressed that independent assortment is a major factor in generating new combinations of alleles at (unlinked) loci, the implication being that independent assortment and the resulting variation is an adaptive feature of meiosis. However, we disagree with this view.

Linkage probably evolved initially to facilitate the assortment of a complete set of genes into daugher cells (Bernstein et al., 1984). Before genes became linked into chromosomes, "repair" of a damaged gene may have resulted from replication of an undamaged copy received from another cell after fusing with it (for discussion, see Bernstein et al., 1984). Once linkage evolved, this strategy could no longer work, and the reason is easy to see. The whole chromosome would have to be discarded if it contained a single damaged gene. The only option at this point is to take out the damaged information and obtain the homologous information from a chromosome containing a good copy of the gene. The mechanism that evolved is physical recombination. Depending on the level of recombinational repair, there is a chromosome size beyond which increased linkage would have no effect on variation, since the loci at the ends of the chromosome already behave as if they are unlinked. In other words, the arrangement of the genome into multiple chromosomes, rather than a single long chromosome, does not necessarily generate more variation than already exists because of the effect of recombinational repair on linkage. Given multiple chromosomes, they must be assorted into daughter cells by some process. Random assortment achieved by random alignment of chromosomes on the metaphase plate is the simplest solution.

POTENTIAL PROBLEMS WITH THE REPAIR HYPOTHESIS

In this section we take up potential problems with the repair hypothesis, admitting at the outset that we do not have conclusive answers to all the issues discussed here. However, we want to point out that these issues relate only to the repair hypothesis and do not relate to, or mollify, the criticisms made earlier of the variation hypothesis as an explanation for meiotic recombination.

Maynard Smith (in this volume) raises several objections to the repair hypothesis. His first objection is that there is no logical reason for physical recombination to result in allelic recombination (his term "crossing over" means the same as our term "allelic recombination"). In support, he cites mating-type change in yeast as an example of physical recombination that avoids allelic exchange. His second objection raises the issue of how double-strand damages are handled in the many mitotic divisions in the germ line of organisms with meiotic recombination. His third objection is that "there are at least some cases in higher eukaryotes in which double-strand repair [i.e., physical recombination] leading to homozygosity does *not* happen in the germ line." We will deal with these objections in turn.

Why isn't all recombination cryptic?

To address Maynard Smith's first objection we must answer the question, Why isn't all recombination cryptic? To answer this question we must consider the costs and benefits of carrying out physical recombination while at the same time preventing allelic recombination. While we agree with Maynard Smith that there is no logical reason why physical recombination should result in allelic recombination, we believe that there are probably good practical reasons involving the chemical mechanisms that underlie physical recombination. However, we acknowledge that presently there is limited knowledge concerning these chemical mechanisms to answer his question with any certainty.

Mechanisms and Costs of Achieving 0% Allelic Exchange As noted in the Appendix, with the model of Szostak and coworkers, we expect that about 50% of physical recombinations will result in allelic exchange. One way of biasing the branching frequency is to exploit the slow speed of relaxation to equilibrium. It takes time to get from the first Holliday structure formed at step C of Figure 1 (Appendix) to the equilibrium state in which all configurations are equally likely (steps G–J). To bias the branching frequency towards 0% allelic recombination, the enzyme(s) that cut and rejoin the two Holliday structures must act quickly before equilibrium is reached. The faster the enzyme(s) acts, the more bias there could be toward 0% allelic exchange. However, mistakes made in cutting DNA are extremely costly. To ask why the cutting reaction cannot be made indefinitely rapid is similar to asking why replication cannot go faster. Speed either requires much greater expenditures of energy or risks inaccuracies. In other words, speed has costs.

A second way of biasing the branching frequency is to invent some way of stabilizing the Holliday structures (formed at steps C and F) at the moment of their formation. The costs of stabilizing one of the resonance forms of the Holliday structure are difficult to determine but are likely to be significant.

A third way, which reduces allelic recombination to zero, involves resolving the heteroduplex region (steps F–J) by replication (for mating-type switching in yeast, see Orr-Weaver and Szostak, 1985, p. 54).

If the structure in step F were to be resolved by a further replication during meiosis, any unrepaired single-strand damage in the chromosome acquired since the previous replication would be converted to a lethal double-strand damage that would then require further recombination repair and replication, leading again to more double-strand damage, and so on. Replication also results in extra genomes, which should be costly.

Thus all strategies for avoiding allelic recombination are likely to be associated with significant costs. There may be other costs of 0% allelic recombination in addition to those just discussed. For example, if chiasmata have some structural role in meiotic segregation (Carpenter, 1984), this would keep the percent exchange of flanking alleles away from 0%. In conclusion, the rate of allelic recombination is unlikely to be selected to be 0% unless there is a large benefit of doing so.

Benefits of 0% Allelic Exchange One often discussed benefit of reducing allelic recombination stems from avoiding the breakup of coadapted gene complexes. However, it is difficult to say how large such a benefit would be and whether it would overcome the costs discussed above. In the specific case cited by Maynard Smith of mating-type conversion in yeast, the benefits of reducing allelic recombination at flanking loci to 0% stem from the lethal chromosomal fragmentation associated with exchange of flanking regions.

We have argued that recombinational repair produces, as a by-product, allelic exchange and that this exchange speeds up the expression of deleterious mutations thus selecting for outcrossing. Consequently, one might think that there is a benefit to be derived from eliminating allelic exchange, since this would delay the expression of deleterious mutations. As discussed next, this is true in certain situations. However, these benefits are transient and occur in reproductive systems that are difficult to arrive at through likely evolutionary scenarios.

The optimum state from the consideration of both repairing damage and masking mutations might appear to be some form of diploid apomixis (mitotically produced seed) with a recombinational repair sysem that produces no allelic exchange. However, in such a closed system, physical recombination will still generate homozygosity at the site of repair by gene conversion. As mutations accumulate, this effect will get larger. Eventually mutations will accumulate until the genome is effectively haploid and gene conversion at sites of recombinational repair will generate homozygosity for deleterious recessives. There is a transient benefit to such a system, although as mutations accumulate, this sytem will decline in fitness.

It is also improbable that such an apomict could arise in an outcrossing population. There is no benefit to having 0% exchange for an outcrosser, as most mutations are masked anyway. In addition, there is a large cost to shifting to apomixis if it occurred without reducing the exchange produced by repair. Consequently, there is a benefit to evolving a recombinational repair mechanism with 0% exchange *only* if it were to occur simultaneously with a shift to apomixis. This, of course, is highly unlikely.

Next, consider a selfing population. For a selfing population, there is no benefit to be derived from 0% exchange, since the expression of recessives is due to inbreeding, not allelic recombination. As discussed elsewhere (Bernstein et al., 1985b), selfing is unstable to the evolution of outcrossing under many conditions.

Finally, consider a diploid automictic population with terminal fusion (which maintains heterozygosity if there is no allelic exchange between the centromere and the heterozygous locus). Again, there is a short-term benefit to reducing allelic exchange, but eventually mutations accumulate and express as a result of gene conversion at sites of recombinational repair and new mutation.

Thus, although in certain reproductive systems there are short-term benefits of reducing to zero the allelic exchange associated with repair, these systems are often hard to evolve initially and once evolved are eventually unstable to the evolution of outcrossing or to a decline in fitness through expression of deleterious mutations as a result of either gene conversion or spontaneous mutation.

The basic point we wish to make regarding whether exchange of flanking alleles is reduced to 0% is that this should be determined by the costs and benefits of accomplishing it. If the benefits of completely stopping allelic exchange are small relative to the cost of the needed structures, we do not expect mechanisms to have evolved that totally avoid allelic recombination at flanking loci. On the other hand, if the benefits of stopping it are large, as is the case with mating-type conversion in yeast, we expect mechanisms to evolve that prevent exchange of flanking alleles. The presently unknown mechanisms operating in the site-specific case of mating-type conversion to reduce allelic recombination to near 0% may be costly in the context of general recombination.

Coping with damage in the mitotic divisions leading to meiosis

Maynard Smith's second objection raises the issue of how double-strand damages are handled in the many mitotic divisions in the germ line of organisms with meiotic recombination.

There are two basic ways that organisms can respond to double-strand damage once it has occurred (Bernstein et al., 1984, 1985a,c). The first is recombinational repair, and the second is cellular selection. In multicellular organisms, selection against damaged cells occurs when viable cells replicate and cells with unrepaired lethal damages die. Cellular selection requires that there be undamaged cells that can then replicate. This is more likely when damage rates are low or when the pool of cells is large. In addition, cellular selection is more effective when cell replication rates are high (although rapid replication risks the deleterious effects of mutation). During the many mitotic divisions in the germ line leading up to meiosis, double-strand damages are probably dealt with by cellular selection. Why then is there the need for meiotic recombination during the final division of the germ line when there was no need prior to it?

We think that the answer to this question lies in the fact that a parent contributes a single haploid cell to its offspring and that this cell must be free of all double-strand damages, since only one will kill the cell when it attempts to divide after fertilization. How can a parent guarantee that the one cell it uses to make its offspring is free of all double-strand damages? This is an especially critical problem in light of the high metabolic activity, and hence the high rate of damage, that occurs during the production of gametes, particularly eggs. During the mitotic divisions of the germ line, the ability to successfully replicate certifies that a cell is free of double-strand damages. However, replication of an unrepaired single-strand damage in a parent cell probably leaves a gap opposite it and, consequently, introduces a lethal double-strand damage in a daughter cell. So, although successful replication guarantees that the parent cell was free of double-strand damages, it does not guarantee that the daughter cells are free of them. The only way of accomplishing this is to produce daughter cells by a process that can efficiently repair all damages. This process, we believe, is meiotic recombination.

Coping with damage in the absence of meiosis

Maynard Smith's third objection raises the issue of how double-strand damages are handled in organisms without meiotic recombination. This objection also raises the issue of the association of homozygosity with meiotic recombination. This homozygosity is a direct result of the allelic exchange that occurs during physical recombination. As we have already discussed, we do not believe that it is cost effective in most situations for this allelic exchange to be avoided.

We have already mentioned somatic selection as a factor in coping with lethal damages. We now consider the apparent lack of recombinational repair in mitotic parthenogens and how it bears on the repair hypothesis. The occurrence of recombinational repair should depend upon the level of double-strand damage and the effectiveness of cellular selection, both of which vary with ecological condition and mode of reproduction. It is difficult to determine what ecological factors influence the level of double-strand damage. Cellular selection is probably more effective in vegetative reproduction than it is when reproduction occurs through an egg or seed, since many cells are passed on to the offspring. Mitotically produced seed is relatively common in plants (agamospermy) but rare in animals. In this case, both recombinational repair and cellular selection are limited as strategies of coping with lethal damage. It is important to realize that as an exclusive mode of reproduction, mitotically produced seed is very rare. Although agamospermy is common in plants, it is almost always facultative, so that mitotically produced seed are mixed with seed produced through meiosis. The well-worn example of North American dandelions is an exception to this general rule, since this organism reproduces exclusively through agamospermy. We do not know how double-strand damages are dealt with in this isolated case, although we believe the rarity of such a mode of reproduction is significant from the point of view of its limited capacity for repair. Our hypothesis that recombinational repair of double-strand damage is the function of recombination does not preclude there being other mechanisms in isolated cases.

More generally, all theories of sex that postulate a short-term benefit, whether through repair or variation, must acknowledge the fact that the hypothesized benefit is expendable for asexuals. Consequently, in these cases it appears that efficient double-strand repair is expendable at least in the short term. However, the occurrence of asexuals with limited repair does not by itself rule out a general benefit of repair any more than their occurrence rules out a general benefit for variation.

The case of endomitosis discussed by Maynard Smith (in this volume) requires special attention. Endomitosis, another parthenogenetic system, is characterized by two sequential premeiotic chromosome replications followed by an apparently normal meiosis to produce diploid eggs. Also at the four-chromatid stage, pairing occurs between chromatids derived from only one initial chromosome (Cuellar, 1971; White, 1973; Cole, 1984). This reproductive system is used, for example, by whiptail lizards common in the deserts of the southwestern United States. Because there is no recombination between the nonsister homologues, the maternal genome should be passed on intact to daughters. If recombination between nonsister homologues were allowed, accumulated deleterious recessives would express. Endomitosis might seem to be an ideal strategy, since it reaps the benefit of meiotic repair while avoiding the expression of deleterious recessive alleles. However, double-strand damages occurring before the first premeiotic replication cannot be repaired by endomitosis, as all chromatid pairing partners are derived from the same chromosome and there is no intact template corresponding to the damaged site. This problem does not arise in conventional meiosis, because recombination occurs between nonsister chromatids. Hence, if double-strand damages are a significant problem before premeiotic replication, endomitosis is an unsatisfactory option. Double-strand damages that occur before premeiotic replication in conventional meiosis should give rise to an 8:0 pattern of gene conversion if they occur in the region of a heterozygous marker. Such patterns were shown to occur with a low but measurable frequency in an ascomycete fungus (Lamb and Wickramaratne, 1973).

Variation in allelic recombination between males and females

In general, both sexes have allelic recombination. However, the rates often differ, males having lower rates of recombination than females (Bell, 1982, Chap. 5; Trivers, in this volume). This trend is taken to its extreme in the case of Drosophila males, which do not undergo any allelic recombination or gene conversion (Chovnick et al., 1970). The general trend of males having lower levels of recombination, discussed by Trivers in this volume, can be explained quite simply on the basis of the higher metabolic activity and hence higher levels of DNA-damaging oxidative compounds produced during oogenesis. However, in contrast to this trend, certain Lepidopteran females, such as silkworm moths (Sturtevant, 1915; Tazima, 1964) and wax moths (White, 1945, p. 193), do not appear to undergo recombination, whereas males from these species do. This is particularly troubling to us in light of our explanation for the general trend in terms of the higher expected rates of damage during oogenesis than during spermatogenesis. It should be noted that in Lepidoptera the females are heterogametic rather than the males. The opposite is the case in Drosophila. Thus in Lepidoptera, lack of recombination is associated with heterogamy rather than, as we would predict, a lower expected level of damage.

DISCUSSION OF THE VARIATION HYPOTHESIS

Variation in allelic recombination rates within populations

Allelic recombination rates are known to vary within populations and can be selected for (for example, see Brooks, 1985). A number of workers have cited these facts as support for the variation hypothesis. However, these facts in and of themselves do not distinguish between the repair and variation hypotheses, since variation in allelic recombination may be an indirect consequence of alleles affecting DNA replication or repair. Evidence for this comes from studies showing either positive or negative effects on recombination by alleles altered in DNA metabolism. Recombination is increased by alleles with reduced enzymatic activity for DNA synthesis (e.g., DNA ligase and DNA polymerase alleles [Bernstein, 1968; Berger et al., 1969; Konrad, 1977]) or for correction of mismatched regions of DNA in heteroduplexes (Feinstein and Low, 1986). On the other hand, recombination is decreased by alleles with reduced activity of enzymes involved in recombinational repair (for examples in bacteriophage, bacteria, yeast, and Drosophila, see Bernstein, 1983). Other kinds of alleles that would generate variation in allelic recombination rates independent of the need for allelic recombination may also exist, such as alleles that allow accumulation of higher intracellular levels of oxygen radicals or other endogenous DNA damaging agents.

More generally, the simple fact that a trait, in this case the rate of allelic recombination, varies genetically does not mean it is an adaptation. However, as Brooks points out (in this volume), such variation could be acted on by natural selection, regardless of its origin.

Natural selection has reduced recombinational and mutational variation

The existence of genetic variation is a necessary condition for evolution. There are two principle sources of such variation: mutation and allelic recombination. Mutation results mainly from replication errors, during either chromosome replication or repair synthesis. Despite the evolutionary importance of mutational variation, the replicative machinery has clearly been selected to be highly accurate, so that error rates per replicated nucleotide are of the order of 10^{-8} to 10^{-11}, depending on the organism (Drake, 1974). The protein machinery that carries out replication is complex, and this complexity is considered by enzymologists studying these structures to reflect adaptations for promoting accuracy (Alberts et al., 1980).

We think that just as mutational variation is a by-product of DNA replication, recombinational variation is a by-product of recombinational repair of DNA. Furthermore, just as the replicative machinery has been selected to reduce mutational variation, the recombinational repair machinery of meiosis has been selected to reduce recombinational variation, resulting in cryptic recombination. The main selective pressure operating in both cases, we think, is the immediate reduction in fitness brought about by random changes in the genome. Genetic variation, we think, is basically a kind of informational noise produced as a by-product of genome replication and repair, two processes essential for survival. Our viewpoint that genetic variation is informational noise does not deny the importance of infrequent beneficial variants, either mutational or recombinational, for evolutionary change. However, the fact that genetic variation is necessary for evolution does not mean it is selected (for further discussion, see Michod, 1986). Indeed, the evidence discussed here indicates that selection has reduced the genetic variation produced by both DNA replication and DNA repair.

The fraction of physical recombination events that result in allelic recombination is infinitesimally small

We have argued that the fundamental function of all recombination events is DNA repair, whether these events occur in the germ line or in the somatic line, whether they are between sister or nonsister homologues, or whether, in the case of nonsister exchange, they lead to allelic recombination or not. There is also empirical evidence for this view. For example, damaging agents increase SCEs in the somatic line (for review, see Hollstein and McCann, 1979) as they increase recombination during meiosis (e.g., Prudhomeau and Proust, 1974; Schewe et al., 1971). In light of this general similarity between germ line recombination and somatic recombination, we now estimate the fraction of total recombination events in the human female that result in allelic exchange. Women were chosen because a careful estimate of the total number of oocytes formed has been made (Baker, 1963). Our estimate of the fraction of allelic recombinants is admittedly speculative. However, the estimated fraction is so small that our conclusion that allelic recombination is insignificant is unlikely to be changed by alterations in the assumed numbers.

The number of allelic recombinants in meiosis is the product of the number of oocytes produced during the lifetime of a woman and the average number of chiasmata (presumed to generate allelic recombinants) per oocyte during meiosis. The number of oocytes present at birth is approximately 2×10^6 (Baker, 1963). The average number of chiasmata per bivalent is 1.89 (Jagiello et al., 1976), and humans have 23 bivalents. Thus the total number of allelic recombination events is approximately $2 \times 10^6 \times 1.89 \times 23 = 8.7 \times 10^7$. To estimate the total number of recombination events in a woman during her lifetime, we need to know the average number of somatic cells at full development, the average number of times these cells turn over during a lifetime, and the average number of recombination events per cell, per cell generation. We consider only SCEs, since the number of nonsister exchanges is relatively very small. The frequency of SCE in human cells has been estimated as 0.12/

chromosome/cell cycle (Brewen and Peacock, 1969; Kanda, 1982). Since humans have 46 chromosomes, we estimate the frequency of SCE/cell/cell generation as .12 × 46 = 5.5. We estimate that the number of cells in the body is 6×10^{12}. The average number of times a cell turns over in a lifetime is a difficult number to obtain, since it is complicated by the fact that some cells do not turn over at all and some turn over very rapidly. The average number of turnovers per cell per lifetime is certainly greater than one. The total number of recombination events in somatic cells during a woman's lifetime is therefore greater than $5.5 \times 6 \times 10^{12} \times 50$ or 3.3×10^{13}. The fraction of total recombination events that result in allelic exchange at meiosis is thus less than $8.7 \times 10^{7}/3.3 \times 10^{13}$ or 2.6×10^{-6}. In this calculation we have not included the germ line SCE events in the denominator. Doing so would only make the fraction smaller.

It is clear, in at least this one case in which a rough calculation is possible, that allelic recombination is an infinitessimally small fraction of the total recombination events that occur in all cells throughout the lifetime. Thus it seems unreasonable to argue that allelic recombination is the adaptive function of recombination generally.

Can the variation hypothesis be sustained?

We can conceive of three possibilities for sustaining the variation hypothesis as an explanation for meiotic recombination. First, one could contend that meiotic recombination was originally designed to promote repair but is now primarily an adaptation for producing allelic recombination. Thus it could still retain characteristics associated with DNA repair, so that premeiotic replication and cryptic recombination as detected by SCE and gene conversion could be vestiges that have not yet been lost by selection. We find this view implausible, primarily because it ignores the substantial evidence for recombinational repair in extant organisms, and also because of the many cases of structures that have been reduced or lost after losing their adaptive value. In addition, the evolutionary relict hypothesis is especially unlikely in this case because cryptic recombination is not just neutral, it is disadvantageous from the point of view of producing genetic exchange.

The second possibility is that meiosis may be presently adapted for both repair and allelic recombination, with tradeoffs existing between promoting these two functions. The need for repair could then result in a lower level of allelic recombination than would be optimal from the point of view of variation alone. However, we argued above that, in principle, it should be easier to undergo repair by hypothetical pathways that have 100% allelic recombination (see Figure 2) than by the pathways that actually occur. Indeed, cryptic recombination during meiosis appears to result from a complex adaptation for reducing allelic recombination rather than from an intrinsic requirement of the repair process itself. These considerations contradict the view that allelic recombination is reduced so that repair can be more efficiently accomplished.

Finally, it could be argued that too much variation is disadvantageous and that the level of variation produced by meiosis is optimally adjusted to some intermediate level by the very processes we have considered. However, within the context of the alternative pathways reviewed here, the level of variation produced by repair seems to be as low as possible, given the need for repair and the likelihood of a balance between the costs and benefits of completely preventing allelic recombination. More important, to maintain this hypothesis, or any other hypothesis that assumes that meiosis is designed to produce a particular level of variation, one would have to postulate mechanisms for generating allelic recombination and for regulating its level. There are two possibilities by which allelic recombination could be produced. First, allelic recombination could be generated by the organism actively inducing damage in its own chromosomes. Such a view seems inconsistent with the fact that many plants protect themselves by producing toxic chemicals that damage their predator's DNA (Ames, 1983). It would not benefit plants to do this if DNA damage produced beneficial allelic recombination. Second, a mechanism could exist for producing allelic recombination independent of the need for repair. However, we know of no evidence for such a mechanism.

SUMMARY

We have framed the variation hypothesis for meiotic recombination in terms of the likelihood of allelic recombination at linked loci. This interpretation is identical to that made in all current and past evolutionary models designed to study recombination. We have argued that general features of meiosis, particularly premeiotic replication and cryptic recombination, as detected by SCE and gene conversion, are best explained by the hypothesis that meiosis is an adaptation for recombinational repair of DNA. Genetic variation through allelic recombination appears to be a by-product whose production is reduced.

We conclude that the variation hypothesis does not provide a satisfactory framework for understanding the mechanics of meiotic recombination. In addition, we conclude that the mechanics of meiotic recombination are consistent with the hypothesis that meiotic recombination is designed for repair of DNA and that allelic exchange is an occasional by-product of DNA repair that has been reduced during evolution.

APPENDIX

Double-strand break repair model

There are two points to this appendix. First, in principle the simplest possible mechanism of physical recombination results in allelic recombination all the time. Second, in practice during meiosis, physical recombination is accomplished by a much more complex process that serves to reduce the level of variation produced through allelic recombination.

We base our discussion of recombination on a model for meiotic recombination recently proposed by Szostak et al. (1983) and referred to as the double-strand break repair model. This model was developed to explain the extensive data obtained from fine-structure genetic analyses in fungi (as reviewed by Orr-Weaver and Szostak, 1985), as well as knowledge of the physical properties of DNA and the enzymatic reactions involved in its processing. It has several features in common with a previous model of Meselson and Radding (1975) that has dominated thinking about the mechanism of general recombination for the past decade, but it accommodates recent experimental evidence not readily explained by the older model. We regard it as the most authoritative model for general recombination currently available. By this model an initial double-strand break is converted at the next step into a double-strand gap. Because any double-strand damage can, in principle, be converted enzymatically into a double-strand gap, this model can also serve as a general model for recombinational repair.

The pathway shown in Figure 1 is essentially the same as the model of Szostak and coworkers (as shown in their Figure 8), except that for clarity we have filled in some of the intermediate steps implied, but not shown, in their

FIGURE 1. Model of general recombination adopted from Szostak et al. (1983). Since each recombination event at meiosis involves a pair of chromatids, only two of the four meiotic chromatids are shown. Each chromatid is represented as double-stranded DNA with two antiparallel strands. The 3′ ends are indicated by arrowheads and 5′ ends by circles. The diagram shows details of recombination within a region one or a few genes in length, with the major portions of the chromatids extending to the left and right of the diagram.

(A) A double-strand break is made in one DNA duplex. (B) A 5′ → 3′ exonuclease converts the initial break into a double-strand gap forming 3′ single-stranded ends. (C) One 3′ end invades another homologous chromosome, forming a displacement loop (D-loop) and initiating formation of a Holliday junction. (D) The D-loop is enlarged by elongation of the invading strand until the other 3′-ended strand can anneal with the D-loop from the other side. The striped arrow represents new DNA synthesis. (E) Repair synthesis and ligation fill in the gap in the upper strand. (F) Elongation of the single strand that initially invaded the D-loop results in enlargement of the D-loop by branch migration and strand displacement. The displaced strand migrates to the lower chromosome, forming a heteroduplex region. Exonucleolytic degradation may be required prior to ligation. (G–J) From the point of view of cutting and resolving the Holliday structure, each of the two Holliday junctions can exist in two equivalent forms (Meselson and Radding, 1975). Thus four configurations are possible at this stage. When the Holliday junctions are resolved in the same sense—that is, cutting the inner strands at both junctions (G) or the outer strands at both junctions (H)—two chromosomes are formed that have not exchanged flanking alleles. When the Holliday junctions are resolved in the opposite sense, with one inner pair cut and one outer pair cut (I and J), two chromosomes are formed that have exchanged flanking alleles.

original version. Much of the complexity in the model is present in order to explain the extensive evidence for cryptic recombination. This evidence comes mainly from the analysis of aberrant segregation ratios in the asci of fungi. The key to this explanation is the intermediate structure formed at step F, which has two nearby Holliday junctions (each indicated by a pair of single-strand crossovers). From the point of view of cutting and resolving the Holliday structures, it is convenient to consider four equally likely configurations of the intermediate structure formed at step F, realizing that in reality there is a continuous distribution of configurations due to free rotation about the chemical bonds involved. By resolving both of these in the same way (i.e., cutting the same two strands in each Holliday junction) as in the leftward branches (G and H), two chromosomes are formed that have not exchanged flanking alleles. The alternate branches (I and J) illustrate the result obtained when the two Holliday junctions are resolved by cutting different strands in each Holliday junction. This generates two chromosomes with their flanking alleles exchanged. We use the term branching frequency to describe the frequency with which the two measurably different outcomes occur, exchange versus nonexchange of outside markers.

At equilibrium, resolution by the four pathways should be equally likely, since they represent equivalent forms of a structure. In this case, the measured branching frequency should be 50%. However, a factor that may bias the outcome is that it takes time to reach the equilibrium state of equal probability (in which all configurations are equally likely), and this may bias resolution against the pathways yielding allelic recombination. If resolution of the Holliday structure is rapid, the time needed to reach the state of equal probability may explain why cryptic recombinants are often less than 50%.

The cryptic recombinants have enough genetic information from their partner chromatid to fill the gap in their DNA sequence. Branch migration of the Holliday structures may increase the amount of information obtained from the partner chromatid beyond that just necessary to fill in the original gap. However, the total amount of recombined information for chromosomes that have not exchanged flanking alleles will still be very small compared to the amount of information in the whole chromosome.

Formation of the second Holliday junction at step F is the most complicated step of the model. While the details were not spelled out by Szostak et al. (1983), they are given by Dressler and Potter (1982, Fig. 5), and we have followed this scheme here. The first step involves displacement of a single strand by progression of a replicative growing point along the lower chromosome, resulting in extension of the upper heteroduplex to the left by branch migration. As the migration proceeds, a strand from the upper chromosome is displaced so that it migrates to the lower chromosome, forming another heteroduplex region. To complete the process the replicative growing point must be ligated to the immigrant strand. This joining may require exonucleolytic degradation prior to ligation. Our purpose in describing these reactions is to show that considerable molecular complexity is needed to explain formation of the second Holliday junction.

A simple pathway yielding 100% allelic recombination

In principle, there is a much simpler way to resolve the structure formed in step D than by the steps shown in Figure 1, although it does not explain the genetic data. The simpler pathway given in Figure 2 involves no reactions other than those needed in Figure 1; endonucleolytic cleavage of exposed single-stranded regions and gap filling catalyzed by DNA polymerase and ligase. We include this pathway to show that the complexity of the mechanism needed to explain the data on cryptic recombination is much greater than that needed just to complete the recombination process. In Figure 2, the pathway up to step D is identical to the pathway up to D in Figure 1. Steps E to G illustrate how the

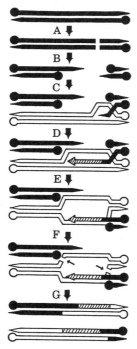

FIGURE 2. Hypothetical model of recombination based on the model of Szostak et al. (1983) up to step D, but resolved in steps E to G by a direct route.

(A–D) Same as in Figure 1. (E) Structure formed in D redrawn in an equivalent arrangement to facilitate illustrating succeeding steps. (F) Cleavage of single strands at positions indicated by small arrows. (G) Strands rejoined as indicated. Repair synthesis and ligation occur where required.

structure formed at D can be readily resolved, but in a way that results in all chromosomes having exchanged flanking alleles. That this can be done in a straightforward way suggests that the complex molecular reactions giving rise to the second invasion are an accessory modification of the basic recombinational process. From the point of view of the repair hypothesis, recombination serves the function of genetic repair and this could be accomplished by the pathway shown in Figure 2. That it is apparently accomplished with complex reactions whose most obvious consequence is to reduce allelic recombination at flanking loci suggests that the mechanism of recombination is designed to serve the primary function of repair while at the same time reducing allelic recombination. From the point of view of the variation hypothesis, the simpler pathway shown in Figure 2 should be preferred because it increases the likelihood of allelic recombination.

CHAPTER 10

THE ROLE OF GENE TRANSFER
IN THE EVOLUTION OF
EUKARYOTIC SEX

Donal A. Hickey
and
Michael R. Rose

INTRODUCTION

Eukaryotic sex is not so much a single biological phenomenon as it is a single concept in biology. This concept covers diverse physiological, behavioral, and genetic phenomena. It is customary to focus on meiotic recombination as the central aspect of sex because it results in genetic variation among progeny, this variation being seen as an adaptation to an uncertain environment. Therefore, the question of what selective forces underlie the evolution of sex is often rephrased in terms of the selective forces favoring increased recombination rates (see East, 1918; Fisher, 1930; Muller, 1932, 1964; Crow and Kimura, 1965, 1969; Turner, 1967; Cavalli-Sforza and Bodmer, 1971; Eshel and Feldman, 1970; Felsenstein, 1974, and in this volume). In this chapter, we will present an alternative view of the evolution of sex, one that does not require selection for increased recombination rates during the early stages of the process.

We distinguish between the origin and the maintenance of sex, and we will deal primarily with the question of origin. For our theory, this distinction is critical. Many attempts have been made to assign a biological "function" to sex, where "function" reflects a fitness advantage to the sexually reproducing organisms. If there is a single function for sex that has not changed over evolutionary time, and if this function is the production of genetic variants through meiotic recombination, then selection for recombination would explain both the origin and the maintenance of sex. The problem with such a scenario has always been that genetic variation is a feature of an evolutionary lineage rather than of a single individual; thus, selection for increased levels of variation can act only indirectly. Moreover, recombination tends to separate the genes for recombination from the favorable genetic combinations that these genes brought about (Strobeck et al., 1976). These problems could also be most serious in the early stages of the evolution of sex. Consequently, we find it useful to consider the possibility that recombination is an evolutionary consequence but not a selective cause of eukaryotic sex. We shall deal later with the problem of the cost of meiosis for the maintenance of sex among anisogamous higher eukaryotes.

We regard the evolution of sex as a multistep process, where each step evolved due to individual selection on genes that were favored under the conditions that existed at a particular stage. Even though recombination rates may be currently very important, we cannot believe that the early phases evolved in a goal-oriented fashion determined by the adaptive advantages of the end result. We argue that selection for efficient horizontal gene transfer initiated the process, which then continued through a series of coevolutionary interactions to produce the extant forms of eukaryotic sex (see also Brooks, in this volume).

Historically, the term "sex" was used to describe the type of biparental reproduction exemplified by vertebrate animals. It is only relatively recently that the genetic consequences of sex have been understood, along with an appreciation of its ubiquity among all eukaryote groups (see Ghiselin, in this volume). All forms of "true" eukaryotic sex involve cycles of gamete fusion and meiosis. Since chromosomal recombination occurs during meiosis, this part of the cycle has been the main focus of interest in the past. It has generally been assumed that the whole cycle, including the fusion of gametic cells, evolved in concert. We will first focus on the evolutionary origin of cell fusion per se and show that it may have evolved independently. Implicit in our argument is the notion that the modern form of eukaryotic sex was perfected after the evolution of haploid eukaryotic cells. Genome mixing—i.e., sex in some form—is probably much older than eukaryotes. However, in the overall context of long-term evolution, eukaryotic sex is relatively specialized and recent. If we accept that life originated approximately 3000 million years ago and that eukaryotic cells evolved roughly 1500 to 1000 million years ago (Margulis et al., 1985; Margulis and Sagan, 1986), then we can confine our discussion of eukaryotic sex to events that took place during the second half of evolutionary history. Thus we are not dealing with the phenomena of early evolution such as freely recombining, polyploid RNA genomes. When dealing with the initial stages of eukaryotic sexual origins, we will concentrate on those evolutionary forces that might have come into play in the ancestors of modern eukaryotes about 1000 million years before the present.

PARASITIC DNA AND THE ORIGIN OF SEX

As stated in the introduction to this chapter, an implicit presumption of most theories of the evolution of sex is that it is an adaptation, that is, that sex is somehow beneficial for those organisms that undergo it. The last 15 years of research have shown, at the very least, that the source of such net benefit is not obvious (for recent overviews of the topic, see Ghiselin, 1974; Williams, 1975; Maynard Smith, 1978; Bell, 1982; Halvorson and Monroy, 1985; Margulis and Sagan, 1986). Therefore, adaptive analyses of sex have grown greatly in subtlety.

An alternative approach to the origin of sex (Hickey, 1982) states that sex could be the result of the evolution of parasitic DNA sequences that exploit the opportunities for horizontal transmission afforded by cycles of germ cell fusion and fission to spread horizontally through populations. Moreover, such parasitic elements could, in theory, enhance their own fitness by promoting gamete fusion. This idea has since been subject to formal analyses where both the origin and the maintenance of sex are concerned (Rose, 1983; Tremblay and Rose, 1985; Krieber and Rose, 1986b). These analyses suggest that such gene transfer could indeed play an important role in the evolution of eukaryotic sex, although they also indicate that adaptive benefits to the host cells might also play a critical role. We would like to stress at the outset, however, that we do not wish to suggest that the evolution of sex involves "nothing but" gene transfer mechanisms. A similar argument for the role of transmissible genes in the evolution of bacterial sex has recently been outlined by Zinder (1985). Here we will outline the basic biological ideas involved in our research, as well as some of the elementary features of the mathematical findings.

The existence of transposable genes was first inferred from the results of genetic studies in maize and later from the observation of unstable mutations in prokaryotes. The discovery of horizontally transmitted antibiotic resistance among medically important bacteria gave a major impetus to the extensive research on bacterial plasmids and transposons. More recent work on the molecular biology of higher eukaryotes has led to the surprising finding of a large array of transposable element families in these genomes (for review, see Shapiro, 1983). In addition to their variety and ubiquity, the eukaryotic elements can occur in impressively large numbers of copies per cell. Despite the early suggestion of McClintock that transposable genes were important controlling elements within the cell, an adaptive function has not been identified for the majority of these elements in eukaryotes. This has led to the suggestion that many, perhaps all, of these transposable elements may have initially spread as genomic parasites, or "selfish DNA" (Doolittle and Sapienza, 1980; Orgel and Crick, 1980). The question addressed by Hickey (1982) was why such parasitic DNAs should be most abundant in the genomes of sexually reproducing outbreeding organisms. In answering this question we get a clue as to how and why the outbreeding phenomenon might have originated, not as an adaptation of the organisms or cells themselves, but of the genetic elements that parasitize them.

Some mathematical points

A major problem in understanding the spread of transposable elements in natural populations is that although such elements are capable of over-replication, and although this allows them to spread within a single genome, it does not facilitate their spread to other genomes. Only when replicative transposition is combined with cycles of gamete fusion and fission can the intragenomic multiplication of the elements be converted into intergenomic spread. This is because zygote formation allows the elements to colonize a new set of chromosomes (Hickey, 1982, 1984). In cases where the transposition rate is very high, this could result in a doubling every generation of the frequency of genomes containing the element. It is important to realize that these calculations (Hickey, 1982) assume that the element is neither harmful nor beneficial to its host cells. Those elements that, in addition to their replication advantage, also code for beneficial host functions would, of course, spread at an even more rapid rate. The more interesting possibility to consider is the case where the replication/transposition advantage is offset by a negative effect of the transposon on its host cell. Here, it can be shown that there is an upper limit on this negative effect; beyond this limit, the element will not be able to spread despite its ability to self-replicate. This upper limit on negative selection at the host level is very large, however, and thus moderate levels of negative selection will not prevent the spread of these elements within a population. Such genetic elements could be classified as parasitic DNA. The important conclusion is that transposable elements that have positive, neutral, or negative effects on host fitness can all spread within sexual populations in a way that would not be possible within an asexual population. Thus, this advantage of sexuality for the transposable elements implicates them in the origin of sex.

The main features of Hickey's model (1982) are as follows. Assume that gametes containing a copy of a self-replicating element occur with frequency p. Random mating will result in $2p(1 - p)$ zygotes formed from one element-containing gamete and one element-free gamete. Among such zygotes the element has the potential to over-replicate in such a way that all gametes produced by these individuals in the following generation contain the element. With high transposition rates and low initial values of p, this will result in an approximate doubling of the frequency of element-bearing gametes each generation. If the element confers an advantage on host cells, it will spread even more rapidly than this. If, however, the element is deleterious, it will spread only if the selective coefficient is less than a specified maximum. With negative selection and discrete generations, the change in the frequency of element-bearing gametes becomes

$$\frac{p(1 - p)\{1 - s[1 + (1 - p)]\}}{\overline{W}}$$

where s is the selection coefficient against individuals carrying the element, and $\overline{W}$ is the mean fitness of individuals in the population. This frequency change will be positive, provided

$$s < \frac{1}{2 - p}$$

Note that when p is close to zero, the maximum value of s is 0.5. In other words, the automatic doubling in frequencing of element-bearing gametes can only be cancelled if element-bearing individuals have their fitness reduced by 50%.

To address the problem of the origin of cell fusion among unicellular forms, a different mathematical formulation of the interaction of transposable element spread and host fitness was developed by Rose (1983) and Tremblay and Rose (1985). Consider the following pair of equations,

$$dx/dt = xg(x) + uy - ym_1(x)$$
$$dy/dt = yq(y) - uy + ym_2(x)$$

where the g and q functions give rates of increase of element-free (x) cells and element-bearing (y) cells, u is the rate of segregational or mutational loss of the element, and the m_i combine any intertype competitive effects with the rate at which single element-bearing cells mate with element-free cells. Invasion of the populations by the transposable element requires only that

$$m_2(x^*) + q(0) - u > 0$$

where x^* is the population density of element-free cells. The interpretation of this relationship is simply that the net effect of element-free cells, both as competitors and as potential hosts, together with the initial rate of increase of element-bearing cells, must be greater than the rate of loss of elements from element-bearing cells. Note that it is not a requirement that

$$q(0) > g(0)$$

or even that $q(0)$ be positive. Again, this means that elements that produce deleterious effects can spread, provided that they induce cell fusion, or exploit preexisting forms of gene transfer. In many ways, the dynamics of this system resemble those of infectious plasmids and viruses (see Stewart and Levin, 1977, 1984; Levin, in this volume). In fact, plasmids could be the genetic elements operating to engender cell fusion in this model; these models are not specific to one type of gene-transfer element (Rose and Redfield, in press).

Evidence for the spread of nonfunctional DNA in sexual populations

We cannot obtain direct evidence that the origin of eukaryotic sex was correlated with the spread of transposable elements over 1000 million years ago. We can, however, provide evidence that sexual reproduction favors the spread of non-functional transposable genes. It should be understood that we use the term "nonfunctional" only in the sense of organismal fitness. The effects of the transferring genes can, of course, be functional in terms of the spread of these elements themselves.

The advantage that zygote formation conferred on self-replicating genetic elements over 1000 million years ago should still hold for contemporary transposable elements. Consequently, we would predict that the genomes of sexually outbreeding species should harbor a great number of such genes. This is indeed the case. By the same reasoning, one would expect asexually reproducing organisms, such as *Escherichia coli*, to harbor relatively few such elements. This is also the case. Moreover, one would expect that bacterial transposable elements, when they do occur, might code for some essential cellular function such as antibiotic resistance or resource utilization. This latter expectation is based on the fact that "beneficial" transposons need not be dependent on over-replication alone for their evolutionary spread. In other words, accessory genetic elements may follow either of two survival strategies: positive contribution to the fitness of their host cells, on the one hand, or self-replication at the expense of their hosts, on the other. A relevant observation is that many bacterial accessory genetic elements for which a function has not been found (i.e., the "cryptic" plasmids) often code for the ability to promote their own replication and horizontal transmission through conjugation.

Among the eukaryotes, the retroviral-like transposable elements are perhaps the best example of parasitic DNA. They appear to form a continuum with infectious viruses, which highlights their parasitic nature. Recently we have argued (Hickey and Benkel, 1986) that many introns, another hallmark of eukaryote genomes, could have originated as a family of parasitic reverse-transcribed elements.

It is difficult to provide direct experimental evidence for any evolutionary process, including the spread of transposable elements. The best "natural" experiment to date is the observation of temporal changes in the distribution of transposable P elements in natural populations of *Drosophila melanogaster*. There is good epidemiological evidence that these elements have spread rapidly in natural populations during the past 50 years (Kidwell, 1983). No positive function has been identified for the P element, and there is ample evidence of deleterious effects upon fertility and viability. Because of its apparent rapid spread, coupled with its significant deleterious effects and lack of positive function, this element has often been used as an example to illustrate models of parasitic DNA (Hickey, 1982; Ginzburg et al., 1984). Recent experiments (Kiyasu and Kidwell, 1984; Good and Hickey, 1986) have provided direct evidence that in spite of their deleterious effects, P elements can spread rapidly in laboratory populations.

Sex is the key to the spread of genomic parasites

Although the laboratory experiments and population surveys of P elements show that parasitic DNAs can spread rapidly within sexual populations, they do not prove that the rapid spread is a result of sexual outbreeding. Experimental evidence for a direct link between DNA parasitism and outbreeding comes from studies of the 2μ plasmid of the yeast *Saccharomyces cerevisiae* (Futcher and Cox, 1983; A. B. Futcher, E. Reid, and D. A. Hickey, unpublished data). This plasmid, like the P element transposon, provides no obvious function for its host cells and can be shown to reduce host fitness (Futcher and Cox, 1983). The advantage of the yeast system is that one can experimentally modify the mating system and thus compare the fate of a single plasmid under various patterns of host cell reproduction in a single host species. The experimental results show that the plasmid does not spread in populations undergoing asexual reproduction or sexual inbreeding, but spreads very rapidly when there is sexual outbreeding of the yeast cells. These results indicate that plasmid survival in nature depends on its ability to exploit the yeast mating process for its own horizontal transfer.

Both the theoretical calculations and the experimental observations support the notion that self-replicating, intragenomic elements can gain a large advantage from the sexual outbreeding of their host genomes. This means that the evolution of outbreeding sexuality allowed these genomes to be invaded by a whole new category of genetic parasites. It seems paradoxical that a trait such as gamete fusion should have evolved if its immediate effects can be negative. This paradox can be resolved by hypothesizing that such fusion, which we see as the first step in the evolution of the outbreeding process, is an adaptation of horizontally transmitted genetic elements rather than an adaptation of the cells that become infected with these elements. This is why sex can begin to evolve among organisms that initially derive no adaptive advantage from the process at the level of cell or organism. We will now review some of the evidence that sex is not only of benefit to horizontally transmitted genetic elements, but also probably a product of genes that were once part of such elements.

Lessons from bacteria

Our best clues as to the probable nature of primitive eukaryotic sex come from the study of living prokaryotes rather than eukaryotes. In eukaryotes, a single specialized sexual system based on cycles of syngamy and meiosis is virtually ubiquitous (Margulis and Sagan, 1986). In contrast, the prokaryotes still display a wide variety of sexual and asexual reproductive systems, and prokaryotic sexual systems are both conjugative and nonconjugative.

It is informative to consider the genetic control of conjugation in bacteria such as *E. coli* (see Willetts and Skurray, 1980). The observation of conjugation between bacterial cells was taken as direct evidence for sexual mating in this species. Only after extensive study of this process was the mating understood to be genetically controlled by a self-transmissible conjugative plasmid, the F factor (Hayes, 1953). As pointed out by Redfield (1984), it is especially interesting to consider the experimental systems of conjugation that yield recombination of chromosomal markers in *E. coli*. The transfer of genes between the *Hfr* donor cell and the F⁻ recipient cell is controlled by the *tra* operon of the F element, whereas the integration of these genes into the chromosome of the recipient cell is controlled by chromosomally encoded enzymes. The fact that bacterial conjugative sex is the result of an interaction between plasmid functions and chromosomal functions lends credence to the view that other sexual systems originated along similar lines.

The idea of a relationship between bacterial parasites and a form of bacterial sex is not a new one. Those bacteriophages that act as generalized transducing phages are potentially important in recombination, yet they are clearly bacterial parasites. Dougherty (1955) was one of the first to point out that phages, although they are parasites, could also facilitate a form of bacterial sexuality. The essence of our view is that not only can intracellular parasites provide a form of sexuality among prokaryotes, but also that "conventional" eukaryotic sex itself began with a type of intracellular parasitism (Hickey, 1982; Rose, 1983).

EVOLUTIONARY ELABORATION OF EUKARYOTIC SEX

Although there is good evidence that bacterial conjugation is an adaptation of horizontally transmitted genes, the link between self-replicating genetic elements and sexuality in modern eukaryotes is not obvious. This is not surprising if we assume that primitive eukaryotic mating, or syngamy, was the first step in a complex evolutionary process. During the course of the ensuing process, syngamy has taken on a new significance. Thus the evidence for the initial stages of the process gradually became obscured. One case where the connection between genetic mobility and sexuality in eukaryotes has not been lost is in the mating-type locus of *Saccharomyces cerevisiae* (Klar et al., 1981). It is no accident that there are not many examples available of mobile genetic elements promoting conjugation in eukaryotes; there is simply no selective advantage in promoting a phenomenon that is already ubiquitous within eukaryotes. The selective advantage, in terms of an increased potential for horizontal gene transfer, existed only at that point in evolutionary history when syngamy among eukaryotic cells was still rare or absent. Such conditions still exist among the prokaryotes. Our starting premise is that the largely asexual prokaryotes are characterized by a variety of mechanisms that cause relatively rare gene exchange between genomes (see the discussion of prokaryotic sexual systems by Levin, in this volume). One such mechanism, namely, syngamy, developed in complexity and frequency among the eukaryotic ancestors and results in what we now call eukaryotic sex. Other types of bacterial "sexuality," such as transformation, may be equally or more important in bacteria, but they do not have eukaryotic counterparts. In this section, we will review the chain of events that could have led to the development of modern eukaryotic sex.

The evolution of meiosis

An important difference between eukaryotic and prokaryotic gene transfer is that among the eukaryotes, there is cell fusion or, at least, nuclear fusion. Conjugative gene transfer between bacterial cells, by contrast, usually involves a physical association of two or more cells, but not cell fusion. This difference fits with the model of horizontal gene transfer. Since prokaryotes possess a single cellular compartment, genetic parasites need only pass from cell to cell; this can be achieved through a simple conjugation pilus. Eukaryotic genomic parasites are faced with the problem of getting from within the nucleus of one cell to within the nucleus of another cell. This can be achieved by contact of the two nuclei, but not necessarily by contact of the two cytoplasms (unless the element also has the ability to traverse the nuclear–cytoplasmic boundary). Thus, horizontally transmitted elements in eukaryotes would benefit from the type of sexual process one actually observes in eukaryotes.

Repeated cycles of cell fusion, without subsequent fission, would allow a eukaryotic parasitic DNA to colonize new chromosomes. Such a system would, however, have serious disadvantages both for the cells involved and for the parasitic elements themselves. First, these cells would be subject to repeated rounds of polyploidization; such a rapid increase in genome size would quickly become deleterious. Second, the parasitic element cannot spread by such fusion alone. Consider single haploid element-bearing cells. After cell fusion, there will be a single diploid element-bearing cell. After a second round of fusion, there will be a single triploid cell, and so on. In other words, this process would impose a burden on the host cells without increasing the frequency of element-bearing cells. This illustrates the point that only a temporary contact or fusion, followed by separation or fission, will favor the spread of horizontally transmissible elements.

The evolution of a primitive meiotic mechanism could function both as a cellular adaptation to reduce the negative effects of cell fusion and as an element-specific adaptation, because it could foster an increase in the actual number of element-bearing cells in the population by ensuring efficient fission. If meiosis evolved as a mechanism to resolve cell-fusion products, it might be expected to occur immediately after syngamy. This is indeed what we see in many simple eukaryotes, though not in complex multicellular higher eukaryotes. It is not unreasonable to suppose that the simpler systems reflect more closely the primitive situation.

The earliest forms of meiosis would function to reduce chromosome number rather than to promote recombination. Chromosome pairing would ensure the orderly segregation of chromosomes and thus prevent the production of maladapted aneuploids. Once this process was perfected, the deleterious effects of syngamy would be minimized, allowing high rates of survival of element-bearing cells and, consequently, the rapid spread of the elements themselves. It is possible that pairing of homologous chromosomes at meiosis could also have evolved, at least in part, as an adaptation of horizontally transmitted elements, as suggested by the fact that many prokaryotic transposons require physical contact between the source copy of the element and the target site for the new copy.

DNA repair and the evolution of sex

Primitive syngamy/meiosis cycles may be disruptive for the cells that undergo them; however, some of the negative effects on the cell might be offset by a number of possible benefits. The most obvious benefit is genetic complementation of recessive mutations in the diploids that result from syngamy. In cases where gamete fusion is immediately followed by meiosis, however, the benefits of diploidy cannot be exploited. On the other hand, cells could still benefit from syngamy by segregating out wild-type genotypes from the mating of cells that carried deleterious mutations on different chromosomes. Such segregation does not require the ability to recombine genes within a chromosome. In this way, even very primitive sexuality would allow a type of "genetic rescue" by regenerating nonmutant cells. As pointed out by Tremblay and Rose (1985), such a benefit to the host cell would facilitate the spread to fixation of a horizontally transmitted element.

Another type of genetic rescue, DNA repair, has been advocated as an important factor in the evolution of sex. Presumably the enzymology involved in DNA repair was perfected long before the evolution of conjugation and meiosis, given its prevalence among prokaryotes (for review, see Hanawalt et al., 1979). The evolutionary advent of syngamy would have allowed these enzymes to function in important new ways because of the availability of new templates within the cell. As pointed out by Bernstein (1977; Bernstein et al., 1981, 1984), this would be especially important for the repair of double-stranded DNA breaks (see Bernstein et al., in this volume). Thus selection for syngamy, which would occur initially on the self-transmissible genes that promote it, could be reinforced because of the benefits of DNA repair to the host cell. DNA repair can become a very important selective force once a genetically efficient mating system has evolved, and cell fusion promoted by horizontally transmitted genes provides a plausible mechanism for the evolution of such mating processes initially.

Chromosomal recombination and the evolution of sex

A population in which there was frequent syngamy followed by meiosis, with the concomitant opportunity for DNA repair, would provide the basis for the evolution of chromosomal recombination. Indeed, most of the sexual cycle would already be in place at this stage. The pairing of homologous chromosomes, necessary for orderly segregation, and the enzymatic cleavage and ligation of DNA involved in the repair process would automatically result in some recombination events. At this stage, the medium- and long-term benefits of genetic recombination could become important in the perpetuation of the sexual cycle (see Maynard Smith, in this volume). This is not to say that other factors, such as horizontal gene transfer and DNA repair, would not continue to play a part in the evolution of sex. As already mentioned, a problem with the role of recombination in the origin of sex is that its benefits are often long-term rather than immediate. By invoking other forces for the origin of sex, we overcome this difficulty. Using the terminology of Levin in this volume, we suggest that many aspects of eukaryotic sex arose by coincidental evolution, that is, they are the by-products of selection for gene transfer and DNA repair.

Traditionally, the advantage of recombination is seen in terms of its ability to produce an array of different genotypes that could act as an adaptation to an unpredictably changing environment (Maynard Smith, 1971, 1976, 1977; and see chapters by Ghiselin, Felsenstein, Brooks, Bell, and Maynard Smith, in this volume). Closer examination of these models, however, shows that their validity depends on unusual patterns of propagule dispersal and environmental heterogeneity (for recent overviews, see Williams, 1975; Maynard Smith, 1978; Bell, 1982). In our view, such patterns are not necessary for the evolution of sex, either its origin or maintenance, but could nonetheless have arisen and played an important role evolutionarily from time to time.

GENOME EVOLUTION IN SEXUAL POPULATIONS

We have tried to show how horizontally transmitted genes might have set in motion a chain of evolutionary events that led to the elaboration of the eukaryotic sexual cycle. The ubiquity of sexuality among diverse groups of eukaryotes indicates that these processes were already fully evolved many hundreds of million years ago. Therefore, a large portion of the recent evolutionary history of eukaryotic sex has to do with maintenance of these phenomena, along with the development of several other processes that depend on the preexistence of sexuality.

Horizontal gene transfer in the maintenance of sex

Even if both mathematical and biological arguments suggest that there is no appreciable problem with hypothesizing an initially parasitic origin of sex, it is highly unlikely that sex has since continued to be simply parasitic. As we have outlined above, evolution could take advantage of the opportunities for adaptation provided by syngamy and meiosis, even if they have initially come about because of evolutionary parasitism. A useful analogy can be made with the evolution of mitochondria. According to the endosymbiosis theory, mitochondria originated as free-living cells that were later the prey, or parasites, of the ancestors of modern eukaryotic cells. Proponents of the endosymbiotic theory would not, however, consider modern mitochondria as intracellular parasites; they have obviously become an integral part of the eukaryotic cell. Likewise, eukaryotic sex, regardless of its origin, is now an established form of eukaryote reproduction.

Even if the genes that gave rise to syngamy have long since become an integral part of the eukaryotic genome, more recently evolved transposable elements still depend on the existence of outbreeding for their spread. It is not unreasonable to suggest that some of these genes may contribute to the perpetuation of the syngamy/meiosis cycle on which they depend for survival. Such elements may also contribute to the evolution of chromosomal recombination, since it has recently been shown by Charlesworth and Langley (1986) that the selective constraints on genetic transposition are relaxed in organisms with higher recombination rates. This occurs because recombination will protect the source copy of an element from the possible deleterious effects of mutations caused by the insertion of new copies elsewhere on the same chromosome. It is ironic that for many years a paradox was seen in the fact that the genes that promoted recombination would be separated, by recombination, from the genotypes they affected. This was based on the assumption that the effects of such genes were adaptive for the cell. Now it seems that those genes that were involved in the initial stages of the evolution of sex may have benefited directly from recombination, in that it separated them from their negative effects on the host cell. In other words, parasitic "recombinator genes" are protected from cellular-level negative selection by recombination.

The cost of meiosis and the cost of fertilization

An adequate theory of the evolution of sex must include not only an explanation of the origin of sex, but also an explanation of its maintenance among anisogamous higher eukaryotes. As pointed out by Maynard Smith (1978), there is a genetic cost to anisogamous sex among higher eukaryotes; this cost would give an immediate advantage to efficient parthenogens that arose spontaneously within such populations. It has proven difficult to explain how the rather uncertain benefits of recombination could counter such a large disadvantage of sexuality (see Charlesworth, 1980; Uyenoyama, 1984).

One possibility is that there may simply be no functional genetic variants with the capacity for asexual reproduction in many sexual taxa; for instance, there are no known parthenogenetic variants in the Mammalia (Rose, 1982). In such cases, there may be critical reproductive adaptations that are bound up with anisogamy (Rose, 1982; cf. Margulis et al., 1985).

Here we present another evolutionary mechanism that can maintain sex even if fairly efficient asexual reproduction arises; it relates back to our view that eukaryotic sex is a complex multistage process. Just as syngamy without meiosis would be deleterious during the evolutionary development of sex, the spontaneous loss of meiosis, without the concomitant loss of fertilization and gamete fusion, would be equally deleterious for modern eukaryotes. In other words, the simple disappearance of meiosis may eliminate the cost of meiosis, but in so doing it automatically creates a cost of fertilization for rare parthenogens if sexual males successfully fertilize them.

The cost of fertilization (and resultant zygote abortion) to organisms that produce unreduced progeny in lieu of reduced gametes has been mathematically analyzed by Krieber and Rose (1986b) for diploid metazoa subject to discrete generations. The results show that if males are sufficiently successful at fertilizing parthenogenetically reproducing females, giving rise to aborted triploids, then such females will not successfully invade sexual populations. If conditions are such that parthenogenetic females can invade initially (e.g., if there is a low probability of fertilization of parthenogens), then they tend to spread to fixation. Since the progeny wastage arises only in matings of sexual males with asexual females, the dynamics of the system are similar to those of the case of heterozygote disadvantage. Thus a corollary of this model is that anisogamous sex and parthenogenesis should only rarely coexist in a population, at least when these reproductive alternatives are dependent on different genotypes; the model does not preclude the kind of phenotypic alteration exhibited by aphids and rotifers. Finally, the model shows that once parthenogenesis has been fixed, it is highly resistant to the subsequent invasion of males, because it is then sexual reproduction that suffers the greatest wastage.

The mathematical description of the cost of fertilization is simplest if we consider the case of unicellular organisms

$$dx/dt = x \left[a_1 - b \left(x + y \right) - dy \right]$$
$$dy/dt = y \left[a_2 - b \left(x + y \right) - dx \right]$$

where the a_i gives the intrinsic rate of increase of sexual cells (x) and asexual derivatives (y); we let $a_2 > a_1 > 0$ to illustrate the point that sex need not be beneficial to be maintained; the positive b parameter includes density-dependent competition effects, assumed to be uniform between the two types (the Tangled Bank model of Bell [1982] would have this parameter smaller for the sexual form, but we want to show how sex can be maintained without such advantages);

and finally the d parameter reflects the loss of cells from both subpopulations due to the fertilization of y progeny by x gametes (all parameters are strictly positive). There must be a k_1 such that $(x, y) = (k_1, 0)$, $k_1 > 0$, is an equilibrium; this equilibrium is unstable when

$$a_2 > k_1 (b + d) = a_1 + dk_1$$

which shows that a_2 must be greater than a_1 by an amount that depends on d, the "fertilization wastage" parameter. Although this is an extremely simplified model, the basic conclusion it affords remains robust under perturbation.

Circumstantial evidence in favor of the cost of fertilization comes from the observation that many "parthenogenetic" species are in fact automictic, thus retaining the elements of meiosis and fertilization. Second, parthenogenetic vertebrate species are often sparsely distributed hybrids, whose ancestors might have a low probability of mating (e.g., asexual lizard species). In densely populated regions, the probability of fertilization would be higher and, consequently, the probability of survival of a parthenogenetic race would be lower (cf. Lynch, 1984).

Effects of evolutionarily recent genetic parasites

In addition to the transposable elements that promoted sex among the eukaryotic ancestral types, it is obvious that there have been several subsequent cycles of evolution in which new transposons have evolved to exploit the opportunities provided by mating. We have already mentioned the P elements of Drosophila, one of the most transparent examples.

Hickey's (1982) model for the spread of transposable elements in a sexual population is formally similar to mathematical models of meiotic drive (Prout, 1953), although the biological processes are quite different. Interestingly, a classic example of meiotic drive, the Segregation Distorter system of *Drosophila melanogaster* (Hiraizumi et al., 1960), may itself be caused by the activity of a transposable element (Hickey et al., 1986). The survival strategy of the SD element is a novel one in that although the element is self-replicating, it does not spread because of the accumulation of new copies but because these new copies destroy competing chromosomes. These "killer" copies are then eliminated along with the chromosomes that they destroy. It is of interest that, as illustrated in this case, the elements that are the basis for the evolution of Mendelian segregation may, in variant form, be the basis for some deviations from Mendelism.

Likewise, we have stressed in this chapter that mating, and consequently the formation of gene pools, is a property of parasitic elements. Nevertheless, it is also possible that barriers to gene flow may arise from the activities of such elements (Rose and Doolittle, 1983; Krieber and Rose, 1986a).

Finally, the mosaic gene structure that is the hallmark of eukaryote genomes may also be due in part to parasitic elements. Many authors (Cavalier-Smith, 1978; Crick, 1979; Chambon, 1981) have suggested that introns may be the remnants of transposable elements. Hickey and Benkel (1985) pointed out that if such elements were self-splicing and reverse transcribed, they could easily invade sexual, but not asexual, populations. Parasitic introns would illustrate the phenomenon of acquired dependence of cells on a transposable element. For instance, if a self-splicing intron produces a number of nonautonomous copies within the cell, then the splicing machinery, and the intron that encodes it, will be actively maintained by natural selection.

In conclusion, we have argued that horizontally transmissible genetic elements have played an important role in the evolution of eukaryotic sex. They are not, in our view, the sole evolutionary factor molding this complex phenomenon. We can draw a useful parallel between the evolution of mutation and that of recombination, the two principal sources of the genetic variability on which all evolution depends. Despite their importance, it is likely that neither the processes of mutation nor those of recombination evolved primarily because of their immediate adaptive benefits. Mutations arose inevitably as accidents of DNA replication, and sexual recombination in eukaryotes arose as an accidental by-product of the interaction between parasitic gene-transfer systems and cellular DNA repair mechanisms. Since the evolution of transposons and the evolution of sexuality are interdependent, it is not surprising that sexual eukaryotes display a wealth of transposable element families, far in excess of what one observes in the largely asexual prokaryotes. We would also suggest that the study of tranposable elements, conjugative plasmids, and other such systems of horizontal gene transfer could reveal a great deal of information that would be of fundamental value for our understanding of the evolution of genetic systems in general.

SUMMARY

In this chapter we have emphasized the potential importance of gene transfer as a selective force during the initial stages of the evolution of eukaryotic sex. Other factors, such as the possibilities for DNA repair and the generation of new recombinant genotypes, might have gained in importance during the later phases of this process. We have presented a broad outline view of the evolution of eukaryotic sex as a complex, multistage process.

Using the perspective suggested here, we can better understand the recent finding of abundant nonfunctional DNA sequences in outbreeding sexual eukaryotes. We also get new insights into the factors that make the spontaneous loss of sexual reproduction improbable.

In contrast to many existing theories that imply population or species-level selection in the evolution of sex, our theory for the origin of sex involves selection at the subgenomic level. In other words, we propose that rather than being imposed by selection at higher levels of organization (population or species), sexual reproduction was initially imposed on individual organisms by selection at a subindividual level, that is, selection on parasitic DNA sequences.

CHAPTER 11

PARASITES AND SEX

Jon Seger and W. D. Hamilton

INTRODUCTION

Parasites of many kinds have long been recognized as important regulators of population size (e.g., May, 1983b), but only during the last decade or two have they been widely viewed as the protagonists in fast-paced (and long-running) evolutionary thrillers involving subtle features of the biochemistry, anatomy, and behavior of their hosts. On this view, their power as agents of evolution derives from their ubiquity and from the great amounts of mortality they can cause (which are also the properties that make them effective agents of population regulation) and, just as importantly, from their *imperfect* (but improvable) abilities to defeat the *imperfect* (but improvable) defenses of their hosts. Thus each party is expected to experience the other as a changeable (and generally worsening) part of its environment. In principle, prey and predator species have the same kind of relationship. But predators usually have generation times as long or even longer than those of their prey, while parasites may have generation times many orders of magnitude shorter than those of their hosts. If this asymmetry allows parasites to evolve improved methods of attack much faster than their hosts can evolve improved methods of defense, then the hosts' best defense may be one based on genotypic diversity, which, if recombined each generation, can present to the parasites what amounts to a continually moving target (e.g., Haldane, 1949; Levin, 1975; Glesner and Tilman, 1978; Jaenike, 1978; Bremermann, 1980, 1985; Bremermann and Pickering, 1983; Hamilton, 1980, 1982, 1986; Hamilton et al., 1981; Anderson and May, 1982; Bell, 1982, 1985; Price and Waser, 1982; Tooby, 1982; Rice, 1983).

In this chapter we discuss the idea that parasites may often play an important role in the maintenance of sexual reproduction. First, we distinguish the problem of maintaining full-fledged sex from that of maintaining genetic recombination in a species that always reproduces sexually. Then we describe the kinds of arguments and evidence that have been advanced to support the view that parasites may be uniquely able to generate the large selective differences that are required to pay the "cost of sex" in most species. Finally, we discuss a few of the many specific predictions that can be derived from different versions of the host–parasite hypothesis. Whatever weaknesses this hypothesis may have, untestability does not seem to be one of them (see Levin et al., 1982).

We use the term "recombination" to mean the creation of new gametic associations of existing alleles at different loci, through the mechanisms of crossing over and reassortment of chromosomes. Because the nucleotide positions within a single functional gene can be viewed formally as separate loci, some forms of intragenic recombination are included in our definition. We use the term "sex" to mean nominally biparental reproduction involving differentiated male and female individuals or reproductive functions. This definition includes hermaphroditism, and even selfing, although selfing is in some respects a partial retreat from sex (as discussed more fully below).

Felsenstein (1985, and in this volume) argues that all ecologically motivated theories for the evolution of sex and recombination fall into one of two categories, depending on the cause of the maladaptive linkage disequilibrium to be lessened by recombination. Theories belonging to the Fisher–Muller category invoke random genetic drift, while those of the Sturtevant–Mather category invoke selection that periodically changes direction. Models of host–parasite coevolution show a generic tendency to cycle, or to move incessantly in some other, more complicated way, because any change that increases the average fitness of one species tends to lower the average fitness of the other (e.g., Person, 1966; Clark, 1976; Eshel and Akin, 1983). The idea that sex is a major weapon in the war against parasites would therefore seem to be an instance of the Sturtevant–Mather theory. But genetic drift caused by finite population size can also give rise to varying frequency-dependent selection mediated by parasites and thereby to an advantage for sex. Thus, in its most general form, the host–parasite coevolution hypothesis seems to be simultaneously an instance of both of Felsenstein's categories.

COSTS OF SEX AND RECOMBINATION

The problem of sex and the problem of recombination are closely related, but they are not simply two names for the same thing. Given that a population reproduces sexually, there still remains the vexing question as to why its recombination rates do not evolve downward toward zero (e.g., Nei, 1967; Feldman, 1972; Feldman and Libermann, 1986; Felsenstein, in this volume), and more generally, there remains the question as to why its recombination rates should have equilibrium values other than zero and one-half (e.g., Charlesworth, 1976; Hutson and Law, 1981; Brooks and Marks, 1986; Brooks, in this volume). But the conditions that favor recombination, given sex, may be much less stringent than those that favor sex itself, given fully viable asexual mutants (e.g., Maynard Smith, 1978).

Under outcrossing, half of a population's parental investment will go into males (or, more generally, male reproductive functions). If males do not themselves rear offspring, then an asexual form that produced entirely female progenies would have a rate of increase that was twice that of its sexual counterparts, and it would drive them to extinction in very few generations (Maynard Smith, 1971). This is the twofold cost of sex. It is sometimes referred to as the cost of meiosis, but it is less a consequence of meiosis than it is of the sex ratio, in species where only the females rear offspring. If males contribute as much as females do to the rearing of offspring, then there is no cost of sex in this ecological sense, because an all-female asexual clone would have no reproductive advantage over an equivalent sexual species. Nonetheless, a new parthenogenic mutation arising within the sexual species could increase, *if* the sexual males unwittingly paired with the parthenogenic females and helped to rear their offspring. But as this mutation increased in frequency, the number of available males would decrease, and in the end there would be a new all-female clone with no reproductive advantage over an equivalent sexual species whose males mated only with their sexual conspecifics (e.g., Uyenoyama 1984). Selfing reduces the cost of sex by permitting the evolution of strongly female-biased patterns of reproductive allocation, but it also reduces the potential benefit of recombination by creating extensive homozygosity. In many respects, partial selfing can be viewed as a continuously adjustable approach to asexuality.

It is sometimes argued that obligately outcrossed species lack the genetic variation that would easily allow them to give up sex, and that except for this constraint, many would do so. This presumed inability to experiment with asexuality is often viewed as a product of group or species selection, on the assumption that sex may permit the long-term survival of a population, despite its short-term disadvantages. But many species of cyclically or facultatively parthenogenic animals (and self-compatible plants) could easily go literally (or effectively) asexual, if selection were pushing them in that direction (Williams, 1975; Maynard Smith, 1978). It follows that outcrossed sexuality, with its attendant sex-ratio penalty, must somehow be paying its own way in these species, and that a satisfying *general* explanation for the prevalence of outcrossed sex should not appeal to long-term group or species selection, but should instead identify short-term benefits of sexual reproduction that give it something like a compensating twofold advantage over asex.

Nonetheless, strong developmental barriers against an easy switch to asexuality could exist in some taxa, and these barriers could have evolved through group selection. A sexual lineage that easily gave rise to viable asexual forms might often find itself driven to local extinction through competition with its own asexual derivatives. If the evolutionary inflexibility of the conquering asexual forms in turn doomed *them* to early extinction, then the lineage might not leave many descendants, compared to an equivalent lineage in which there happened to be no developmentally feasible route to asexuality. But the fact that asex and selfing *are* viable alternatives in some taxa shows that short-term advantages to sex must exist, at least in those taxa. And there is no reason to suppose that such advantages exist *only* in taxa showing lapses from exclusively outcrossed sexuality. Thus even if we knew that group-selected barriers to asex had evolved in some taxa, the problem of the twofold cost would still be with us.

These arguments are well known, and they are discussed in several other chapters in this volume. We have rehearsed them here to emphasize that a full explanation for sex requires that it often have large and persistent selective advantages over asex. The attraction of parasites is that they seem likely to be able to generate such advantages.

PARASITES AND POLYMORPHISM

There can be no benefit in reducing linkage disequilibrium unless ecologically significant genetic polymorphism actually exists. Thus we need to ask first, whether host–parasite interactions are expected to cause the accumulation of such polymorphism, and second, whether there is evidence that they do so.

Theory

Host–parasite coevolution can be viewed metaphorically as an "arms race," in which each side is continually searching for new and improved methods of defense or attack. If the new methods are unconditionally better or worse than the existing methods, then the mutations giving rise to them will either sweep to fixation or be lost, and there will be no tendency to accumulate polymorphism. But if better methods of defense or attack tend to *cost* more than their alternatives (in that they drain resources away from reproduction), then a "better" defense will be of net benefit to a typical host individual *only* if the host is likely to be attacked by a parasite against which no weaker (and cheaper) defense will work. The parasite faces a similar dilemma, and thus the two species find themselves playing an evolutionary game that is closely related to the well-known "war of attrition" (Maynard Smith, 1974, 1982). Similarly, if the differences among phenotypes are *qualitative*, such that particular defenses simply work best against particular attacks, and vice versa, with no differences of intrinsic cost, then host and parasite can be viewed as a pair of coupled multiple-niche models, in which each species provides a variable environment for the other. In either case, the relative fitness of a given defense (or attack) will depend on the frequencies of the different attacks (or defenses) currently being employed by the other species.

Under these circumstances a polymorphic equilibrium may exist (e.g., Mode, 1958; Gillespie, 1975), but if the full genetic and population dynamics of both species are included in the model, the equilibrium is likely to be unstable (e.g., Person, 1966; Jayakar, 1970; Yu, 1972; Clarke, 1976; Rocklin and Oster, 1976; Auslander et al., 1978; Lewis, 1981a,b; Anderson and May,

1982; May and Anderson, 1983a,b; Eshel and Akin, 1983; Levin, 1983; May, 1985; Bell and Maynard Smith, 1987; see also Maynard Smith and Brown, 1986). The boundaries are usually unstable as well, which implies that the two species will engage in some kind of permanently dynamical "chase" through the gene-frequency and population-size planes. As one host genotype increases in frequency it favors the increase of the parasite genotype best able to exploit it, whose subsequent increase lowers the fitness of that host genotype, allowing a different host genotype to increase, which favors a different parasite genotype, and so on.

Levin (1975) applies Whittaker's (1969) famous coevolutionary metaphor to the special case of host and parasite, who sweep back and forth across the evolutionary "dance floor." This captures the sense of lively, coupled movement, and almost makes it sound like fun. But do the partners spend most of their time out in the middle of the floor? Or do they tend to bump into the walls? In particular, do the dynamics tend to keep the *host* species polymorphic? If not, then the host will usually have little to gain from recombination.

In the simplest one-locus models without mutation or migration, the two species either circle endlessly in a neutrally stable orbit determined by the initial conditions (if the model is cast in continuous time), or else they spiral outward toward the boundaries (if the model is cast in discrete time). Figure 1 illustrates the dynamics of one such model. In most models of this kind, as in this one, the fitnesses of the host genotypes depend only on the current frequencies of the parasite genotypes, and vice versa. But the current state of the parasite population reflects the recent history of the host, so the fitnesses of the host genotypes depend, indirectly, on their *own* frequencies over many *previous* generations. The same is true of the fitnesses of the parasite genotypes. Thus any genotype that was common in the recent past is likely to suffer relatively low fitness at present, because of the evolutionary change that its commonness induced in the other species. In effect, the current position of each species is a "memory" of the recent history of the other, and so the fitnesses of the genotypes within each species appear to exhibit negative frequency dependence with a time delay, even though there is no *explicit* intraspecific frequency dependence in the model.

In general, there are no stable internal equilibria in models of this kind unless they incorporate some form of explicit intraspecific frequency dependence, density dependence, or heterozygote advantage. Thus in a finite world, their cyclical dynamics would be likely to degenerate into irregularly spaced episodes of monomorphism, punctuated first in one species, then in the other, by the reintroduction of the lost allele and its rapid passage to fixation. This would not seem to be very favorable for sex, since any given locus would tend to be monomorphic for long periods of time. But there are several ways to rescue the situation.

First, there is the appeal to mutation and migration. The tendency to spiral outward can be arrested even in the simplest discrete-time models by remarkably

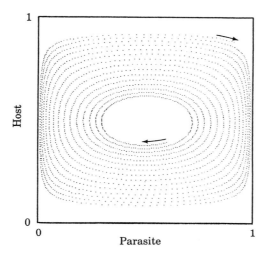

FIGURE 1. Gene-frequency trajectory of a simple 1-locus host-parasite model. Each species has a single haploid locus with two alleles, at frequencies h_1 and $h_2 = 1 - h_1$ in the host and p_1 and $p_2 = 1 - p_1$ in the parasite. Hosts and parasites encounter each other at random, so the probability that any given host individual is attacked by parasite type 1 is proportional to p_1. Parasite type 1 is most successful on host type 1, and parasite type 2 is most successful on host type 2, while hosts are most successful against parasites of opposite type. Thus the expected fitness of a type 1 host is negatively proportional to the frequency of type 1 parasites: $W(host\ 1) = (1 - s)p_1 + p_2$, where s is the penalty, to the host, caused by successful parasitism. Conversely, the expected fitness of a type 1 parasite is positively proportional to the frequency of type 1 hosts : $W(parasite\ 1) = h_1 + (1 - t)h_2$, where t is the penalty, to the parasite, caused by the host's successful defense. The fitnesses of type 2 hosts and parasites are constructed in exactly the same way. Given these four fitnesses, it is easy to write down the recurrence equations for h_1 and p_1. For $0 < s < 1$ and $0 < t < 1$, the central equilibrium at $(0.5, 0.5)$ is unstable, as are the boundaries. The case illustrated here is $s = 0.05$, $t = 0.15$. Each point shows the gene frequencies of parasite and host (p_1, h_1) in one generation, and the entire trajectory is 2500 generations long.

small inputs of genetic variation uncorrelated with the current state of the population (Figure 2). A low rate of mutation or migration gives rise to a stable limit cycle near the boundaries, and as the rate is increased the cycle shrinks inward toward the central equilibrium point, which is finally stabilized at rates above a certain critical value (see legend to Figure 2).

Second, there is the appeal to multiple alleles. The two-allele model of Figures 1 and 2 always cycles in a highly stereotyped and regular way, but the equivalent three-allele model has very complex dynamics that depend more strongly on parameter values and initial conditions than do those of the two-allele models (Figure 3). Without mutation or migration, the three-allele gene-frequency trajectories eventually become stuck near the boundaries, as in the

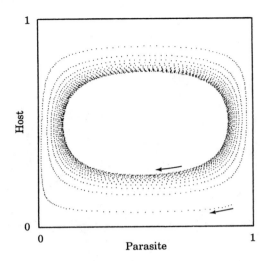

FIGURE 2. Gene-frequency trajectory of a simple 1-locus host-parasite model with mutation in the parasite. This model is exactly the same as the one described in the legend to Figure 1, except that the parasite species experiences a mutation rate m (which can also be thought of as a migration rate). If the mutation rate exceeds $0.25st/(2 - s - t + st)$, then the central equilibrium at $(0.5, 0.5)$ becomes stable. Lower mutation rates give rise to stable limit cycles, such as the one illustrated here for $s = 0.05$, $t = 0.15$, $m = 0.0005$. As in Figure 1, the points show the joint gene frequencies of parasite and host in successive generations, and the total length of the trajectory is 2500 generations.

two-allele model, but the time to quasifixation may be longer than in the two-allele case. This suggests that the relatively chaotic dynamics of a highly multiallelic system might be less inclined to drive particular alleles to very low frequencies than are the more regular dynamics of a system in which there are only two possible allelic states in host and parasite.

Third, there is the appeal to multiple loci. The argument here is that although most loci may be monomorphic most of the time, enough of them will be polymorphic enough of the time to give an advantage to recombination. In effect, this is the Fisher–Muller view of multilocus evolution: A favorable new mutation is almost guaranteed to be out of linkage equilibrium with alleles at other loci, and this may retard its progress to fixation. The argument applies to every kind of transient polymorphism, no matter what its cause, so parasites retain a special importance only to the extent that they are a frequent cause of adaptive gene substitutions (Hamilton, 1986).

Finally, there is the appeal to biological complexities not represented in the simplest models. These range from molecular and physiological details of the way in which host and parasite interact (e.g., mechanisms of acquired immunity), through their life history patterns (e.g., parasite life cycles involving more than one host species), to their population structures (e.g., subdivided host

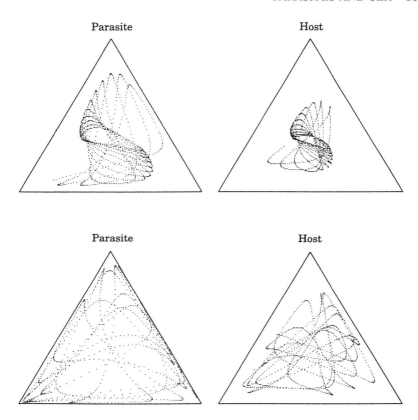

FIGURE 3. Gene-frequency trajectories of a simple 3-allele host-parasite model. The model illustrated here is the 3-allele generalization of the model described in the legend to Figure 1. Each of the three parasite genotypes successfully attacks one of the three host genotypes, and suffers a fitness penalty t when associated with either of the other two host types. Likewise, each host suffers a fitness penalty s when successfully attacked by the one parasite type that can penetrate its defenses. There is no mutation in the model shown here, although mutation in the parasite has essentially the same kind of stabilizing effect in the 3-allele case as it does in the 2-allele case shown in Figure 2. Separate gene-frequency trajectories for parasite and host are shown here, since a phase diagram can only show the frequency of one allele in each species. The fitness parameters s and t have the same values as in Figures 1 and 2, and the trajectories are again 2500 generations long (but here *every other* generation is plotted, rather than every one). The upper pair of trajectories begin at a point chosen to be similar to the starting point of Figure 1; the lower pair are the continuation of the trajectory shown in the upper pair. Thus 5000 generations are shown in all. All meaningful values of s and t and all starting points apparently lead eventually to chaotic gene-frequency dynamics, in the absence of mutation or migration. Both species may eventually become stuck near the boundaries most of the time, but each continues to make at least occasional passsages out through the middle of its gene-frequency space.

populations with limited migration among subdivisions). In many of the cases studied to date, the addition of realistic detail has reduced either the occurrence or the severity of cycling (e.g., May and Anderson, 1983a,b; Bremermann and Fiedler, 1985), but in some cases it has increased the tendency to cycle (e.g., May, 1985).

One very important detail is the generation time of the parasite (Anderson and May, 1982). If this is much shorter than that of the host (as is often the case), then the parasite population may more or less fully adapt, within each *host* generation, to the current distribution of host genotypes. In the limit, each host generation faces an array of parasite attack strategies that depends only on the distribution of genotypes in the *previous* generation of hosts. This greatly shortens the effective time delay in the frequency dependence experienced by host genotypes, and thereby gives rise to shorter cycles more likely to produce sustained polymorphism at loci controlling the host's defenses. Indeed, under various kinds of simplifying assumptions it all but eliminates the need even to model the actual dynamics of the parasite population, which can be represented as a simple phenomenological frequency dependence of the genotypic fitnesses of the host population, perhaps with a short time delay. This is the route taken by many "host–parasite" models, especially those that focus on the possible advantages of sex and recombination in the host (e.g., Hamilton, 1980, 1982; Hamilton et al., 1981; Hutson and Law, 1981; May and Anderson, 1983a,b; May, 1985). In some models this process of abstraction is carried even farther, and the parasite population is represented as a regime of *externally* imposed alternating fitness differences among the various host genotypes (e.g., Eshel and Hamilton, 1984; Kirkpatrick, 1985).

Hamilton (1980, 1982) and Hamilton et al. (1981) explore one-locus diploid and two-locus haploid models with phenomenological negative frequency dependences of the form

$$W_i = \exp[d(1-xp_i)]$$

where d is a parameter that sets the strength of the frequency dependence, x is the number of different genotypes (two or four), and p_i is the frequency of genotype i, either in the present generation or in the previous one. May and Anderson (1983b) examine similar models in which the fitnesses are derived from standard epidemiological models for infectious microparasites such as viruses and bacteria. Parameter values corresponding to mild frequency dependence tend to give stable polymorphic equilibria, but more extreme values give rise to two-point cycles and, in some cases, to higher-order cycles and finally chaos (see also May, 1985).

In the two-locus haploid models, these cycles may involve alternating coefficients of linkage disequilibrium, where an excess of coupling gametes (AB and ab) in one generation is followed by an excess of repulsion gametes (Ab and aB) in the next, without any gene-frequency changes at all! Here the advantage of recombination is easy to see, since it allows the common (favored) genotypes in one generation to produce, among their progeny, reasonably large numbers of the rare (disfavored) genotypes that *will* be favored in the next. As a result, the geometric mean fitness of a sexual population can be much larger than that of the corresponding asexual population. In effect, the sexual population "hedges its bets" by *retarding* the rate at which its *genotype* frequencies respond to selection. These models are extremely artificial, but they show that intense frequency dependence can generate temporally varying linkage disequilibria of the kind that may strongly and persistently favor recombination (Charlesworth, 1976; Hutson and Law, 1981; see also Bell and Maynard Smith, 1987).

But if the frequency dependence is not so extreme, so that the host's genotype frequencies cycle only weakly or not at all, then recombination may actually be selected against. To see why, consider again the two-locus haploid model with four genotypes (AB, Ab, aB, and ab) and suppose that the fitnesses of these genotypes are identically frequency dependent according to a scheme such as the one mentioned above, so that there is a stable polymorphic equilibrium with all four genotypes present in equal frequencies. Then there will be no linkage disequilibrium and no advantage (or disadvantage) to recombination. But if the pattern of frequency dependence is made less symmetrical, so that the equilibrium genotype frequencies are *not* in linkage equilibrium, then recombination will tend to generate too many of the genotypes with the lower equilibrium frequencies, and modifiers of recombination that tighten linkage will tend to be favored by selection (e.g., Feldman and Libermann, 1986; Felsenstein, in this volume). Indeed, a mixture of four asexual clones would easily keep itself at the equilibrium frequencies, and given the sex ratio advantage discussed above, such a mixture would overwhelm even a nonrecombining sexual population.

In all of the models discussed so far, the negative frequency dependence of fitnesses is caused by the presumed complementary specificity of the interactions between hosts and parasites. From the point of view of an individual host, it is bad to be common because the parasites best able to evade your defenses are themselves likely to be common. With two alleles at each of two loci, no genotype can remain rare for long. We need to ask whether any qualitatively new behavior is likely to arise in more complex models that permit real rarity, which is to say, in models with many alleles at each of many loci.

Given an overall pattern of negatively frequency-dependent genotypic fitnesses and a very large population size, it is clear that (1) many alleles could be maintained at each locus, and (2) a system that involved several loci in the determination of the host's defensive phenotype might have great advantages over a system that involved only one or two loci. Under these assumptions the number of functionally distinct host genotypes might be very large. In an infinite world this would make no difference; a cloud of clones, each at low frequency, would still defeat an equivalent sexual species, as long as the dynamics of interaction between host and parasite did not give rise to vigorous cycling. But in a finite world there are limits to the number of genotypes that can be maintained, even in the absence of cycling, in either a sexual or an asexual population. In particular, rare asexual clones are always at risk of going extinct (Treisman, 1976). Rare sexual genotypes may also disappear, of course, but if their constituent alleles remain in the population, then they can be recreated in subsequent generations. As is often remarked, only in a sexual population can every individual be unique. With respect to defense against parasites there may be no particular advantage in being unique, but there may be great benefit in being very rare.

Will a recombining sexual population actually maintain the multilocus allelic diversity required to give it an average genotypic diversity greater than that maintained by an equivalent asexual population of the same finite size? Intuition suggests that it should, but many intuitively reasonable arguments about recombination have turned out to be wrong. Here one might also imagine that in a system with many loci, each individual locus is so unimportant that it could easily slide into monomorphism if unconstrained by linkage to other, functionally related loci (e.g., Lewontin, 1964b, 1980; Franklin and Lewontin, 1970). To explore this question we constructed the simplest possible Monte Carlo simulation of a finite population subject to frequency-dependent selection with respect to an eight-locus, two-allele haploid genotype. Each of the 256 possible genotypes is assumed to determine a unique phenotype, with a fitness inversely proportional to its frequency. For a wide range of population sizes, rates of mutation or migration, and strengths of selection, more genotypic diversity is maintained under sexual than under asexual reproduction, and this is reflected in higher average fitnesses of the sexual populations. The disparity in genotypic diversity (and hence average fitness) between sexual and asexual reproduction becomes very large for population sizes on the order of 100. Some typical results are shown in Table 1, with the model described more fully in the legend.

In summary, the dynamics of host–parasite interaction tend to give an advantage to rare host genotypes, under the usual assumption that coevolution between host and parasite tends to produce complementary attack and defense phenotypes. But this advantage of rarity may or may not cause large amounts of variation to accumulate in the host, depending on many details of the life histories, population structures, and genetic systems of both species. The relative generation time of the parasite, its mode of transmission, its average virulence, and its effect on the population density of the host have all been identified as important variables, as has the host's ability to mount immune reactions. But polymorphism can apparently be maintained if there is some degree of complementarity between the genotypes of host and parasite, and if there exist one or more complicating factors sufficient to prevent runaway cycling of the kind that leads to effective monomorphism.

Before looking more closely at the ways in which parasite-induced polymorphisms might give an advantage to sexual reproduction, we will briefly

TABLE 1. Equilibrium genotypic diversities and average fitnesses in an eight-locus simulation of frequency-dependent selection[a]

N	m	Reproductive System	Average Number of Genotypes	Average Genotypic Diversity	Average Fitness
1024	10^{-3}	sex	222	131	0.99
		asex	68	34	0.97
	10^{-5}	sex	201	108	0.99
		asex	18	16	0.94
256	10^{-3}	sex	96	56	0.98
		asex	21	13	0.92
	10^{-5}	sex	60	37	0.97
		asex	8	7	0.86
64	10^{-3}	sex	25	15	0.93
		asex	8	6	0.82
	10^{-5}	sex	8	7	0.85
		asex	3	3	0.66

[a]The model species is either hermaphroditic or asexual. There are 256 possible genotypes (eight haploid loci, each with two alleles). The fitness of each genotype is $W_i = 1 - p_i$. The distribution of progeny sizes is Poisson. N is the total population size, and m (or migration) is the mutation rate per locus per generation. Each set of conditions was run to approximate equilibrium (1000 generations), and then the number of genotypes present, the genotypic diversity, and the mean fitness was calculated every 20 generations, for the next 200. Each number given in the table is the average of these 11 figures, averaged again over four independent runs. Genotypic diversity is calculated as $1/\Sigma p^2$. Results were highly consistent within and between runs.

mention (without attempting to review) the various lines of evidence indicating that such polymorphisms exist.

Evidence

Complementary "gene-for-gene" systems appear to be fairly common in certain crop plants and their fungal pathogens (e.g., Flor, 1956; see Day, 1974; Barrett, 1983, 1985; Bell, 1985; Bremermann 1985). These systems motivate most of the fully coevolutionary models that have been published to date. Barrett (1985) argues that these systems are usually more complicated and less symmetrical than is commonly believed and that the equivalent systems in undomesticated species are even messier. Thus a one-to-one relationship between genes in the host and genes in the parasite is an extreme instance of relationships that are probably more often one-to-many, many-to-one, or even many-to-many (i.e., fully polygenic on both sides). But even though the genetics of these systems are usually more complicated than the simple gene-for-gene hypothesis would suggest, phenotypes still tend to exhibit complementary specificity.

Variation in innate resistance to protozoans and helminths has been documented for several animal species, especially mice (see Hamilton, 1982; May and Anderson, 1983a,b; Holmes, 1983; Blackwell, 1985; Wakelin, 1985a,b; Wassom, 1985; Sher et al., 1986), but in only a few animal systems is there yet any evidence for the complementarity that motivates the models discussed above (e.g., Benjamin and Briles, 1985). Several genetic complexes assumed on functional grounds to affect disease resistance are notoriously polymorphic (e.g., HLA in human beings), and there is epidemiological and other genetic evidence that different genotypes may vary in their susceptibility to different diseases (for entries to the literature on HLA, see Ryder et al., 1981; Thomson, 1981; Bodmer, 1986a,b; Hedrick et al., 1986). But showing that a system is polymorphic, or even that there is variation for resistance, is not the same as showing that the polymorphism is maintained by frequency-dependent interactions with particular species of parasites (Levin et al., 1982). It may be difficult to imagine what *else* could be maintaining all that polymorphism, but as yet there seems to be little direct evidence, even of the limited sort that exists for crop plants and their fungal pathogens.

At the phenotypic level there is abundant evidence of negative frequency dependence, mainly from experiments on grasses (e.g., Allard and Adams, 1969; Antonovics and Ellstrand, 1984; see Bell, 1985). Although these experiments show clearly that individuals may be fitter when surrounded by unrelated nearest neighbors than when surrounded by close relatives, for the most part they say nothing about the mechanisms generating the frequency dependence. There are, however, a few experiments showing that mixtures of inbred lines may suffer less damage from pathogens than do monocultures (Barrett, 1981), and suggesting that this may be one reason for their superior yields (Wolfe and Barrett, 1980; Wolfe et al., 1981).

Many patterns in the geographical distribution of plant breeding systems and animal parthenogenesis conform to the general expectation that sex and recombination should be most valuable in stable, biotically rich environments, and least valuable in physically harsh, disturbed, or otherwise biotically impoverished environments (e.g., Ghiselin, 1974; Levin, 1975; Glesener and Tilman, 1978; Maynard Smith, 1978; Bell, 1982, 1985; but see Lynch, 1984, for a critique). This association is consistent with the view that parasites are most troublesome in biotically rich environments (e.g., in the tropics), but it is also consistent with the view that sex is an adaptation to straightforward competitive and prey–predator interactions.

Annual plants are more often self-pollinating or apomictic than are perennials (Levin, 1975). This is consistent with the idea that perennials should be more troubled by parasites than should annuals, because they are easier to find and have longer generation times. But perennials should also be more troubled by competitors, so again the comparative evidence tends to be ambiguous.

The strongest evidence of complementary coadaptation between hosts and parasites in nature comes from the work of Edmunds and Alstad (1978, 1981) on the black pine leaf scale, a homopteran that infests Douglas fir and several species of pines in western North America. Scales show limited dispersal, and they are completely sedentary once settled on a host. Adjacent trees often differ enormously in their total load of scales, but most trees become more seriously infested as they grow older. Through a series of reciprocal transplantation experiments, Edmunds and Alstad have shown that the increased infestation of older trees is explained mainly by the local adaptation of their indigenous populations of scales, and not by a general weakening of defenses with age.

Scales are haplodiploid (males are haploid, and females diploid). Alstad and Edmunds (1983) show that where two adjacent trees touch each other, the sex ratio tends to be lower than it is on the opposite sides of the same trees. Alstad and Edmunds interpret this as evidence of "outbreeding depression" caused by gene flow between the two populations of scales, each of which is better adapted to its own host than to the other; males, being haploid, are expected to suffer worse from the effect than are females. Pines and firs defend themselves with extremely complex and individually variable mixtures of terpenes and other toxic compounds (e.g., Sturgeon, 1979), so it is possible that scales benefit by adjusting their own defenses to the particular mixtures produced by their host trees. In principle, this hypothesis could be tested experimentally.

On balance, the existing evidence is favorable to the idea that parasites are often a cause of polymorphism at loci controlling certain aspects of the defenses of their hosts, but it is not yet decisive as to the generality or the importance of the phenomenon. The main problem is that different kinds of evidence tend to come from different systems—genetics here, population biology there, physiology somewhere else. When the chain of causation has been tied together at all these levels for even one system, the fragmentary evidence from other systems will probably seem more coherent, and thus more compelling, than it does at present.

POLYMORPHISM AND SEX

Given polymorphism, there remains the question as to how it favors sex and recombination. As Felsenstein (1985, and in this volume) has emphasized, recombination accomplishes only one thing: the reduction of linkage disequilibrium. If this is to be advantageous, then there must be epistatic fitness interactions between loci whose linkage disequilibria periodically change sign, either because of drift or because of changing patterns of selection.

Complementary attack and defense interactions of parasites and hosts could generate epistasis on the fitness scale, but we are not aware that this has ever been demonstrated, even in the well-studied gene-for-gene systems. To the extent that rarity per se is favored, epistasis is almost guaranteed, since particular combinations of alleles may be very rare even if each of the constituent alleles is itself fairly common. This would seem to be, at least in principle, a special strength of the host–parasite hypothesis.

Fluctuating disequilibria can easily be generated by random drift, giving rise to the "Fisher–Muller" version of host–parasite coevolution, as exemplified by the simple model discussed earlier and illustrated in Table 1. Because host–parasite models have an innate tendency to cycle, the perturbations caused by sampling in finite populations may also set off spiraling gene-frequency changes that generate additional, selectively induced linkage disequilibria, even where the interactions are not of a form that would sustain such cycles in the absence of stochastic perturbations (Figure 2). These selectively induced linkage disequilibria would also change over time, depending on the phase of the cycle at which the population found itself, propelled by a combination of random and deterministic forces. No such effects are seen in the stochastic model described above and illustrated in Table 1, because the parasite population is represented implicitly by a simple fixed pattern of negatively frequency-dependent genotypic fitnesses in the host. A finite-population model with evolving parasites would be very difficult to analyze, but might prove interesting. In any event, such a model would apparently be one in which randomly induced and selectively induced linkage disequilibria were inseparably entwined; it would therefore be simultaneously a Fisher–Muller model *and* a Sturtevant–Mather model, in Felsenstein's taxonomy.

In an infinite population governed entirely by deterministic dynamics, cycles giving rise to changing linkage disequilibria can also be sustained, as emphasized by Hamilton (1980, 1982, 1986), but the interactions between host and parasite need to be stronger than they do in the case of a finite population. Extreme parameter values are needed to generate two-fold fitness advantages for sexual reproduction in the simple two-locus models studied to date, but more complicated multilocus or multiallele models are likely to produce large advantages for sex under reasonable assumptions about the fitness differences associated with different host genotypes (May and Anderson, 1983b; Weinshall, 1986). In principle, several independent mechanisms, each of which produced a small advantage for sex and recombination, could be combined to produce a cumulative advantage of almost any desired size. This argument applies to all kinds of mechanisms, not just those defending hosts against parasites. But the members of a typical species probably face parasitic threats from several quarters, and the defenses involved seem likely to be at least partly distinct from each other.

Where sex involves active mate choice it can do more than reduce linkage disequilibria. In theory it can actually *generate* linkage disequilibria, but more plausibly, it can change gene frequencies. If hosts and parasites are engaged in coevolutionary gene frequency cycles of intermediate length and severity, then much of the time there is likely to be heritable variation for fitness within the host population (Eshel and Hamilton, 1984). Hamilton (1980, 1982) has argued that under these circumstances, females in polygynous species might benefit from attempting to choose mates that were relatively free of parasites, and thus relatively likely to have genotypes conferring above-average resistance to the currently dominant strains of parasites. Kirkpatrick (1985) describes a three-locus model in which female choice for a "showy" male trait that reveals parasite burdens can be driven to fixation, under an externally imposed regime of alternating selection at the locus controlling resistance. Such a pattern of female choice might pay part of the cost of sex in polygynous species (which tend to suffer the full twofold cost because they typically have no male parental invest-ment), but it is not clear how large the benefit might actually be, since the best resistance genotypes are being favored by natural selection anyway.

Regardless of the extent to which female choice could help to pay the cost of sex, it provides an opportunity to test specific hypotheses that arise as impli-cations of the more general hypothesis that host–parasite interactions generate heritable fitness differences. For example, Hamilton and Zuk (1982) and Read (1987) show that brightly colored bird species tend to carry more genera of blood parasites than do duller species, as might be expected if sexual selection tends to be relatively strong in species that are relatively prone to infection. Like most comparative studies, this one cannot rule out alternative schemes of causation, but these can be examined experimentally, and several such experi-ments are now under way or soon to be reported (e.g., Zuk, in press; J. A. Endler, personal communication).

SUMMARY

Selectively important linkage disequilibria involving loci that affect the inter-actions between hosts and parasites could be caused either by selection or by drift (or both), and they could vary either in time or in space (or both). Thus parasites, as agents of selection, are not tied even in principle to any particular category of models for the evolution of sex and recombination. As Bell (1985) points out, they could play as important a role in Tangled Bank models (which emphasize spatial variation) as they do in Red Queen models (which emphasize temporal variation). The asymmetry would appear to lie in the greater depen-dence of Red Queen models on a role for parasites, since it is difficult to imagine what other selective agency could provide sufficiently large and rapidly changing fitness differences, involving epistatically interacting loci.

There remain many interesting theoretical issues to be explored, particularly those involving realistic details of host and parasite life histories (both of which can be very complicated), in the context of fully coevolutionary treatments of the dynamics of both species or, even better, *several* species of hosts and parasites (see Hamilton, 1986). These models will be frighteningly complex. Artful simplifications will undoubtedly be the key to making their behavior understand-able.

But the main need, as we see it, is for more evidence concerning the actual interactions between hosts and parasites, at both the individual and the population levels. In particular, it seems important to know much more than we do about the costs of various attack and defense mechanisms, ideally for both members of a pair of interacting species (but see Levin and Lenski, 1983, 1985, for bacteria and viruses), and it also seems important to know how far we can generalize from the complementary genetic systems of plants and their fungal parasites (Barrett, 1985). Without such evidence there are too few constraints on models intended to answer questions about the amounts of ecologically significant polymorphism that might be maintained by host–parasite interactions. Many of the relevant experiments are ecological and evolutionary in scope, so they will require large population sizes and large numbers of generations. Levin et al. (1982) consider the kinds of experimental systems that are most likely to prove both tractable and useful for these purposes.

By contrast, there seem to be few limits (other than imagination and knowledge of natural history) on the number of potentially testable comparative predictions that could be generated from the basic premise that host and parasite may be engaged in a fast-moving coevolutionary struggle. For example, if infections tend to spread in epidemic fashion within large social insect colonies, then we might expect social species to engage more frequently in multiple mating, and to have higher rates of recombination, than do their solitary relatives (Tooby, 1982; Hamilton, 1987; Sherman et al., in press). For similar reasons, butterfly species that live at low population densities might be expected, other things being equal, to distribute their eggs singly or in small groups among a large number of host plants, rather than piling them together on a few plants, where there is greater risk that an epidemic could take hold among a large group of relatively homozygous and genetically similar siblings. We expect that many interesting new predictions will soon be made concerning the ecological and demographic correlates of mating systems in various groups of plants and animals. Comparative studies will not address the quantitative questions that arise from the abstract theory, but they may nonetheless derive a great deal of power from the way they exploit distinctive features of the biologies of particular groups of organisms.

After this was written, Burt and Bell (1987) reported that excess chiasma frequency in the males of 24 species of undomesticated mammals is positively correlated with age of sexual maturity. Excess chiasma frequency is defined as the total number of chiasmata in excess of one per bivalent. The raw correlation is very strong ($r = 0.88$), as is the partial correlation taking out the effect of body size ($r = 0.69$). Neither excess chiasma frequency nor age of maturity is correlated with chromosome number, and excess chiasma frequency is negatively correlated with litter size. Burt and Bell interpret this pattern as evidence "that crossing-over may function to combat antagonists with short generation times but does not function to reduce sib competition."

This hypothesis is similar in spirit to the one mentioned above, concerning the recombination rates of social insects and their solitary relatives, with life span in mammals playing the role of colony size in insects. In each case, the factor expected to promote recombination is one that is expected to make the species a relatively easy target for fast-evolving pathogens. Social insects appear to have higher chromosome numbers than their solitary relatives (Sherman 1979, Seger 1983), but Burt and Bell (1987) find no evidence that chromosome number is related to age at maturity in mammals. It will be interesting to see whether this apparent inconsistency between the two groups of organisms can eventually be resolved, and whether similar patterns can be found in other groups.

CHAPTER 12

THE EVOLUTION OF SEX IN BACTERIA

Bruce R. Levin

INTRODUCTION

If one defines sex to include all processes where genes from separate sources recombine in a single organism, bacteria are sexual. Indeed, from this qualitative perspective, bacteria are particularly sexy organisms. Not only are they able to exchange genes with each other, their communities abound with viruses, plasmids, and naked DNA carrying genes that they can pick up and express. In addition to their capacity for acquiring chromosomal genes by homologous recombination, there are at least two mechanisms by which recombination can occur without extensive homology, thus opening the possibility of sex between phylogenetically distant organisms. Finally, genes acquired by infection with plasmids and temperate phage can be permanently maintained and expressed without ever becoming incorporated into the bacterial chromosome.

In this chapter I (1) describe the major variations on the theme of sex observed in bacteria, (2) present and critically evaluate some hypotheses for the evolution and maintenance of these mechanisms for mixing genetic material from different sources, and (3) consider the role of sex in the adaptation and evolution of bacteria.

My emphasis (bias if you like) is evolutionary mechanisms, that is, population processes and selection pressures, rather than evolutionary history. For a consideration of the latter, I suggest the books by Bell (1982) and Margulis and Sagan (1986). While I have tried to be comprehensive in my treatment of the biology of bacterial sex, whenever possible I have avoided consideration of the

194

more molecular details of recombination. For these, the reader can consult the chapter by Devoret in this volume and the review articles by Bennett (1985) and Radding (1985).

I have restricted this consideration to recombination between genes borne on the chromosomes of bacteria. Not considered are recombination among the plasmids, phage, and transposons that infect bacteria, or bacteria acquiring and maintaining of genes that are permanently on these accessory genetic elements. This restriction in scope is, to some extent, arbitrary and done to limit the length of this chapter. The plasmids, phage, and transposons that infect bacteria can be considered prokaryotes and do recombine with each other as well as with their host's chromosome. Much of bacterial adaptation is through the expression of genes borne on accessory genetic elements (Falkow, 1975; Reanny, 1976; Broda, 1979; Campbell, 1981), and recombination among these elements is certainly important for their evolution. However, there is also a more academic justification for this restriction of the scope of this chapter. The use of accessory element–borne genes for bacterial adaptation is more akin to symbiosis than to sex in the sense that it is treated in the rest of this volume. That coevolutionary process has, to some extent, been considered in Levin and Lenski (1983).

SEX IN BACTERIA

Sex in bacteria is not tied to reproduction. Genes are acquired by infection by one of three basic mechanisms: *transformation, conjugation,* and *transduction.* With transformation, free DNA is taken up by the bacterium and incorporated into its genome. Conjugation is a more intimate process, with the transfer of genes requiring contact between a donor and a recipient cell. In transduction, the movement of genetic material between cells is accomplished by bacterio-phage vectors that pick up DNA from a donor cell and transmit it to a recipient.

There are at least three mechanisms by which donor DNA can be incorporated into the recipient chromosome: homologous recombination, site-specific recombination, or transposition. In *Escherichia coli,* homologous ("legitimate") recombination requires sequences of a minimum of 20 identical base pairs between the donor and recipient DNAs, with the rate of recombination increasing exponentially up through 74 base pairs and linearly beyond that (Watt et al., 1985). For site-specific recombination and transposition little (or possibly no) homology is required ("illegitimate recombination") (Lewin, 1985). Homologous recombination is mediated by enzymes that also function in the repair of replicating DNA, such as the *rec*A, B, and C enzymes of *E. coli* (see chapters by Devoret and Bernstein et al., in this volume). Site-specific recombination and transposition are catalyzed by enzymes whose function appears to be specific for the insertion of defined sequences of DNA, such as the genomes of temperate phage, *prophage,* or transposable elements, into other DNA molecules (Lewin, 1985).

Transformation

The first real (genetic) evidence for sex in bacteria was for transformation in pneumococcus (now *Streptococcus pneumoniae*) (Griffith, 1928). Mice injected with either a living culture of a virulent, noncapsulated (rough, R) strain of pneumococcus or a heat-killed culture of a virulent, capsulated (smooth, S) strain, generally remained healthy. When injected with mixtures of living R and heat-killed S, they often acquired a lethal pneumonia. The bacteria isolated from afflicted mice that had been injected with mixtures of R and heat-killed S were of the virulent, capsulated, S phenotype. Subsequent studies demonstrated that this transformation from rough to smooth could be obtained in vitro, by treating living R cells with sterile extracts of heat-killed S, from which all cells and cell debris had been removed. In a now classic study, Avery, MacLeod, and McCarty (1944) demonstrated that the biologically active component of the pneumococcus R–S transforming material, "consists principally, if not solely, of a highly polymerized, viscous form of deoxyribonucleic acid."

Transformation occurs naturally (under physiologically realistic conditions) in some members of both the Gram-positive and Gram-negative eubacteria, the two major classes. Among the Gram-positive bacteria, transformation of chromosomal genes has been most extensively studied in *Streptococcus pneumoniae*, *Streptococcus sanguis*, and *Bacillus subtilis*. For the Gram-negative bacteria, much of what is known about the mechanisms of transformation has come from studies with *Hemophilus influenzae* and *Hemophilus parainfluenzae*. (For recent reviews of transformation, see Smith et al., 1981; Stewart and Carlson, 1986.)

To facilitate its description it is convenient to divide the transformation process into four stages: (1) the development of *competence* (the capacity to take up exogenous DNA), (2) the binding of DNA to the cell surface, (3) the uptake of DNA by the recipient, and (4) the integration of that DNA into the recipient chromosome (Figure 1). For naturally transforming bacteria, the development of competence is an active and complex process involving substantial changes

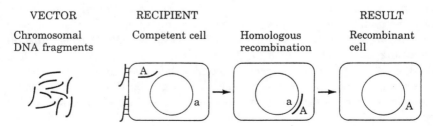

VECTOR	RECIPIENT		RESULT
Chromosomal DNA fragments	Competent cell	Homologous recombination	Recombinant cell

FIGURE 1. Gene transfer by picking up free DNA (natural transformation). The bacterial cell wall is indicated by a rectangle and its genome by a circle. The normal substrate of transformation is thought to be double-stranded linear DNA in the environment. Competent cells bind the DNA and take it up (see text for details). Once inside the cell, the picked-up DNA may be permanently incorporated into the recipient chromosome by homologous recombination.

in cell chemistry and morphology. Competence is generally induced by changes in growth conditions of a sort that could be interpreted as the decay of or dramatic changes in environmental conditions, such as shifts to media that do not support growth.

In the Gram-positive bacteria there seem to be proteins with receptor-like functions, but no apparent DNA-sequestering structures on the cell surfaces. In Gram-negative transforming bacteria such as Hemophilus there are specific DNA uptake organelles, "blebs" (or more formally, transformasomes) that form on cell surfaces upon the induction of competence. In the Gram-positive bacteria, such as naturally transforming Bacillus, long pieces of double-stranded DNA bind to the cell surface and are cleaved into shorter lengths (about 13 kilobases) before uptake. In the Bacillus all double-stranded DNA molecules can bind and, presumably, are equally capable of being taken up by the cell. In the Hemophilus there are specific recognition (uptake) sites, consisting of 11 base pair sequences, that substantially augment the likelihood of a DNA molecule being taken up. The Hemophilus genome has approximately 600 of these uptake sites, much greater than the two or three that would be expected by chance alone.

In *B. subtilis*, *S. pneumoniae*, and *S. sanguis*, only one strand is taken up by the cell, with the other being released into the environment or destroyed by exonucleases associated with the cell envelope. The single-stranded DNA molecules entering the cytoplasm are bound to specific proteins. In Hemophilus, relatively short lengths of double-stranded DNA are taken into the blebs and then injected into the cytoplasm as single-stranded molecules, with the other strand being degraded and released into the medium. All naturally transforming bacteria have procedures for handling DNA, such as bringing it in as single strands or keeping double-stranded molecules in blebs, that have the effect of protecting these genetic molecules from degradation by cellular endonucleases.

Although there are differences in some of the details, once the single-stranded DNA molecules enter the cytoplasmic space, the mechanisms for their integration into the genome appear to be similar for both Gram-positive and Gram-negative bacteria. These short single-stranded molecules are thought to form triplexes with homologous regions of the chromosome. Some of these triplexes then turn into heteroduplexes in which the donor strand has replaced a segment of the recipient DNA (for an alternative model, see LeClerc and Setlow, 1974). By standard DNA replication the heteroduplexes thus formed give rise to homoduplexes with regions of exogenous DNA. These are the transformants. In both these groups of bacteria, the integration of exogenous DNA involves *rec*A-like recombination pathways.

Conjugation

While bacterial cells in apparently intimate contact had been seen by a number of micrographic voyeurs, the first genetic evidence for sex via conjugation was obtained by Lederberg and Tatum (1946a,b). An auxotrophic mutant of *E. coli*

K-12 that required biotin and methionine (B^-, M^-, P^+, T^+) and another that required threonine and proline (B^+, M^+, P^-, T^-) were mixed and allowed to grow in a media that permitted the growth of both clones. When these mixtures were plated on a selective media (one that required synthesis of these vitamins and amino acids for growth), stable prototrophic clones (B^+, M^+, P^+, T^+) were isolated. Since these prototrophs could not be isolated from single clone cultures, Lederberg and Tatum concluded that they were produced by recombination rather than mutation. Since recombinants did not obtain when the auxotrophic mutants were mixed with sterile filtrates of the strains that produced recombinants in mixed culture, they concluded that this form of sex required some sort of cell–cell contact, that is, conjugation, rather than transformation.

It took almost ten years of intensive work before the current view of *E. coli* sex mediated by conjugation was elucidated (Jacob and Wollman, 1961). Still, 40 years after the first observations by Lederberg and Tatum, there are many unanswered questions about the nature of conjugation, especially at the molecular level (Clark, 1985). Nevertheless, for *E. coli* (the species in which conjugation has been most extensively studied), the major details of recombination via conjugation are now known. (For general reviews of this literature, see Willetts and Wilkins, 1984; Willetts, 1985; and Clark, 1985.)

The capacity of *E. coli* K-12 to transfer chromosomal genes by conjugation, the conjugation organelles (sex pili), and the variety of changes in the donor cell surface associated with the transfer process are determined by genes carried by a conjugative plasmid denoted F (for fertility factor). This plasmid is permanently derepressed for conjugative pili synthesis (Willetts, 1985) and carries a series of transposable elements that are also present on the K-12 chromosome. An autonomous F plasmid can mediate its own transfer (Figure 2A,) or, more rarely, by *recA*-dependent, homologous recombination, it can enter the bacterial chromosome. The integration of the plasmid and chromosome, forming a state known as an "Hfr" (high-frequency recombination), can occur in a number of places along the circular *E. coli* chromosome (Figure 2B).

For *E. coli* maintained in well-agitated liquid culture, conjugation appears to occur by random contact between plasmid-bearing and plasmid-free cells (Levin et al., 1979). The sex pilus serves either as the bridge for the transfer of donor DNA (as suggested in Figure 2) or as an embracing organelle that brings the participants into intimate contact. Only a single strand of DNA moves to the recipient, with the transfer process being accompanied by DNA synthesis. Transfer is polar, originating with a specific sequence on F, not surprisingly known as the origin of transfer (*ori*T), and immediately followed by the regions of the F plasmid associated with replication. The genes responsible for the self-transmissibility of the plasmid enter the recipient last. In integrated plasmid–chromosomes, the entire bacterial chromosome (about $50 \times$ the length of F) separates the origin of transfer from the genes required for conjugation. As a result of environmental turbulence and other tribulations of pair-bonding, the

DONOR   RECIPIENT   RESULT

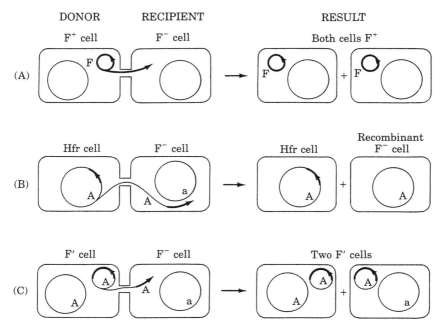

FIGURE 2. Gene transfer mediated by F plasmid–determined conjugation. Heavy lines represent the plasmid genome; light circles, the host chromosome. The origin of conjugative DNA transfer is indicated by an arrowhead. Donor and recipient cells are shown in the process of conjugation, joined by the pilus. (A) F plasmid conjugation. Only a copy of the F plasmid is transferred. (B) Hfr-mediated host gene transfer. The F plasmid of the donor is integrated into the host chromosome. During conjugation, a copy of a portion of the donor chromosome is transferred to the recipient, where it may replace parts of the recipient chromosome by homologous recombination. (C) F′-mediated host gene transfer. A fragment of the bacterial chromosome is carried on the F′ plasmid. A copy of the entire F′ plasmid is transferred by conjugation. The recipient becomes diploid (merozygous) for the chromosomal genes carried on the F′ plasmid, which can be maintained as an independent element.

complete F plasmid in an Hfr donor is rarely transferred to the recipient. One consequence of this is that the transmitted DNA is generally incapable of autonomous replication or of mediating its own transfer.

Occasionally, the F plasmid of an Hfr will excise from the chromosome, become an autonomous element once again, and bring host genes with it. In that state this plasmid is known as an F prime (F′) factor and can transmit the genes it picked up as well as itself (Figure 2C). The recipients of these F′ factors will be converted into donors and will be heterozygous for the chromosomal regions borne on the F′ plasmid. The F′ plasmid can (1) be maintained in this autonomous state, or (2) become incorporated into the host chromosome (now with a bias for integration into the region of homology with the chromosomal segment it picked up), or (3) the chromosomal region borne by the plasmid can replace the homologous region on the host chromosome.

Conjugative plasmids other than F are capable of mediating chromosomal gene transfer (Cooke and Meynell, 1969). While the mechanisms by which these other plasmids mobilize host genes have not been as well studied as those for F, it seems reasonable to anticipate that they are similar.

Transduction

In an effort to ascertain how common sex is among the bacteria, Zinder and Lederberg (1952) performed experiments with strains of *Salmonella typhimurium* that were analogous to those Lederberg and Tatum had done with *E. coli* K-12. The results of these experiments were positive, in that they obtained evidence for the transfer and stable persistence of traits from one clone to another. However, the Salmonella recombination results differed from those of *E. coli* in two ways: only one trait was transmitted to individual recipient cells, and the transfer could be mediated by "filterable agents," that is, it did not require cell–cell contact. Since the agent responsible for the infectious transfer of donor genes was still effective when treated with deoxyribonuclease (DNAase), transformation of the sort observed for pneumococcus was ruled out. Since "weakly lytic phages" were involved in the production of the agent responsible for the gene transfers, and the gene transferring substance seemed to be particulate (could be removed with 0.1-micron filters), Zinder and Lederberg suggested that phage could function as the "passive carriers of the genetic material," *transduce* genes from one bacterium to another. Later studies indicted that the DNAase-resistant filterable agent responsible for this transduction in *Salmonella typhimurium* was the bacteriophage P22.

In the contemporary view, transduction is of two classes, generalized and specialized (Figures 3B and 3C, respectively). The P22-mediated transduction observed by Zinder and Lederberg is an example of the former; virtually any chromosomal gene can be moved. In specialized transduction, the only host genes transmitted are those adjacent to the site at which the *prophage*, the latent form of the *temperate* bacteriophage vector, integrates into the chromosome. Phage that are unable to form stable associations with their hosts, and kill as a necessary part of their reproductive cycle (*virulent*, or *lytic*, phage) (Figure 3A), can also serve as vehicles for the generalized transduction of host genes, as can some temperate phage. Two conditions seem to be required for generalized transduction: the host DNA has to remain intact during phage development and the phage must have the capacity to package host DNA molecules. (For recent reviews of bacterial transduction, see Masters, 1985; Smith, 1985.)

Generalized and specialized transduction differ in the way the transducing particle is formed and the way that the phage DNA is incorporated into the

(A) NORMAL PHAGE INFECTION

(B) GENERALIZED TRANSDUCTION

(C) SPECIALIZED TRANSDUCTION

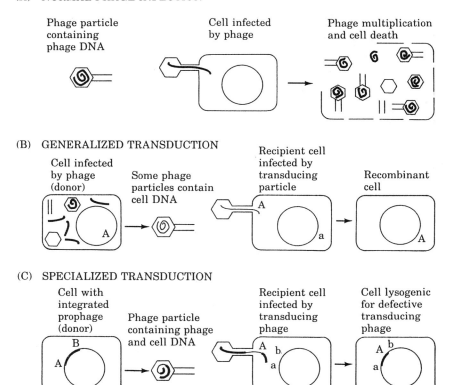

FIGURE 3. Infection and host gene transfer by bacteriophage (transduction). Phage genomes are indicated by heavy lines and bacterial genomes by light lines. (A) Lytic phage replication. The phage particle injects phage DNA into the cell, where its expression leads to the production of progeny phage and cell lysis. (B) Generalized transduction. A small fraction of the progeny phage particles contain random fragments of host DNA instead of phage DNA. These particles can inject this bacterial DNA into new cells, where it may replace resident genes by homologous recombination. (C) Specialized transduction by integrating (temperate) phage. During the induction of a lysogen, as a consequence of imperfect excision of the prophage, part of the phage genome is replaced with flanking sections of host DNA. When phage carrying these flanking regions of the bacterial chromosome inject that DNA into new hosts, phage-specified, site-specific recombination can insert those bacterial genes into the chromosome of the new host.

recipient chromosome (Masters, 1985). In the case of generalized transduction (Figure 3B), (1) the transducing particles arise during lytic growth, as apparent accidents of DNA packaging, (2) all of the DNA borne by the transducing particle is that of the host, and (3) the replacement of the homologous recipient DNA is by a double crossover mediated by the bacterial *rec* system. In specialized transduction (Figure 3C), (1) the transducing particle arises during the excision of the prophage, (2) in addition to the host DNA, the transducing particle includes a segment of phage DNA in a configuration that does not preclude its ability to lysogenize, and (3) the replacement of the chromosomal DNA is by site-specific integration of the prophage, a process that is independent of the *rec* system.

The number of genes moved in any single transduction event is limited by the capacity of the phage head, that is, the size of the normal phage genome. For the best studied generalized transducing phage, P1 and P22, this is between 1% and 2% of the host genome.

HYPOTHESES FOR THE EVOLUTION OF SEX IN BACTERIA

For reasons that I hope will become apparent to the reader, it is convenient to treat the evolution of vector-mediated (plasmid- and phage-mediated) recombination separately from the evolution of transformation. For both vector-mediated recombination and transformation, I consider four classes of hypotheses: (1) coincidental evolution, (2) parasitic DNA, (3) individual selection for recombination, and (4) group (population-level) selection for recombination. By and large, these hypotheses are variations of those considered by other authors for the evolution of sex in higher organisms. In the case of coincidental evolution, recombination is a by-product of selection for some other character(s) rather than the object of this selection. The hypothesis that recombination is by-product of DNA repair (see Bernstein et al., in this volume) is one of coincidental evolution. With the parasitic DNA hypotheses, sex evolved for the horizontal transfer of those portions of the genome that coded for the machinery needed for this transfer. Hickey and Rose (in this volume) postulate a major role for selection on parasitic DNA sequences in the origins of sex in eukaryotes.

For both the coincidental evolution and the parasitic DNA hypotheses, the advantages of recombination to individual organisms or populations (if any) are secondary and not essential to the evolution of sex. This is not the case for either the individual selection or the group selection hypothesis. In accord with these more classical hypotheses, the generation of new genotypes by recombination in some way augments the rate of survival or reproductive yield of individual organisms or increases the probability of survival or rate of growth and spread of whole populations. These two classes of hypotheses have been considered by a number of authors for the evolution of sex in eukaryotes (see chapters by Brooks, Bell, Crow, Maynard Smith, and Williams, in this volume).

Plasmid- and phage-mediated recombination

Coincidental evolution Plasmid- and phage-mediated recombination of chromosomal genes in bacteria can be explained as a by-product of the infectious transfer of these replicons and the host DNA repair systems (see Levin and Lenski, 1983; Halvorson, 1985; Zinder, 1985; Clark, 1985; Margulis and Sagan, 1986). This mechanism is parsimonious, provides a sufficient explanation for all that is currently known about vector-mediated recombination of bacterial genes, and is consistent with observations about the frequency of recombination in bacteria with vector-mediated recombination. The coincidental evolution hypothesis differs from that of parasitic DNA as considered by Hickey and Rose (in this volume), in that the transfer of host genes is not necessary for the maintenance of plasmid and phage and, as I argue below, is to the disadvantage of these vectors.

The evolution and maintenance of mechanisms for the infectious transfer of conjugative plasmids and virulent and temperate phages can be explained without invoking their role as vectors for the horizontal transmission of host genes (see Levin and Lenski, 1983). The *rec* enzymes responsible for homologous gene recombination are part of an extensive DNA repair system (see Devoret, in this volume). The role of the *rec* genes in maintaining the fidelity of the genetic material provides a seemingly sufficient explanation for their evolution and maintenance.

The mechanisms responsible for forming plasmid–chromosome complexes (Hfrs)—*rec*-mediated, homologous recombination—operate in the absence of vector-mediated recombination (for the repair of DNA). The selective pressures responsible for evolution of temperate phage and the integration of the prophage into bacterial chromosomes (lysogeny) (Stewart and Levin, 1984) provide a sufficient explanation for the evolution of the site-specific recombination. The formation of phage particles carrying host genes adjacent to the site of integration—specialized transducing phage—would be anticipated to occur by accident in course of prophage excision. As long as the bacterial DNA is not destroyed, it seems reasonable to assume that during lytic replication there would be occasional errors where phage heads are filled with segments of host DNA rather than phage DNA. Since the infectious properties of progeny phage is determined by their parental genomes, rather than the genes these progeny phage are carrying (Stent and Calendar, 1979), it is not surprising that phage particles carrying only bacterial genes are capable of adsorbing to bacteria and injecting that DNA.

The relative rates of plasmid transfer and plasmid-mediated, host gene recombination are consistent with the coincidental evolution hypothesis for vector-mediated sex. For an F′ *lac* plasmid in *E. coli* K-12 growing exponentially in broth, the rate constant of plasmid transfer is approximately three orders of magnitude greater than that for the transfer of genes near the *lac* region (*thr* and *leu*) (B. R. Levin and C. Laursen, unpublished data). The proportion of a population of generalized transducing phage such as P1 that carry specific host genes is on the order of 10^{-5}.

If host gene recombination is not the object of the selection leading to the evolution of vector-mediated gene transfer, recombination could be a rare event. This is certainly the case for *E. coli*.

In their original study of recombination, Lederberg and Tatum (1946a,b) examined only a single strain of *E. coli* K-12 and obtained relatively high rates of recombination. In retrospect, their one-try success seems to be more a matter of serendipity (coupled with some classy experiments) rather than the discovery of a ubiquitous and frequent phenomenon. There have been a number of studies of the incidence and frequency of recombination among *E. coli* from natural sources (Cavalli and Heslot, 1949; Lederberg, 1951; Lederberg et al., 1951; Ørskov and Ørskov, 1961). The results of these surveys indicate that (1) donor ability is rare among naturally occurring *E. coli*, and (2) among bacteria capable of serving as donors of host chromosomal genes, the rate at which these genes are transferred is low.

In the Ørskov and Ørskov study, 35% of the 199 distinct serotypes examined served as recipients for Hfr strains of *E. coli* K-12. However, only six of these natural isolates were able to donate chromosomal genes to F⁻ strains of *E. coli* K-12 and seemed to do so at rates substantially lower than K-12 Hfrs. In single experiments, four of these six fertile donors produced less than 50 recombinant colonies and the other two less than 200 on the sampling plate. The majority of the crosses with the *E. coli* K-12 Hfrs produced more than 200 recombinant colonies in cultures of similar densities to those employed for matings with these wild strains. Although there are an abundance of high-molecular-weight, potentially conjugative plasmids in *E. coli* from natural sources (e.g., see Caugant et al., 1981), most naturally occurring self-transmissible plasmids are repressed for conjugative pili syntheses (Watanabe, 1963), which may be one of the reasons for the low rate of recombination with naturally occurring donors (Cooke and Meynell, 1969; but also see Lundquist and Levin, 1986).

The results of enzyme electrophoretic studies of genetic variation in *E. coli* are also consistent with the hypothesis that recombination is a rare event in natural populations of this bacterial species. In spite of a genic diversity of nearly 50%, the same multilocus genotype is frequently isolated from different sources (Selander and Levin, 1980; Caugant et al., 1981, 1983; Ochman and Selander, 1984). Included among these recurrent genotypes are recently isolated *E. coli* strains that are identical, for all 20 loci examined, to *E. coli* K-12 (Selander and Levin, 1980). *E. coli* K-12 was established as a laboratory strain in the 1920s. One explanation for the long-term maintenance of genotypes of these bacteria (the "clone concept"; see Ørskov and Ørskov, 1983) is that the rate at which genes are shuffled by recombination is too low to overcome the purging of variants by random extinction of populations (Maryuama and Kimura, 1980) or periodic selection within populations (Levin, 1981).

Parasitic DNA If all else were equal, it would be to the advantage of a bacterium's genome to infectiously transmit copies of itself to other cells. Thus, it is conceivable that selection would favor bacteria with higher probabilities of transmitting copies of their genomes to the marauding plasmids and phage that infect them. In the case of lytic infections with phage or the induction of prophage, where the cell is fated to die, bailing out by becoming incorporated into the phage genome would provide DNA with a chance for persistence.

I see three problems with this prokaryotic variant of the parasitic DNA hypothesis. First, the genes promoting this promiscuous (and egoistic) behavior would only have an advantage when they themselves are transmitted. In specialized transduction and some plasmid–mediated chromosomal gene transfers (Cooke and Meynell, 1969), there are specific regions of the *E. coli* chromosome that are more likely to be transmitted than others. However, this is more readily explained as a property of the vector than that of specific host genes, especially in view of the low rate at which this gene transfer seems to occur. Second, these expansionist genes would have to replace different genes in the recipient. If these bacterial populations are maintained as colonies or exist in an otherwise physically structured habitat, the most likely recipient of the transfer-promoting genes is going to be a member of the same clone, who already have those genes. Third, although it may be to the advantage of the host genes to be picked up and transmitted by marauding plasmids and phage, as I discuss in the following section, service as vehicles for the movement of host genes is likely to be to the disadvantage of the vector plasmid or phage. Thus, there would be selection against plasmids and phage that are amenable to this kind of host gene opportunism.

Individual selection for recombination Individual selection could lead to the evolution of vector-mediated recombination in at least two nonexclusive ways: (1) by increasing the fitness of the plasmids and phage that serve as vectors for host gene transfer, or (2) by favoring bacteria with increased probabilities of receiving chromosomal genes transmitted by conjugation or phage infection.

From what is known about plasmid- and phage-meditated recombination, it is unlikely that the infectious transfer of host genes will increase the fitness of individual conjugative plasmids or transducing phage. Indeed, the opposite is more likely. In an Hfr (integrated plasmid–chromosome complex), the plasmid genome can be maintained by vegetative reproduction, but its capacity for "overreplication" (Campbell, 1981) by infectious transfer is impaired, as it is rarely transferred in that state. Thus, unless integration into the chromosome substantially reduces the likelihood of plasmid loss by vegetative segregation or, in some yet-to-be-determined way, augments the individual fitness of bacteria carrying a plasmid in its chromosome, selection would not favor plasmid integration.

The transfer of host genes is certainly to the disadvantage of a transducing virus. For most phage responsible for generalized transduction, the viral genome is not carried by the transducing particle (the phage mu and the phenomenon of mini-muduction [Toussaint, 1985] may be an exception). While parts of the prophage of most special transducing viruses may be transmitted to the recipient, in general the entire phage genome is not.

Selection favoring individual bacteria with an enhanced capacity to receive and incorporate chromosomal genes from external sources is a formal possibility. This type of recombination does not engender the twofold cost in the future representation of genome copies that obtains meiotic, anisogamous sex in diploids (Maynard Smith, 1978). One can also concoct (and actually construct) situations where individual recombinant bacteria are more fit than the parental cell types (which is how bacterial genetics is done). However, I see little reason to assume that an increased capacity to receive chromosomal genes from marauding plasmids and phage would, on the average, confer an advantage on individual recipient cells. One could in fact champion the position that the acquisition of a random gene would, on the average, reduce fitness by upsetting adaptive gene combinations that have evolved by clonal selection.

The low rate of vector-mediated recombination itself argues against individual selection favoring the evolution of mechanisms for augmenting the probability of their receiving chromosomal genes. Even if we assume that all genes received enhanced the fitness of the recipient, or that copies of the transfer-promoting regions are particularly likely to be picked up, the fitness differential favoring individuals with enhanced recombination rates would be on the order of the probability of recombination. As discussed earlier, this is low, of a magnitude similar to that of mutation (Selander and Levin, 1980; Levin, 1981).

Group selection for recombination Although generally not favored as a mechanism for evolution, except as a last resort (Fisher, 1958), group or population-level selection is a relatively appealing process for the evolution of sex in bacteria, for the following reasons:

1. From what is known about these processes, it seems that they would not engender much of a cost in the fitness for individual bacteria engaged in this form of sexuality.
2. Although contingent on the nature of the formulation (Kondrashov, 1984; Evans, 1986), there are certainly situations where the capacity to generate variation by recombination would increase the likelihood and rate at which populations adapt to particular habitats.
3. Since they often maintain their populations as colonies of genetically identical cells (clones) that are relatively isolated from other colonies of the same genotype, the physical structure of bacterial populations is particularly amenable to the operation of group selection (for example, see Chao and Levin, 1981).
4. Due to the broad host range of some plasmid and phage vectors and mechanisms for nonhomologous gene recombination, bacteria can acquire chro-

mosomal genes from distantly related species. Thus, when entering new habitats, bacterial clones with the capacity to receive genes from members of the adapted, resident populations may be more likely to become established than bacterial clones without this capacity.

5. Finally, one can produce models in which under broad (and seeming realistic) conditions, group selection can lead to the evolution and persistence of characters in clonal populations, even when those characters engender a disadvantage within populations (Levin, 1986; R. Evans, R. Lenski and B. Levin, in preparation).

Having said all of these favorable things about group selection, and thereby illustrating how open-minded I am, I can now admit to not believing that group selection is the primary mechanism responsible for the evolution and maintenance of plasmid- and phage-mediated recombination. I believe that the coincidental evolution mechanism provides a sufficient explanation for this type of bacterial sexuality. On the other hand, group selection would operate in a synergistic manner with other processes responsible for the evolution of vector-mediated recombination and may provide some positive force for maintaining that form of bacterial sexuality.

The evolution of transformation

Coincidental evolution Even with the modest detail presented earlier in this chapter, it should be apparent that transformation is a complex and highly evolved process in both the Gram-positive and Gram-negative bacteria. However, it is still possible that recombination was not the object of the selection leading to the evolution and maintenance of transformation, but rather a by-product of it. Indeed, as with vector-mediated recombination, the evolution of the processes responsible for the integration of transformed DNA, the *rec* system, can be explained without invoking their role in recombination. But what about the mechanisms for uptake, handling, and transportation of DNA?

One possibility is that bacteria are taking up exogenous DNA as a source of nucleotides or nutrients (Stewart and Carlson, 1986). This seems unlikely for three reasons. (1) In both the Gram-positive and Gram-negative bacteria, DNA is taken up in a manner in which it is not subject to degradation by the cell's restriction endonucleases, that is, as single-stranded molecules or in envelopes (the blebs). Why protect DNA, if it is only going to be degraded anyway? (2) Only one strand of DNA is taken up by Gram-negative bacteria. Although double-stranded DNA is taken in by transforming Gram-negative bacteria such as Hemophilus, one strand seems to be excreted. This would seem to be profligate behavior for an organism that requires nucleotides for growth. (3) In the Hemophilus, there are specific recognition sites (the 11 base pair sequences) that substantially increase the likelihood of taking up DNA from closely related organisms. Yet if the DNA is being used as a supply of nucleotides for nutrition, wouldn't any source be equally good?

Another possibility for the coincidental evolution of transformation is that the exogenous DNA is being used as template to repair damage to cellular DNA. This repair mechanism has been presented as a hypothesis for the evolution of meiotic recombination (see Bernstein et al., 1985a and in this volume) and, on first consideration, is an attractive hypothesis for the evolution of transformation. If it were to the advantage of bacteria to use exogenous DNA as template for the repair of damage to their own DNA, then mechanisms for the uptake and handling of DNA similar to those observed in naturally transforming bacteria would be anticipated. The observation that the Gram-positive bacteria take DNA from any source may seem inconsistent with this hypothesis, since *rec*-dependent recombination requires homology. However, that may not be problematic; since bacteria are likely to be living in colonies, most of the DNA available to them is likely to be from members of their own clone. Thus, they would not need specific mechanisms for the recognition of homologous DNA.

I see two potential problems with the DNA repair hypothesis. First, it assumes that the cells are unable to use their own DNA as template for repair. Second, the probability of randomly picking up the right segment and the appropriate strand of that segment for repairing lesions may be too low to confer an adequate individual selective advantage to evolve and maintain all of the complex machinery needed for obtaining these templates.

I do not consider these potential problems to be particularly grave and view DNA repair as a reasonable selective force for the evolution of transformation. When bacteria stop growing due to the kinds of shift-downs in nutrient availability that induce competence, they generally have fewer copies of DNA per cell than in growing cultures. In *Bacillus subtilis*, competent cells have only one copy of their chromosomes (Dubnau, 1982). Thus, there is reason to assume that when naturally transforming bacteria are competent, there would be less DNA redundancy and consequently less capacity to use internal templates for DNA repair than when they are not competent for transformation. Not so clear is whether competent cells can acquire a sufficient advantage by using randomly sequestered segments of homospecific DNA for this repair, or whether they have to (and are able to) selectively pick up the right sequences for this advantage. Nevertheless, the DNA repair hypothesis remains appealing because it can be tested, at least as the mechanism responsible for the maintenance of transformation in extant bacteria.

Parasitic DNA It is possible that transformation evolved as a by-product of the evolution of mechanisms for the infectious transfer of free DNA. In a free state, bacterial DNA is, of course, incapable of replication and fated to degradation. If, however, that DNA is taken up by a bacterium and incorporated into its chromosome, then even though it is incapable of autonomous replication, it would survive and continue to replicate. Therefore, it would seem that selection would favor free DNA molecules with the ability to enter cells and do so in a manner that would protect them from degradation by cellular endonucleases.

One seemingly major problem with this hypotheses is that the mechanisms for the uptake and handling of DNA in naturally transforming organisms are properties of the cell and coded for chromosomal DNA. Therefore, one has to assume that the chromosomal genes coding for these processes either (1) evolved and are maintained by selection for replication of homospecific DNA that is excreted or released following death, or (2) have other functions and are simply exploited by the exogenous DNA. These are not mutually exclusive mechanisms, and it is possible that both have played a role in the evolution of the DNA uptake and handling in transformation.

One difficulty in accepting the premise that the mechanisms for DNA uptake and handling evolved and are maintained by selection for the replication of exogenous DNA is that relatively short and presumably random pieces of chromosomal DNA are taken up. Unless the genes coding for these DNA uptake and handling functions are present in many copies (a potentially testable hypothesis), these transformation-determining genes would have a relatively low probability of being picked up. On the other hand, the hypothesis that the mechanisms for DNA uptake and handling have other functions is more appealing. It is especially attractive in the case of Hemophilus, where there are physical structures, the blebs (transformasomes), that are responsible for the uptake of exogenous DNA, and where sequences of 11 base pairs, which are present in many copies, serve as DNA uptake sites. These 11 base pair sequences could well be parasitic DNA. The demonstration of some alternative function for the blebs would certainly provide support for this hypothesis.

Individual selection The arguments for and against transformation evolving by individual selection favoring cells with the ability to pick up and incorporate exogenous DNA into their genomes are analogous to those for individual selection for the acquisition of genes by vector-mediated recombination (see earlier discussion). While one can construct scenarios where this type of selection would work, the arguments against this hypothesis seem more compelling. If the rate of recombination mediated by transformation is low and most chromosomal gene adaptation is by mutation and selection, it would seem that, on the average, it is more likely to be to the disadvantage of the individual to receive a random gene from an external source than to its advantage. Even if, on the average, most genes received enhanced the fitness of the recipient, the probability of an individual acquiring these genes may be too low to generate a fitness advantage of sufficient magnitude to evolve and maintain the machinery needed for transformation.

Nevertheless, at this time, I do not believe there is any justification for advocating a strong position against individual selection being responsible for the evolution of transformation. The fact that I cannot readily conceive of compelling arguments for this may be no more than my own lack of imagination and personal biases. Furthermore, unlike in *E. coli*, where both experiments and natural population data suggest that recombination rates are low, there are few data that provide estimates of the recombination rates in populations of naturally transforming bacteria. In fact, the existing data suggest that recombination in transforming bacteria occurs at a higher rate than vector-mediated recombination in *E. coli*. Under laboratory conditions, more than 1% of populations of *Hemophilus influenzae* can pick up and express genes borne on exogenous DNA (Herriott et al., 1970). While natural populations of *H. influenzae* do maintain a clonal structure (Musser et al., 1985; Porras et al., 1986), there is evidence to suggest that the persistence time of clones of this transforming species is less than that of clones of *E. coli* (Porras et al., 1986). One interpretation of the latter is that recombination occurs at higher rates in natural populations of Hemophilus than in those of *E. coli*. Finally, without specific known selection, high frequencies of recombinants are obtained in mixed populations of *Bacillus subtilis* maintained in semirealistic conditions (Graham and Istock, 1979).

Group selection For the reasons considered earlier, bacterial populations are particularly amenable to group or population-level selection. Nevertheless, in the case of vector-mediated recombination, I felt that the a priori appeal and evidence for the coincidental evolution hypothesis were sufficiently strong to relegate group selection to a secondary, supporting role. For transformation, on the other hand, at this juncture I do not consider any other hypothesis to be adequately compelling to relegate group selection to a secondary position.

THE ROLE OF RECOMBINATION IN BACTERIAL ADAPTATION AND EVOLUTION

In an earlier, and much briefer, consideration of the evolution of sex in bacteria, Lenski and I used the phrase "much ado about very little" in reference to the low frequency of chromosomal gene recombination in *E. coli* (Levin and Lenski, 1983). While the returns are not in for many other species, at this time, it seems unlikely that gene shuffling occurs at very much higher rates in natural population of most bacteria than in *E. coli*. The results of enzyme electrophoretic studies of *Legionella pneumophila* (Selander et al., 1985) and *Hemophilus influenzae* (Musser et al., 1985, 1986; Porras et al., 1986) also indicate the maintenance of a clonal population structure and thus low rates of recombination.

It is, however, important to emphasize that even if the rate of chromosomal gene replacement by recombination is as low as that by mutation, this does not mean that this form of bacterial sex is not important for the adaptation and evolution of bacterial populations. It may well be extremely important. Unlike mutation, recombination can result in the substitution of gene(s) that have successfully traversed the gauntlet of natural selection. Theoretically, in the course of a single gene transfer event, a clone can acquire new catabolic pathways, resistance to antibiotics, and any of a vast array of other characters it did not previously possess. This is certainly the case for plasmid-borne and prophage-borne characters; is this also true for chromosomal gene recombination?

At this time, I do not believe that we can answer this question. The critical data are not yet available. While there is evidence that at least some plasmids are chimeras of genes from many sources (Cohen, 1976), I am unaware of evidence to indicate whether this is also true for the genomes (or parts of the genomes) of bacteria. Although the rate of gene shuffling may be too low to randomize the genomes of bacteria, it could well be that different regions of bacterial chromosomes have different ancestries. Hopefully, the data addressing this issue will soon become available. I would like to know that answer and hope this chapter will stimulate further investigations of this and other questions of sex and evolution in bacteria.

CHAPTER 13

ON THE EVOLUTION OF GENETIC INCOMPATIBILITY SYSTEMS: INCOMPATIBILITY AS A MECHANISM FOR THE REGULATION OF OUTCROSSING DISTANCE

Marcy K. Uyenoyama

INTRODUCTION

Bengtsson's (1978) conceptual approach to the evolution of mate choice elucidated the conflict between parent–offspring relatedness and inbreeding depression. Genotypes that promote high parent–offspring relatedness are favored by greater fidelity of transmission across generations. However, because high parent–offspring relatedness implies inbreeding in the offspring, the most closely related offspring are subject to the greatest inbreeding depression.

The linear regression coefficient of the additive genotypic value of offspring on the additive genotypic value of the parent that controls mate choice increases linearly with m, the correlation between mates:

$$b_{P \to O} = (1 + m)/2 \tag{1}$$

(see Uyenoyama and Bengtsson, 1982). The parent–offspring correlation (Wright, 1921) converges asymptotically to this value. The viability of offspring derived by selfing relative to offspring derived by random outcrossing declines as the level of inbreeding among selfed offspring increases. If the effect of alleles contributing to inbreeding depression is nonadditive (e.g., recessive), then the average viability among offspring depends on F, the correlation between uniting gametes (Morton et al., 1956). In the absence of epistasis, the log of mean viability declines approximately linearly with F among the offspring (Morton et al., 1956; Latter and Robertson, 1962). These considerations indicate that relatedness increases linearly and the log of viability decreases linearly with the correlation between mates. Considering only completely recessive deleterious mutations and very low mutation rates, the fitness of offspring produced by selfing relative to offspring produced by outcrossing to unrelated individuals (ϕ_S) is approximately

$$\phi_S = 1 - n\mu F_S/F \tag{2a}$$

where n represents the number of loci contributing to inbreeding depression, μ the rate of deleterious mutation, F_S the inbreeding coefficient of offspring derived by selfing, and F the average inbreeding coefficient in the offspring generation (see May, 1979; Lande and Schemske, 1985; Bernstein et al., 1985). In general, the relative viability of offspring produced by biparental inbreeding (ϕ_I) under the same assumptions is approximately

$$\phi_I = 1 - n\mu m F_S/F \tag{2b}$$

where mF_S represents F_I, the inbreeding coefficient among those offspring (see May, 1979; Uyenoyama, 1986). Transmission of genes between generations depends upon the number of surviving offspring and their genetic similarity to their parents. Comparison of Equations 1 (increasing in m) and 2b (decreasing in m) suggests that the optimal mate choice lies at an intermediate genealogical distance. "Outbreeding depression" resulting from disruption of coadapted gene complexes or fine-scale local adaptation, as has been reported in natural populations of *Delphinium nelsoni* and *Ipomopsis aggregata* (Price and Waser, 1979; Waser and Price, 1983, 1985), may contribute to the selective pressure favoring outcrossing at intermediate *physical* distances as well by reducing the viability of offspring derived from crosses between widely separated parents (see Bateson, 1980; Shields, 1982).

While this comparison serves to introduce the essential elements under discussion, the evolutionary dynamics are likely to be complex. Because inbreeding both purges deleterious mutations and increases genetic correlations among genealogical classes (e.g., siblings and first cousins), the optimal outcrossing distance is expected to evolve along with mate choice. Similarly, changes in physical outcrossing distance engender changes in the genetic structure of the population with respect to interacting loci affecting viability, thereby modifying the subsequent evolution of outcrossing distance (Waddington, 1983; Campbell and Waser, 1987; see also Crowe, 1971). Further, the correlations between mates that appear in Equations 1 and 2 in fact refer to different sets of loci: The selective advantage of high parent-offspring relatedness depends upon similarity at loci controlling mate choice, while the level of inbreeding depression depends upon homozygosity at the loci responsible for inbreeding depression. Natural selection on genetic variation within both sets of loci will also affect the measures of relatedness.

This chapter assesses the effectiveness of genetic incompatibility systems as a mechanism for the regulation of outcrossing distance. In this discussion, incompatibility in the broad sense refers to postmating mechanisms that generate variation among families in the offspring genotypic distribution. Under the definition to be presented, incompatibility subsumes interactions between genetically determined pollen and style specificities (gametophytic and sporophytic self-incompatibility) as well as immunologically based systems of maternal–fetal recognition or rejection (histoincompatibility). I explore the proposal that the primary function of genetic incompatibility systems is not so much to distinguish self from nonself, but rather to distinguish offspring likely to suffer inbreeding depression from those with better prospects.

The remainder of this chapter comprises four major sections. In the first, I describe the results of an analysis of the selective pressures bearing on the origin of specificities (antigens) that evoke a partial rejection of gametes that share specificities with the maternal (or seed) parent. Three major components of selection govern evolutionary changes at the antigen locus itself: gametic selection, modification of parent–offspring relatedness, and tradeoffs in offspring number across mating distances. In the second section, I present a definition of incompatibility in the broad sense and address immunological systems of maternal–fetal incompatibility within this framework. The contrast between the stringency of the conditions for the origin of the rejection response and the existence of functionally similar incompatibility systems in hermaphroditic angiosperms and (gonochoristic) mammals provokes a deeper consideration of the interactions between incompatibility loci and the loci responsible for inbreeding depression. The third section addresses the means by which organisms can use incompatiblity systems to assess or amplify variation in offspring quality. In the fourth section, I suggest that a phenomenon closely related to associative overdominance (see Ohta and Cockerham, 1974) can generate a correlation between inbreeding depression and the level of concordance between parents and offspring at incompatibility loci. These elements form the basis of the proposal that integrated incompatibility systems, comprising antigen loci, modifiers of the intensity of the incompatibility reaction, and loci contributing to inbreeding depression, can regulate outcrossing distance by serving as a prospective means of assessing genomic homozygosity and inbreeding depression.

COMPONENTS OF SELECTION ON INCOMPATIBILITY

Mather (1943) and Bateman (1952) argued that self-incompatibility arose much more plausibly through the gradual modification of the intensity of the rejection reaction rather than through the abrupt appearance of a fully functional S-gene expressing activity in both pollen and style. Charlesworth and Charlesworth (1979) reviewed a number of studies reporting quantitative variation in stylar response. Nasrallah (1974) detected a suppressor locus in *Brassica oleracea* that promotes self-compatibility by attenuating the production of the receptor protein that recognizes the S-locus antigen. In this section, I summarize the results of an analysis (described in greater detail in M.K. Uyenoyama, in preparation) examining the conditions for initial increase of an allele that exhibits a partial stylar rejection response in an incompletely self-compatible population. Charlesworth and Charlesworth (1979) analyzed a similar model involving the segregation of fully functional and fully nonfunctional S-alleles.

Description of the model

Each individual in a partially self-compatible hermaphroditic population receives pollen from itself, from one related individual, and from the population at large. The proportions of these three classes are s (selfing), $(1 - s)k$ (biparental inbreeding), and $(1 - s)(1 - k)$ (random mating), respectively. In order to model biparental inbreeding, I assume that the relative that donates pollen shares its seed parent with the recipient. These individuals may be considered half-sibs, although either may have been derived from any of the three pollen classes. Offspring derived by selfing have viability ϕ_S and offspring derived by biparental inbreeding have viability ϕ_I relative to offspring produced by random mating.

Two alleles, A and a, segregate at the incompatibility locus. The relative fertilization success of A and a pollen tubes in AA styles are a_1 and a_2. In styles of genotypes Aa and aa, these rates are b_1 and b_2, and c_1 and c_2, respectively. I assume that all individuals set the same number of seeds; the fraction of seeds derived from A pollen depends upon the proportion of A pollen received and its relative fertilization success. For example, a seed parent with genotype AA coupled with a half-sib pollen donor with genotype Aa receives a proportion s of its pollen from itself (all of which carry only A), $(1 -s)k$ from its half-sib (A and a in equal proportions), and $(1 - s)(1 - k)$ from the population as a whole (A and a in frequencies p and q, respectively, where $p + q = 1$) (Table 1). Among the seeds of this individual, the proportion that are AA is equal to the product of the frequency of A pollen received and $a_1/a(2)$, where $a(2)$, given by

$$a_1[s + (1 - s)k/2 + (1 - s)(1 - k)p] + a_2(1 - s)[k/2 + (1 - k)q] \quad (3)$$

represents the average fertilization rate among the pollen received by the individual. The distributions of genotypes among the seeds produced by AA individuals paired with AA or aa half-sibs depend upon $a(1)$ and $a(3)$, which are defined in a similar way. Functions $b(i)$ and $c(i)$ ($i = 1, 2, 3$) correspond to seed parents having genotypes Aa and aa, respectively. In the limit approaching complete exclusion of alleles carried in the style (e.g., a_1 nearing 0), this formulation converges to the "pollen elimination" model of Finney (1952).

TABLE 1. Number of offspring produced by a seed parent with genotype AA paired with a half-sib of genotype Aa

	Offspring Genotype[a]	
Pollen Source	AA	Aa
Self	$s\phi_S a_1/a(2) - X_S$	—
Half-sibling	$(1 - s)k\phi_I a_1/[2a(2)] - X_I$	$(1 - s)k\phi_I a_2/[2a(2)] - X_I$
Random outcross	$(1 - s)(1 - k)p a_1/a(2) - X_R$	$(1 - s)(1 - k)q a_2/a(2) - X_R$

[a]X_S, X_I, and X_R denote the average numbers of offspring produced by selfing, biparental inbreeding, and random outcrossing, respectively.

Inbreeding depression, which depends solely on the genealogical relationship between the seed parent and the pollen source, is expressed in offspring only after seed germination.

Table 1 records the numbers of mature offspring produced in the three classes, expressed as a deviation from the mean in each class, for a seed parent with genotype AA paired with a half-sib with genotype Aa. The distributions of offspring produced by the five other mating types are obtained in a similar fashion. To each genotype for the seed parent I associate three character values, corresponding to the numbers of the three kinds of offspring produced by that seed parent. The average effect of substitution of the A allele on the number of offspring derived by random mating is denoted $(\alpha_1 - \alpha_2)$, by biparental inbreeding $(\beta_1 - \beta_2)$, and by selfing $(\gamma_1 - \gamma_2)$.

The covariance method

In order to enumerate the components of selection on incompatibility, I consider the covariance between fitness and the additive genotypic value with respect to the number of offspring produced by outcrossing (see Li, 1967, 1976; Price, 1970, 1972). The components of selection with which this additive genotypic value is positively correlated promote outcrossing, and those with which it is negatively correlated discourage outcrossing. This covariance is equal to the change in mean additive genotypic value with respect to outcrossing, which in turn can be represented by a sum of covariances and the change in mean additive genotypic value between offspring and parents:

$$\begin{aligned} \text{Cov}(FA) &= 2T\Delta p(\alpha_1 - \alpha_2) \\ &= \text{Var}(M_\alpha)[b_{M \to R} + G/\text{Var}(M_\alpha) \\ &\quad + b_{M \to S}(\gamma_1 - \gamma_2)/(\alpha_1 - \alpha_2) + b_{M \to I}(\beta_1 - \beta_2)/(\alpha_1 - \alpha_2)] \end{aligned} \tag{4}$$

where $b_{M \to S}$, $b_{M \to I}$, and $b_{M \to R}$ represent parent–offspring regressions, and G, the component of gametic selection (see Appendix) (M. K. Uyenoyama, in preparation).

Equation 4 summarizes the components of selection on incompatibility: (1) tradeoffs in offspring number among classes, (2) parent–offspring relatedness, and (3) gametic selection. Tradeoffs in offspring number among the classes are represented by the ratios of the average effects of substitution with respect to those characters. For example, the partial exclusion of similar genotypes by incompatibility generates a negative correlation between the numbers of offspring derived by selfing and by random outcrossing. Selection on incompatibility systems also depends on the genetic similarity between parents and offspring derived by each mode of reproduction. At neutral loci, parent–offspring relatedness increases linearly with the correlation between mates (see Equation 1). This correlation assumes the value unity under selfing, m under biparental inbreeding, and zero under random mating. Incompatibility reduces the similarity between parents and offspring produced by biparental inbreeding. Finally, gametic selection disfavors genes carried in common by offspring and parents.

Application to the introduction of an incompatibility allele with full activity

To illustrate the effects of incompatibility on the various components of selection, I place within the framework described here the conditions derived by Charlesworth and Charlesworth (1979) for the initial increase of a fully functional S-allele in a monomorphic, fully self-compatible population in which no biparental inbreeding occurs ($k = 0$). The resident allele (A) accepts both pollen genotypes ($a_1 = a_2$), while the invading genotype (Aa) excludes the rare allele ($b_2 = 0$). Because pollen bearing the rare allele never fertilizes a heterozygous seed parent, the aa genotype is absent. Charlesworth and Charlesworth (1979) found that incompatibility is favored only if it sufficiently reduces the rate of selfing of the invading genotype (s') relative to the resident (s):

$$s' < s(1 - 2\phi_S)/(1 - \phi_S) \tag{5}$$

where ϕ_S replaces $(1 - \delta)$ in their notation. They observed that in order for incompatibility to increase, inbreeding depression must be greater than the twofold difference expected for other mechanisms regulating selfing (Kimura, 1959; Maynard Smith, 1977).

The covariance analysis indicates that incompatibility reduces parent–offspring relatedness in the invading genotype. Because the rare allele acting in the style completely excludes pollen carrying that allele, offspring produced by selfing are as distantly related as offspring produced by random outcrossing ($b_{M \to R} = b_{M \to S} = \frac{1}{2}$). In completely self-compatible individuals, parent–offspring relatedness retains its usual values ($b_{M \to R} = \frac{1}{2}$, $b_{M \to S} = 1$). The fitness of resident genotypes represents an average between closely related offspring produced by selfing and outbred offspring:

$$s\phi_S + (1 - s)/2 \tag{6a}$$

while the fitness of the invading genotype reflects the reduction in relatedness as well as selfing rate:

$$s'\phi_S/2 + (1 - s')/2 \tag{6b}$$

Equation 6b exceeds 6a under the condition of Equation 5.

The other two components, tradeoffs in offspring number and gametic selection, are subsumed by the change in the rate of selfing. In fully self-compatible individuals, the selfing rate equals the proportion of self-pollen received, while in Aa individuals, it is nearly

$$s' = sb_1/[2b(1)] = s/(2 - s) \tag{7}$$

Substitution of Equation 7 into Equation 5 produces

$$\phi_S > (1 - s)/(3 - 2s) \tag{8}$$

Under the assumptions of the model, the components of selection enumerated in Equation 4 reduce to

$$\begin{aligned} b_{M \to S} &= \tfrac{1}{2} \\ b_{M \to R} &= \tfrac{1}{2} \\ (\gamma_1 - \gamma_2)/(\alpha_1 - \alpha_2) &= -\phi_S \\ G/\mathrm{Var}(M_\alpha) &= -\phi_S(1 - s/2)/(1 - s) \end{aligned} \tag{9}$$

Equation 8 is obtained by substitution of Equation 9 into Equation 4.

Regulation of mating distance by incompatibility systems

Incompatibility systems modify rates of biparental inbreeding in addition to selfing (see de Nettancourt, 1977, Chap. 2; Lewis, 1979). Bateman (1952) compared a number of homomorphic systems of gametophytic and sporophytic incompatibility with respect to the reduction in sibmating relative to random outcrossing. Fisher (1965) calculated the proportion of parent–offspring matings and sibmatings that would be prevented by a two-locus system of tristyly. Both studies portrayed incompatibility as a mechanism for promoting crosses with unrelated individuals. This section considers whether incompatibility systems can promote outcrossing at intermediate genealogical distances.

The average effects of substitution reflect the expected changes in the numbers of offspring produced by random mating, biparental inbreeding, and selfing resulting from the substitution within individuals of one resident allele by one invading allele. Consider the invasion of a completely self-compatible population ($a_1 = a_2 = 1$) by a completely dominant incompatibility allele with weak activity ($b_1 = c_1 > b_2 = c_2$, with the b_i nearly equal to 1). Relative to the invading allele, the resident allele decreases the number of offspring produced by random mating $[(\alpha_1 - \alpha_2) < 0]$ and increases the number produced by selfing $[(\gamma_1 - \gamma_2) > 0]$. The ratios of the average effects of substitution express the tradeoffs in offspring number among classes:

$$(\beta_1 - \beta_2)/(\alpha_1 - \alpha_2) = [1 - F_I/F]k\phi_I/(1 - k) \tag{10a}$$

$$(\gamma_1 - \gamma_2)/(\alpha_1 - \alpha_2) = [1 - F_S/F]s\phi_S/[(1 - s)(1 - k)] \tag{10b}$$

where F_S and F_I represent the coefficients of inbreeding at the incompatibility locus among offspring produced by selfing and biparental inbreeding; and F the average inbreeding coefficient

$$\begin{aligned}
F_S &= (1 + F)/2 \\
F_I &= m(1 + F)/2 \\
F &= sF_S + k(1 - s)F_I
\end{aligned} \tag{11}$$

(see Uyenoyama, 1986; Uyenoyama and Antonovics, 1986). Relative to the change in the number of outcrossed offspring, the change in the number of each inbred offspring class depends upon the level of inbreeding in those offspring compared to the average level of inbreeding:

$$(F - F_D)/F \tag{12}$$

where F_D corresponds to F_S or F_I given in Equation 11 for offspring derived by selfing or biparental inbreeding, or to zero for offspring derived by outcrossing. Because offspring derived by selfing are the most inbred, Equation 10b is always negative, indicating that incompatibility increases the number of offspring produced by outcrossing and reduces the number by selfing. However, Equation 10a can be positive, which implies that the number of offspring produced by biparental inbreeding may actually increase with the rate of outcrossing. These results hold under the assumption that variation at the incompatibility locus is not associated with variation in seed set. Parameter sets that produce positive values for Equation 10a involve high rates of selfing (M.K. Uyenoyama, in preparation). Equations 10a and 10b indicate that incompatibility systems can influence outcrossing distance by differentially altering the relative proportions of offspring derived by selfing, biparental inbreeding, and outcrossing according to the level of similarity between the maternal genotype and the paternal gamete.

GENETIC INCOMPATIBILITY SYSTEMS IN MAMMALS

Genetic incompatibility systems, broadly defined to include mechanisms that permit the early detection of inbreeding depression, may evolve to distinguish offspring derived by biparental inbreeding as well as by selfing. In particular, such systems could amplify variation in offspring quality in dioecious plants and gonochoristic animals. Conventional wisdom suggests that the evolution of extensive postpollination mechanisms of offspring choice in plants reflects the inability to exercise much control over mate selection at an earlier stage. However, the existence of functionally analogous systems in mammals suggests that postzygotic control of parental investment is important in organisms with well-developed social systems as well.

Definition of incompatibility

de Nettancourt (1977, Chap. 1) defined self-incompatibility in angiosperms as the absence of zygote production after self-pollination, placing emphasis on prezygotic mechanisms in order to avoid confusion with inbreeding depression. Seavey and Bawa (1986) expanded this definition to include incompatibility expressed at the ovary or after embryo formation. Their definition distinguishes between inbreeding depression suffered by offspring and maternal rejection, which evolves in response to inbreeding depression. Introducing an ultimate function (response to inbreeding depression) into the definition complicates its application compared to those (e.g., Charlesworth, 1985) that depend on only the genotype (maternal or offspring) to which failure of self-pollination is attributed.

In spite of the practical difficulties associated with defining processes in terms of their adaptive functions, for the purposes of this discussion I adopt a definition of incompatibility that includes postzygotic effects in order to address discrimination among related individuals (in addition to self and nonself) within the same conceptual framework. I recognize as a component of incompatibility any mechanism that promotes termination of parental resources in certain offspring in order to permit reallocation toward offspring with better prospects. Under this definition, modifier loci that cause the expression of deleterious genes earlier in development would be regarded as components of incompatibility, provided that expression occurs sufficiently early to benefit the surviving offspring. Hamilton's (1966) analysis of the evolution of senescence showed that although individual selection favors the late expression of deleterious genes, early expression may evolve under family selection if parents can replace inviable offspring. Coyne (1974) invoked similar reasoning to argue that decreased viability of interspecific hybrids may evolve in populations exhibiting extensive parental care. Labov (1981) has proposed that in rodents, pregnancy blocking (abortion following exposure to unfamiliar males) may be advantageous even to females if it avoids investment in broods subject to aggression by the male. Lloyd's (1980) hypothesis of serial adjustment of maternal resources by elimination of offspring during the course of a single reproductive episode holds that early detection and abortion is advantageous to the extent that it permits the redirection of resources toward offspring having higher fitness. This same principle forms the basis of a component of selection favoring incompatibility.

Postzygotic incompatibility in mice

Results of experiments on inbred mice, while conflicting in part, provide evidence of incompatibility systems of the kind under discussion. Billington (1964) reported that placental size (interpreted as an indication of the quality of the fetal environment) is larger in crosses between inbred strains than within inbred strains. James (1965, 1967) demonstrated that placental size and fetal weight increase with the ability of the mother to react immunologically to the strain from which its mate was derived. Injection of spleen cells at the appropriate stage of the females' development rendered them immune or tolerant to the strain to which they were mated. Placental size and fetal weight of hybrids carried by tolerant mothers did not differ significantly from inbred offspring carried by untreated mothers, eliminating hybrid vigor as an important factor. Comparisons among interstrain crosses indicated that placental size and fetal weight increased significantly with degree of maternal sensitization (immune > untreated > tolerant), even though litter size (which is negatively correlated with placental size) did not differ significantly among these groups.

Clarke (1971) failed to confirm these results, even though the same inbred strains studied by James were used; on the contrary, maternal immunization significantly reduced fetal weight and litter size in one experiment. Breyere and Sprenger (1969) observed a significant reduction in size of litters produced by females that were immunized against tumor cells from the strain from which their mates were derived. They suggested that because both allograft rejection and fetal recognition require immunological responses, the effects of maternal sensitization may have depended upon the particular genetic combination involved or the immunization procedures used.

Frequencies of heterozygotes at the H-3 locus (Hull, 1969) and the H-2 locus (Hamilton and Hellstrom, 1978) in excess of Mendelian expectations were observed in broods produced by homozygous females that had been sensitized to alloantigens during previous pregnancies. In both studies, the absence of significant reductions in litter size or offspring weight in affected broods was interpreted as an indication that selection favoring offspring bearing histocompatibility alleles that differed from those of their mothers occurred early in development, perhaps soon after (Hull, 1969) or even before (Hamilton and Hellstrom, 1978) conception.

Correlation between infertility and HLA concordance in humans

In humans, similarity between spouses at loci within the major histocompatibility complex (particularly in the HLA-D/DR region) is associated with spontaneous abortions due to unknown causes (Kolmos et al., 1977; Beer et al., 1981; Gill, 1983; Tiwari and Terasaki, 1985, Chap. 14). This effect contrasts with the association between abortion and dissimilarity of ABO or Rh antigens (reviewed by Gill, 1983). The deleterious effects associated with Rh incompatibility may simply represent an unfortunate consequence of confronting a highly developed immune system with unusually high levels of heterozygosity resulting from recent admixture of largely monomorphic or oligomorphic populations (see Haldane, 1942). In contrast, the extraordinary levels of polymorphism within the HLA complex, which steadily increase with the development of new sera (see Albert et al., 1984), appear to characterize all human populations. Sharing of HLA-A or B antigens is associated with longer intervals between births among the Hutterites, who proscribe birth control (Ober et al., 1983). However, because sharing of HLA antigens was confounded with coancestry in this isolated community, further interpretation is complicated by the possibility of inbreeding depression.

Sharing of HLA antigens may be correlated with the diminution of an immunosuppressive response by the mother that involves the production of plasma-borne blocking factors (gamma immunoglobulins) that prevent rejection of the fetus (Rocklin et al., 1976; Stimson et al., 1979; McIntyre and Faulk, 1979a). The inhibition of mixed lymphocyte culture (MLC) reactions by blocking factors suggests recognition of antigens encoded by the HLA-D region loci (Stimson et al., 1979; Beer et al., 1981). Blocking factors that inhibit MLC reactions by cross-reacting with antigens borne on lymphocytes have been isolated from placental (trophoblast) membranes (McIntyre and Faulk, 1979b). These tissues lack β_2 microglobulin, the invariant chain of antigens encoded by the HLA-A, B, and C loci (Faulk et al., 1978). Faulk and colleagues (1978) have proposed that inadequate production of blocking antibodies permits a second set of antigens borne on trophoblast membranes to provoke the immune response that results in fetal rejection.

Three of four women with histories of spontaneous abortions produced apparently normal children after undergoing repeated transfusions of leukocytes and lymphocytes from unrelated (but erythrocyte-compatible) donors throughout their pregnancies (Taylor and Faulk, 1981). The investigators hypothesized that sharing between mother and fetus of the antigens recognized by blocking factors may have resulted in an inadequate response in the women, each of whom shared two or more HLA antigens with her spouse. Transfusions of foreign antigens apparently stimulated the production of the blocking antibodies that prevent fetal rejection.

Abundant evidence supports the correlation between concordance at histocompatibility loci and infertility. Until recently, the confounding of concordance and consanguinity obscured the interpretation of this correlation by introducing the possibility that it could be attributed entirely to inbreeding depression. The transfusion experiments in humans and the (questionable) immunization experiments in mice have established that a distinct system of fetal rejection, apart from the viability of the offspring itself, contributes to the observed correlation. The existence of this elaborate double recognition system, together with the high levels of polymorphism characteristic of histocompatibility complexes in mammals at the population level, suggests that termination of certain pregnancies may represent an evolved response, rather than malfunction of a system that evolved for a different purpose, as may be the case for Rh incompatibilities.

CORRELATIONS BETWEEN INCOMPATIBILITY AND OFFSPRING QUALITY

Were it possible for parents to evaluate and discriminate among offspring of varying quality, natural selection would clearly favor the development of genetically based mechanisms of this kind (see discussions and reviews in Willson, 1979, 1983, Chap. 3; Stephenson, 1981; Willson and Burley, 1983, Chap. 3; Stephenson and Bertin, 1983). This section examines the means by which parents can amplify existing variation in offspring quality or predict at an early stage subsequent performance of offspring.

Intensity of pollen competition and sporophytic vigor

Mulcahy (1979) reviewed the experimental literature, which demonstrates that the vigor of the zygote improves as the opportunity for pollen competition increases (for reviews and additional studies, see Mulcahy et al., 1986b). The opportunity for pollen competition has been experimentally manipulated by controlling the proximity of pollen deposition to the ovary (Mulcahy and Mulcahy, 1975) or the amount of pollen applied (Ter-Avanesian, 1978). More directly, sporophytic quality has been shown to be correlated with rate of pollen tube growth (Mulcahy, 1974; Sari Gorla et al., 1975).

Mulcahy (1979) interpreted these observations as evidence of a prezygotic system of gamete choice capable of assessing genetic quality of zygotes at the gametophytic stage. However, variation in pollen quality due to entirely environmental causes could also contribute to this phenomenon. For example, accidents during meiosis or pollen formation could produce pollen grains bearing morphological defects that impair growth during the phase of pollen competition as well as genetic deficiencies that would be expressed in offspring derived from such pollen.

The heterosis model

Mulcahy and Mulcahy (1983) proposed that incompatibility derives from the expression of several closely linked loci that influence zygotic viability as well as pollen tube growth. This heterosis model falls within the class of overlapping models (Mulcahy, 1979), in which the set of loci expressed in gametophytes overlaps with the set expressed in sporophytes. Several recent studies have reported extensive overlap among loci expressed in the two stages (reviewed by Mulcahy et al., 1986a). About 60% of the isozymes scored in the tomato (*Lycopersicon esculentum*) were expressed in both pollen and vegetative tissue (Tanksley et al., 1981). A comparable estimate was obtained by hybridizing mRNA from pollen and vegetative shoots in *Tradescantia paludosa* (Willing and Mascarenhas, 1984).

Lawrence and coworkers (1985) have challenged the reinterpretation of incompatibility in terms of the heterosis model (see reply by Mulcahy and Mulcahy, 1985). Their critique cited a number of studies that clearly demonstrated that failure of self-pollination was due to maternal rejection rather than passive replacement of subviable zygotes. Seavey and Bawa (1986) observed that under the heterosis model, virtually no distinction remains between incompatibility and inbreeding depression. While variation in vigor among pollen tubes or zygotes would not itself be regarded as incompatibility under the definition adopted in the preceding section, such variation could contribute to the selective pressure favoring the evolution of mechanisms that encourage competition for maternal resources or amplify differences among offspring. Such mechanisms, together with the loci contributing to inbreeding depression, would constitute an incompatibility system.

Endosperm as a component of incompatibility

Endosperm competition or dysfunction provides a possible mechanism for amplifying variation in vigor among offspring. In species to which Lloyd's (1980) serial adjustment hypothesis applies, small differences in vigor among offspring may engender large differences in success as fewer offspring compete for greater levels of maternal investment at each stage. Temme (1986) explored the effect of variation in offspring quality on variation in maternal provisioning among seeds. Endosperm dysfunction represents a major cause of failure of interploid hybrids at the seed stage (Brink and Cooper, 1947). Johnston et al. (1980) have proposed that the effective ploidy of the embryo is determined by the endosperm, with abnormal endosperm development and abortion following detection of a deviant ratio between maternal and paternal contributions. Seavey and Bawa (1986) recognized endosperm collapse as a form of late self-incompatibility.

Brink and Cooper (1939, 1940, 1947) characterized endosperm as an "aggressive" tissue that competes for maternal resources. In their work (1939, 1940) they compared embryos and endosperm derived from self- and cross-fertilizations of alfalfa (*Medicago sativa*). While the rate of growth (estimated by daily counts of cells or nuclei) of embryos derived from the two crosses did not differ significantly, outcrossed endosperm increased at a significantly higher geometric rate than selfed endosperm. In order to examine the effect of the shorter interval between pollination and fertilization in the outcross treatment, the number of nuclei in selfed and outcrossed endosperm were counted at identical stages of embryo development and found to support the same conclusion. These studies demonstrated that endosperm greatly amplifies variation in vigor among offspring.

This interpretation contrasts strongly with the hypothesis that endosperm evolved to reduce genetic differences among siblings, thereby attenuating an evolutionary conflict between the parent, which is equally related to each of its offspring, and the selfish interests of the offspring themselves (Charnov, 1979; Cook, 1981; Kress, 1981; Westoby and Rice, 1982; Queller, 1983, 1984). The uniformity of relatedness of parents to their offspring does not necessarily imply that parents or the offspring themselves evolve indifference toward variation among offspring in vigor or other components of fitness (see also Temme, 1986). If endosperm evolved to intensify rather than attenuate sibling competition, then endosperm qualifies as a component of incompatibility under the definition adopted in this discussion. Because both the maternal and paternal complements are expressed in endosperm, this tissue cannot be unequivocally regarded as an organ of the seed parent as opposed to the offspring. Under the definition introduced in the preceding section, the designation of endosperm as a component of incompatibility does not require parental control or manipulation.

Implication of HLA in both predisposition to disease and maternal–fetal incompatibility

Associations between HLA haplotypes and various genetic and infectious diseases in humans have received intensive investigation (reviewed in Thomson, 1981). Many of these diseases exhibit particularly strong associations with antigens encoded by loci in the HLA-D region (McDevitt, 1977), while other diseases (e.g., anencephaly, Schacter et al., 1984) are more strongly associated with HLA-A or B. Of the several hypotheses that have been advanced (see discussions in McDevitt and Bodmer, 1972; Zinkernagel and Doherty, 1977; Amos and Ward, 1977), close linkage between HLA loci and loci controlling specific immune responses (McDevitt and Bodmer, 1972, 1974) best appears to account for both the associations and certain attributes (such as autoimmunity) of the diseases involved.

These associations with predisposition to disease are not directly responsible for the negative maternal–fetal interactions described in the preceding section. Such associations would tend to generate selection disfavoring particular haplotypes rather than antigens held in common. Further, the women studied by Taylor and Faulk (1981) produced apparently viable offspring after having received transfusions of foreign leukocytes. The associations of HLA with diseases and with fetal rejection represent two distinct evolutionary issues. While the disease associations appear to reflect close linkage between the HLA region and immune response (IR) loci, a second question concerns why HLA is involved in fetal rejection.

Bateman (1952) proposed that incompatibility may originate with the recognition of certain antigens already segregating in the population. Specific recognition of HLA may have been favored because of the association between HLA and loci prone to deleterious mutations. In particular, if mutations occurring at IR loci greatly reduce fitness, then mechanisms permitting early monitoring of normal function of IR genes would be strongly favored. Exclusion of similar HLA genotypes would moderate inbreeding depression to the extent that homozygosity at HLA loci is a reliable indicator of homozygosity at loci at which deleterious mutations segregate. The advanced age of onset characteristic of the diseases associated with HLA suggests that the selection pressure they induce is weak. However, associations can be observed only for diseases that mechanisms promoting higher offspring quality failed to prevent. The definitive test of the association between offspring quality and maternal–fetal incompatibility requires subversion of all incompatibility mechanisms in order to permit comparison between offspring viability in the presence and the absence of incompatibility.

Maternal–fetal incompatibilities involving HLA may have arisen in response to the association between HLA and IR genes rather than the diseases themselves. The selection pressure favoring outbreeding at IR genes would derive from the expression of mutations that result in the absence of function or dysfunction of generalized immune responses. Absence of expression of immune response genes is recessive (Benacerraf and McDevitt, 1972), as required by this interpretation. However, abnormal expression may be dominant (ankylosing spondylitis, multiple sclerosis) as well as recessive (hemochromatosis) (Thomson, 1981). Further, recent analysis indicates synergism among HLA-DR alleles associated with predisposition to insulin-dependent diabetes mellitus (Thomson et al., 1986).

ASSOCIATIVE OVERDOMINANCE CONFERRED ON INCOMPATIBILITY LOCI BY DELETERIOUS MUTATIONS

Associative overdominance describes the apparent fitness advantage of heterozygous combinations caused by associations with a distinct set of selected genes rather than from the expression of the primary loci themselves. In this section, I explore the proposal that deleterious mutations throughout the genome may generate selective pressures favoring incompatibility. Concordance between mates at incompatibility loci can serve as a prospective indication of inbreeding depression to the extent that the levels of homozygosity at incompatibility loci and at loci responsible for inbreeding depression are correlated.

Muller's hypothesis for the inactivation of genes borne on the Y chromosome proposes that the enforced heterozygosity of the sex chromosomes permits the maintenance of deleterious recessive genes (see Fisher, 1935; Nei, 1970). To test this hypothesis, Fisher (1935) studied the evolution of the association between the sex chromosomes and a locus prone to recessive lethal mutations. Because the conditions for the development of complete association between the Y chromosome and the recessive lethal include extraordinary assumptions on the mutation rates, Fisher concluded that Muller's theory was implausible. However, Nei (1970) showed that in populations of finite size, fixation of the lethal gene on the Y chromosome can occur under genetic drift if the rate of recombination is sufficiently low. (Charlesworth [1978] developed another suggestion by Muller, showing that the absence of recombination between the X and Y chromosomes can result in the accumulation of deleterious mutations on the Y chromosome.) The question of whether incompatibility loci can serve as prospective indicators of inbreeding depression inverts this classical debate: The issue concerns not the sheltering of lethals by enforced heterozygosity, but rather whether deleterious genes can impart an advantage to heterozygosity at incompatibility loci.

The role of population structure in the generation of associations among loci

In randomly mating populations, genetic drift can generate linkage disequilibrium between neutral loci and a locus under overdominant selection or selection disfavoring partially recessive deleterious genes (Sved, 1968; Ohta and Kimura, 1970; Ohta, 1971, 1973). This association can increase the level of heterozygosity at neutral loci.

Ohta and Cockerham (1974) demonstrated that a balance between mutation and selection can impart associative overdominance to a neutral locus in populations undergoing partial selfing, even in the absence of linkage disequilibrium. The magnitude of this effect primarily depends on identity disequilibrium (Cockerham and Weir, 1968), a measure of the excess of two-locus inbreeding beyond the expectation based on the single locus levels of inbreeding. Partial selfing generates positive equilibrium levels of identity disequilibrium between two neutral loci, even in the absence of linkage and linkage disequilibrium (Weir and Cockerham, 1973). This excess of doubly homozygous and doubly heterozygous combinations can cause an apparent heterosis at the neutral locus under purifying selection at the associated locus (Ohta and Cockerham, 1974).

The development of associations between incompatibility systems and other loci depends upon population size, the mating system, and the rate of recombination. Strobeck (1980) found that in randomly mating populations the level of heterozygosity at a neutral locus linked to a locus controlling heterostyly or to a translocation exceeds the expectation based on the effects of drift and mutation only if the product of effective population size and the recombination rate is small. Holsinger and Feldman (1981) showed that linkage disequilibrium between a translocation and a heterotic locus affecting viability evolves in a population undergoing partial selfing if linkage is sufficiently tight.

Identity disequilibrium between a neutral locus and an incompatibility locus

As a preliminary investigation into the magnitude of associative overdominance between loci subject to inbreeding depression and incompatibility loci, I computed identity disequilibrium between a neutral locus and a locus causing partial incompatibility in a population undergoing selfing and random mating (but no biparental inbreeding). As assumed in a preceding section, the two alleles at the incompatibility locus (A and a) occur in equal frequencies, with homozygotes inhibiting pollen bearing the same allele ($a_1 = c_2 < a_2 = c_1$) and no net gametic selection in heterozygotes ($b_1 = b_2$). Let r represent the rate of recombination between the incompatibility locus and a neutral locus at which two alleles (B and b) segregate. Zero linkage disequilibrium is assumed between the two loci.

The coefficient of inbreeding at the incompatibility locus is

$$F_A = [1 - (1 - s)g_2]/[1 + (1 - s)g_2] \tag{13}$$

where s represents the fraction of self-pollen received and g_2 the fertilization rate of pollen bearing an allele different from the one held by a homozygous seed parent relative to the average received by that parent,

$$g_2 = 2a_2/[a_1(1 + s) + a_2(1 - s)] \tag{14}$$

In the absence of incompatibility ($a_1 = a_2$, $g_2 = 1$), Equation 13 reduces to the correlation between uniting gametes expected for neutral loci in partially selfing populations: $F_A = s/(2 - s)$ (Wright, 1921, with $m = s$). In the limit approaching complete exclusion of the same allele ($a_1 \to 0$), Equation 13 converges to $-\frac{1}{3}$. (As complete incompatibility cannot occur in a biallelic population, a_1 necessarily remains positive.) Incompatibility causes an excess of heterozygosity over the expectation based on the selfing rate; in fact, the locus is more outbred than expected under random mating if the ratio of the success rates of same and different pollen exceeds the relative frequencies in which they occur on stigmas of homozygotes:

$$a_2/a_1 > (1 + s)/(1 - s) \tag{15}$$

Incompatibility also affects the inbreeding coefficient at the neutral locus:

$$F_B = s/(2 - sg_1) + s(1 - s)(g_1 - g_2)\{1 - s/2 \\ + sr(1 - r)[1 - (1 - s)g_2]\}/E \tag{16}$$

where $g_1 = g_2a_1/a_2$ represents the success rate of pollen bearing the same allele relative to the average received by homozygous seed parents (see Equation 14), and E is

$$[2 - s + 2sr(1 - r)][1 + (1 - s)g_2](2 - sg_1)$$

In the absence of incompatibility ($a_1 = a_2$, $g_1 = g_2 = 1$), F_B reduces to the neutral value as expected. While F_B always lies below the neutral value (locus B is more outbred), it remains above the random mating value of zero for all levels of incompatibility.

Identity disequilibrium between the incompatibility locus and the neutral locus is

$$\eta = 2s(1 - s)g_2\{2[1 + \lambda^2(1 - s)] [1 + (1 - s)g_2] $$
$$+ (g_1 - g_2) (1 - s) (2 - s\lambda^2)\}/E' \tag{17}$$

where λ replaces $(1 - 2r)$ (in Cockerham's notation; see Weir and Cockerham, 1973), and E' is

$$[4 - s(1 + \lambda^2)] [1 + (1 - s)g_2]^2(2 - sg_1)$$

In the absence of incompatibility, Equation 17 reduces to the expression obtained by Weir and Cockerham (1973) for neutral loci:

$$\eta_N = \frac{4s(1 - s) [1 + \lambda^2(1 - s)]}{(2 - s)^2[4 - s(1 + \lambda^2)]} \tag{18}$$

As noted by Weir and Cockerham (1973), identity disequilibrium declines as linkage decreases. The value approached by Equation 17 as incompatibility becomes intense ($a_1 \to 0$) exceeds the neutral expectation (Equation 18) if

$$\lambda^2(2 - s) (1 + s) (2s - 1) + (1 - \lambda^2) [s^2 - 5(1 - s)] > 0 \tag{19}$$

Equation (19) is satisfied for high rates of selfing (s greater than ½) and sufficiently tight linkage. This result suggests that incompatibility can generate stronger identity disequilibrium than that expected between two neutral loci.

Incompatibility reduces the level of inbreeding at both the incompatibility locus and the neutral locus. Further, even in the absence of linkage disequilibrium, identity disequilibrium between an incompatibility locus and a neutral locus evolves under partial inbreeding. Positive identity disequilibrium implies an excess of doubly homozygous and doubly heterozygous genotypes, and a deficiency of single heterozygotes. In particular, individuals that are heterozygous at the incompatibility locus are likely to be heterozygous at the neutral locus as well. If these conclusions hold for loci that contribute to inbreeding depression, then identity disequilibrium confers an advantage in viability on the evolution of incompatibility.

SUMMARY

The analysis of the components of selection (Equation 4) presented in this study indicates that considerable selective barriers confront the evolution of incompatibility. Gametic selection directly opposes alleles expressed in the style that cause their own exclusion among pollen. Further, by reducing relatedness between parents and their offspring derived from uniparental and biparental inbreeding, incompatibility causes a decline in the fidelity of transmission between generations. Incompatibility influences the relative rates of production of offspring derived from various outcrossing distances under mixed pollen loads.

Tradeoffs in offspring number depend upon the relative level of genetic concordance between the style and the pollen classes (Equation 13) as well as the availability of the pollen classes. For example, higher rates of incompatibility can increase the relative rate of production of offspring derived by biparental inbreeding if the average level of inbreeding exceeds the level of inbreeding among those offspring (Equation 10).

Anderson and Stebbins (1984) have suggested that dioecy furnishes a more versatile and efficient means of avoiding selfing than does gametophytic self-incompatibility in a variety of ecological settings. The analytical results reviewed here support the view that if avoidance of selfing were the only function of incompatibility, the evolution of other mechanisms (including morphological or phenological changes) would seem to require less stringent conditions.

In contrast, Seavey and Bawa (1986) enumerate numerous examples of functionally similar late-acting systems that reduce concordance between offspring and parent. Late-acting incompatibility appears to represent a general feature of maternal–fetal interactions in mammals as well. Mulcahy and Mulcahy (1983) and Seavey and Bawa (1986) suggest that subtle forms of incompatibility may be more common than traditionally suspected.

A paradox arises between the apparent prevalence of partial or quantitative incompatibility and the selective barriers opposing its evolution. The preliminary analysis described here suggests that two factors may promote incompatibility. First, the effect of incompatibility on the relative rates of biparental inbreeding may provide a mechanism for regulating outcrossing distance. The extensive microgeographic differentiation found in natural populations of plants indicates that outcrossing is highly localized and likely to involve related individuals (Jain and Bradshaw, 1966; Ehrlich and Raven, 1969; Bradshaw, 1972; Levin and Kerster, 1974). Biparental inbreeding may represent the best compromise between increasing parent–offspring relatedness and avoiding inbreeding depression (Bateson, 1980). Incompatibility may be favored in highly inbred populations by simultaneously decreasing the rate of selfing and increasing the rates of both random outcrossing and biparental inbreeding.

Second, incompatibility may provide a mechanism for the assessment of offspring quality by serving as a means of amplifying variation in offspring vigor or as an indicator of general genomic homozygosity. Early expression of deleterious genes may be advantageous if it permits reinvestment of resources in offspring with better prospects (Hamilton, 1966). Incompatibility loci that are genetically and functionally distinct from the loci that cause inbreeding depression can be used to accomplish the same end as early expression to the extent that the levels of homozygosity within the two sets of loci are correlated. The nature and magnitude of this correlation determine the selective advantage of incompatibility. In the absence of inbreeding, linkage disequilibrium alone contributes to the correlation between incompatibility and offspring quality. However, inbreeding generates identity disequilibrium among loci, even in the absence of linkage disequilibrium (Weir and Cockerham, 1973). Identity disequilibrium between a neutral locus and a locus held in a balance between mutation and purifying selection can cause associative overdominance at the neutral locus (Ohta and Cockerham, 1974). The proposal considered in this chapter suggests that inbreeding depression can confer associative overdominance on an incompatibility locus. This association contributes to a correlation between the level of incompatibility and offspring quality. A preliminary analysis indicates that identity disequilibrium between an incompatibility locus and a neutral locus evolves under partial selfing.

The adaptive value of sexual reproduction as a means of generating variation among offspring and novel recombinants depends in large part on parent–offspring relatedness and offspring quality. Viewed as one endpoint of a continuum of breeding systems, the asexual–sexual transition engendered enormous possibilities for evolutionary responses to the variable and conflicting selective pressures bearing on reproduction. Parent–offspring relatedness and offspring quality govern the evolution of breeding systems subsequent to the establishment of sexual reproduction as well. Integrated genetic incompatibility systems comprise antigen loci, modifiers of the intensity of the incompatibility reaction, and loci contributing to inbreeding depression. By serving the dual functions of monitoring the correlation between mates and assessing offspring quality, incompatibility systems may provide a means for the regulation of outcrossing distance.

APPENDIX

The numbers of individuals surviving to reproductive age may be obtained from information similar to that shown in Table 1. Let Tu_1', Tu_2', and Tu_3' denote the numbers of AA, Aa, and aa among adults of the next generation; u_1', u_2', and u_3' the frequencies of those individuals; and T the normalizer that ensures that the frequencies sum to unity. For each genotype, define fitness as the proportional excess (see Fisher, 1941):

$$F_i - \bar{F} = T(u_i' - u_i)/u_i \qquad \text{(A.1)}$$

where $F_i - \bar{F}$ denotes the deviation in the character value from the mean and u_i the frequency of genotype i among adults of the current generation. The covariance between fitness as defined in Equation A.1 and the additive genotypic value with respect to the number of offspring produced by outcrossing is

$$\text{Cov}(FA) = \sum_i u_i A_i T(u_i' - u_1)/u_i \qquad \text{(A.2a)}$$

$$= 2T\Delta p(\alpha_1 - \alpha_2) \qquad \text{(A.2b)}$$

where A_i denotes the additive genotypic value associated with genotype i (see Robertson, 1966; Falconer, 1966; Li, 1967, 1976; Price, 1970, 1972; Crow and

Nagylaki, 1976). Equation A.2a comprises weighted averages of offspring additive genotypic values:

$$\text{Cov}(FA) = E(S_\alpha M_S) + E(I_\alpha M_I) + E(R_\alpha M_R) - TE(M_\alpha) \qquad (A.3a)$$
$$= \text{Cov}(S_\alpha M_S) + \text{Cov}(I_\alpha M_I) + \text{Cov}(R_\alpha M_R) +$$
$$T[E(0_\alpha) - E(M_\alpha)] \qquad (A.3b)$$

where S_α, I_α, and R_α denote the additive genotypic values of offspring derived by selfing, biparental inbreeding, and random mating; M_S, M_I, and M_R the genotypic values (dominance and additive components) of maternal parents with respect to those three characters; and $E(M_\alpha)$ the average additive genotypic value among maternal parents. The last bracketed expression in Equation A.3b, representing the component of gametic selection (G in Equation 4), is defined as the average difference over seed parents and over offspring classes between the maternal additive genotypic value and the additive genotypic values among its offspring in that class. For example, for the class of offspring derived by selfing, this difference is zero except in the case of heterozygous parents, for which the average additive genotypic value among offspring is

$$\{b_1[2\alpha_1 + (\alpha_1 + \alpha_2)] + b_2[(\alpha_1 + \alpha_2) + 2\alpha_2]\}/[2(b_1 + b_2)] \qquad (A.4)$$

For the other offspring classes, the difference between the additive genotypic values of the seed parent and the mean among offspring departs from zero in the presence of genetic variation among offspring.

Define parent–offspring relatedness as the ratio of the covariance between offspring additive genotypic value and parental genotypic value to the covariance between these components within parents:

$$b_{M \to D} = \text{Cov}(D_\alpha M_D)/\text{Cov}(M_\alpha M_D) \qquad (A.5)$$

where D represents the offspring classes (S, I, or R) and M_D the parental genotypic value with respect to production of that offspring class (see Michod and Hamilton, 1980; Orlove and Wood, 1978). Each of the covariances in Equation A.3b can be written as a product of parent–offspring relatedness and another covariance:

$$\text{Cov}(D_\alpha M_D) = b_{M \to D}\text{Cov}(M_\alpha M_D) \qquad (A.6a)$$
$$= b_{M \to D}\text{Var}(M_\alpha) (\epsilon_1 - \epsilon_2)/(\alpha_1 - \alpha_2) \qquad (A.6b)$$

where the last ratio represents the ratio of the average effects of substitution for the two characters. In previous studies (Uyenoyama and Bengtsson, 1982; Uyenoyama, 1984, 1985, 1986), ratios of average effects of substitution were interpreted as measures of relative cost. Equation A.6b follows from A.6a because the additive and dominance components are by definition independent within parents and the three additive genotypic values associated with each genotype are proportional to one another in biallelic populations. Using Equation A.6, Equation A.3 produces Equation 4.

CHAPTER 14

BENEFITS AND COSTS OF

BIPARENTAL AND UNIPARENTAL

REPRODUCTION IN PLANTS

David G. Lloyd

INTRODUCTION

Studies of sexual strategies in plants and animals have emphasized a small number of major topics. Among these, the relative advantages of sexual and asexual reproduction has emerged as one of the central concerns of evolutionary biologists, as this volume attests. Botanists in particular have given prolonged attention to a second topic, the evolution of self-fertilization. A change from outcrossing ancestors to frequently selfing descendants has evolved numerous times (at least 300 times in the Onagraceae alone [Raven, 1979]), and it may well be the most common evolutionary change in plants. A third topic, the allocation of limited parental resources to male and female offspring or functions, has recently become one of the most productive areas of "strategy thinking" (Charnov, 1982).

This chapter considers the evolution of sexual allocations, asexual reproduction, and self-fertilization in flowering plants. Previous studies have tended to compartmentalize the three subjects. I attempt to provide links between the topics and to include a number of factors, particularly those concerned with pollination ecology, that have not always received the attention they deserve. The first two sections emphasize that there are many reproductive expenses other than those to pollen and seeds. These accessory structures constitute a major and sometimes predominant part of the reproductive allocation, and are incorporated into an allocation model for outcrossing species. The third section analyzes the selection of asexual reproduction and self-fertilization in a single model that treats the major similarities and differences between the two methods of reproduction. The final section examines the effects of the occurrence of uniparental reproduction on the selection of allocations to various reproductive structures.

REPRODUCTIVE ALLOCATIONS

The most widely discussed reproductive allocation strategies concern "sex allocation" (Charnov, 1982), the apportionment of resources by sexually reproducing parents to male and female offspring or to offspring derived from male and female gametes. Most sex allocation studies have considered the sex ratios of dioecious populations, starting with Fisher's (1930) key argument that parents are selected to invest equally in male and female offspring. A large majority of plant populations however, consist of a single morph, a cosex, that produces both male and female gametes and on average acquires equal fitness through both functions (Lloyd, 1980b). In cosexual populations, gender allocations are concerned with maternal versus paternal investment. If the fitness curves relating maternal or paternal fitness to the expenditure on each function are linear, equal allocations to maternal and paternal functions are selected (Maynard Smith, 1971), paralleling Fisher's conclusion. Various factors, such as local mate or resource competition, self-fertilization, or interference between functions can select unequal allocations (Charnov, 1979, 1982; Charlesworth and Charlesworth, 1981; Lloyd, 1984).

The "direct" products of sex allocations are the gametes and offspring that transmit the genes of parents to future generations. Besides these direct allocations to pollen and seeds, successful reproduction requires considerable expenditure on "accessory" activities that do not contribute directly to the next generation, such as flower stems and petals. Little attention has been paid to the accessory costs of reproduction. They have been included in discussions of sex allocation in only three contexts. Heath (1977) considered the effects of "fixed" unilateral costs that are outlaid in full before any fitness accrues from male or female expenditure (see also Charlesworth and Charlesworth, 1981; Lloyd, 1984). Schoen and Lloyd (1984) showed that the degree to which the expenditure on the corolla and other attraction organs is reduced in cleistogamous (closed, automatically self-fertilized) flowers affects the likelihood that cleistogamous self-fertilization is selected. Recently, Charnov and Bull (1986) incorporated the costs of attraction into a model of gender allocation in angiosperms, using the technique of Lagrange multipliers.

Similarly, most measurements of reproductive allocations in cosexual plant populations have concentrated on the proportions of paternal and maternal expenditure. Some of the studies have assumed that the gender allocations are restricted to the stamens (containing the pollen) and carpels (seeds and fruits), excluding or ignoring the costs of organs other than the sporophylls. Other studies have assigned accessory structures to one or both sexual functions without any rigorous justification. The costs of attracting and rewarding pollinators, in particular, have sometimes been split equally between maternal and paternal functions (Cruden and Lyon, 1985), sometimes assigned solely to the paternal function (Charnov and Bull, 1986), and sometimes calculated by both methods (Schoen, 1982; Bell, 1985).

The view adopted here is that reproduction is a complex process involving many structures that contribute to reproductive fitness in diverse ways. Selection determines the allocation of the various structures in proportions such that the fitness of the individual plants cannot be exceeded and is evolutionarily stable. To understand reproductive allocations, we must look at the selection of the individual structures involved before we can interpret the total sexual functions.

The numerous reproductive structures can be grouped in several ways, for different purposes. The most obvious classification is into male and female allocations. In dioecious species, the distinction between male and female allocations is easy to make on the basis of resources invested directly in male and female offspring. In cosexual species, however, maternal and paternal fitness are achieved by the same parent in different ways, and it is extremely difficult to partition structures such as petals and sepals into unequivocal male and female contributions.

Other classifications of the diverse reproductive structures are sometimes helpful. Allocations may be grouped into those concerned with preflowering mating strategies and postflowering parental investment. Allocations may also be classified according to their functions, including pollen and seed production, support (floral stems, the filaments of stamens), servicing pollination (attractants and rewards), and dispersal (fruit walls and sometimes other organs). Another functional division, already alluded to, is between direct allocations to pollen and seeds and allocations to all other (accessory) organs. The models presented below distinguish between "unilateral" costs that benefit either maternal or paternal fitness and "bilateral" costs that benefit both, although not necessarily to equal extents. All these classifications, like the division into male and female allocations, run into practical difficulties concerning the boundaries between the alternative classes and should not be used inflexibly.

Measurements of reproductive allocations

To compare the magnitudes of the direct maternal and paternal allocations to pollen and seeds with the assorted accessory costs, I searched the literature on allocation measurements. Unfortunately, few studies have separated pollen from the remainder of the stamens, or seeds from fruit. Hence, the data have been assembled into three broad categories (Table 1). The "paternal" allocation to stamens and the "maternal" allocation to seeds and fruits include some accessory costs. The assorted accessory costs of all other organs is an underestimate of the true allocation to all accessory structures.

Estimates of at least some of the accessory expenses have been published for 15 cosexual species that are frequently outcrossed (see Table 1), including

TABLE 1. Proportionate allocations to stamens, seeds plus fruits, and other organs in angiosperms

Species	Proportionate Allocations (%)		
	Stamens	Seeds plus Fruits	Other Organs
COSEXUAL SPECIES WITH OPEN FLOWERS			
Amaryllis hybrid[a]	5	64	36
Impatiens pallida[b]	7	49	25
Impatiens biflora[b]	7	45	31
Trillium grandiflorum[c]	6	56	37
Erythronium albidum[c]	12	67	21
Podophyllum peltatum[c]	10	66	24
Hibiscus trionum[c]	2	80	19
Gilia achilleifolia[d]	5	83	12
Geranium maculatum[e]	8	62	29
Oxalis violacea[e]	4	74	22
Sisyrinchium campestre[e]	5	72	23
Hesperis matronalis[e]	7	73	20
Solanum dulcamara[e]	5	86	9
Epilobium angustifolium[e]	6	80	14
Phormium tenax[f]	3	34	66
SPECIES WITH CLOSED, SELFED FLOWERS			
Impatiens pallida[b]	0.5	98	2.0
Impatiens biflora[b]	0.6	98	1.2
MALE PHASE OF A SEX-CHOOSING SPECIES			
Arisaema dracontium[g]	1.4	0	98.5
FEMALE MORPH OF A DIOECIOUS SPECIES			
Silene alba[h]	0	92	8

[a]Data from Smith and Evenson (1978). [b] Data from Schemske (1978). [c] Data from Lovett Doust and Cavers (1982a). [d] Data from Schoen (1982). [e] Data from Cruden and Lyon (1985). [f] Data from C. Aker (unpublished data). [g] Data from Lovett Doust and Cavers (1982b). [h] Data from Gross and Soulé (1981).

separate estimates for the open and closed (cleistogamous) flowers in two species of Impatiens (Schemske, 1978). The only estimates that I found for functionally unisexual plants are those of the male phase of a diphasic (sex-choosing) species, *Arisaema dracontium* (Lovett Doust and Cavers, 1982b), and the female morph of a dioecious species, *Silene alba* (Gross and Soulé, 1981).

Few of the data sets have included all accessory structures. In particular, flower stems and nectar were rarely included. Among the few studies that have separately itemized the cost of flower stems, these varied from only 1% to 4% of the *total* reproductive costs in the two floral types of Impatiens species up to 54% and 78% of all costs in *Phormium tenax* and *Arisaema dracontium*. In some species, nectar is also a major item of reproductive expenditure (South-wick, 1984), and its omission further reduces the estimates of accessory allocations below their true value. All estimates in Table 1 are based on dry weights, except for the data on Amaryllis and Impatiens, for which the figures were calculated from calorie values.

Despite the inadequacies of the measurements, the data on the 17 species are informative. For the 15 cosexual species, including the open flowers of Impatiens, the estimates of the assorted accessory costs vary between 9% and 83% of all reproductive costs, even though fruit walls are transferred to the "fruits and seeds" category. In all 15 species, the accessory costs exceed the costs of stamens (even though these include the accessory items, anther walls and filaments) and approach or exceed the costs of fruits and seeds. The accessory costs may exceed direct paternal costs in most angiosperms. In a study of 39 species ranging from "outcrossing" to "facultatively autogamous," Cruden and Lyon (1985) found that the weights of the calyx and corolla alone exceeded the *total* weight of stamens in 36 of the species. Unfortunately, they measured fruit and seed weights for only 6 species (those in Table 1), so the maternal costs cannot be calculated for all 39 species.

The two estimates for closed, selfed (cleistogamous) flowers show considerably lower accessory allocations (1% to 2%), associated with the greatly reduced corollas of these flowers. The single estimate for a functionally male plant, the male phase of *Arisaema dracontium*, shows by far the highest allocation to accessory structures (98.5%) of all 17 species, caused principally by heavy stems and low pollen production. In contrast, the only estimate of accessory costs for a female plant, the female morph of *Silene alba* (8%), is lower than those for the open flowers of all 15 cosexual species.

Although the amount of information on allocations to reproductive structures is frustratingly small, three generalizations seem justified. First, the accessory expenses constitute a sizable fraction of the total reproductive expenditure. In some species accessory structures absorb more than half the total reproductive allocation. Second, in all 15 cosexual species, the costs of stamens are much less than the expenditure on seeds and fruits. Third, there are tantalizing suggestions that the size of the allocation to accessory structures varies with the sex and breeding system of flowers. (The differences between the groups in Table 1 are in agreement with the predictions of the models below.) There is an urgent need for more fully itemized studies of additional species, so that the effects of gender and frequency of self-fertilization on the direct and accessory allocations can be documented more accurately.

SELECTION OF ALLOCATIONS IN OUTCROSSING COSEXES, FEMALES, AND MALES

The models in this section examine the selection of the allocations to various reproductive structures in plants that are obligately outcrossing. Five types of reproductive structures are considered: direct and accessory structures that contribute to either maternal or paternal fitness and bilateral accessory structures that contribute to both functions. The effect of each type of structure on paternal or maternal fitness is assumed to be proportional to the allocation to that structure (a relative fraction represented by a letter of the alphabet), raised to a power designated by the corresponding or nearest Greek letter. The costs and fitness effects of the allocations are:

> direct paternal cost, a_i, where $p_i \propto (oa_i)^\alpha$
> direct maternal cost, b_i, where $m_i \propto (nb_i)^\beta$
> accessory bilateral cost, g_i, where $p_i \propto (c_g g_i)^\gamma$ and $m_i \propto (c_e g_i)^\epsilon$
> accessory paternal cost, k_i, where $p_i \propto (c_k k_i)^\kappa$
> accessory maternal cost, l_i, where $m_i \propto (c_l l_i)^\lambda$

Here p_i and m_i are the paternal and maternal fitness of individual i, and the sum of the allocations, $a_i + b_i + g_i + k_i + l_i = 1$. The terms within the parentheses are the proportional allocations adjusted by a scaling factor. Thus, o is the number of pollen grains that would be produced if the entire reproductive effort was invested in pollen ($a_i = 1$), n is the number of seeds produced if $b_i = 1$, and c_g, c_e, c_l, and c_k are proportionality constants that scale the appropriate accessory allocations. If an exponent, α, β . . . λ, is greater (or less) than 1, the fitness curve relating the appropriate allocation to maternal or paternal fitness is positively accelerating (or decelerating, showing diminishing fitness gains).

The various direct and accessory allocations affecting paternal fitness (a, g, and k) or maternal fitness (b, g, and l) are assumed to have independent, multiplicative effects, that is

$$m_i = (nb_i)^\beta (c_e g_i)^\epsilon (c_l l_i)^\lambda \text{ and}$$
$$p_i \propto (oa_i)^\alpha (c_g g_i)^\gamma (c_k k_i)^\kappa$$

The paternal fitness of a plant is the seed fitness of its mates multiplied by the fraction of its mates' ovules that it fertilizes. The latter is its own male competitiveness, $(oa_i)^\alpha (c_g g_i)^\gamma (c_k k_i)^\kappa$, divided by that of the total K plants competing for the ovules of each plant. The fitness of a phenotype, w_i, is the sum of its maternal and paternal fitness, that is, $w_i = m_i + p_i$.

Allocations of cosexes

If there is a single sexual morph in a population, it must contribute genes on average equally through its male and female gametes. The allocation of such cosexes (which include hermaphrodite and monoecious floral conditions) are examined first.

The set of allocations that constitutes an evolutionarily stable strategy, an ESS (Maynard Smith, 1982), is found by comparing the fitness of a resident phenotype, phenotype 1 with allocations a_1, b_1, g_1, k_1, and l_1, with that of a rare mutant of phenotype 2 with allocations a_2, b_2, g_2, k_2 and l_2. If K is large, all individuals outcross with and compete in pollen pools only with individuals of phenotype 1, and the fitnesses of resident and mutant cosexual phenotypes are respectively

$$w_1 = (nb_1)^\beta (c_e g_1)^\epsilon (c_l l_1)^\lambda + K(nb_1)^\beta (c_e g_1)^\epsilon (c_l l_1)^\lambda \cdot \frac{(oa_1)^\alpha (c_g g_1)^\gamma (c_k k_1)^\kappa}{K(oa_1)^\alpha (c_g g_1)^\gamma (c_k k_1)^\kappa}$$

$$w_2 = (nb_2)^\beta (c_e g_2)^\epsilon (c_l l_2)^\lambda + K(nb_1)^\beta (c_e g_1)^\epsilon (c_l l_1)^\lambda \cdot \frac{(oa_2)^\alpha (c_g g_2)^\gamma (c_k k_2)^\kappa}{K(oa_1)^\alpha (c_g g_1)^\gamma (c_k k_1)^\kappa}$$

The ability of the mutant to increase is expressed by its fitness advantage, $w_2 - w_1$ (Hamilton, 1967). A necessary condition for a set of allocations to be an ESS is that the fitness advantages from slight increases in each of the allocations, their "marginal advantages," are equal (Lloyd, unpubl.), that is,

$$\frac{\partial(w_2 - w_1)}{\partial a_2} = \frac{\partial(w_2 - w_1)}{\partial b_2} = \frac{\partial(w_2 - w_1)}{\partial g_2} = \frac{\partial(w_2 - w_1)}{\partial k_2} = \frac{\partial(w_2 - w_1)}{\partial l_2} \quad (1)$$

Obtaining $w_2 - w_1$, differentiating it with respect to each of the allocations, and equating the marginal advantages gives stationary conditions only when

$$\hat{a} : \hat{b} : \hat{g} : \hat{k} : \hat{l} = \alpha : \beta : \gamma + \epsilon : \kappa : \lambda \quad (2)$$

Equation 2 provides a simple solution to the proportionate allocations to direct and accessory items of reproductive expenditure. The allocation to each item depends only on its own effects, specified by the shape of the fitness curve relating expenditure on the item to fitness returns from it. More precisely, the allocation to an item is proportional to the exponent of its fitness curve, which measures the extent to which fitness benefits from further increments of investment continue at higher allocations.

Another feature of the allocations shown by the bilateral accessory costs is that the allocation to an item is proportional to the *sum* of its separate effects on paternal and maternal fitness ($\gamma + \epsilon$).

An important result of Equation 2 is that the *ratio* of any two allocations is independent of the sizes of the other allocations or even of whether they are included. Thus the predicted ratio of direct paternal:direct maternal expenditure, $\hat{a}:\hat{b} = \alpha:\beta$, is the same as that previously derived when all accessory costs are excluded (Charnov, 1979; Charlesworth and Charlesworth, 1981; Lloyd, 1984). The effect of including accessory costs is to show how the absolute sizes of the direct costs are reduced as a proportion of the total reproductive investment, although their ratio remains the same.

The ratio $\hat{a}:\hat{b}$ considered in previous theories of sex allocations (see Charnov, 1982) refers only to expenditure on pollen and seeds, not to the total male and female expenditures, which include the costs of a number of accessory structures. The accessory costs may be assigned to total gender allocations if this is desired. The unilateral costs, k and l, can simply be included in the total paternal and maternal costs, respectively, and bilateral accessory costs, g, may be partitioned by assigning $(\gamma/\gamma + \epsilon)$ to total paternal costs and $(\epsilon/\gamma + \epsilon)$ to total maternal costs. Then the ratios of total gender allocations are

$$\hat{A} : \hat{B} = \alpha + \gamma + \kappa : \beta + \epsilon + \lambda \tag{3}$$

Since the exponents vary independently, the sum $\alpha + \gamma + \kappa$ may be larger than or smaller than the sum $\beta + \epsilon + \lambda$. Hence there is no universal reason why total maternal costs should be larger than total paternal costs, or vice versa. Moreover, even approximate equality of total maternal and paternal allocations is a special condition achieved only when the sums of the two sets of exponents happen to be almost equal. Similarly, Equations 2 and 3 show there is no general reason why the investment by a cosexual plant in its stamens should approximate the investment in its carpels, or why the total cost of flowers up to flowering should equal the total cost of fruits and seeds, as some authors have assumed.

In many plant species, increasing expenditure on pollination costs (g) such as petals and nectar, may cause the maternal fitness to decelerate faster than the paternal fitness $(\epsilon < \gamma)$. This is expected as a corollary of Bateman's principle that the fitness of males is limited more by their ability to achieve fertilizations than is that of females (Bateman, 1948). The experiments of Willson and colleagues (e.g., Willson and Price, 1977; Willson et al., 1979) and Bell (1985) confirm that higher levels of expenditure on organs of attraction increase paternal fitness more than maternal fitness. But even if this effect is marked, it does not justify assigning *all* pollination costs to the paternal function, since maternal parents must attract pollinators to obtain their fitness.

Allocations of females and males

The ESS allocations of females to the various classes of structures are not the same as those of cosexes. The ESS allocations of strictly unisexual females may be found by comparing the fitnesses of two female phenotypes, x and y, with slightly different allocations. Then

$$w_x = (nb_x)^\beta \, (c_g g_x)^\epsilon \, (c_l l_x)^\lambda \text{ and}$$
$$w_y = (nb_y)^\beta \, (c_g g_x)^\epsilon \, (c_l l_x)^\lambda$$

Subtracting, differentiating, and equating the marginal advantages of b, g, and l gives

$$\hat{b}_\female : \hat{g}_\female : \hat{l}_\female = \beta : \epsilon : \lambda \tag{4}$$

Females optimally spend nothing on unilateral paternal items, a and k, and have an altered allocation to the previously bilateral structures, g, compared with a cosex (cf. Equation 2). The allocations specified by Equation 4 hold for females present in any frequency in a population.

The optimal allocation of a male can be obtained similarly by comparing the fitnesses of two male phenotypes with differing allocations and equating the marginal advantages of the various allocations. The optimal allocation for unisexual males at any frequency in a population is then found to be

$$\hat{a}_\delta : \hat{g}_\delta : \hat{h}_\delta = \alpha : \gamma : \kappa \qquad (5)$$

Comparative pollination costs of cosexes, males, and females

It has been claimed that cosexual plants have an advantage over unisexual males and females because the pollination costs of cosexes serve both maternal and paternal functions, so the costs are shared (Ghiselin, 1974; Charnov et al., 1976). We can compare the pollination costs in cosexes, males, and females by examining the ESS allocations to g in the results obtained above. From Equations 2, 4, and 5,

$$\begin{aligned}
\hat{g}_{co} &= (\gamma + \epsilon)/(\alpha + \beta + \gamma + \epsilon + \kappa + \lambda) \\
\hat{g}_\varphi &= \epsilon/(\beta + \epsilon + \lambda) \\
\hat{g}_\delta &= \gamma/(\alpha + \gamma + \kappa)
\end{aligned} \qquad (6)$$

The comparative values of g in the three morphs depend on the magnitude of γ and ϵ relative to each other and to the other exponents. For instance, suppose that all the exponents ($\alpha \ldots \lambda$) are equal. Then $\hat{g}_{co} = \hat{g}_\varphi = \hat{g}_\delta = \frac{1}{3}$. Alternatively, suppose that all the coefficients are equal except that ϵ approaches zero (higher allocations to attractants and rewards increase seed fitness very little). Then $\hat{g}_{co} = \frac{1}{5}$, $\hat{g}_\varphi = 0$, $\hat{g}_\delta = \frac{1}{3}$. The pollination costs for cosexes are then less than those for males but greater than those for females.

The examples show that cost sharing does not in general make the pollination costs of cosexes more economical than those of males and females. The reason why cost sharing does not lead to economies in expenditure on servicing pollinators in cosexes is that the pollination costs benefit both sexual functions, and the ESS allocation, $\hat{g}_{co}$, is proportional to the additive marginal benefits.

SELECTION OF UNIPARENTAL REPRODUCTION

The previous models assumed that reproduction occurred by outcrossing and was therefore biparental. Many seed plants, however, reproduce partly or wholly by a uniparental mode of reproduction, asexual reproduction or self-fertilization. In this section, the principal factors affecting the evolution of asexual or self-fertilizing angiosperms are examined. For brevity, the evolution of uniparental reproduction is considered only from cosexual ancestors, as has usually happened in plants. The treatment of asexual reproduction is confined to asexual reproduction by seeds, agamospermy. Vegetative reproduction is omitted because it involves quite different structures and adaptations from those used in sexual reproduction.

The following models incorporate four features that often distinguish outcrossing from uniparental reproduction by seeds, and consist of two advantages for each type of parentage.

1. *Intrinsic advantages. The intrinsic advantages* of uniparental reproduction may arise from either of two distinct sources (Treisman and Dawkins, 1976). In some modes of uniparental reproduction discussed below, asexual or selfing parents are favored because they contribute two sets of genes to each offspring and thereby retrieve the "cost of meiosis," as Williams (1971) proposed. One uniparental mode of reproduction benefits from a reduced "cost of producing males," the argument put forward by Maynard Smith (1971).

   Some methods of producing selfed or asexual seeds cause a concomitant decrease in the ability of the parent plants to succeed as outcrossing male parents (Nagylaki, 1976; Holsinger et al., 1984). If the decrease in cross-fertilizing ability of male gametes, "male discounting," is equal to the increase in uniparental reproduction, the cost of meiosis is completely nullified. This occurs in plants in which selfing occurs in specialized closed (cleistogamous) flowers that have only minimal expenditure on pollen and accessory structures. These selfed flowers have full male discounting, although they show a large (but not exactly twofold) advantage from economies in producing males and in mating costs.
2. *Reproductive assurance.* Whenever the production of outcrossed seeds is limited by pollinator activity, an increased success in reproduction occurs in species in which uniparental reproduction does not require pollinators.
3. *Parental fertility.* Successful asexual reproduction by agamospermy requires the circumvention of two complex processes, meiosis and fertilization. Particularly when agamospermy first evolves, some ovules fail to produce embryos (Gustafsson, 1946–1947; Heslop-Harrison, 1972), causing a disadvantage from reduced fertility.
4. *Offspring quality.* The offspring resulting from uniparental reproduction often have reduced average fitness, either because they are less variable (applicable to asexual progeny especially, but also to selfed progeny to a lesser extent) or because they express inbreeding depression (selfed progeny only).

The magnitude of the selective forces generated by these four factors varies widely among both asexual and self-fertilizing modes of reproduction. The following models for the selection of uniparental reproduction make the primary division among the diverse modes on the basis of whether they operate autonomously or require the activity of a pollinating agent. The models encompass uniparental reproduction in general and are applied to specific modes of asexuality or self-fertilization by inserting particular values of certain parameters.

Autonomous uniparental reproduction

A proportion, u_i, of the ovules produced by an individual of phenotype i begin to develop uniparental embryos *before* there are any opportunities for cross-fertilization. A proportion, f, of these ovules are fertile and produce progeny with an average fitness, q. The fertility and average fitness of outcrossed embryos are defined as one. Only a fraction, e, of the $(1 - u_i)$ ovules available for outcrossing are fertilized when pollinator activity is limited. All individuals produce m male gametes, but the effective number of male gametes is reduced in proportion to the frequency of uniparental reproduction by a factor, $1 - xu_i$, where x measures the extent of male discounting.

Assuming that all male gametes in a population have the same prospects of achieving cross-fertilization after discounting is taken into account, the proportion of each mate's ovules fertilized by an individual is its discounted number of male gametes, $m(1 - xu_i)$, divided by the discounted total of male gametes in the gamete pool from K paternal parents competing for each outcrossed ovule. The population consists of a prevalent resident phenotype ($i = 1$) and a single mutant ($i = 2$) that respectively reproduce uniparentally in proportions u_1 and u_2 of their ovules ($u_2 > u_1$). When K is large, the discounted pool of competing male gametes is $Km(1 - xu_1)$, and these compete for $K(1 - u_1)$ ovules. Each individual produces n^* seeds when seed set is not limited by pollinator activity.

The fitness of an individual is the sum of two sets of genes contributed to each uniparental offspring plus one set of genes to each maternally- and paternally-derived outcrossed offspring. The fitness of individuals of phenotype i ($= 1$ or 2) is thus

$$w_i = n^* \left[2u_i fq + e(1 - u_i) + Ke(1 - u_1) \cdot \frac{m(1 - xu_i)}{Km(1 - xu_1)} \right]$$

Substituting for $i = 1$ and 2 and subtracting gives the fitness advantage of a mutant increasing the proportion of uniparental reproduction,

$$w_2 - w_1 = n^*(u_2 - u_1) \left\{ 2fq - e \left[1 + \frac{x(1 - u_1)}{1 - xu_1} \right] \right\}$$

When the resident and mutant phenotypes differ only slightly ($u_1 \doteq u_2 \doteq u$), a small increase in uniparental reproduction is favored when $w_2 - w_1 > 0$, that is,

$$fq > \frac{e}{2} \left[1 + \frac{x(1 - u)}{1 - xu} \right] \tag{7}$$

The level of outcrossing effected, e, is equal to $(c_e g)^{\epsilon}$ in the allocation models described above for outcrossing populations. Hence, uniparental reproduction is favored less when there is higher expenditure on attracting and rewarding pollinators and a higher level of outcrossing resulting from this expenditure. The values of the other parameters in Equation 7—f, q, and x—are often different for asexual reproduction and self-fertilization, so the conditions for their selection are considered separately.

In asexual individuals, the success of male gametes is unlikely to be affected by a mutation altering the frequency of sexual and asexual embryos. Putting $x \doteq 0$ for the absence of male discounting, Equation 7 becomes

$$fq > \frac{e}{2} \qquad (8)$$

All four of the selective forces incorporated in the general model affect the selection of autonomous asexual reproduction. It is favored when the multiplied effects of reduced parental fertility and offspring quality are not too severe and outweigh the reductions in the fitness of outcrosses caused by the exactly twofold cost of meiosis and the frequency of cross-fertilization.

Self-fertilization can be increased by mutations decreasing the level of physiological self-incompatibility or by bringing the presentation of pollen and stigma in a hermaphrodite flower closer together in space or time. None of these changes is likely to affect ovule fertility (i.e., $f \doteq 1$) or to have an appreciable effect on the ability of pollen to succeed in outcrossing (i.e., $x \doteq 0$). Substituting these values in Equation 7 gives

$$q > \frac{e}{2} \qquad (9)$$

Autonomous selfing that occurs before any opportunities for outcrossing in a flower (e.g., by self-pollination in flower buds) has dual advantages derived from retrieving the cost of meiosis and more assured fertilization compared with the uncertainty of outcrossing. If pollen discounting is significant $(x > 0)$, a higher fitness of inbred progeny is required before selfing is selected (Equation 7; cf. Nagylaki, 1976; Holsinger et al., 1984).

In a number of self-fertilizing species, flowers open in good weather and may receive and donate pollen for cross-fertilization, but remain closed in poor weather and are self-fertilized (Müller, 1883). Equation 7 is applicable to such species where u represents the proportion of flowers that remain closed. When selfing is induced in this way, the pollen of selfed flowers is unavailable for outcrossing and it must be completely discounted from the male outcrossing fitness. Putting $x = 1$ in Equation 7 gives if again $f = 1$

$$q > e \qquad (10)$$

This type of "induced" selfing has no intrinsic advantage and can be selected only when it increases the seed set sufficiently to outweigh the effects of inbreeding depression.

In other autonomously self-fertilized angiosperms, selfing occurs in closed flowers that spend very little on producing pollen and accessory structures other than fruit walls (i.e., $a \doteq 0$, $g \doteq 0$). Such cleistogamy has been reliably documented in more than 120 species of angiosperms (Darwin, 1877; Lord, 1981). The selective forces are similar to those for induced selfing, with the addition that savings on male costs and mating costs allow higher allocation to seeds and hence the production of more offspring. Again, there is full male discounting ($x = 1$) for the pollen in the selfed flowers (proportion u_i). If the open outcrossed flowers allocate a proportion b^* to seed and fruit production, and it is assumed that $b^* = 1$ for cleistogamous flowers,

$$w_i = n \left[(1 - u_i)b^*e + K(1 - u_1)b^*e \cdot \frac{m(1 - u_i)}{Km(1 - u_1)} + 2u_iq \right]$$

$$= 2n[1 - u_i)b^*e + u_iq]$$

The fitness advantage of a mutant increasing cleistogamy is positive when

$$q > b^*e \tag{11}$$

Cleistogamy is the only mode of uniparental reproduction whose selection depends on the cost of producing males (rather than a cost of meiosis) and on mating costs. Since the seed and fruit costs, b^*, may be less than half the total reproductive allocation (evidence reviewed previously), cleistogamy may have an intrinsic advantage that is *more* than twofold, as well as a further advantage from assuring reproduction.

The final type of autonomous self-fertilization occurs only after all opportunities for a flower to be outcrossed have passed. For example, selfing may occur when a senescent corolla closes or falls (Müller, 1883; Lloyd, 1979). When selfing is delayed, the fitness of resident and mutant phenotypes is given by

$$w_i = n \left[e + \frac{Kem}{Km} + 2(1 - e)u_iq \right]$$

Putting $i = 1$ and 2 gives the fitness advantage

$$w_2 - w_1 = 2nq(u_2 - u_1)(1 - e)$$

Delayed self-fertilization is advantageous ($w_2 > w_1$ when $u_2 > u_1$) when

$$q > 0 \text{ and } e < 1 \tag{12}$$

Conditions for delayed selfing are extremely lenient because it is simply a bonus that adds to a plant's fitness if cross-pollination is limited.

Pollinator-dependent uniparental reproduction

In some species, uniparental reproduction is as dependent on pollinators as is outcrossing. The fitness of resident and mutant phenotypes is then given by

$$w_i = ne \left[2u_i fq + (1 - u_i) + K(1 - u_1) \cdot \frac{m(1 - xu_i)}{Km(1 - xu_1)} \right]$$

Substituting $i = 1$ and 2 gives a fitness advantage to a mutant that slightly increases the frequency of selfing ($u_1 \doteq u_2 \doteq u$) when

$$fq > \frac{1}{2} \left[1 + \frac{x(1 - u)}{1 - xu} \right] \tag{13}$$

The advantages of pollinator-dependent modes of uniparental reproduction come solely from retrieval of the cost of meiosis.

First consider pseudogamous agamospermy in which pollen tube growth is required for embryo or fruit development but not for fertilization (Gustafsson, 1946–1947). As for autonomous agamospermy, $x = 0$ and $q \leq 1$. Asexual reproduction is then favored (from Equation 13) when

$$fq > \frac{1}{2} \tag{14}$$

If pollinator activity limits seed production, the conditions for the selection of asexual reproduction are more stringent when pseudogamy occurs (compare Equation 8). Hence there will be selection to eliminate pseudogamy, so that agamospermy operates independently of pollinator activity.

The special case of a mutant that produces only asexual seeds invading a population of a completely sexual phenotype is instructive. Here $u_1 = 0$ and $u_2 = 1$, and again $x = 0$. Then $w_1 = 2n^*e$ and $w_2 = n^*e(2fq + 1)$. With these simplified fitness expressions, the relative fitness of the asexual mutant is

$$\frac{w_2}{w_1} = \frac{2fq + 1}{2} \tag{15}$$

The result shows the source of the intrinsic advantage of asexual reproduction very clearly. An asexual embryo preempts the second set of genes that a separate paternal parent would contribute to outcrossed embryos, without diminishing the ability of the asexual plant to contribute as a male to the outcrossed progeny of strictly sexual parents. Hence the cost of meiosis is fully retrieved, but at the possible expense of reduced parental fertility and offspring fitness. If the latter are unimportant ($f = q = 1$), Equation 15 becomes

$$\frac{w_2}{w_1} = \frac{3}{2} \tag{16}$$

as Charlesworth (1980) concluded.

Pollinator-dependent selfing sometimes occurs when the transfer of pollen from an anther to a stigma of the same flower requires the actions of a pollinator ("competing" selfing [Lloyd, 1979]). Assuming that an increase in selfing does not affect fertility or outcrossing pollen success ($f = 1$, $x = 0$), Equation 13 then becomes

$$q > \tfrac{1}{2} \tag{17}$$

Competing selfing is the only one of the eight modes of uniparental reproduction considered in this chapter for which selection involves a simple balance between average offspring fitness favoring outcrossing and an exactly twofold intrinsic advantage of uniparental reproduction. Even here, the intrinsic advantage would be less than twofold if there is any male discounting.

One of the most common forms of self-fertilization involves the transfer of pollen from one flower to the stigma of another flower of the same plant (geitonogamy). Pollen deposited on stigmas of the plant that produced it is unavailable for cross-pollination. Hence paternal outcrossing success is fully discounted by the frequency of geitonogamy ($x = 1$), and with $f = 1$ Equation 13 becomes

$$q > 1 \tag{18}$$

Unlike the other modes of uniparental reproduction previously considered, geitonogamy has no intrinsic advantage and no advantage from assured repro-duction. It is selected against if there is any inbreeding depression ($q < 1$). Nevertheless, it occurs frequently in many species of angiosperms as an un-avoidable consequence of adaptations for outcrossing (Arroyo, 1976).

EFFECTS OF UNIPARENTAL REPRODUCTION ON REPRODUCTIVE ALLOCATIONS

The occurrence of uniparental reproduction affects the ESS allocations to pollen, seeds, and accessory structures servicing pollinators. In this section, the fitness of a resident phenotype with allocations a_1, b_1, and g_1 is compared with that of a mutant with allocations a_2, b_2, and g_2 when a proportion of the seeds of a cosexual plant are produced by uniparental selfing or asexual reproduction.

Autonomous uniparental reproduction

Suppose a proportion, u, of the ovules of a plant are committed to develop uniparentally and autonomously before a fraction $e = (c_e g_i)^\epsilon$ of the remainder are outcrossed. Assuming that the proportion of uniparental embryos may vary independently of the allocations, a_i, b_i and g_i, the fitnesses of resident and mutant phenotypes ($i = 1$ and 2) are given by

$$w_i = (nb_i)^\beta[2ufq + (1 - u)(c_{e}g_i)^\epsilon] + K(nb_1)^\beta(1 - u)(c_{e}g_1)^\epsilon \cdot \frac{(oa_i)^\alpha(c_{g}g_i)^\gamma}{K(oa_1)^\alpha(c_{g}g_1)^\gamma}$$

Equating the marginal advantages of the three allocations as before gives an ESS when

$$\hat{a} : \hat{b} : \hat{g} = \alpha(1 - u) : \beta(2ufq + 1 - u) : (\gamma + \epsilon)(1 - u) \qquad (19)$$

As the frequency of uniparental reproduction increases, the ESS allocations to pollen, $\hat{a}$, and to servicing pollination, $\hat{g}$, decrease to zero when $u = 1$, while the allocation to seeds increases. The ratio of pollen to seed allocations was derived by Charlesworth and Charlesworth (1981). The reason why the allocations depend on the frequency of selfing or agamospermy is that in uniparental reproduction expenditure on seeds has twice the reproductive value of that on pollen and outcrossing pollination mechanisms, because two sets of genes are contributed to each seed progeny. The relationship is not due to greater efficiency of uniparental reproduction or to local mate competition, as suggested by Cruden (1977) and Charnov (1979), respectively. The nature of the allocations in self-pollinating species is considered further in Lloyd (1987).

The other three modes of autonomous self-fertilization considered in the previous section cause selection of ESS allocations that are identical to those specified in Equation 19 (Lloyd, 1987).

Pollinator-dependent uniparental reproduction

When a proportion, u, of embryos develop uniparentally only if pollen is deposited on the stigmas by pollinators, the fitnesses of resident and mutant phenotypes are

$$w_i = (nb_i)^\beta(c_{e}g_i)^\epsilon \left[2ufq + 1 - u + K(nb_1)^\beta(c_{e}g_1)^\epsilon(1 - u) \cdot \frac{(oa_i)^\alpha(c_{g}g_i)^\gamma}{K(oa_1)^\alpha(c_{g}g_1)^\gamma} \right]$$

When the marginal advantages of the allocations are equal, the ESS allocations are in the ratio

$$\hat{a} : \hat{b} : \hat{g} = \alpha(1 - u) : \beta(2ufq + 1 - u) : \gamma(1 - u) + \epsilon(2ufq + 1 - u) \qquad (20)$$

The ESS ratio of pollen to seed allocations, $\hat{a}:\hat{b}$, is the same as when uniparental reproduction is autonomous (cf. Equation 19). The allocation to outcrossing pollination mechanisms, $\hat{g}$, is more complex. Bateman's principle that male fitness is more limited than female fitness by the ability of individuals to achieve fertilizations is widely applicable in plants (Bell, 1985). Then $\beta > \epsilon$ in the present model, and the allocation to pollinator servicing decreases as uniparental reproduction increases. In contrast to the pollen allocation, however, there is still an allocation to attracting and rewarding pollinators ($\hat{g} > 0$) even when there is no outcrossing ($u = 1$).

DISCUSSION AND FUTURE DIRECTIONS

Many different structures contribute to the fitness of a reproducing plant. The allocation models presented above show that each of these structures is allocated a certain proportion of the total reproductive expenditure because of its own effects on maternal or paternal fitness or both. The various structures may be grouped into categories on several criteria—male versus female, structures concerned with mating versus those involved in parental care for the developing seeds, or direct versus accessory structures. Such classifications are a means of simplifying the diversity of structures rather than a reflection of how selection operates. The pollen, anther walls, corollas, and other structures that contribute to paternal fitness, for example, are not selected as a bloc, "the male allocation," but are selected for their own contributions.

At present, we have very little understanding of the allocations to particular structures in even a single species of angiosperms. Hence we cannot critically compare composite categories, such as total male versus female allocations, in a cosexual species. Without a knowledge of the parts, we lack a firm basis to compare the wholes. Instead, with the present state of knowledge it is preferable to consider single structures, or their simple ratios, in different species. There are several such comparisons by which the allocations predicted above can be tested.

The most precise tests of allocation theory for plants concern the changes that accompany increasing self-fertilization. There is considerable evidence that the predicted decreases in the allocations to pollen and pollination mechanisms and the expected increase in the seed allocation do occur in nature. Decreases in the number of pollen grains per flower and the pollen:ovule ratio with increasing frequencies of selfing have been observed in many genera (Cruden, 1977). Recent measurements of the pollen:fruit expenditures in several genera show an excellent agreement with expected trends (Charnov, 1982; McKone, in press). In addition, it has long been known that regularly self-fertilized plants spend less resources on attracting and rewarding pollinators, but there are no data at present that can test the quantitative predictions for allocations to structures that service pollination.

Another direction in which allocation theories could readily be tested is the comparison of the costs of servicing pollination in males and females of the same species. While it is problematical to partition the pollination costs of cosexual species into unequivocal male and female components, the pollination costs of males and females of dioecious species can be compared without the same ambiguity. The models presented above predict that when Bateman's principle applies, males should be selected to spend more resources on pollination than females. There are too few measurements of actual costs available at present to confirm these predictions quantitatively, although linear measurements of the corollas of males and females show that in most dimorphic species the corrollas of males are larger (and presumably more expensive) than those of females (Darwin, 1877; Baker, 1948). There is, however, an alternative non-adaptationist explanation of larger male corollas. In *Glechoma hederacea* and *Geranium anemonifolium*, the emasculation of hermaphrodite flowers results in corollas of similar size to those of natural female flowers (Plack, 1957). Application of gibberellic acid to emasculated flowers restores corolla size (Plack, 1958).

It would be worthwhile to compare the allocations to structures that attract and reward pollinators in the males and females of a series of dioecious angiosperms and to conduct experiments similar to those of Plack to test whether the differences observed can be attributed to allocation strategies or developmental constraints.

Another potential approach to understanding reproductive allocations is the comparison of single structures among different ecological groups. How, for example, do the total costs of nectar and petals (or their ratio) differ among related species with different pollinating agents, and how does the expenditure on fruit walls vary among species with different types of dispersal mechanisms?

The allocation models presented above might be extended in several directions. The models assume that each structure with a separate allocation has independent effects on fitness. Where there are *alternative* contributions to fitness, as in the case of offspring derived through paternal and maternal expenditure, the contributions were added together. Where different structures are *both necessary*, as when success of a male requires production of pollen and its transfer by a pollinator, their fitness effects were combined multiplicatively. Various types of interactions, including interference or facilitation between male and female functions (Lloyd, 1984), or partial substitutability of structures (nectar and petals?) could be investigated. Shapes of fitness curves other than the exponents considered above (e.g., approaches to asymptotes) could be modelled. Historical, ecological, or developmental constraints could also be included.

The models of selection of uniparental versus biparental reproduction also oversimplify the events in nature. Nevertheless, they show that the comparison involves more than the simple opposition of an exactly twofold advantage of uniparental reproduction and the genetical consequences of outcrossing. The intrinsic advantage of uniparental reproduction may be greater or less than a factor of two, and it may derive from either the cost of meiosis or the cost of producing males, or it may be absent altogether. The other factors examined—reproductive assurance, the fertility of uniparental reproduction, and the quality of the resultant offspring—also vary among different classes of uniparental reproduction. These variations may explain a number of features of the natural occurrence of uniparental modes of reproduction.

First, self-fertilization is much more frequent than asexual reproduction by seeds in the angiosperms. The disparity occurs despite the fact that selfing carries an extra handicap, inbreeding depression. Self-fertilization is much easier to achieve in developmental terms, however. It may become more frequent by the weakening or loss of self-incompatibility or by simple changes in the position or maturation of the stigmas and anthers. In contrast, the circumvention of meiosis and fertilization in asexual reproduction is much more difficult to achieve and is often associated with infertility (Gustafsson, 1946–1947; Heslop-Harrison, 1972; Lloyd, 1980a).

The various types of selfing (and those of asexual reproduction) differ markedly in their selective advantages. This is expressed in the average fitness that selfed or asexual progeny must reach before each mode of reproduction is favored. In particular, autonomous modes of uniparental reproduction are expected to be selected more easily than pollinator-dependent modes. Among asexual species, pseudogamy may persist as a historical constraint in species in which no system that bypasses the pollen function of triggering seed or fruit development has evolved. The two types of pollinator-dependent self-fertilization may exist primarily as unavoidable consequences of adaptations for outcrossing.

The four modes of autonomous selfing also differ in their ease of selection. Delayed selfing is most advantageous and might be expected to prevail. Developmental constraints may prevent its evolution in some species, however. Alternatively, there may be additional factors that have not yet been taken into account. For example, early pollination in buds may allow some fitness when flowers open in bad weather and pollen is spoiled by rain. At present, we know too little about the ecology of self-fertilization to explain the distribution of its various types.

There may be additional ecological factors that influence the selection of uniparental reproduction among plants in general. The disparity between the disperal of progeny derived from a plant's seeds and those derived from outcrossing pollen may be one such factor (Lloyd, 1980a). The seed progeny of a plant disperse the parent's genes only once, during seed dispersal. In contrast, pollen progeny disperse a plant's genes in two episodes, during pollen dispersal and seed dispersal. This factor has been quantified to date in only one context, cleistogamy, where it predicts the selection of intermediate frequencies of self- and cross-fertilization in some situations (Schoen and Lloyd, 1984).

The reproductive allocations and the modes of reproduction that have been considered in this chapter are still inadequately known and explained. If the features and distributions of outcrossed, self-fertilized and asexual species are to be understood more fully, a more eclectic approach is required. Further ecological, developmental, and historical factors should be pursued alongside the genetical factors that have been emphasized in the last generation.

SUMMARY

Expenditure on reproduction may be divided into the "direct" costs of structures that contribute genes to the next generation and "accessory" costs of structures that contribute to maternal and/or paternal fitness indirectly. In angiosperms, the direct costs are those of pollen and seeds, and accessory costs include those of flower stems, sepals, petals, nectar, and parts of the sporophylls. Measurements of accessory costs in 17 species show they are considerable, but they vary widely. Phenotypic models of the selection of allocations to reproductive structures show that the allocation to any direct or accessory structure depends on the shape of the fitness curve relating expenditure to the paternal or maternal fitness rewards. Comparison of the ESS allocations of outcrossing cosexes, males, and females reveals that cosexes do not necessarily utilize pollination costs more efficiently than unisexual morphs. In many dioecious species, males are likely to be selected to spend more on pollination costs than females.

The selection of uniparental modes of reproduction, self-fertilization, and asexual reproduction is examined in models that incorporate four factors—intrinsic advantages and more assured reproduction versus reduced parental fertility and reduced average offspring fitness. Various modes of uniparental reproduction differ markedly in their advantages, and they do not always have a twofold intrinsic advantage.

As the proportion of uniparental reproduction carried out by an individual increases, the allocation to diaspores increases and those to pollen and structures that attract and reward pollinators decrease.

CHAPTER 15

SEX AND ADAPTATION

William M. Shields

INTRODUCTION

Sex has two opposite, but not mutually exclusive, consequences that may influence the evolutionary process. Depending upon a host of auxiliary factors, sex can act as a progressive or conservative evolutionary force, or it can act as both simultaneously. By sex, I mean any of the many processes that result in a single organism containing a genome that is a mixture of genetic material drawn from at least two independently replicating sources. While usually coupled with reproduction, the production of a new individual from parent stock, sex can occur independent of reproduction. As defined, sex includes many forms of genetic fusion, exchange, or both. In prokaryotes, parasexual processes like transformation, plasmid or episome exchange, partial chromosome exchange, or nuclear fusion would qualify. In eukaryotes, nuclear fusion (as in some fungi), the classic conjugation of many protophytes and protozoans, and the postfertilization syngamy of chromosomes from different metaphyte or metazoan parents (or from different replicating chromosomes in diploid selfers) would also qualify. Finally, traditional crossing over between homologous chromosomes during meiosis in diploids would also be classed as sex.

Historically, adaptive theories have emphasized the creativity of sex in generating adaptation in new or changing environments. More recent, and currently minority, views have focused on the conservatism of sex in maintaining adaptation (for reviews, see Shields, 1982a; Stearns, 1985; Ghiselin, in this volume). All adaptive theories, however, still imply a causal relationship between sex and either the process or the state of adaptation.

SEX AND ITS CONSEQUENCES

As defined, sex has many surface manifestations, but all stem from its sole consequence of shuffling genetic material. Sex generates combinations of alleles that differ from parental combinations (Felsenstein, 1974, and in this volume). Since many of the chapters in this volume, and most of the recent books on the subject, comprehensively review the consequences of sex, I will not reiterate the details here (for my perspective, see Shields, 1982a,b). Rather, I will briefly review the major consequences of sex that impinge on questions of information processing, storage, and the process and state of adaptation.

Traditional discussions of the adaptive value of sex focused on three major costs: (1) a twofold cost of meiosis, (2) segregational load, and (3) recombinational load; and two potential benefits: (1) more efficient combinatorial production of adaptive genomic variants, or (2) more efficient removal of new deleterious genetic variants or combinations. The original assumption that sex involved unrelated donors led to the conclusion that it carried a twofold cost, in that sexually produced progeny were only half as related to their parents ($r = 0.5$) as asexually produced progeny were to theirs ($r = 1.0$) and asexual females could produce twice as many productive female progeny as could sexual females forced to produce unproductive males (Williams, 1975, 1980; Maynard Smith, 1978). It also implied that whenever well-adapted constellations of alleles were brought together into single individuals via mutation, recombination, and/ or syngamy, sex immediately tore them apart at its next occurrence, inducing significant segregational and/or recombinational loads (Table 1) (Shields, 1982a).

Even qualitative estimates of the relative magnitudes of the benefits and costs of sex could permit fairly strong statements. For sex to be favored, then the combined cost of asexuality's higher mutational and damage loads, and its higher conservatism (i.e., its inability to generate sufficient combinatorial diversity), must exceed the combined costs of sex's genetic cost of meiosis and ecological cost of males, and its segregational and recombinational loads (Table 1).

The diversifying benefits of sex or the conservative costs of asexuality occur only if it is beneficial to possess greater efficiency in creating and recreating genetic diversity throughout the genome. This emphasis resulted in a search for environments that could favor a gambling strategy of creating novel combinations every generation. Such diversity could be useful in time (e.g., between parents and progeny, important in most biotic interaction models of sex), in space (e.g., among a single female's progeny, most important in sibling competition models of sex, like Ghiselin's tangled bank theory, in this volume), or in both (e.g., in any environment that varies sufficiently in time and space that the gamble of sex is necessary to produce the Sisyphian genomes that are required to win; Williams, 1975).

TABLE 1 The relative values of the genetic costs hypothetically associated with alternative reproductive strategies[a]

Potential Costs	Reproductive Strategy		
	Outbreeding	Inbreeding	Asexuality
Cost of meiosis	high	low	none
Cost of males	high to none	high to none	none
Recombinational load	high	low to none	none
Segregational load	low	high	none
Mutational load	low	low	high
Damage load	low	low	high
Cost of conservatism[b]	low	moderate to high	high

[a]Modified from Shields, 1982a.
[b]The degree of conservatism is an estimate of the capacity for a particular mode of reproduction to faithfully transmit parental genomes to progeny. It is an inverse measure of the degree of genetic differentiation between parents and their progeny and among the progeny of single females.

Since the potential conservative costs of asexuality are explored throughout this volume, I will focus here on the alternative, but not mutually exclusive, repair costs of asexuality. My narrower focus is not meant to imply that I doubt the potential importance of the creative side of sex. In fact, I find the arguments convincing as partial explanations for the origin and especially the maintenance of sex, particularly in higher-fecundity species for which the models have been validated (e.g., Ghiselin, 1974; Williams, 1975).

A BENEFIT FOR SEX: GENETIC ERROR REPAIR

Since sex is a shuffling process, its consequences are usually complementary. Every time that sex produces an individual that combines novel mutations, it also produces an individual that varies from its parents and its complementary siblings by not carrying the same novel mutations. The dual potential of sex for creating new combinations and reconstituting old combinations of alleles has a long history in evolutionary thought (e.g., Geddes and Thompson, 1914; Dougherty, 1955; Grant, 1958, 1971).

More recently, Walker and Williams (1976; Walker, 1978; Williams and Walker, 1978) provided logical and mathematical analyses along these lines. In their most explicit treatment, Walker stated that "The theory is presented that the sexual process is a repair mechanism which maintains redundancy within the sub-structure of hierarchical, self-reproducing organisms," and that "The theory of repair implies that sexual reproduction is essentially a conservative mechanism: a damaged system is *brought back* to its former functional state" (Walker, 1978).

Despite continued reiteration that sex can repair genetic error (Muller, 1964; Felsenstein, 1974; Felsenstein and Yokoyama, 1976; Manning, 1976; Bernstein, 1977; Martin, 1977; Maynard Smith, 1978; Blute, 1984), it is only recently that a number of workers, essentially independently and from a variety of disciplines, have begun to suggest that repair may be the primary or even sole *function* of sex in many organisms (Walker, 1978; Williams and Walker, 1978; Shields, 1979, 1982a,b; Bernstein et al., 1981, 1985; Kondrashov, 1982, 1984a,b; Margulis and Sagan, 1986). Despite the common theme, however, there are important differences in emphasis within the repair camp.

Sex and damage

Bell (in this volume) distinguishes between models of endogenous and exogenous error repair. In his usage, endogenous repair includes all of the molecular machinery used in recombinational repair of the kind of error that Bernstein and his colleagues (Bernstein, 1977; Bernstein et al., 1981, 1985, and in this volume) call DNA damage. They are careful to distinguish between damage, which includes chemical changes in DNA that interfere with replication and result in the death of cells with damaged DNA, and mutation. In its traditional genetic sense, a mutation is by definition a replicable error and is, if not lethal, transmissible to progeny. As such, it requires exogenous repair (sensu Bell), if it is not to result in the decay of adaptation.

I will not comment much on the elegant and persuasive damage repair hypothesis (reviewed by Bernstein et al., in this volume), other than to note that repair alone is not a likely explanation for the origin of the outcrossing aspects of meiosis for the reasons given by Bernstein et al. (1981) and Maynard Smith (in this volume). As Bernstein et al. (1981) note in discussing cross-over between sister homologues in some parthenogenetic species, diploidy is sufficient for damage repair. It is only when there is no template for molecular repair, either because the error is cryptic, and thus a transmissible mutation, or because no homologue is available as a repair template (as in haplonts), that sexual exchange would be *necessary* for error repair.

Sex and mutation

Muller's (1964) ratchet provided an early and intuitively appealing argument for sex as an exogenous repair mechanism. He noted that a finite asexual group "incorporates a kind of ratchet mechanism, such that it can never get to contain, in any of its lines, a load of mutations smaller than that already existing in its at present least-loaded lines." In addition, such least-loaded lines can be lost by chance or become more heavily loaded by mutation. The result could be a continuous decline in adaptation owing to ever-increasing mutational loads in asexual lines and their ultimate failure in competition with sexual lines that can regenerate less-loaded individuals via recombination in every generation.

In this vein, sex acts as an editor. It takes parental mutations and reassorts them into progeny in a way that can, in concert with selection, minimize mutational load. Many have felt (e.g., Maynard Smith, 1978; Walker, 1978; Bell, 1982) that this editing effect seems to apply to populations, perhaps requiring group selection. I suggested (Shields, 1982a, p. 122), however, that "the advantage also applies to a female which produces a 'population' of progeny in her lifetime, since her individual success is measured by comparing her population of progeny with those produced by others."

This individual effect can be illustrated by examining the distribution of parental mutations after sexual or asexual reproduction. Assume that single-diploid parents initially carrying two mutations are founders. Half reproduce asexually via ameiotic parthenogenesis. Half produce gametes via meiosis with a 50% crossover rate between a single pair of homologous chromosomes. In the sexuals, zygotes result from self-fertilization.

With these starting assumptions, families of progeny produced sexually would show greater variation in the number of classes carrying different numbers of mutations per individual than would the asexually produced families (Table 2). While the numbers presented here would certainly vary with mean and variance differences in mutation and crossover rates, a family of progeny produced sexually would *always* be expected to show greater variance in the individual dosage of parental and novel mutations than would any family of progeny produced asexually under the same conditions.

In this example, if we assume that each new mutation results in a reduction in fitness in heterozygous condition and that some form of truncation or threshold selection is operating, then in a population where sexual and asexual individuals competed ecologically, sexuality would quickly replace asexuality. The stronger the selection, the more quickly sex would reach fixation. In a series of papers, Kondrashov (1982, 1984a,b) has done numerical analyses indicating that such purifying selection can operate over a wide range of population sizes and parameter values (reviewed by Maynard Smith, in this vol-

TABLE 2 Frequency of progeny with different mutation loads after asexual or sexual reproduction by parents carrying two mutations

Mode of Reproduction	Number of Mutations per Progeny						
	0	1	2	3	4	5	6
Asexual	0	0	0.75	0.25	0	0	0
Sexual	0.04	0.16	0.31	0.30	0.15	0.04	0.004

ume). While he reports his models in terms of group effects and explicitly discusses group selection, I believe that they could entail individual benefits and selection as well.

It is possible that exogenous repair can provide direct benefits for sexual *individuals* (cf. Bell, in this volume). In essence, sex shuffles novel deleterious mutations, so that individual mutation load will not interfere with the positive selection of otherwise well-adapted progeny (thus ameliorating the Hill–Robertson effect, Felsenstein, 1974, and in this volume; Shields, 1982a). It allows a sexual parent to produce *some* progeny that do not carry the parent's deleterious mutations. An asexual parent is incapable of reducing the number of mutations transmitted to any of its progeny. Under many conditions, this would provide a direct benefit to the sexual parent. As a fortuitous side effect, the sexual *population* would carry fewer deleterious mutations than the asexual *population*, thereby obviating the ratchet, and insuring greater longevity for the sexual population.

Only additional modeling of sex's consequence of increasing the variance in mutation dosage under a broader range of conditions and parameter values can inform us further about its plausibility as a general or sufficient explanation of sex (for beginnings that are couched in population terms, see Williams and Walker, 1978; Kondrashov, 1984a; and Bell, in this volume). If repair is the primary function of sex, however, one could conclude that the diversifying influence of sex was either a side effect or a secondary function that originated in some taxa after sex had become ubiquitous owing to the benefits of repair.

Currently the potential exogenous repair benefits of sex are thought to depend on the relatedness of sexual partners in a straightforward way (Heller and Maynard Smith, 1979; Bell, in this volume; Maynard Smith, in this volume). Bell may be overstating the case when he asserts, "Moreover, automixis, selfing, or close inbreeding will not do, since the ratchet will operate on homozygous lines (Heller and Maynard Smith, 1979)—outcrossing is indispensable." Bell is following the argument that a ratchet operates in selfers "because an individual homozygous for i mutations cannot, by selfing, produce offspring homozygous for fewer mutations." As Maynard Smith states (in this volume), "The reason is easy to see. Every deleterious mutation in a selfing population either becomes fixed ($p = \frac{1}{2}$) or is eliminated: if it is fixed, it is equivalent to a mutation in an asexual haploid."

While the statements are true, they depend on homozygosity as much as on selfing. The argument that a sexual parent can increase the dispersion of mutational load, thereby producing more well-adapted progeny than a competing asexual parent, assumes that mutants occur independently in sexual partners, that is, that they are *not* fixed at their moment of origin. If they are deleterious, and especially if they are deleterious in heterozygous condition, they are likely to remain at low frequencies, even in selfers, and so they will *only* occur in heterozygous condition.

As Heller and Maynard Smith (1979) also note, even in selfers "no ratchet operates on the heterozygous loci, because by selfing a heterozygote can give rise to a normal homozygote." Thus, homologous chromosomes, whether in separate cells, as in haploid exchangers, or in the same cell, as in diploids, would *not* carry the same mutations at their origins. If they were deleterious as heterozygotes, sex would increase the variance in mutational load and increase the opportunity for purifying selection, regardless of the relatedness of mates.

Error repair

Sex would be of value to individuals if the cost of the greater mutational and damage loads of asex, exceeded the relatively higher costs of meiosis and males and segregational and recombinational loads of sex (Table 1). At its origin, primitive sex probably involved the exchange of chromosome (or DNA molecule) pieces, as well as simple fusion of complementary or homologous DNA molecules. The former would reduce, and the latter mask, the effects of damage *and* mutation quite effectively (for a discussion of masking, see Bernstein et al., 1985, in this volume). Thus, damage and mutation repair and masking are complementary effects and all could have independently favored the origin and maintenance of primitive sexual exchange and fusion.

Once masking benefits produced a semipermanent state of fusion (e.g., diploidy alternating with the ancestral haploid state), however, the pairing of homologues, crossing over during gamete production, and the reassortment of gametes associated with meiosis would not be necessary for endogenous repair. Given diploidy, molecular repair would require only a redundant DNA molecule or chromosome, undamaged at the site damaged on its homologue, as a template for repair (Bernstein et al., 1981; Maynard Smith, in this volume). In contrast, if mutations occurred often enough, and were deleterious, then crossover and syngamy would be necessary for, and could have originated owing to, the benefits of exogenous mutation repair or masking or both.

Once meiosis originated to allow mutational repair, however, there is no reason to believe that molecular damage repair would not work more efficiently if it was temporally and mechanically associated with meiosis (Bernstein et al., 1981, 1985, and in this volume). Once damage repair was physically associated with meiosis (mutation repair), then the loss of meiosis would entail a simultaneous loss of the capacity for damage repair. The increased mutational and damage loads that resulted would reduce the probability that a successful asexual lineage could evolve from a sexual ancestor. In this sense, then, damage control might not be sufficient to explain the origin of meiotic sex, but it still could be critical in explaining the maintenance of meiosis.

It is at least a tenable hypothesis that sex, in its many forms, originated and is currently maintained in many taxa by individual selection because it allows a sexual parent(s) to produce *some* progeny that carry fewer genetic errors than would *any* of the progeny produced asexually. The genetic errors favoring more efficient sexual repair, then, could include mutation or damage and most likely would include both. Regardless of the relative importance of mutation and damage, however, the primary or sole benefit of sex, whether inbreeding or outbreeding, would be error repair (Table 1).

Predictions and evidence

As I have explicitly noted for mutational loads (Shields, 1982a,b), if the primary or sole benefit of sex were repair, then the benefits of sex (or the costs of asex) would increase with the rate of error production per generation per individual. Since both damage and mutation are physicochemical changes in DNA molecules, they will share causes and their occurrence rates should covary. Thus, what I have predicted for mutation should also apply to damage and thus to error in general.

Since most of the physical factors causing genetic error (e.g., radiation, chemical mutagens, and the physical process of replication) occur in time, and errors rarely return to their original state spontaneously, the absolute number of errors per individual will increase with absolute time. Thus, the number of novel errors carried by an individual should increase with increasing generation time. In line with this, estimated per locus mutation rates per generation are much smaller for prokaryotes $(10^{-9}$ to $10^{-6})$ than for eukaryotes with much longer generation times $(10^{-6}$ to $10^{-3})$ (reviewed in Dobzhansky et al., 1977; Wright, 1977). Similarly, if errors occur independently at different loci, then increasing the number of functional loci will increase the number of errors per individual per unit time. Thus, individuals with larger functional genomes are expected to generate and carry more errors than otherwise similar individuals with smaller genomes.

This analysis of expected error rates permits predictions about the occurrence of sexuality and asexuality. If the primary or sole benefit of sex is error repair, then sex should be rare in organisms with the lowest error rates per generation per individual (Table 3). The extant organisms with the smallest genomes and shortest generation times (e.g., bacteria, blue-green algae, and other unicellular prokaryotes and eukaryotes) do show the least reliance on sex (reviewed in Shields, 1982a; Bell, 1982). Conversely, sex should be obligate for the organisms with the highest mutation rates per generation per individual (Table 3). In line with this, most organisms with large functional genomes and long generation times are exclusively sexual (e.g., most higher vertebrates) (reviewed in Shields, 1982a; Bell, 1982). The hypothesis also makes a novel, and as yet untested, prediction about heterogonic species. Within the domain of moderate error rates favoring heterogony, decreasing error rates should increase the relative frequency of asexual generations (Table 3) (Shields, 1982b, p. 268).

TABLE 3 Predicted associations among fecundities, error rates, and reproductive strategies if reproduction functions to maintain adaptation[a]

Error Rate per Generation per Individual[b]	Lifetime Fecundity[c]		
	Low	**Moderate**	**High**
Low	Asexual	Asexual	Asexual
Moderate	Heterogonic[d]	Heterogonic	Heterogonic
High	Inbreeding	Mixed[e]	Outbreeding

[a]Modified from Shields, 1982a.
[b]The error rate per generation per individual is equal to the error rate per locus per generation (ranging from 10^{-9} to 10^{-3} multiplied by the number of functional loci per individual (thought to range from 10^2 to 10^5) and so is expected to range from about 10^{-7} to 100 errors per generation per individual.
[c]Precise estimates of the fecundities that would favor different modes of reproduction are not yet available, but roughly, fewer than 500 progeny per female per lifetime would be classed as low fecundity; more than 10,000 progeny, as high fecundity; and from 1000 to 5000 progeny, as moderate fecundity.
[d]Heterogonic is alternation of sexual and asexual generations. The number of asexual generations between sexual events is expected to increase with decreasing error rates.
[e]Mixed mating systems would include alternation between or mixtures of inbreeding and outbreeding during progeny production.

Finally, if we assume that for most organisms sex is necessary to repair genetic error, then a final prediction emerges. If a population that is normally sexual or heterogonic, and presumably subject to moderately high error rates, is forced into obligate asexuality, either through experimental manipulation or because it loses its capacity for sex, then its members should accumulate errors over time, with a concomitant decline in adaptation and fitness (reviewed in Wright, 1977, p. 147, Shields 1982b, p. 256). Bell (in this volume) has recently performed a more extensive review of the literature on forced asexuality and has reached the same conclusion.

THE COSTS OF SEX: INBREEDING VERSUS OUTBREEDING

Whether error repair is sufficient to explain the origin and maintenance of sex will depend on whether sex's combined benefits exceed its combined costs. The benefits of repair will accrue regardless of whether sexual individuals inbreed or outbreed. The costs of sex, however, as well as any potential for additional benefits, will vary, both in kind and in magnitude, with the mating system (Table 1; Shields, 1982a). The mating system, in turn, also varies from the intense inbreeding associated with selfing or biparental incest, through moderate inbreeding in random-mating but small populations ($N_e < 1000$), to the relatively wide outbreeding that occurs in random-mating, large ($N_e > 10,000$) populations (for comprehensive reviews of mating systems, see Shields, 1982a; 1987; Chepko-Sade and Shields, 1987).

Cost of meiosis

Since the genetic cost of meiosis stems from parental sharing of progeny by sexual parents, it decreases with the degree of inbreeding (Table 1; Williams, 1980; Shields, 1982a). Obviously, selfers do not share progeny, while truly unrelated mates would suffer the full 50% loss in genetic representation discussed by Williams (1975; 1980). The ecological cost of producing males applies to any sexual parent, regardless of whether they inbreed or outbreed, unless the sex ratio is biased towards females (Table 1; Maynard Smith, 1978; Williams, 1980).

Recent analyses by Uyenoyama (1984, 1985, and in this volume) indicate that the two costs are separable and behave in the ways postulated by earlier workers. She concludes that inbreeding will reduce the genetic costs but will exacerbate the ecological costs by increasing the reproductive value of females. This implies that in many diploid species the mating system will not produce a predictable net effect on the cost of meiosis. Increased inbreeding would reduce the genetic cost, but this could be balanced or outweighed by increases in the ecological cost of sex. In species with males that contribute to female success, however, either through direct parental investment or via control of important resources limiting female reproduction, inbreeding could reduce the genetic cost of meiosis below that suffered by outbreeders.

Segregational load

Sex will entail a segregational load relative to asexuality if combinations of different alleles at single loci (heterozygotes) are better adapted than combinations of identical alleles (homozygotes) at those loci. An asexual and heterozygous parent produces only heterozygous progeny. In contrast, heterozygous sexual parents will always segregate homozygous progeny, regardless of whether they inbreed or outbreed. At loci with two alleles, 50% of the progeny of heterozygous parents are expected to be homozygous, whether they self or outbreed widely. At loci with more alleles, however, outbreeders are expected to produce fewer homozygous progeny than inbreeders. Thus, sex will always entail a segregational load relative to asexuality, but it will vary with the mating system, increasing with inbreeding intensity (Table 1), if heterozygosity is favored either because of its ability to mask error or because variation is beneficial per se (Shields, 1982a; Bernstein et al., 1981, 1985).

Recombinational load

Sex will entail a recombinational load if particular combinations of alleles at *different* loci are better adapted than alternative combinations (Crow and Kimura, 1970). As Wright (1931) noted many years ago, sex can destroy adaptation because "a successful combination of characteristics is attained in individuals only to be broken up in the next generation by the mechanism of meiosis itself." Specific interlocus combinations, in turn, can be better adapted than alternatives for different reasons.

For example, a novel interlocus combination of *rare* alleles could represent an unconditional improvement over all ancestral combinations. If sex tore the new combination apart, it would generate a cost relative to asexuality. Alternatively, particular combinations could represent local, and therefore conditional, adaptations, with one combination being favored in habitat A and a second in habitat B. If mixtures of alleles from these two adaptive peaks (sensu Wright, 1978) were maladapted in all habitats, sex would entail a load if it created novel mixed combinations that disrupted such local adaptation (Shields, 1983).

Similarly, if alleles at different loci were jointly responsible for the production of phenotypes, that is, they interacted epistatically, then selection could favor different "coadapted" complexes, even in the same environment. For example, the same adaptive level of biochemical activity could be achieved by possessing an allele at a regulatory locus directing for the synthesis of a large amount of low-activity form of an enzyme at a second locus or by a low regulator calling for lesser amounts of a more active form of the enzyme. Sex would disrupt such coadapted complexes if it produced genomes with new combinations, like the low regulator with the low-activity enzyme, that failed to function adequately (for actual examples, see Shields, 1982a, Templeton et al., 1986).

Thus, when phenotypic expression, and hence adaptation, depend on the identity of interacting alleles carried at different loci, sex can generate a recombinational load. Sex takes alleles from successful parental combinations and shuffles them during gamete production. If the syngamy that follows is also random, fewer proven parental combinations will be transmitted to progeny. Sex reduces the heritability of adaptation and fitness, as the correlation between the observed fitness of a parent and the expected fitness of its progeny declines relative to an asexual parent.

Of course this conclusion assumes outbreeding. By inbreeding, sexual parents can reduce recombinational load to nil (Shields, 1982a). Any well-adapted combinations of alleles at different loci broken apart by recombination have a higher probability of being reconstituted during syngamy when the gametes or genetic material fused are drawn from relatives. This would be true for combinations of rare alleles, locally adapted complexes, or coadapted complexes of alleles, especially when the interacting loci were homozygous. Only adaptations that depended on interaction between heterozygous genotypes at different loci might do better with reduced inbreeding. But even here, the outbreeding would have to be limited in order to insure that heterozygotes identical to the parents, rather than untried combinations, were produced (Shields, 1982a).

In the end, the costs of sex will vary with mating system. At the inbred end of the mating continuum, segregational loads would reach their maximum for loci carrying multiple alleles, but the genetic costs of meiosis and recombinational load would be minimized and could actually be eliminated (Table 1). At the outbred end of the continuum, the segregational load would be minimized but could never be eliminated, while the expected costs of meiosis and recombinational load would be maximized (Table 1).

If repair provided the primary benefit of sex, and the increased segregational load of inbreeding were less costly than the increased recombinational load and costs of meiosis of wider outbreeding, then inbreeding could be favored over outbreeding sex. This would be most likely in species where epistasis (interlocus interactions) was more important than heterosis (intralocus heterozygosity) in determining fitness, in those living in stable (and not necessarily constant) environments, or in both. In contrast, if diversification were the primary benefit of sex, and/or a decreased segregational load were more important than increases in the cost of meiosis or recombinational load or both, then outbreeding could be favored over inbreeding. This, in turn, would be most likely for species living in the kinds of chaotic or varying environments that could favor genetic diversity per se. Such species, of course, would also be expected to outbreed as widely as possible.

ADAPTATION AND SEX

One of the core assumptions of the Darwinian, Neo-Darwinian, and synthetic paradigms is that reproduction can and does occur. The concept of reproduction is so central to any evolutionary theory that we often fail to examine its assumption or implications. For example, in Darwin's (1859) thought, the essence of reproduction was contained in the observation that, in toto, progeny usually resemble their parents more than they resemble others. That is, parents appear to *reproduce* (themselves) when generating progeny, rather than to simply *produce* descendants that are random samples of all the potential traits or trait-states in a parent pool.

This observation resulted in Darwin's assumption that variation in traits that were important in meeting environmental challenges (adaptations) could cause cumulative differences in survival and reproduction that resulted in adaptive evolution. If progeny more closely resembled their parents with respect to adaptation and maladaptation, the result would be natural selection. With our modern knowledge of genetics, we have translated this into the explicit assumption that heritable genetic variation in traits important to adaptation was, and continues to be, a necessary condition for adaptive organic evolution.

In this context, one can imagine two kinds of progeny production as alternative transmission tactics. Faithful reproduction would entail replication of genetic material and balanced transmission of the resulting copies to progeny. Random production, in contrast, would entail transmission of more or less random samples of parent genetic material to progeny. Random production of progeny is at least conceivable in the primordial soup. Suppose that a group of protocells, coacervates, or proteinoids carried random samples of all of the chemical species to be found floating about in their environment. If the protocells or coacervates continuously expelled many chemicals before splitting in two, or budding off new entities, and the resulting empty shells gathered new sets of chemicals at random from the environment, we could speak of random progeny production. Similarly, random asexuality would occur if during parental fissioning daughter cells received random samples of parental genomes.

Adaptation consists of knowledge about those aspects of environmental features that are constant or vary within "known" limits or both. If the environmental features an adaptation matches were constant, then perfect replication would always be the ideal. The information contained in such an adaptation would always be true. For example, an individual with traits that caused it to survive a specific temperature could do no better than to reproduce that adaptation perfectly, if temperature remained constant.

Most would agree with this assessment, but would add that faithful reproduction might fail if the environment varies. If features vary, however, they can vary in limited or predictable ways and/or their consequences can be constant and therefore predictable. Knowledge of this kind of predictable variability would remain true and therefore useful. For example, temperature varies, but usually remains within a limited and stable range of values, in particular habitats. Individuals whose most critical chemical constituents are more efficient at the experienced range of temperatures should outperform competitors consisting of chemicals that work more efficiently at temperatures outside that range.

Well-adapted parents that faithfully transmit their adaptations to predictably varying temperatures, or any other predictably varying features in their environment, should be more successful than any truly random progeny producers. One can conceive of random production being more valuable in such circumstances, but only for individuals that initially are maladapted. It is only when environments or their features vary in an unpredictable, and therefore, chaotic fashion, that faithful tranmission would always fail. In such an unstable environment, the absence of a history useful in correctly predicting the future would favor the random production of enormous numbers of highly variable progeny as a sort of shotgun approach to creating and recreating adaptation.

We can define *equilibrium* environments as those with a preponderance of constant and/or predictably varying features (i.e., features that vary within relatively constant bounds for two or more generations of the lineage in question) with predictable consequences for the lineages in that environment. In such equilibrium environments, faithful reproduction will be the transmission tactic of value. This implies that organismic heritability is only useful insofar as environmental features are also heritable. Since adaptation is an interactive mapping of the features of organisms onto specific features of specific environments, the transmission and continued existence of adaptation presupposes that progeny can, in some fashion, inherit *both* the appropriate genome and the corresponding environmental features upon which it maps correctly (for review, see Oyama, 1985).

This implies that as long as the *association* between a lineage and a particular environment is stable, or at least in temporary equilibrium, faithful reproduction will be favored (Shields, 1982a). Given this and the assumption that equilibrium lineage–environment associations are not rare, one can ask how is such fidelity to be achieved. Given small genomes and short generation times, balanced asexuality (mitotic reproduction that includes a doubling by replication and the transmission of balanced genome copies) can transmit parental genomes with great fidelity. This kind of reproduction is commonplace in short-lived organisms with small genomes (Table 3). Truly random progeny reproduction, in contrast, is not known in nature, implying that the kind of chaotic lineage–environment associations that could favor it may be rare or absent in nature.

Given large genomes and long generation times and stable associations, inbreeding sex is to be expected (Table 3). Given sufficient error rates, asexuality would fail the fidelity test owing to its inability to prevent mutational diversification. Outbreeding would allow for error repair but could fail the fidelity test because of the disruption associated with higher recombinational loads relative to inbreeding. Mild inbreeding, then, could conserve adaptation by minimizing both mutational and recombinational loads, and only then optimizing the segregational load within this constraint (Table 1).

If environment–lineage associations were less stable, or key features varied unpredictably, then the less faithful reproduction associated with wider outbreeding could be favored. Outbreeding sex would first minimize mutational load and reduce the cost of fidelity in an unpredictably varying environment by editing mutation and creating novel allele combinations, and only then optimizing recombinational load within these constraints (Table 1). As the state of the environment or its key features became less predictable, then this more creative approach to adaptation might be required (see Bell, Maynard Smith, and Seger and Hamilton, in this volume).

Of course, inbreeding and outbreeding are not mutually exclusive alternatives. If the lineage–environment association were stable and almost all of the key features predictable, then what worked yesterday should work tomorrow. Under these conditions, faithful reproduction is not a gamble, but a necessity. Only a few progeny need to be produced to meet this challenge, but those should be the product of inbreeding. Thus, genetically complex, long-lived organisms that produce relatively few progeny in their lifetimes should inbreed exclusively (Table 3).

Organisms in more chancy circumstances must produce more progeny. As fecundity rises, the reproductive excess relative to the limited number of spaces in the environment (a higher stake) would allow for increased gambling with at least some progeny. Here gambling implies generation of genetic diversity. In this context, most have focused on recombinational diversity, but Slobodchikoff (1982) is certainly correct that in long-lived and genetically complex organisms asexuality promotes mutational diversity as a result of its associated ratchet. A mixed strategy, then, with some inbreeding and some outbreeding or some asexuality, would faithfully transmit parental adaptations to some progeny and creatively generate prospective adaptations in others. When some young are produced by inbreeding, in case the unpredictable does not occur, and some are produced by outbreeding or asexually, in case it does, some winners are more likely to be produced, thereby favoring a mixed strategy (Table 3).

As the association between the adaptive features of an organism and more key features in its less predictably varying environment destabilizes, fecundity and the need to gamble should both increase. Extremely high fecundities allow for extreme creativity. Thus, organisms with the highest fecundities are expected to gamble the most. They should produce greater proportions of their progeny by outbreeding (and/or include asexuality more frequently) and outbreed more widely than organisms with lower fecundity (Table 3). If there is any possibility that conditions will remain the same or vary predictably, however, then even high-fecundity organisms should conserve adaptation by producing some inbred progeny.

I have presented the basic outline of this theory and extensively reviewed many of its predictions in detail elsewhere (Shields, 1982a, 1983). I will only note here that despite some controversy about definitions and implications, the data are generally consistent with the predictions. Thus, I showed, for both plants and animals, that at least on a broad front, high-fecundity individuals were more likely to outbreed, and outbreed more widely, than low-fecundity organisms. Similarly, the prediction that almost all vertebrates should be at least mildly inbred was confirmed by the high frequency of philopatric dispersal and generally small effective size of their breeding populations that resulted (Wright, 1978; Shields, 1982a; Chepko-Sade and Shields, 1987).

Since these initial explorations, others have added to the data. For example, in a more detailed analysis of marine invertebrates, Jackson (1985, pp. 336–337) noted, "The resulting clear correlation between clonality, philopatry, long generation time, low fecundity (at least on the basis of biomass), and environmental stability is consistent with the argument of Shields (1982) regarding the frequency and adaptive significance of inbreeding in natural population." In an article intended to be quite critical of what they asserted were my views, Ralls and colleagues (1986, p. 51) concluded that with my definitions, "inbreeding would be the rule in birds and mammals."

They concluded that the observed frequencies of incestuous pairs (0 to 19.4%) were low enough to state that "matings between close relatives are uncommon in most populations of birds and mammals" (Ralls et al., 1986, p. 55). I certainly disagree. In a stable population an individual can expect to have, on average, one opposite sex progeny plus one opposite sex sibling alive as a potential mate. This permits a rough estimate of random expectations of incest, a null hypothesis. This probability would be calculated by taking the two that would yield incest divided by the number of opposite sex individuals in the *entire* random mating deme. Thus, in a large population (e.g., $N_e = 1000$), the expectation would be 2/500 or 0.4%. A breeding population of 100 would be necessary to generate 4% incestuous matings at random. Thus, their data are consistent with the prediction that vertebrates are random mating in small semi-isolated demes.

SUMMARY

An epistemological view of adaptation implies that the correspondence between organisms and environments reflects true information, that is, phylogenetic *knowledge*, about the probable states of key features of the environment important to the survival and reproduction of those organisms (Pittendrigh, 1958; Campbell, 1974; Plotkin and Odling-Smee, 1981). Thus, adaptation reflects the history of interaction between lineage and environment, is more or less complex, is always improbable, and by definition is, on average, successful in predicting environmental challenges.

Our universe appears to be sufficiently lawful that information about the past usually permits correct predictions about the present and future. Thus an organism carrying an adapted genome would do well to transmit it intact to as many of its progeny as it could, if the rules were unchanged. In such a universe, knowledge is power, and the probability of success in such a universe is likely to increase as much or more by conserving and using knowledge about the past as it is by generating new knowledge.

Adaptation to variation in such environments could entail creative genetic responses (e.g., different genes or gene combinations that match different feature states in the environment) or, if the variation has been experienced in a lineage's history, a fixed genetic substrate that permits a less costly (in terms of maladapted progeny) phenotypic response (Slobodkin and Rapoport, 1974). In the latter case the genetic information that informs the phenotypic response would be as valuable to progeny as it was to its parents. Thus, environmental variability does not require the creation of new genetic adaptations. The challenge of variation, as long as the variation is bounded and has characterized the environment in the past, can be met with adaptations that can be faithfully and profitably transmitted to progeny.

In this context, genetic error can be considered noise that reduces the transmission fidelity of reproduction. Mitotic asexuality and sex, at least inbreeding sex, could have originated and still be maintained in many organisms because it conserves adaptation by reconstituting parental genomes in the face of damage or mutation or both. If doing what has worked in the past is a good strategy in the future, then inbreeding sex is the only reproductive strategy available to long-lived organisms with large genomes.

The fact that much of the world's biota is intensely inbreeding (e.g., selfing plants and incestuous arthropods) is inconsistent with hypotheses that sex functions *solely* to generate new allele combinations, since inbreeders do not generate the new combinations as required. The question, What use is sex?, is likely to have multiple answers. In order to develop a complete answer, then, more careful consideration must be given to the very different consequences of inbreeding and outbreeding and how both would affect the process and state of adaptation. Since knowledge is a precious commodity, I would vote for the primacy of sex as a preserver rather than a creator of adaptation.

CHAPTER 16

SEX DIFFERENCES IN RATES OF RECOMBINATION AND SEXUAL SELECTION*

Robert Trivers

There is a very widespread sex difference in the underlying genetic system which has gone nearly completely unnoticed in our recent efforts to understand sexual selection and the evolution of sex (but see Bell, 1982, and Bull, 1983). That sex difference is a difference in the rates at which genes in the two sexes recombine during meiosis in the production of the two gametes. Although it has long been appreciated that the sex chromosomes themselves are associated with differences in recombination (e.g., XX chromosomes recombine freely while XY or XO do so little or not at all), much more striking is the widespread occurrence of a sex difference in rates of *crossing over* between paired autosomes. In almost every species studied, the sexes differ in rates of crossing over, and data from numerous species form a complex and interesting pattern which invites explanation. Even if the reader sees little merit in the theory I advance to explain these facts, I hope at least to show the potential value in the genetical facts reviewed here for our understanding of sexual selection and sex.

The facts concerning sex differences in recombination, to my mind, are most easily accommodated by imagining that sexual selection often acts adaptively from the female's standpoint; that is, it often causes superior genes to be passed in the male sex. This, in turn, selects for tighter linkage, in order to preserve the more highly favored combinations of genes being revealed by sexual selection. Twenty years ago the assumption that in species lacking male parental investment processes of sexual selection would raise to breeding status in males

*This chapter is taken from a book in preparation, *Intragenomic Conflict*, University of California Press.

270

superior genes from a female's standpoint (as measured by an increase in the survival and fecundity of her resulting offspring) would have been controversial. Indeed, the common bias in this century has been the assumption that sexual selection usually acts maladaptively from the female's standpoint. That is, it gives her genes from the noninvesting males worse than those she would get from pairing at random with another female (were that possible). This assumption has been based on a keen appreciation of the pervasiveness and strength of male–male competition, especially aggressive, which, if unguided by female choice, would easily seem to generate extremes in male morphology and behavior useful only in a male–male competitive context, such that the other genes thereby elevated might actually be worse for a female's *daughters* than the genes of an average male.

In addition, female choice was given a male bias. When imagined to operate at all, female choice was usually assumed to favor traits in males which were useful predictors of their *sons'* future success. To put this in the vernacular: either females choose a "bully" as a mate in order to (produce) sons good at excluding other males, or they prefer a "pretty boy," a male preferred by many other females, in order to (produce) sons attractive to the daughters of these females. By contrast, a renewed appreciation of the importance of female choice, combined with the demonstration that systems of female choice are expected to evolve with a bias toward the interests of daughters, suggests that sexual selection may often act adaptively (Seger and Trivers, 1986; Trivers, 1985). In any case, our image of the possible adaptive value of sexual selection should affect our expectation regarding rates of recombination. If the logic presented in this chapter is accepted, then the pattern of evidence regarding sex differences in recombination provides additional reason to believe that sexual selection may often act adaptively. This is based on the assumption that a sex difference in recombination measures in part the degree to which, in one generation, selection has acted more adaptively (from the standpoint of resulting progeny) in one sex compared to the other. Put another way, if linkage is tighter in males, we are permitted the assumption that breeding males possess superior genes, on average, compared to breeding females.

Finally, I will emphasize that just as the genetic system may affect the operation of selection, so natural selection molds the genetic system. As Ernst Mayr (1963, 1982) has emphasized, Darwin's theory of evolution was a *two-factor* theory: two independent factors, genetic variation and natural selection, interact to produce evolutionary change over time. Since the rediscovery of Mendel's work, it has been common to emphasize the relevance of genetics for the operation of natural selection. Thus, details of the genetic system such as dominance, linkage, epistasis—and especially, mode of inheritance—may affect the direction and intensity of natural selection. The direction of causality in these arguments can be summarized as follows: genotype → phenotype → selection. That is, details of the genotype have some effect on the phenotype, which in turn affects selection. Or, as in the case of mode of inheritance, genes

affect selection directly by affecting the proportions with which alternate genotypes are inherited (e.g., sex chromosomes vs. autosomes). An example of the
former causal chain is: heterogamety → higher mortality → sexual selection.
That is, heterogamety (the XY or XO sex) causes higher mortality (due to the
breakdown of diploidy and subsequent genetic defenselessness against the appearance of "lethal" recessives) which, in turn, alters the adult sex ratio, thereby
affecting the degree of intrasexual competition for members of the opposite sex.

Much less emphasized has been the possibility that natural selection molds
the genetic system, either via a phenotypic trait or directly. In the above
example, sexual selection → higher mortality → heterogamety. That is, sexual
selection causes higher mortality (Trivers, 1972, 1985) and this more severe
selection—if oriented in the right direction—favors tighter linkage which, in
turn, may predispose that sex to the evolution of heterogamety (Bull, 1983).
On the latter connection, Haldane (1922) had argued from the genes outward:
heterogamety causes tighter linkage on the autosomes. We argue the other way
around: an initial sex difference in recombination across the autosomes predis-
poses the sex with tighter linkage to the appearance of heterogamety in order to
preserve combinations of sex factors or genes having sex limited benefits (Bell,
1982; Charlesworth and Charlesworth, 1978). Increased selection for even
tighter linkage on the incipient sex chromosomes induces further genetic isolation and, hence, divergence in self-interest leading to increased conflict between the X and the Y chromosomes and eventual reduction and nullification
of the Y (Hamilton, 1967).

SEX DIFFERENCES IN RATES OF RECOMBINATION

Rates of recombination are affected by two variables. On the one hand, non-
homologous pairs of chromosomes assort themselves independently during
meiosis, so that increasing chromosome number will, with overall length of the
genotype held constant, increase rates of recombination. On the other hand,
homologous chromosomes may exchange segments during meiosis so that linked
genes (located on the same chromosome) show some frequency of recombination above zero. Typically the sexes do not differ in chromosome number, but
in haplodiploid systems males have only half as many chromosomes as a
female—a haploid set—and there is no recombination, while females freely
recombine. In all haplodiploid species (and parahaplodiploid species—see Bull,
1983) the male is the haploid sex, or reproduces as if he were (parahaplodip-
loidy = paternal genome loss). Systems having related effects are multiple sex
chromosomes and reciprocal translocation heterozygotes (see below). Likewise,
in the XO/XX means of sex determination (which is common in many insect
groups) the heterogametic sex has one less chromosome (an X) than the homogametic sex. This is usually the male.

In addition to the above factors, whose effects on total recombination are
typically small (e.g., XX vs. XY), the sexes also usually differ in the degree to

which linked genes located on homologous pairs of autosomes recombine. As is now well known, this kind of recombination results from a process termed crossing over. Crossing over occurs in mid-prophase of meiosis, when homologous chromosomes form intimate connections seen cytologically as "chiasmata," after which the homologous chromosomes typically switch chromosegments located "below" the connecting point. More than one chiasma may form between two homologous chromosomes, but smaller chromosomes typically show a single chiasma. Were this true for all the chromosome sets in an individual, and were the chiasmata always located in the exact midpoint of each chromosome, then this degree of crossing over would be exactly equivalent to cutting all the chromosomes in half at the midpoint and thereby doubling chromosome number.

Sex differences in rates of crossing over can be detected in two ways. They may be seen directly by counting chiasmata in the two kinds of sex cells photographed at parallel stages in meiosis, or they may be detected by counting the frequencies of various combinations of linked markers among progeny depending on the sex bearing the markers (for both methods applied to a marsupial, see Bennett et al., 1986). Each method has shown that there may be striking heterogeneity in sex differences in recombination depending on the section of the genotype being compared. For example, in the mealworm *Tribolium castaneum* studies of genetic markers reveal three linkage groups, in which adjacent sections show a reversal in the sex with tighter linkage (Dawson and Berends 1985). Likewise, cytological studies of chromosomes forming chiasmata show that these are sometimes distributed in a complementary fashion between the two sexes. For example, in the grasshopper *Stethophyma grossum*, chiasmata in males are procentrically located (that is, close to the centromeres), while in females only 6 percent of chiasmata are procentrically located, the remainder being interstitial or distal (White, 1973; Perry and Jones, 1974).

A remarkable feature of complementary sex differences in recombination is that the complementarity may differ markedly in closely related species. For example, in newts (*Triturus helveticus*), males show proterminal chiasma localization: almost all chiasmata are found at the ends of chromosomes (Watson and Callan, 1963). Although chiasmata frequency is similar in females, these are not localized. A partial reversal of this pattern is found in *Triturus cristatus*, in which chiasmata in male meioses are spread along the length of the chromosomes, while chiasmata in females are located near the centromeres.

In spite of this heterogeneity, in many species there are clear *average* differences between the sexes in rate of recombination across the autosomes. For example, across a wide variety of taxa, crossing over may be regular in one sex but completely absent in the other (meiosis achiasmatic: e.g., male *Drosophila*, female butterflies and moths). In species with crossing over in both sexes, chiasmata *number* may differ consistently between the sexes or the majority of linkage groups may show similar sex differences in linkage rates. For example, in the house mouse, 23 intervals measured across 10 linkage groups showed significant sex differences in recombination. These were distributed within linkage groups such that nine groups always showed tighter linkage in males, while one group always showed tighter linkage in females (Dunn and Bennett, 1964). Even when the distribution of chiasmata within one sex differs from the other, average differences in chiasmata number often vary in the same direction. For example, in *Triturus*, chiasmata number are always slightly higher in the sex showing nonlocalized chiasmata, so that on both counts this sex shows higher rates of recombination.

The facts concerning average sex differences in autosomal recombination form an interesting pattern, as revealed by the valuable reviews of Dunn and Bennett (1964), Perry and Callan (1977), and Bell (1982). The most striking generalizations are these: linkage is typically tighter in males or in male tissue (a rule to which there are numerous exceptions); there is a strong—but not universal—tendency for the heterogametic sex to show tighter linkage; and only a few species are known to show no sex difference at all.

1. *Recombination is typically greater in females than in males.* This is true of most mammals, such as humans, laboratory mice, and horses, all of which typically show about 30 percent higher recombination across linkage groups in females than in males (Dunn and Bennett, 1964; Andersson and Sandberg, 1984). Achiasmatic meiosis is in the majority of insect orders confined to the male sex (Bell, 1982). Besides the well known case of *Drosophila* and some related Diptera, achiasmatic male meiosis is also found in various grasshoppers (White, 1965), in some bugs (Nokkala and Nokkala, 1983, 1984), in a beetle (Serrano, 1981) and in a mantid (White, 1938).

2. *This rule extends to male gonadal tissue compared to female in hermaphrodites.* This is true of the majority of plants that have been tested, e.g., *Lilium* spp. and species of *Allium* (Ved Brat, 1966). It is also true of a turbellarian worm (Pastor and Callan, 1952). The importance of this finding is that it suggests that the *phenotype* of the individual may control rates of recombination more than the genotype of the cells undergoing meiosis (since genotype in the two kinds of cells is identical). This supposition is strengthened by the remarkable finding of Yamamoto (1961): by hormone treatment he turned XY male fish (*Oryzias latipes*) into phenotypic females. When such a male reproduced, he showed five times as much crossing over between his X and Y chromosomes as did phenotypic males. For our purposes, it would have been more striking if Yamamoto had shown an effect on recombination across the autosomes, since it can be argued that an X in a female normally undergoes strong recombination with another X and is "fooled" in the XY female into thinking she is recombining with another X chromosome. In either case, however, a controlling role of the phenotype is established.

3. *There are numerous exceptions.* For example, unlike the placental mammals mentioned above, the marsupial fat-tailed insectivore *Sminthopsis crassicaudata* shows tighter linkage in females (Bennett et al., 1986). The salamander

Triturus cristatus shows tighter linkage in females. Although six orders of insects show achiasmatic male meiosis in at least some species, the Lepidoptera and Trichoptera (themselves closely related) invariably show achiasmatic meiosis limited to females (e.g., Turner and Sheppard, 1975; Suomalainen et al., 1973; Suomalainen, 1966). Among other invertebrates a few scorpionids and acarines are known to have achiasmatic meiosis limited to males, but several copepods show achiasmatic meiosis limited to the female. In hermaphroditic plants, *Pinus radiata* shows 43% higher recombination across one linkage group in male tissue compared to female and a similar (but not significant) trend in a second linkage group (Moran et al., 1983). These exceptions are critical to a test of any theory. I will argue that the exceptions will be associated with (1) substantial male parental investment (Lepidoptera/Trichoptera); (2) substantial male mating cost (copepods, *Triturus*); or (3) a sharp reduction in the efficacy of sexual selection (*Pinus*).

4. *There is a strong—but not universal—association between heterogamety and tighter linkage.* For example, copepods and Lepidoptera/Trichoptera are female heterogametic and achiasmatic in female meiosis. Indeed, there is a one-to-one correspondence between the sex showing achiasmatic meiosis (when only one sex does; see below) and the sex which is heterogametic (Bell, 1982). When both sexes show crossing over, however, exceptions begin to appear. Male marsupials are XY, yet *Sminthopsis* females show tighter linkage. Chickens are female heterogametic, yet show tighter linkage in males (Fisher and Laundauer, 1953; Warren and Hutt, 1936; Warren, 1940). *Triturus helveticus* is female heterogametic, yet shows tighter linkage in males. Nevertheless, in species in which chiasmata occur in both sexes, the general pattern is for heterogamety to be associated with tighter linkage.

5. *Cases in which no sex difference in recombination exists are relatively rare.* Although seven genera of oligochaete worms are known to have achiasmatic meiosis in both sexes (thus, no sex difference in recombination: Christiansen, 1961), all other cases of achiasmatic meiosis are restricted to one sex (Bell, 1982). Likewise, although scattered species, both hermaphroditic and dioecious, have failed to show a sex difference in recombination (Callan and Perry, 1977; Bell, 1982), the great majority of species investigated show consistent, significant differences.

SEX DIFFERENCES IN RECOMBINATION ACROSS THE SEX CHROMOSOMES

The sex difference in recombination across the autosomes is supplemented by a sex difference in rates of recombination across the sex chromosomes. The X and the Y chromosomes typically show low rates of recombination. Although especially true for X's and Y's that differ markedly in size and structure, a sharp reduction in recombination sometimes precedes structural divergence of the incipient X and Y (Schmidt et al., 1979). When one sex is XO, there is no recombination across the sex chromosomes, while the XX may show normal recombination. Haplodiploid and parahaplodiploid species (Bull, 1983) are extreme examples of this. Intermediate examples are systems of multiple sex chromosomes, either multiple X's or multiple Y's; the former tend to increase the proportion of the genotype inheriting in a haplodiploid fashion (see White, 1973). Another intermediate case is sex-linked translocation heterozygotes limited to the male sex, e.g., many species of termites (Luykx and Syren, 1979) and possibly all of the monotremes (Murtagh and Sharman, 1977). Similar translocation heterozygotes have been described for staminate mistletoes (*Viscum*: Wiens and Barlow, 1979). These facts can be summarized by saying that the mode of inheritance typically causes at least a small sex difference in recombination (measured across the entire genotype) according to the rule that the heterogametic sex shows little or no crossing over on the sex chromosomes (entire genotype for haplodiploid species).

Haldane (1922) was the first to produce a logic linking sex differences in recombination on the sex chromosomes to sex differences in recombination on the autosomes. He argued that the sex chromosomes were primary; that selection had favored a sharp reduction in crossing over (for example, to bind two independently segregating sex factors to each other); and that this had had a spill-over effect onto the autosomes, either because an absence of recombination on the sex chromosomes mechanically interfered with smooth recombination across the autosomes, or because selection to reduce recombination on the sex chromosomes had often acted on the genome at large, thereby increasing linkage on the autosomes. In hindsight, this argument has the form of the evolutionary tail wagging the evolutionary dog. There is no evidence for a mechanical interference, and there is no a priori reason for supposing that natural selection could not separate the two variables as, indeed, in exceptional cases we know it has.

The reverse logic seems more appealing (Bull, 1983): that an initial sex difference in recombination across *all* chromosomes predisposed the sex with tighter linkage to evolve heterogamety. This would occur if sex were determined by two or more independent loci located along the incipient sex chromosomes (as in plants: Charlesworth and Charlesworth, 1978), or if there existed genes with strong sex-specific effects on reproductive success along the incipient sex chromosomes which would benefit from tight linkage to the appropriate sex factor. At the same time, the frequent evolution of haplodiploidy, parahaplodiploid systems, and intermediate systems involving multiple sex chromosomes or translocation heterozygotes suggests that there has been selection to increase the proportion of the genotype undergoing little or no recombination in the heterogametic sex.

At this point it is worth emphasizing that this haplodiploid portion of the genotype, in addition to restricting recombination in one sex, also generates a novel pattern of degrees of relatedness among offspring and, perhaps more relevant to this discussion, increases the proportion of genes in the heterogametic sex which are inherited in the first generation only by the homogametic sex. In the typical case, that is, *it increases the proportion of genes in males which are inherited only by daughters.* This, as we shall see, may become important under certain kinds of female choice and sexual selection.

SEXUAL SELECTION AND SEX DIFFERENCES IN AUTOSOMAL LINKAGE

Two facts are worth noting at the outset. First, the autosomes are equally inherited by sons and daughters and are, except where linked to the sex chromosomes, distributed at random to the two sexes. This means that being male or female predicts nothing about the sex in which one's autosomes will reside in the future. Second, an individual's autosomes are equally likely to have been inherited from either parent. Thus being a male or female implies nothing about one's past life as either. Hence, if natural selection has molded different optimal rates of recombination in the two sexes, this can only reflect the intensity and direction of selection that has occurred in one generation: from the moment of conception to the moment of breeding. The chief variable affecting this will be sexual selection. Conceptually, it is valuable to distinguish three components of sexual selection: differential mortality by sex, intrasexual competition, and intersexual choice. For the great majority of species—that is, those lacking male parental investment—these typically translate into differential male mortality, male–male competition, and female choice (for a recent review see Trivers, 1985).

In species lacking male parental investment we expect to find greater variation in male reproductive success compared to that of the female (Bateman, 1948; Trivers, 1972). This means that the autosomal genes enjoying reproductive success on the male side are a more restricted sample of the original set of genes with which the generation began than are the genes in breeding females. If this additional restriction in males is in the right direction from the standpoint of resulting offspring—that is, if it is in the same general direction as the original restriction—then the genes and combinations of genes being passed in males will be superior on average, compared to genes passed in females. (Superior, that is, as measured by their effects on survival and reproductive success of the resulting offspring.) Insofar as the actual *combinations* in which a male's genes appear are important to their success, then he will be selected to reduce rates of recombination (compared to females) in order to preserve these beneficial combinations. This explains the primary rule in nature regarding rates of recombination: in dioecious species with no male parental investment, these are commonly lower in males. Note that the argument depends crucially on the assumption that sexual selection improves the quality of genes being passed in males, an assumption that is consistent with a growing body of evidence from both plants and animals (see below) but is by no means a necessary feature of nature.

At first glance, the facts concerning sex differences in recombination in hermaphroditic individuals would appear to contradict the theory being proposed for dioecious species. A hermaphroditic plant passes the same genes through pollen as through ovules; why not link them equally tightly within individuals? If sexual selection is operative, we might expect a hermaphrodite who was of high female quality to be even more favored as a male. The plant should show equally tight linkage, however, in its two kinds of gonadal tissue because they are genetically identical. We might expect variation in quality of hermaphrodite to be matched by variation in frequency of recombination, but within each individual we would expect both kinds of sex cells to receive the same amount of recombination. But in fact, recent evidence from plants strongly suggests that sexual selection acts in hermaphroditic species, and that an individual's success as a male and as a female may not be tightly coupled (Stephenson and Bertin, 1983; Bertin, 1982).

If the organism is to some degree uncertain about the quality of its genes, it could reason as follows: "If I have high success as a male, I should assume that the quality of my genes is good and, since I'm unable to predict this in advance, I will link my genes more tightly in pollen production than in ovule production. If I have low quality genes, my pollen will not be used much in any case, so that the inappropriately tight linkage will not be an important factor overall." Evidence regarding this interpretation of plants will be reviewed below; the comparable situation in hermaphroditic animals is much less clear, though cases of reciprocal egg trading such as has been discovered in sea bass in which an individual's success as male and female are presumably tightly linked are probably the exception and not the rule.

Cases of tighter linkage in females appear to be associated with male parental investment (e.g., birds, Lepidoptera/Trichoptera) or with male mating effort (salamanders, copepods). The argument for these correlations runs as follows: in species with high male parental investment, one might initially expect rates of recombination to be similar in the two sexes. But the situation in birds suggests that when male parental investment is substantial (e.g., more than one-half female parental investment) but is less than female parental investment, there may be a sharp reduction in sexual selection on males while the higher female parental investment induces differential *female* mortality. Thus, we expect breeding females to be the more restricted sample and, providing this restriction is in the right direction (improves the genetic quality of offspring), they will wish to recombine their genes less. Although the evidence is less clear from butterflies and moths (see below), differential *female* mortality is at least more common in this group than other groups of animals (with the exception of birds), so that a similar explanation may apply.

Variation in male reproductive success may also be reduced when copulations are expensive for males, even though males invest nothing in offspring.

For example, in salamanders costly spermatophores are produced which are, however, low in proteins and lipids and are not digested by females. Likewise, in copepods and some other marine invertebrates, expensive spermatophores are produced which appear to function as a mechanism of sperm transport in an aqueous medium (Mann, 1984). These are not digested by the female, but are still expensive for the male to produce. In any case, as noted above, there seems to be a crude correlation between the production of such expensive but nondigested spermatophores and female heterogamety.

EVIDENCE THAT SEXUAL SELECTION MAY OFTEN ACT ADAPTIVELY FROM THE FEMALE'S STANDPOINT

The only direct experimental evidence regarding the adaptive value of sexual selection in animals comes from the work of Partridge (1980) on *Drosophila melanogaster*. When females were assigned mates at random, their larvae suffered 2–4% greater mortality in competitive circumstances in the lab, compared to the larvae of females housed in large enclosures with many adult males. Direct evidence from the wild comes from a study by Clutton-Brock (1983) on red deer. He showed that those males who defended larger harems during their years of rutting survived longer than those males that defended smaller harems, suggesting that sexual selection and selection for survival were aligned in the same direction.

More convincing experimental evidence comes from the study of plants (see especially Stephenson and Bertin, 1983; Willson and Burley, 1983). In angiosperms, at least, pollen competition acts in an adaptive fashion, selecting for genes which result in plants that survive and grow better (Mulcahy and Mulcahy, 1987; Mulcahy, 1983). Selective fruit abortion is often aligned in such a way as to compound the positive effects of pollen competition: greater pollen competition results in more seeds set per fruit and fruits with relatively few seeds are preferentially aborted (e.g., Winsor et al., in press; Stephenson and Winsor, 1986; Bookman, 1984; see also Marshall and Ellstrand, 1986). There is growing evidence that flower coloration and size in hermaphroditic plants works primarily to favor pollen dispersal (Bell, 1985; Schoen and Clegg, 1985). Unlike sperm which express only paternal gene effects, more than 50% of the haploid genotype is expressed during pollen tube competition (e.g., Tanksley et al., 1981) so that there is ample opportunity for much of the genotype to be tested during pollen competition.

On the theoretical side, two advances are notable. Seger and Trivers (1986) showed that there is an intrinsic defense to runaway selection favoring traits beneficial to males but disadvantageous to females, in systems guided by female choice: in such systems males will more easily evolve structures and behavior that reveal the quality of their genes for *daughters* than their sons, because female choice genes benefitting daughters spread more quickly than similar genes benefitting sons. The reason for this is that female choice genes are expressed only in females and when they benefit daughters they increase in frequency in the choosing sex (females) within one generation. This increase, in turn, increases the reproductive success of males revealing high quality genes for daughters, and such males have a disproportionate number of the female choice gene for these traits. In short, a female choice gene benefitting daughters more quickly reinforces its own spread. By contrast, a similar female choice gene benefitting sons will increase in frequency among males in the first generation only, where it will fail to be expressed. Only in the following generation will we see an increase in the number of females choosing in this fashion. Thus, such genes lag in their effects a full generation behind those choice genes benefitting daughters. Some evidence in support of these assertions is reviewed in Trivers (1985).

A second advance was the appreciation that parasites may have played an important role in selecting for sexual reproduction (Hamilton et al., 1981) and molding mate choice (Hamilton and Zuk, 1982). Specifically, it was shown that species of birds which suffer higher loads of brood parasites tend to be more brightly colored in both sexes (especially in males) and to show more complex male song. Since bright coloration and complexity of song were assumed to reveal absence of parasites, and since mate choice in most birds is expressed by both sexes, the positive correlations were taken to support the assumption that species more heavily parasitized emphasized bright coloration and complexity of song more strongly in choice of mates. As noted by Hamilton and Zuk (1982) parasite selection, insofar as it conforms to certain cyclical features, will tend to maintain considerable genetic variability even while showing strong selection on the variants.

OTHER CORRELATES OF CROSSING OVER

If tighter linkage in males is really explained by sexual selection, then it follows that *within* a sex individuals may be able to rank themselves according to relative expected reproductive success and adjust their level of recombination accordingly. Remarkable evidence consistent with this expectation has been presented by Tucic et al. They showed that female fecundity in *Drosophila melanogaster* was inversely correlated with recombination rates: those females laying 40 or more eggs during a 48-hour period reduced by about 30% their rates of recombination in producing these offspring, compared to females who produced between 0 and 10 eggs during the same period of time. Fertility estimates in males were also inversely associated (with recombination rates in females of similar genotype) but the trend was not significant, probably because in this experimental design, male–male competition and female choice was sharply reduced (male fertility being estimated as the number of females out of ten showing sperm after enclosure with a single male for 48 hours). So far as I know, these are the only data available from any organism linking recombination rates with variation in reproductive success. Unfortunately, these results have not yet been repeated and are subject to the criticism that they may be a secondary consequence of variation in degree of hybrid dysgenesis, a condition affecting some laboratory strains when exposed to matings with wild-caught individuals in which, among other traits, low fertility co-occurs with high recombination rates. (For a recent paper on hybrid dysgenesis see Simmons, 1986.)

Other known correlates of recombination show confusing patterns which, at this stage in our knowledge, defy explanation. For example, in the tulip, frequency of chiasmata vary in pollen mother cells according to position on the anther, those developing first, at the base of the anther, showing fewer chaismata per cell (Couzin and Fox, 1974). Since there is only a trivial age difference in the plant at which different sections of the anther mature, an adaptive explanation for the facts would have to consider the form of sexual selection operating at different points along the anther. Is it possible, for example, that different intensities of sexual selection are associated with different sections on the anther, so that a cell could logically adjust its chiasma frequency to position on the anther based upon assumptions about its genetic quality if it is successful at that position? A large literature on chiasma frequency in relationship to temperature shows many of the conceivable patterns without any clear logic for the variation (Yanney and Wilson, 1959). Likewise, correlations with age fail to show a consistent pattern within species (Valentin, 1972) or across species (Mayo, 1974). For additional correlates, see Bell (1982).

THE EVOLUTION OF HETEROGAMETY

Let us begin by reviewing the facts that need to be explained.

1. *The distribution of heterogamety by sex.* It is a striking fact of biology that sex at the chromosomal level is oppositely determined in a variety of organisms. In general, species are male heterogametic (XY or XO). In dioecious plants most species are male heterogametic, but some are female heterogametic (Bull, 1983). Mammals and most fish and frogs are male heterogametic, but birds, some fish, and all snakes are female heterogametic. Most insects are male heterogametic, but the Lepidoptera and Trichoptera are female heterogametic. And so on. We must first explain the distribution of heterogamety by sex. It would also be nice if we could explain why vertebrates are usually XY, while insects are usually XO.

2. *Degeneration of the Y.* Relative to the X chromosome and to the autosomes, and whether the female or the male is heterogametic, the Y appears often to have degenerated: it is often sharply reduced in size, in gene content, and has been invaded by repeat elements (Bull, 1983). Why has this occurred?

3. *Conservation of the X.* In contrast to the Y, the X chromosome is conserved in both size and genetic content (Bull, 1983; Ohno, 1967). The X often seems to be slightly larger than the average autosome (in mammals it is 5%

of the total genome, in birds 10%). Why has the X done relatively well compared to the Y, and even compared to the autosomes—prospering, so to speak?

4. *Haldane's rule.* In the same paper in which he first drew attention to the association between tighter linkage on the autosomes and heterogamety, Haldane (1922) enunciated a famous rule: when in a distant cross within a species or a cross between closely related species one sex is absent, rare, or sterile, this is the heterogametic sex. Why should this be true?

5. *X–Y heteromorphism and rates of morphological evolution.* In snakes there appears to be an association between rates of morphological evolution (and hence taxonomic status: "primitive" or "advanced") and degree of dissimilarity between the X and the Y (Jones and Singh, 1985). The Boidae are least advanced taxonomically and have morphologically indistinguishable X's and Y's (females heterogametic). The Elapidae and Viparidae, by contrast, are highly advanced and show a strongly degenerate Y. The Colubridae are morphologically intermediate and are also intermediate in X–Y differentiation: the X and the Y differ often in a single pericentric inversion, so that they are similar in length but differ in the position of the centromere. There is weaker evidence of a similar trend in birds: the "primitive" ratites have morphologically similar X's and Y's while more advanced birds show a degenerate Y (female heterogametic; see, for example, de Boer, 1980). Why should this be true?

6. *Modes of achieving dosage compensation.* Since the homogametic sex will have two X's and the heterogametic sex only one, some adjustment is necessary so that development will proceed smoothly in both even though one sex has two doses of each gene on an X while the other has only one. In placental mammals, this is achieved by the random inactivation of one X cell in each of the somatic cells of the female. This, in itself, is a surprising fact, because it means that female development is, in effect, being adjusted to male development; given the primacy of females in evolution, one would have expected the reverse. In *Drosophila* the more logical adjustment appears to take place, single X's producing as much gene product as two X's do, yet in birds (female heterogametic) there appears to be no dosage compensation, males producing roughly twice the gene products of their X's as females do. Even among mammals there is unexplained variation: in marsupials, females inactivate one X in their somatic tissue but, unlike placental mammals, this is always the *paternal* X (Cooper et al., 1977).

7. *Kinds of genes located on the sex chromosomes.* There is evidence that genes involved in spermatogenesis are disproportionately located on the Y and *also* the X (e.g., Livak, 1984; Lifschytz and Lindsley, 1974). Why should this be so?

In attempting to explain the above facts by reference to the notion of conflict within the genotype (as first outlined in this context by Hamilton, 1967), I emphasize that some facts remain completely unexplained, e.g., the comparative facts concerning dosage compensation and the genetics of sex determination. I believe the next round of progress in understanding sex chromosome evolution will come from understanding these two areas. In the meantime, I suggest that the key variable in explaining the facts outlined above is an initial sex difference in rates of crossing over on *all* chromosomes due to sexual selection. Notice that this sex difference should evolve in an otherwise genetically homogenous world, lacking sex chromosomes but possessing two sexes, whether monoecious or dioecious. Note also that the efficacy of sexual selection (= tendency to benefit offspring) may have improved slowly at first, so that selection for tighter linkage likewise grew slowly. In any case, once tighter linkage appears in one sex, that sex should show a predisposition toward heterogamety. This should occur whenever two or more linked loci determine sex, or whenever genes at one or more sex linked loci show strong sex-specific effects on reproductive success (Charlesworth and Charlesworth, 1978; Bull, 1983). Either of these two causes leads to further selection for tight linkage across the incipient Y and X. This additional selection for linkage effectively isolates the X and Y from each other in subsequent evolution: insofar as allelles are no longer exchanged via recombination, the incipient X and Y diverge in (1) function, (2) mode of inheritance, and (3) shared self-interest.

Regarding function, isolation means that new mutations (including translocations, transposable elements, et cetera) appearing on one sex chromosome do not, within a few generations, automatically appear on the other. With divergence in genetic content comes the breakdown of loci themselves, so that in the heterogametic sex, there is an increasing proportion of loci on the X and Y which are unguarded or hemizygous.

With lack of recombination, all genes on the Y chromosome are passed from father to son only. Thus the Y should become a repository of genes beneficial only to males, such as those involved in sperm function. (This, however, poses a threat to the X—see below—which may generate genes for sperm function of the X.) By contrast, genes on the X chromosome of a male are all passed to daughters only. Thus, the X is a perfect repository for genes benefitting daughters preferentially. Insofar as sexual selection is oriented in this direction, the X may be selected to grow in size. This possibility is important to emphasize, because conflict between X and Y may lead to selection for the diminution in size of each (Y more so than X—see below; Hamilton, 1967), yet comparative evidence suggests that the X chromosome is often average or larger than average in size.

With lack of recombination, there also comes a striking reduction in shared self-interest. With each generation X and Y will view each other as less related. Although inbreeding will increase relatedness between paired autosomes, it leaves r between X and Y at or near zero. With lack of shared self-interest comes increasing conflict over representation among offspring. Genes on a recently separated Y chromosome might reason as follows: "None of us are found on the X, nor will we be in the future. We best act together to favor our own spread, even if this means the destruction of the X chromosome." Of course, genes on the X in a heterozygote are expected to "reason" in a similar way, but such genes spend two-thirds of their evolutionary life in females (who are XX), while genes on the Y invariably appear in males only. Thus selection for narrowly selfish behavior on the Y should be three times as intense as similar selection on the X (Hamilton, 1967). In addition, recombination between X's in females may occur at normal levels, while the Y shows at best very low levels of recombination.

To state the matter again, in the heterozygous individual genes on either sex chromosome will see little relatedness to the other sex chromosome and virtually no chance of being associated in progeny, so that all genes on a sex chromosome will be selected to act in concert to bring about preferential inheritance of that chromosome (meiotic drive). By contrast, genes on autosomes—while also tempted towards meiotic drive—will be restrained by some past relatedness (which, through variation in degree of inbreeding, may be high or very low) and *by a future chance, through recombination, of being associated together in progeny.* If these two forces are strong enough, we are led to clear expectations regarding the frequency of meiotic drive in nature: most frequent among sex chromosomes (especially Y), less frequent among autosomes, and least so in the sex having highest rates of crossing over. For fruit flies and most mammals this means that we would expect frequency of meiotic drive to decrease as follows: Y > X > autosome in male > autosome in female.

Although cases of meiotic drive are by their nature difficult to detect (requiring the detection of biased frequencies of genes among progeny), many well-studied cases are now known from animals (Crow, 1979). Cases of sex chromosome drive are, as expected, especially common, e.g., in *Aedes aegypti, Drosophila pseudoobscura, Nasonia vitripennis,* as well as a butterfly and two species of lemmings (see Trivers, 1985 for a review and references). Autosomal drive has been less frequently reported, as expected, but it is much more difficult to detect (see below). Famous cases are segregation distortion on the fourth chromosome of *Drosophila melanogaster* and the + system on the seventeenth chromosome in mice (*Mus musculus* and *M. domesticus*). By contrast, cases of meiotic drive in *female* mammals and *Drosophila* are nonexistent. The only case of meiotic drive in female animals occurs on the X of a butterfly *Aoraea acedon.* Of course, in butterflies females are XY, so this exception is another confirmation of the general pattern. Although exactly as expected, the facts themselves are still very few from animals, and I doubt that the facts concerning meiotic drive in plants can as easily be explained.

Meiotic drive operating on sex chromosomes in the XY individual is special in several ways. Such drive is easier to detect, because the sexes themselves are usually easy to distinguish and strong deviations among progeny (from, for example, an expected value of 1:1) should stand out. By contrast, the *t* haplotype in wild mice, though known to have an antiquity of at least a few million years and to have undergone a complex evolution, is classically detected in phenotype (by humans) only when paired with a laboratory-maintained dominant marker gene for tail length (short in non-*t* mice, absent when paired with *t* haplotype). Of course, relative ease of detection may also affect the creatures themselves, though such abilities are expected to evolve: the mice themselves detect *t* haplotypes via smell and make very subtle discriminations. Genes for altering the sex ratio will change the relative frequency of two well-developed and co-adapted morphs, the two sexes. Initially counterselection is slight (since effect on the population sex ratio is small). By contrast, the *t* haplotype appears to be otherwise disadvantageous at *all frequencies* and to be maintained only because of a very strong meiotic drive in males (inherited by about 95% of the offspring of a heterozygous male). In this context, it is also worth noting tht the sex ratio may, especially under conditions of sib-mating, be selected to deviate from 1:1, usually towards an excess of females. Under such conditions, genes inducing the appropriate meiotic drive will, initially at least, be favored at both levels of selection. This appears to have been the case in the lemmings and butterfly mentioned above.

A most intriguing correlation—should it hold true—is that between degree of sex chromosome heteromorphism (degeneration of Y) and degree of morphological specialization (taxonomic rank). Cause and effect could go in either direction. One possibility goes as follows: the more sexual selection acts adaptively, the faster should be the rate of adaptive evolution. At the same time, chromosome degeneration will proceed more quickly because selection will be more intense for tight linkage. Against this view is the fact that it appears to be most valid only early in sex chromosome evolution. Put another way, given that a sharp reduction in crossing over occurs early in sex chromosome differentiation, is it really true that subsequent changes reflect differences in overall selection for linkage due to differences in the adaptive orientation of sexual selection?

SUMMARY

In almost all species examined there is a sex difference in rates of recombination across the autosomes. In dioecious species males usually show tighter linkage and in hermaphrodites cells giving rise to sperm (or pollen) typically show in meiosis tighter linkage than cells giving rise to eggs (or ovules). There are numerous exceptions, most notably in Lepidoptera/Trichoptera and in copepods, in all of which meiosis is achiasmatic in females while showing crossing over in males. These species are female heterogametic and, in fact, in species showing achiasmatic meiosis in one sex, this sex is invariably heterogametic. However, examples are known (e.g., *Triturus helveticus*) in which the heterogametic sex shows *more* recombination across its autosomes than the homogametic sex.

These are explained by arguing that sexual selection often acts adaptively from the female's standpoint and, if so, males are selected to link their genes more tightly in order to preserve their more highly selected beneficial combinations. This also applies to hermaphroditic species, as long as sexual selection is operating, for which there is good evidence in plants. Exceptions are explained by (1) substantial male parental investment, (2) the high cost of male copulation, or (3) the relative weakness of sexual selection.

CHAPTER 17

RETROSPECT ON SEX AND

KINDRED TOPICS

George C. Williams

It is certainly a pleasure to be able to bestow a benediction and to have the last word on such a fine collection of writings about a topic of such deep and continuing interest. Some of the authors have been among my favorite heroes for many years. Others are newcomers I have never met but now have abundant cause to admire. Their different chapters have aroused my interest and aided my understanding in many ways. There really are many possible kinds of understanding of a topic such as the evolutionary biology of sexuality, as several of the chapters make clear, especially the one by Ghiselin. Any particular kind of understanding can be reached only after that type of problem has been recognized and then formulated as a conceptually answerable question. The attainment of even a naive understanding of this sort then makes possible a deeper appreciation of the problem and more rigorous formulation of the question. The great clarity of the questions framed by Felsenstein, Maynard Smith, and others in this volume would not have been possible a decade ago and is possible today only because of recent progress in provisionally answering and then reformulating earlier questions.

One example of recent clarity comes from the realization that there may be genetic conflict not only between different individuals in a population, but also between different stages of the life cycle. As Uyenoyama's chapter shows, such conflict (e.g., between pollen and style) may be a key determinant in the evolution of incompatibility systems. Another example may be noted in progress away from a simplistic assumption underlying some of my own early inquiries (e.g., Williams and Mitton, 1973). Mitton and I assumed that if we understood how natural selection determines a strawberry's allocation of resources to the competing demands of sexual and vegetative reproduction, we might thereby understand the forces that have molded and maintained such allocations since the Cambrian and perhaps before. The distinction between problems of phylogenetic origins and of current evolutionary equilibria seems obvious, but we had an inadequate appreciation of the nature and importance of this distinction for the evolution of sexuality.

Another difficulty was our preoccupation with long-lived multicellular organisms, such as angiosperms and vertebrates, and with ecological aspects of life histories. This was and is the main focus of my interest, but I am entirely willing to concede that we may have missed much of importance with this limited perspective. The work of Levin and of Devoret on recombination in prokaryotes, and that of Holliday and Bernstein, Hopf, and Michod on various aspects of sexuality in relation to DNA repair, show the fruitfulness of a broadened perspective. They make it clear that the machinery of sexuality may have had a rather different kind of significance, early in the history of life, from that which Mitton and I postulated for cladoceran or strawberry life cycles.

Indeed, it would not be surprising to find, over the coming years, that there may have been an elaborate succession of modifications, in meiotic prophase and other cytological machinery, for novel functions. Some of the new uses for older mechanisms may have replaced obsolete earlier functions, while others may have required that the modified machinery solve new problems while continuing to solve the old. Perhaps there was a time when machinery of DNA repair or related housekeeping incidentally generated recombination within chromosomes, and this new process then was selected for optimized rates of progeny diversification, while the original sorts of housekeeping still had to be done.

A number of chapters suggest that the beginnings of allelic recombination arose as a necessary but functionally incidental consequence of DNA repair. Recombination would have started as a spandrel, in the sense of Gould and Lewontin (1979). However it may originate, any feature of any organism that varies genetically in a way that may influence fitness can be co-opted for a useful function. Gould and Lewontin recognize the human chin as a likely spandrel, but different people to different degrees find this structure useful for holding telephones. I will concede that it may be some time before this usage results in significant evolutionary change in the human chin. A new function for meiosis, such as genetic diversification of progeny, need not imply that the more primitive functions become any less important. For this reason an understanding of the phenomena of mutation and recombination in prokaryotes may provide clues to the forces that led to the first appearance of synapsis, segregation, and syngamy. The details of these phenomena in the simpler protists may be even more likely to lead to such insights. Some of the functions of sexuality that served the earliest eukaryotes may still be adaptive in long-lived multicellular organisms, even if, as I believe, they are not adequate to account for all quantitative details.

LEVELS OF SELECTION IN RELATION TO SEXUALITY AND RECOMBINATION

Another example, of progress in my own understanding, is the realization that to know the evolutionary basis of a species' resource allocations is only to know about evolution within the lineage leading to that species. It implies nothing about why that species and its adaptations are here for inspection, while others, in which quite different allocations might have been favored, have gone extinct. The generally low taxonomic rank of exclusively asexual multicellular animals and plants certainly suggests that selection in entities more inclusive than single evolving lineages has been operative. Within any such lineage, selection operating on individuals and recorded by changing allelic frequencies in the gene pool may be the only kind of selection that needs recognition. Selection at the level of species or higher groups (taxon selection of Williams, 1985) may be required to explain the global prevalence of sexual groups and the paucity and low rank of the exclusively asexual. This conclusion is implied in many discussions throughout this century, including Muller's (1930) classic paper on the evolutionary significance of sexuality. In my opinion it was not convincingly argued prior to the work of Van Valen (1975) and Maynard Smith (1978).

I once thought (e.g., Williams, 1966) that the distinction between individual and group selection would always be obvious to everyone, but that was because I was thinking mainly about animal behavior and mainly of the higher animals. In such organisms, physiologically independent individuals have unique genotypes, and selection among them is based on their relative contributions to a common gene pool. Like everyone else two decades ago, I equated group selection with selection among demes, that is, among gene pools within a species. I believe that these meanings should normally be retained, for reasons outlined in Janzen's (1977) analysis of the concepts of individuals and groups in species with clonal reproduction.

So I am inclined to disagree with Levin's discussion of individual and group selection, because the gene pool concept is inapplicable to bacteria or to any other organisms in which there are no regularly occurring bouts of genome-wide recombination. Unlike bacteria, most of the eukaryotes that are regularly clonal also indulge in meiosis and syngamy often enough to make the gene pool concept entirely applicable. A bryozoan colony or vegetatively spreading seed plant is ultimately derived from a zygote produced by sampling from the local gene pool. By their occasional sexual reproduction, members of a clone derived from such a zygote attempt to maximize their contribution of genes to that same pool. Individual selection here would mean selection among genotypes, however multiple and dispersed each may be. This is the meaning urged by Janzen (1977) and seconded by a number of contributers to Harper, Rosen, and White (1986). The concept of group selection, in the original sense of selection among demes with separate gene pools, is applicable to bryozoans and clonal angiosperms, but not to bacteria.

Group selection in another sense would be applicable to any collection of organisms that interact ecologically. Wilson (1980) introduced the concept of trait groups for such entities. Levin must have this concept in mind when he refers to selection among clones as group selection. If members of a clone encounter and interact with each other much more often than with members of other clones, a clone might profitably be considered a trait group. Trait group selection in Wilson's ecological sense would be applicable, but in the genetic sense the selection would surely be among individuals. If groups were formed by members of different clones there could be natural selection among these heterogeneous trait groups too. This could result in changing proportions of competing clones, if some clones have more favorable effects on their trait groups than others. This is the main point of Wilson's theory of trait group selection.

There is a prevalent semantic difficulty here in the tendency to use natural selection to refer both to the events underlying one entity's being favored over another and to the genetic recording of such events. The first refers to the history taking place, the other to the writing of the history. There could be a high rate of such events as the extinction and proliferation of trait groups, but these events will not influence evolution unless the trait groups differ genetically. I have discussed this problem at length elsewhere (Williams, 1985). Arnold and Wade's (1984) distinction between selection and response to selection is related.

Following Janzen (1977), I would equate individual selection in bacteria to selection among clones. A single genetically unique bacterium may, one day later, be represented by a hundred descendant cells. Even if they are widely scattered, I would be inclined to regard the hundred as constituting a single individual from the standpoint of natural selection. Fitness would be measured for each genotype by its phenotypic capability for proliferation in competition with other genotypes in the habitat, and its capability for successful colonization of other habitats.

SOME OTHER CONTROVERSIES

A refreshing new approach, new at least to the analysis of cellular details of sexuality, is the reverse engineering method explicitly applied by Bernstein, Hopf, and Michod to the machinery of meiosis. Surely a reading of this intricate machinery ought to tell us the function for which it was most recently modified and, perhaps, provide clues to earlier functions or even to that for which it originally arose. Their conclusion, that synapsis was originally evolved and is still maintained as a mechanism for repairing DNA, and not as a mechanism for generating variation among descendant chromosomes, strikes me (as well as Maynard Smith and Bell) as too extreme.

Random recombination of genes on nonhomologous chromosomes, which Crow emphasizes as much the more important source of Mendelian recombination, can hardly be a by-product of the mechanisms of DNA repair. It takes precise engineering (or elaborate computer programming) to design a system that will choose among alternatives in a completely unbiased fashion. I cannot imagine such a system being the simplest way to complete meiosis, as Bernstein, Hopf, and Michod contend. The known examples of meiotic drive show that meiosis can be biased. That it is normally unbiased I would attribute to selection establishing a stalemate as the ESS for intergenomic conflict. Reiss (1987) provides discussion on the special case of non-Mendelian sex ratios, and Eberhard (1980) and Cosmides and Tooby (1981) propose more general ideas on conflict among replicators within a cell. I would suggest that some of these ideas are relevant to the interpretation of meiosis and the many provocative phenomena of bacterial recombination discussed by Devoret.

I find myself quite happy with some of the discussion by Bernstein, Hopf, and Michod, especially on the function of premeiotic replication. A convincing refutation of their view might be accomplished by someone able to rise to the challenge of producing a better interpretation of the details of the meiotic machinery. A possible candidate is Ettinger (1986), who interprets meiosis as evolved for purging the genotype of parasitic DNA. He suggests that this evolution proceeded by modifying earlier mechanisms of DNA repair.

This volume presents many other new interpretations of the evolution of sexuality, or at least refinements of ideas that were newly presented in recent works by the same authors. Holliday argues for repair of a specific kind of DNA damage as important in the early development of sexual reproduction. Chapters by Brooks, Levin, Uyenoyama, Maynard Smith, and Bell analyze processes by which genes can be favorably selected by means other than enhancing the fitness of their individual carriers. Some of these, such as Muller's rachet and hitchhiking effects, have been recognized for some time. Others, such as the suggestions of Hickey and Rose that rates of recombination are subject to manipulation by transposable elements or plasmids, are new to me and are surely worth further exploration.

Having recognized the value of new approaches in interpreting the phenomena of sexuality, I would also like to urge that attention may still be worth channeling into other approaches, such as the fitness consequences of recombination, or its absence, in relation to ecological factors affecting a parent or likely to affect offspring. I doubt that we have entirely mined out the insights that can be gained from this approach for the organisms for which it has traditionally been used, such as Daphnia and Viola. I would also concede that the most important new insights in the near future may arise more readily from applying such old approaches to less traditional organisms, such as prokaryotes.

Levin's discussion of the likelihood of fitness reduction by random recombination in bacteria parallels arguments formulated many years ago by Eschel and Feldman (1970). They analyzed a generally applicable model, but clearly had multicellular eukaryotes in mind. Eschel and Feldman's most provocative conclusion, that recombination can be expected to retard adaptive change in an evolving population, was not received with great enthusiasm by a scientific community desperate to find ways in which recombination might be favored. Levin's discussion of fitness reduction by recombination in bacteria says, in effect, that Eshel and Feldman's unwelcome conclusion has wide applicability. Seger and Hamilton's chapter turns this Eshel–Feldman effect into an advantage. In retarding the advance of favored genotypes, recombination makes a progeny more likely to meet the challenge of reversed selection pressures.

For another example of an old problem that might still be attacked from the traditional approach of reproductive ecology, I return again to one of my favorite examples. A strawberry plant, at a certain stage in its reproductive life, is found to be devoting a proportion p of its reproductive expenditures to sexual reproduction and $1 - p$ to asexual reproduction. Are we to take seriously the idea that this resource partitioning may not represent a frequency-dependent equilibrium between the two processes? Brooks's suggestion that there may be no genetic variability that would affect mode of reproduction is demonstrably inapplicable for this example. Artificial selection, in a historically trivial number of generations, has greatly augmented resources devoted to fruit and produced some varieties with very little expenditure for vegetative spread. I do not see that the solution to this resource allocation problem is likely to be aided by knowing that the basic machinery of sexuality was evolved as a DNA repair mechanism or that prokaryote recombination is usually associated with injury or pathogens. I share Ghiselin's view that the diversity of life cycles is the main theoretical challenge.

However, I do not share his view of how the almost exclusively sexual reproduction of vertebrates and many other groups is most convincingly explained. I wish he had elaborated on the statement that the data of ecology and systematics fail to support phylogenetic constraint as the solution to this problem, because I am unaware of such evidence. I am aware of evidence for the highly relevant generalization that asexual vertebrates never arise by an ordinary (gradualist) evolutionary process. They are created by the saltational event of hybridization. I remain convinced that genetic variation that would constitute the beginnings of a shift from sexuality to parthenogenesis would be universally disfavored in the vertebrates and many other groups. Perhaps many of these animals would have higher fitness with parthenogenesis, at least in the short term, but there is no way for selection to take them there from where they are.

I assume that this is the postulated cause behind Brooks's suggestion that "within most species there is little variation in the mode of reproduction." This should not be understood to mean that major groups, such as the vertebrates, are without genetic variation in the parameters that differentiate the two reproductive modes. Is there no genetic variation in the frequency of nondisjunction leading to eggs with $n + 1$ chromosomes? This is a step $1/n$ of the way towards producing diploid eggs. Is there no variation at all in any vertebrate in the developmental stimulus threshold that must be met by the sperm? A reduced threshold would also be a step towards the higher adaptive peak that parthenogenesis might ultimately provide, but all such steps lead first into the deep adaptive pit of aneuploidy. To borrow a phrase from Lloyd, an asexual vertebrate never evolves, because such animals are unable to achieve "the circumvention of two complex processes, meiosis and fertilization."

I certainly hope that people will continue to exploit the older approaches and try to find better answers to some of the questions that have been around for a long time. I am not convinced by Crow's and Maynard Smith's view that the reasonable answers to the old questions have all been formulated and that the main job now is to decide on their relative importance. Ghiselin describes and Crow provides a formal list of major and widely applicable disadvantages to recombination, and these authors support them with convincing and straight-forward arguments. They are mainly factors understandable as immediately important to natural selection at the individual level.

By contrast, the advantages in Crow's list seem weak and restricted in scope, the arguments in their favor rather devious, and their applications most readily envisioned as long-term effects at the group level. I think it clear that if the world were otherwise—if meiosis and fertilization were rare or unknown and the world full of Lynch's (1984) general-purpose genotypes—there would be no mystery. No one would wonder why these elaborate processes have not been evolved to enable organisms to reverse Muller's rachet, repair DNA, escape pathogens, or increase their potential for niche expansion. Of the contributors to this symposium, only Seger and Hamilton, and (especially) Lloyd, attempt to show that the postulated advantages are quantitatively adequate to balance the disadvantages. Felsenstein is inclined to belittle the crisis that arises from these considerations. I believe that Ghiselin's recognition of the crisis is more likely to lead to important new understandings.

Occasionally the suggestion is made that an adequate advantage for sexuality can be shown by models of strong selection at one or a few loci (Treisman, 1975; Weinshall, 1986). As an extreme case, if an unpredictable one of the three genotypes AA, Aa, and aa is lethal in any given generation, selection for recombination will be strong enough to prevent fixation of parthenogenesis. This is an extreme and implausible model that I would expect to be applicable only briefly in any population. A lethal genotype in high frequency would set up strong selection at all other loci for alleles that might in some way alleviate the lethal condition or make it a facultative response to signals that predict its viability. The strong one-locus selection would disappear quickly on an evolu-tionary time scale. The rarity of strongly selected single-locus polymorphisms in nature supports my position. I would expect the sickle-cell allele to reach near fixation in human populations subject to malaria, because sickle-cell anemia should disappear in a short time (hundreds or thousands of generations) as adaptive modifiers accumulate at other loci.

The contributors to this symposium disagree with each other or with me on many other issues, including some that might appear to be rather simple, with an easily attained consensus. Both Holliday and Maynard Smith maintain that important aspects of Shields's DNA repair by inbreeding would not work. I certainly find it difficult to believe that the shedding of newly arisen mutations by briefly heterozygous inbreeders would do much to decrease mutational load. Several other examples are listed by Maynard Smith and by Ghiselin.

WHAT SORT OF COST IS REALLY AVOIDED BY ASEXUAL REPRODUCTION?

I do not agree with Felsenstein that there would be no cost of meiosis without the prior evolution of anisogamy. At the least I would suggest that the modeling Felsenstein has in mind is not the most instructive that can be devised. I have already published some arguments to this effect (Williams, 1980), but will try another here. Perhaps it is just a matter of time before someone discovers (or invents in the laboratory) an all-male species. It makes diploid sperm that inseminate eggs of a related species and give rise to diploid nuclei that exclude the egg pronuclei. The exclusively sperm-derived genes then direct the development of a male animal with the father's genotype. This could go on generation after generation in a way analogous to the clonal reproduction of gynogenetic fishes (Moore, 1984). Such all-female fishes are considered parasitic on males of the species that provide the sperm, which merely trigger development without fusion with the already diploid (or polyploid) egg nucleus. The all-male species I have described would be parasitic in a far more substantive sense. All parental investment would be provided by the female victims, who get no reproductive payoff from their investment.

The point of the story is that any male of any species that refrains from such egg piracy is paying a cost of meiosis as a direct result of the haploidy and cytologically cooperative behavior of its sperm. The diploid sperm strategy would spread rapidly (for a while) in any species in which it could be introduced. The piracy would have twice the payoff of cooperative syngamy, other things being equal. This is true whether sexual reproduction is by isogamy or by anisogamy. If the gametes are equal in size and nutritive reserves, one that simply takes over the resources provided by the other gamete, without allowing their equal use by the genes of the other gamete, is cheating its own genes of what they might gain by the envisioned parasitism.

It should be noted that while a cost of meiosis is readily recognizable in my all-male species, a cost of males is not, at least not as an aspect of selection at the individual level. The two terms are often used synonymously: Felsenstein and Ghiselin use one and Crow the other, but seemingly with the same meaning. There are other terminological possibilities. Seger and Hamilton use the more general cost of sex, and Uyenoyama (1984) speaks of the cost of outcrossing. Her suggestion is reasonable, because the cost of meiosis can be avoided by selfing, but meiosis is a necessary precondition for outcrossing. I think it best to retain both the cost of meiosis and the cost of males, but with different meanings, as do Shields and Lloyd. The cost of meiosis is usually the better concept if selection within a population is under discussion. As long as producing sons and producing daughters are equally effective tactics for producing grandchildren, there is no individual-level disadvantage in the production of males.

Males (or maleness in hermaphrodites) is costly only at a group level, and the cost is measurable as a decrement in rate of increase. This sort of measure is often used in simple models of natural selection, for instance, with bearers of a mutant gene having one rate of increase and the ancestral genotypes another. These two groups would form a single population, so that no group selection in the usual sense would take place. I assume that this is the sense in which Seger and Hamilton speak of an asexual driving a sexual form to extinction. This sort of modeling is valid for single-locus genetic problems or for simple phenotypic characters (e.g., body size) subject to additive genetic effects. It is not valid for a multilocus character complex, such as a sequence of reproductive activities. Such complex differences require separate populations for their maintenance, and any differences in rates of increase imply group selection.

The cost of males is clearly this kind of group-level phenomenon. I once found it puzzling that so many people maintained that male parental investment made sexual reproduction less costly for females (e.g., Seger and Hamilton, in this volume). Finally I realized that they were assuming that only the offspring of sexual females would get such investments from males. Two characters were always associated: haploid eggs and investing males. Surely these need not have the same genetic basis. If an otherwise normal parthenogenetic female arose in a normal (sexual) population of song birds, she might well get assistance from a male for raising offspring that would be exclusively her own. The male would be cuckolded by an extra genome from his own mate who would thereby have a twofold advantage over her more honest competitors. Male parental investment does nothing to make exclusively haploid eggs an ESS in any population.

When ecological competition between an all-female clone and a Mendelian population (without paternal investment) is being considered, male parental investment would make a difference, Seger and Hamilton's account of why the asexual form would win out would be correct, and the cost of males is the preferred concept. If half the members of the sexual population are males and use all their reproductive allocations in competing among themselves for mates, the population's production of males would be economically wasteful and give it a 50% disadvantage in the competition. The same consideration would apply to bdelloid rotifers versus copepods, or any other problem in group selection or ecological competition. Lloyd's chapter gives a thoughtful and quantitative analysis of these two kinds of cost.

DO SOME OF US STILL COMMIT THE WILLIAMS FALLACY?

I believe that I detect in several chapters some statements reminiscent of the Williams Fallacy (Williams, 1966, pp. 138–141). This unfortunate idea is that, because the great majority of mutations are deleterious, selection can only act to reduce the mutation rate. This error was based on a naive assumption of symmetry between ultimate quantitative effects of favorable and unfavorable mutations. In reality, as Maynard Smith (1978, pp. 112–113) and others have pointed out, the two kinds of events have extremely asymmetrical consequences. An unfavorable mutation, of whatever severity, is a problem with a simple solution, one genetic death. If a favorable mutation happens and escapes stochastic loss, all hell breaks loose. The mutation sweeps through the population and replaces alternative alleles, or at least rises to an appreciable frequency-dependent level. Such a change at the one locus may cause changes in selection and allele-frequency equilibria at other loci. The adaptive advance caused by the incorporation of the new allele would be expected to have at least slight effects on niche parameters and therefore on other species in the community. So the effects of equal but opposite quantitative changes in fitness can be extremely unequal. A population might easily maintain a high level of fitness through normalizing selection, despite a moderate rate of origin of deleterious mutations. In a world ruled by the Red Queen, it could not maintain itself indefinitely if deprived of rare favorable mutations.

The advantage of maintaining an appreciable mutation rate would work best for organisms capable of prolonged clonal reproduction. In them a favorable mutation could reach a high local frequency in the genotype in which it arose, and this would provide a hitchhiking advantage to any mutation rate gene that permitted the favored mutation to occur. The maintenance of an appreciable mutation rate would be especially favored at the individual (clonal) level in bacteria. In exclusively sexual populations it would be favored only at the group level, or for close linkage between the favored mutation and the gene that let it happen.

Thus I am inclined to take exception to the statement by Bernstein, Hopf, and Michod "just as the replicative machinery has been selected to reduce mutational variation, so has the recombinational repair machinery of meiosis been selected to reduce recombinational variation. . . ." For the same reasons I question Crow's and Bell's suggestion that the much greater frequency of deleterious mutations makes the shedding of such mutations a more important function of recombination than is the production of favorable new combinations.

The idea that selection always acts to decrease recombination between synapsed chromosomes is most clearly refuted by the extreme sex differences in crossover rates, a subject mentioned by several contributors and discussed in detail by Trivers. Why should such selection in Drosophila have succeeded perfectly in one sex and still allowed extensive recombination in the other? I am not entirely comfortable with Trivers's idea that one sex, usually the male, is more dependent on coadapted genes for its fitness (apparently Trivers is also not entirely comfortable), but I have no other explanation to offer. I should think that Trivers's theory could be tested with self-fertilizing hermaphrodites, such as some persistently selfing plants or the fish *Rivulus marmoratus* (Harrington, 1975). There can be no selection for suppressing recombination or for mate choice mechanisms in such species. Trivers's theory would be refuted, or at least seriously questioned, if obligate selfers show much more frequent chiasmata in one kind of gonadal tissue than the other.

WHAT USE IS THEORY?

I think it wise to recognize that a search for widely applicable theory, as exemplified by this book, can play more than one role in scientific progress. Its most obviously fruitful role is in providing explicit direction for research. From theory we can deduce conclusions not previously reached and that are occasionally counterintuitive. Consider Brooks's idea that the natural selection of recombination rate can cause a reduction of mean fitness, or Hickey and Rose's inference that selection may increase the frequency of females that prefer to mate with males burdened with some maladaptive character. These are not propositions that many would have seriously considered a few years ago.

If fortune smiles on the theorist, the theoretically derived conclusion will be readily testable by observation, as that of Hickey and Rose could be by a simple mate choice experiment with a suitable organism. Lloyd lists a great wealth of possible investigations for which his models predict specific results. Fortune will be benevolent indeed if the inference from one theory contradicts that of another. Happily, much of the disputation among the authors in this book makes use of such evidence. Ghiselin's and Bell's citing of habitat correlations in recombination frequency as favoring genetic recombination models, and ruling out the complete adequacy of DNA repair models, is one of many examples.

Theory can also be useful, if less directly, if it merely clarifies relations among concepts, even without explicit reference to testable hypotheses. It helps us put our conceptual house in order and prevent self-deception. I think that Ghiselin's, Maynard Smith's, and especially Felsenstein's chapters are immensely valuable in this respect. My understanding is surely enhanced by knowing that some sibling competition models that I have favored are genetically varieties of the Fisher–Muller theory.

It may also be instructive to search beyond our immediate circle (biologists explicitly concerned with the evolution of sexuality) and look for models of processes formally analogous to such things as recombination. For instance, ecologists' models of the function of dispersal may be relevant. This is suggested by the metaphor of a chromosome being the temporary habitat of a gene. If the chromosome duplicates without crossing over, the gene's daughters have not changed habitats. Their fortunes continue to be determined mainly by the activities of all other genes on the unchanged chromosomes. If crossing over takes place, our gene disperses its daughter genes into two new genetic environments. Their fortunes will be determined by the arithmetic mean success of these and all later chromosomal habitats. Is a gene that achieves such dispersal to other habitats more fit than one that inhibits recombination? Much depends on the form of the variation in fitness through time.

Reproductive success in most populations must have a strong positive skew. This conforms to Maynard Smith's idea that two lethals are no worse than one, and to the outcomes of the simulations of sib-competition models written by Mitton (Williams and Mitton, 1973). One possible approach to the formal modeling of skewed variation in reproductive success (from genetic and environmental fitness and luck) is to assume that it is log-normally distributed, with odds more like double-or-half than like double-or-nothing. Genes that disperse to new linkage groups could then have greater fitness than those that keep them intact, for the same reasons proposed in Strathmann's (1974) theory of dispersal. If success at the same time in different habitats is less than perfectly correlated, and if the population as a whole is subject to density-dependent regulation, the wide disperser achieves the arithmetic mean success of the kinds of habitats in which it finds itself. Nondispersers get the lower success represented by the geometric mean.

Another role of theory is to allow clear recognition of instructive anomalies. Maynard Smith's flaunting of the challenge of the bdelloid rotifers is a good example. Another persistent anomaly is the lek paradox, the prevalence of strongly developed female-choice mechanisms in species without paternal investment (Taylor and Williams, 1982; Kirkpatrick, 1986). I believe that it is this phenomenon that goaded Seger and Hamilton into deriving their theory of recombination as a means of escaping from parasites specialized for parental genotypes. The prevalence of sexual recombination itself may represent the most instructive anomaly of all.

Acknowledgments

Chapter 1: Michael T. Ghiselin   This has been an unusually difficult paper to write. Therefore I owe more than the usual thanks to the following persons for their advice and encouragement: Francesco M. Scudo, Suresh Jayakar, Steven C. Stearns, Jacob Koella, the editors, and an anonymous referee.

Chapter 2: Raymond Devoret   Melanie Pierre provided invaluable help for the preparation of the material used in the writing of this chapter. Discussions with Adriana Bailone, Marie Dutreix, Patrice L. Moreau, and Suzanne Sommer provided valuable contributions. Patrice L. Moreau, Suzanne Sommer, and Lone Simonsen are thanked for their suggestions. Gerald R. Smith kindly made available one of his drawings.

This work has been carried out with grants from Euratom, Ligue Francais contre le Cancer, Association pour la Recherche sur le Cancer, and Fondation pour la Recherche Medicale.

Chapter 4: James F. Crow   This chapter is Paper Number 2914 from the Laboratory of Genetics, University of Wisconsin, Madison.

Chapter 5: Joseph Felsenstein   I am grateful to W. G. Hill and Alan Robertson for their discussions with me on these subjects over many years. I also wish to thank the editors for suggestions helpful in clarifying my presentation.

This work was supported by task agreement number DE-AT06-76EV71005 of contract number DE-AM06-76RL02225 between the United States Department of Energy and the University of Washington, Seattle.

Chapter 11: Jon Seger and W. D. Hamilton   We thank E. L. Charnov, A. P. Dobson, A. M. Lyles, R. M. May, N. A. Moran, J. W. Stubblefield, M. Zuk, and the editors for helpful advice and discussion.

Chapter 12: Bruce R. Levin   I wish to thank Richard Condit, Ralph Evans, Judy MacDougall, Richard Michod, Bill Shannon, and Lone Simonsen for stimulating and useful discussions and comments. I owe a particular debt of gratitude to Rosemary Redfield for critical commentary and for designing and preparing the illustrations in the chapter.

This endeavor was supported by a grant from the National Institutes of Health, GM33782.

Chapter 16: Robert Trivers   I am especially grateful to the Harry Frank Guggenheim Foundation for supporting this work. I am also grateful for the encouragement of Betty-ann Kevles and the University of California Press. For discussions and help with the literature I am grateful to Chris Otis and Jon Seger. For much encouragement and numerous helpful suggestions I am grateful to Ernst Mayr. For helpful comments on an earlier draft I am grateful to many people, especially James Bull, Brian Charlesworth, James Crow, Ernst Mayr, Todd Newberry, Uzi Nur, and Jon Seger.

Chapter 17: George C. Williams   This chapter is Contribution No. 634 from the Department of Ecology and Evolution, State University of New York at Stony Brook.

Literature Cited

THE NUMBERS IN BRACKETS THAT FOLLOW EACH ENTRY IDENTIFY THE CHAPTER(S)
IN WHICH THE REFERENCE IS CITED.

Abdullah, N. F. and B. Charlesworth. 1974. Selection for reduced crossing over in *Drosophila melanogaster*. Genetics 76:447-451. [6]

Abugov, R. 1985. Is there a cost of meiosis in life history? J. Theor. Biol. 116:616-623. [1]

Achwal, C. W., P. Ganguly and H. S. Chandra. 1984. Estimation of the amount of 5-methylcytosine in *Drosophila melanogaster* DNA by amplified ELISA and photoacoustic spectroscopy. EMBO J. 3:263-266. [3]

Adams, R. L. P. and R. H. Burdon. 1985. *The Molecular Biology of DNA Methylation*. Springer-Verlag, New York. [3]

Albert, E. D., M. P. Baur and W. R. Mayr (eds.). 1984. *Histocompatibility Testing 1984*. Springer-Verlag, Berlin. [13]

Alberts, B. M., J. Barry, P. Bedinger, R. L. Burke, U. Hibner, C. C. Liu and R. Sheridan. 1980. Studies of replication mechanisms with the T4 bacteriophage in vitro system. In *Mechanistic Studies of DNA Replication and Genetic Recombination*, B. Alberts and C. F. Fox (eds.). Academic Press, New York. [9]

Alberts, B. M. and L. Frey. 1970. T4 bacteriophage gene 32: A structural protein in the replication and recombination of DNA. Nature 227:1313-1318. [2]

Allard, R. W. 1963. Evidence for genetic restriction of recombination in the lima bean. Genetics 48:1389-1395. [6]

Allard, R. W. and J. Adams. 1969. Population studies in predominantly self-pollinating species. XIII. Intergenotypic competition and population structure in barley and wheat. Amer. Natur. 103:621-645. [11]

Allee, W. C., A. E. Emerson, O. Park, T. Park and K. P. Schmidt. 1949. *Principles of Animal Ecology*. Saunders, Philadelphia. [1]

Alstad, D. N. and G. F. Edmunds. 1983. Selection, outbreeding depression and the sex ratio of scale insects. Science 220:93-95. [11]

Ames, B. N. 1983. Dietary carcinogens and anticarcinogens. Science 221:1256-1264. [9]

Amos, D. B. and F. E. Ward. 1977. Theoretical consideration in the association between HLA and disease. In *HLA and Disease*, J. Dausset and A. Svejgaard (eds.). Munksgaard, Copenhagen. [13]

Amundsen, S. K., A. F. Taylor, A. M. Chaudhury and G. R. Smith. 1986. *recD*: The gene for an essential third subunit of exonuclease V. Proc. Natl. Acad. Sci. USA 83:5558-5562. [2]

Anderson, G. J. and G. L. Stebbins. 1984. Dioecy versus gametophytic self-incompatability: A test. Amer. Natur. 124:423-428. [13]

Anderson, R. M. and R. M. May. 1982. Coevolution of hosts and parasites. Parasitology 85:411-426. [11]

Andersson, L. and K. Sandberg. 1984. Genetic linkage in the horse. II. Distribution of male recombination estimates and the influence of age, breed and sex on recombination frequency. Genetics 106:109-122. [16]

Angus, R. A. 1980. Geographical dispersal and clonal diversity in unisexual fish populations. Amer. Natur. 195:531-550. [1]

Antonovics, J. and N. C. Ellstrand. 1984. Experimental studies of the evolutionary significance of sexual reproduction. I. A test of the frequency-dependent hypothesis. Evolution 38:103-115. [1, 11]

Arnold, S. J. and M. J. Wade. 1984. On the measurement of natural and sexual selection: Theory. Evolution 38:709-19. [17]

Asher, J. H. 1970. Parthenogenesis and genetic variability. II. One-locus models for various diploid populations. Genetics 66:369-391. [1]

Asker, S. 1979. Progress in apomixis research. Hereditas 91:231-240. [1]

Attfield, P. V., F. E. Benson and R. G. Lloyd. 1985. Analysis of the *ruv* locus of *Escherichia coli* K12 and identification of the gene product. J. Bacteriol. 164:276-281. [2]

Auslander, D., J. Guckenheimer and G. Oster. 1978. Random evolutionarily stable strategies. Theor. Pop. Biol. 13:276-293. [11]

Austin, C. R. 1972. Pregnancy losses and birth defects. In *Reproduction in Mammals, Book 2: Embryonic and Fetal Development*, C. R. Austin and R. V. Short (eds.). Cambridge University Press. [9]

Avery, O. T., C. M. MacLoed and M. McCarty. 1944. Studies on the chemical nature of the substance inducing transformation of pneumocococcal types. J. Exp. Med. 79:137-158. [12]

Bagdasarian, M., A. Bailone, M. M. Bagdasarian, P. A. Manning, R. Lurz, K. N. Timmis and R. Devoret. 1986. An inhibitor of SOS induction specified by a plasmid locus in *Escherichia coli*. Proc. Natl. Acad. Sci. USA 83:5723-5726. [2]

Bailone, A., A. Levine and R. Devoret. 1979. In vivo inactivation of prophage lambda repressor. J. Mol. Biol. 131:553-572. [2]

Bailone, A., S. Sommer and R. Devoret. 1985. MiniF plasmid-induced SOS signal is RecBC-dependent. Proc. Natl. Acad. Sci. USA 82:5973-5977. [2]

Bailone, A., A. Backman, S. Sommer, J. Celerier, M. M. Bagdasarian, M. Bagdasarian and R. Devoret. 1987. Genetic and functional characterization of Psi polypeptides that counteract the activities of RecA protein in *E. coli*. Proc. Natl. Acad. Sci. USA. [2]

Baker, B. S., A. T. C. Carpenter, M. S. Esposito, R. E. Esposito and L. Sandler. 1976. The genetic control of meiosis. Annu. Rev. Genet. 10:53-134. [6]

Baker, H. G. 1948. Corolla size in gynodioecious and gynomonoecious species of flowering plants. Proc. Leeds Phil. Lit. Soc. 5:136-139. [14]

Baker, T. G. 1963. A quantitative and cytological study of germ cells in human ovaries. Proc. Roy. Soc. London B 158:417-433. [9]

Barash, D. P. 1976. What does sex really cost? Amer. Natur. 110:894-896. [1, 5]

Barrett, J. A. 1981. The evolutionary consequences of monoculture. In *Genetic Consequences of Man-Made Change*, J. A. Bishop and L. M. Cook (eds.). Academic Press, London. [11]

Barrett, J. A. 1983. Plant-fungus symbioses. In *Coevolution*, D. J. Futuyma and M. Slatkin (eds.). Sinauer Associates, Sunderland, Massachusetts. [11]

Barrett, J. A. 1985. The gene-for-gene hypothesis: Parable or paradigm? In *Ecology and Genetics of Host-Parasite Interactions*, D. Rollinson and R. M. Anderson (eds.). Academic Press, London. [11]

Bateman, A. J. 1948. Intra-sexual selection in *Drosophila*. Heredity 2:349-368. [14, 16]

Bateman, A. J. 1952. Self-incompatability systems in angiosperms. Heredity 6:285-310. [13]

Bateson, P. 1980. Optimal outbreeding and the development of sexual preferences in Japanese quail. Z. Tierpsychol. 53:231-244. [13]

Beer, A. E., J. F. Quebbman, J. W. T. Ayers and R. F. Haines. 1981. Major histocompatability complex antigens, maternal and paternal immune responses and chronic habitual abortions in humans. Amer. J. Obstet. Gynecol. 141:987-999. [13]

Bell, G. 1982. *The Masterpiece of Nature: The Evolution and Genetics of Sexuality*. University of California Press, Berkeley. [5, 6, 7, 8, 9, 10, 11, 12, 15, 16]

Bell, G. 1985. On the function of flowers. Proc. Roy Soc. London B. 224:223-265. [14, 16]

Bell, G. 1985. Two theories of sex and variation. Experientia 41:1235-1245. [1, 7, 8, 11, 15]

Bell, G. 1987. *Sex and Death in Protozoa: The History of an Obsession*. Manuscript in review. [8]

Bell, G. In press. Recombination and the immortality of the germ line. J. Evol. Biol. [8]

Bell, G. and J. Maynard Smith. 1987. Short-term selection for recombination among mutually antagonistic species. Nature 328:66-68. [8, 11]

Benacerraf, B. and H. O. McDevitt. 1972. Histocompatibility-linked immune response genes. Science 175:273-279. [13]

Bender, R. A. 1984. Ultraviolet mutagenesis and inducible DNA repair in *Caulobacter crescentus*. Molec. Gen. Genet. 197:399-402. [2]

Bengtsson, B. O. 1978. Avoid inbreeding: At what cost? J. Theor. Biol. 73:439-444. [13]

Bengtsson, B. O. 1985. Biased gene conversion as the primary function of recombination. Genet. Res., Camb. 47:77-80. [4, 7]

Benjamin, W. H., Jr. and D. E. Briles. 1985. Evidence that the pathogenesis of *Salmonella typhimurium* is dependent on interactions between *Salmonella* and mouse genotypes. In *Genetic*

Control of Host Resistance to Infection and Malignancy, E. Skamene (ed.). Alan R. Liss, New York. [11]

Bennett, J. H., D. L. Hayman and R. M. Hope. 1986. Novel sex differences in linkage values and meiotic chromosome behavior in a marsupial. Nature 323:59-60. [16]

Bennett, P. 1985. Bacterial transposons. In *Genetics of Bacteria*, J. Scaife, D. Leach and A. Galizzi (eds.). Academic Press, New York. [12]

Berger, H., A. J. Warren and K. E. Fry. 1969. Variations in genetic recombination due to *amber* mutations in T4D bacteriophage. J. Virol. 3:171-175. [9]

Bernstein, C. 1979. Why are babies born young? Meiosis may prevent ageing of the germ line. Perspect. Biol. Med. 22:539-544. [1]

Bernstein, C. 1981. Deoxyribonucleic acid repair in bacteriophage. Microbiol. Rev. 45:72-98. [1]

Bernstein, H. 1968. Repair and recombination in phage T4. I. Genes affecting recombination. Cold Spring Harbor Symp. Quant. Biol. 33:325-331. [9]

Bernstein, H. 1977. Germ line recombination may be primarily a manifestation of DNA repair processes. J. Theor. Biol. 69:371-380. [1, 4, 10, 15]

Bernstein, H. 1983. Recombinational repair may be an important function of sexual reproduction. BioScience 33:326-331. [1, 9]

Bernstein, H., H. C. Byerly, F. A. Hopf and R. E. Michod. 1984. Origin of sex. J. Theor. Biol. 110:323-351. [3, 9, 10]

Bernstein, H., H. Byerly, F. Hopf and R. E. Michod. 1985. Sex and the emergence of species. J. Theor. Biol. 117:665-690. [1]

Bernstein, H., H. C. Byerly, F. A. Hopf and R. E. Michod. 1985. Genetic damage, mutation and the evolution of sex. Science 229:1277-1281. [3, 7, 8, 9, 13, 15]

Bernstein, H., H. C. Byerly, F. A. Hopf and R. E. Michod. 1985. The evolutionary role of recombinational repair and sex. Int. Rev. Cytol. 96:1-28. [1, 3, 4, 7, 8, 9]

Bernstein, H., H. Byerly, F. Hopf and R. E. Michod. 1985. DNA repair and complementation: The major factors in the origin and maintenance of sex. In *The Origin and Evolution of Sex*, H. O. Halvorson and A. Monroy (eds.). Alan R.Liss, New York. [1, 9, 12]

Bernstein, H., G. S. Byers and R. E. Michod. 1981. Evolution of sexual reproduction: Importance of DNA repair, complementation and variation. Amer. Natur. 117:537-549. [1, 3, 10, 15]

Bernstein, H., F. A. Hopf and R. E. Michod. 1987. The molecular basis for the evolution of sex. Adv. Genet. 24:323-370. [9]

Bertin, R. I. 1982. Influence of father identity on fruit production in trumpet creeper (*Campsis radicans*). Amer. Natur. 119:694-709. [16]

Better, M. and D. R. Helinski. 1983. Isolation and characterization of the *recA* gene of *Rhizobium meliloti*. J. Bacteriol. 155:311-316. [2]

Billington, W. D. 1964. Influence of immunological dissimilarity of mother and foetus on size of placenta in mice. Nature 202:317-318. [13]

Blackwell, J. M. 1985. Genetic control of discrete phases of complex infections: *Leishmania donovani* as a model. In *Genetic Control of Host Resistance to Infection and Malignancy*, E. Skamene (ed.). Alan R. Liss, New York. [11]

Blanar, M. A., S. J. Sandler, M. E. Armengod, L. W. Ream and A. J. Clark. 1984. Molecular analysis of the *recF* gene of *Escherichia coli*. Proc. Natl. Acad. Sci. USA 81:4622-4626. [2]

Blute, M. 1984. The sociobiology of sex and sexes today. Current Anthro. 25:193-212. [15]

Bodmer, W. F. 1986a. HLA today. Hum. Immun. 17:490-503. [11]

Bodmer, W. F. 1986b. Human genetics: The molecular challenge. Cold Spring Harbor Symp. Quant. Biol. 51:1-13. [11]

Bodmer, W. F. and J. Felsenstein. 1967. Linkage and selection: Theoretical analysis of the deterministic two-locus random mating model. Genetics 57:237-265. [6]

Bookman, S. S. 1984. Evidence for selective fruit production in *Asclepias*. Evolution 38:72-86.

Bradshaw, A. D. 1972. Some of the evolutionary consequences of being a plant. Evol. Biol. 5:25-47. [13]

Bremermann, H. J. 1979. Theory of spontaneous cell fusion. Sexuality in cell populations as an evolutionarily stable strategy. Applications to immunology and cancer. J. Theor. Biol. 76:311-334. [5]

Bremermann, H. J. 1980. Sex and polymorphism as strategies in host-pathogen interactions. J. Theor. Biol. 87:671-702. [1, 11]

Bremermann, H. J. 1985. The adaptive significance of sexuality. Experientia 41:1245-1254. [1, 6, 11]

Bremermann, H. J. and B. Fiedler. 1985. On the stability of polymorphic host-pathogen populations. J. Theor. Biol. 117:621-631. [11]

Bremermann, H. J. and J. Pickering. 1983. A game-theoretical model of parasite virulence. J. Theor. Biol. 100:411-426. [11]

Brewen, J. G. and W. J. Peacock. 1969. The effect of tritiated thymidine on sister-chromatid exchange in a ring chromosome. Mutat. Res. 7:433-440.

Breyere, E. J. and W. W. Sprenger. 1969. Evidence of allograft rejection of the conceptus. Transplant. Proc. 1:71-75. [13]

Brink, R. A. and D. C. Cooper. 1939. Somatoplastic sterility in *Medicago sativa*. Science 90:545-546. [13]

Brink, R. A. and D. C. Cooper. 1940. Double fertilization and development of the seed in angiosperms. Bot. Gaz. 102:1-25. [13]

Brink, R. A. and D. C. Cooper. 1947. The endosperm in seed development. Bot. Rev. 13:423-541. [13]

Brink, R. A. 1973. Paramutation. Annu. Rev. Genet. 7:129-152. [3]

Broadhead, R. S. and J. F. Kidwell. 1975. A note on the distribution of the recombination fraction in *Drosophila melanogaster*. J. Hered. 66:309-310. [6]

Broadhead, R. S., J. F. Kidwell and M. G. Kidwell. 1977. Variation of the recombination fraction in *Drosophila melanogaster* females. J. Hered. 68:323-326. [6]

Broda, P. 1979. *Plasmids*. W. H. Freeman, San Francisco. [12]

Brooks, L. D. 1985. The Organization of Genetic Variation for Recombination in *Drosophila melanogaster*. Ph. D. Thesis, Harvard University. [6, 9]

Brooks, L. D. and R. W. Marks. 1986. The organization of genetic variation for recombination in *Drosophila melanogaster*. Genetics 114:525-547. [6, 11]

Browne, R. A. 1980. Competition experiments between parthenogenetic and sexual strains of brine shrimp, *Artemia salina*. Ecology 61:471-474. [1]

Bujarski, J. J. and P. Kaesberg. 1986. Genetic recombination between RNA components of a multipartite plant virus. Nature 321:528-531. [2]

Bull, J. J. 1983. *Evolution of Sex Determining Mechanisms*. Benjamin/Cummings, Menlo Park, California. [16]

Bullmer, M. G. 1982. Cyclical parthenogenesis and the cost of sex. J. Theor. Biol. 94:197-207. [1]

Burt, A. and G. Bell. 1987. Mammalian chiasma frequencies as a test of two theories of recombination. Nature 326:803-805. [11]

Calow, P., M. Beveridge and R. Sibly. 1979. Heads and tails: Adaptational aspects of asexual reproduction in freshwater triclads. Amer. Zool. 19:715-727. [1]

Campbell, A. 1981. Evolutionary significance of accessory DNA elements in bacteria. Annu. Rev. Microbiol. 35:55-83. [12]

Campbell, D. R. and N. M. Waser. 1987. The evolution of plant mating systems: Multilocus simulations of pollen dispersal. Amer. Natur. 129:593-609. [13]

Campbell, D. T. 1974. Evolutionary epistemology. In *The Philosophy of Karl Popper*, P. A. Schlipp (ed.). Open Court Pub., Chicago. [15]

Capaldo, F. N. and S. D. Barbour. 1975. DNA content, synthesis and integrity in dividing and nondividing cells in *Rec* strains of *Escherichia coli* K12. J. Mol. Biol. 91:53-66. [2]

Carpenter, A. T. C. 1984. Meiotic roles of crossing-over and of gene conversion. Cold Spring Harbor Symp. Quant. Biol. 49:23-29. [9]

Case, T. J. and M. L. Taper. 1986. On the coexistence and coevolution of asexual and sexual competitors. Evolution 40:366-387. [1]

Cassuto, E. 1984. Formation of covently closed heteroduplex DNA by the combined action of gyrase and RecA protein. EMBO J. 3:2159-2164. [2]

Catcheside, D. G. 1977. *The Genetics of Recombination*. University Park Press, Baltimore, Maryland. [2, 6]

Catcheside, D. E. A. 1986. A restriction and modification model for the initiation and control of recombination in *Neurospora*. Genet. Res., Camb. 47:157-165. [3]

Cattanach, B. M. 1986. Parental origin effects in mice. J. Embryol. Exp. Morph. 97(Suppl.):137-150. [3]

Caugant, D., B. R. Levin and R. K. Selander. 1981. Genetic diversity and temporal variation in the *E. coli* populations of a human host. Genetics 98:467-490. [12]

Caugant, D. A., B. R. Levin, G. Lidin-Janson, T. S. Whittam, C. Svanborg Eden and R. K. Selander. 1983. Genetic diversity and relationships among strains of *E. coli* in the intestine and those causing urinary tract infections. Prog. Allergy 33:203-227. [12]

Cavalier-Smith, T. 1978. Nuclear volume control by nucleoskeletal DNA selection for cell volume and cell growth rate and the solution of the DNA c-value paradox. J. Cell Sci. 34:247-278. [9]

Cavalli-Sforza, L. and H. Heslot. 1949. Recombination in bacteria: Outcrossing *Escherichia coli* and K12. Nature 166:991-992. [12]

Cavalli-Sforza, L. and W. Bodmer. 1971. *The Genetics of Human Populations*. W. H. Freeman, San Francisco. [9]

Chambon, P. 1981. Split genes. Sci. Amer. 244(5):60-71. [9]

Chandler, V. and V. Walbot. 1986. DNA modification of a maize transposable element correlates with loss of activity. Proc. Natl. Acad. Sci. USA 83:1767-1771. [3]

Chao, L. and B. R. Levin. 1981. Stuctured habitats and the evolution of anticompetitor toxins in bacteria. Proc. Natl. Acad. Sci. USA 78:6324-6328. [12]

Charlesworth, B. 1976. Recombination modification in a fluctuating environment. Genetics 83:181-195. [4, 6, 7, 11]

Charlesworth, B. 1978. Model for the evolution of Y chromosomes and dosage compensation. Proc. Natl. Acad. Sci. USA 75:5618-5622. [5, 7, 8, 13]

Charlesworth, B. 1980. The cost of sex in relation to the mating scheme. J. Theor. Biol. 84:655-671. [1, 10, 14]

Charlesworth, B. 1980. The cost of meiosis with alternation of sexual and asexual generations. J. Theor. Biol. 87:517-528. [1]

Charlesworth, D. and B. Charlesworth. 1975. An experiment on recombination load in *Drosophila melanogaster*. Genet. Res., Camb. 25:267-274. [7]

Charlesworth, B. and D. Charlesworth. 1978. A model for the evolution of dioecy and gynodioecy. Amer. Natur. 112:975-997. [14, 16]

Charlesworth, B. and D. Charlesworth. 1981. Allocation of resources to male and female functions in hermaphrodites. Biol. Jour. Linn. Soc. 15:57-74. [14]

Charlesworth, B. and D. Charlesworth. 1985a. Genetic variation in recombination in *Drosophila*. I. Responses to selection and preliminary genetic analysis. Heredity 54:71-83. [6]

Charlesworth, B. and D. Charlesworth. 1985b. Genetic variation in recombination in *Drosophila*. II. Genetic analysis of a high recombination stock. Heredity 54:85-98. [6]

Charlesworth, B. and D. Hartl. 1978. Population dynamics of the segregation distorter polymorphism of *Drosophila melanogaster*. Genetics 89:171-192. [4]

Charlesworth, B. and C. H. Langley. 1986. The evolution of self-regulated transposition of transposable elements. Genetics 112:359-383. [9]

Charlesworth, B., I. Mori and D. Charlesworth. 1985. Genetic variation in recombination in *Drosophila*. III. Regional effects on crossing over and effects on nondisjunction. Heredity 55:209-221. [6]

Charlesworth, D. 1985. Distribution of dioecy and self-incompatibility in angiosperms. In *Evolution: Essays in Honor of John Maynard Smith*, P. J. Greenwood, P. H. Harvey and M. Slatkin (eds.). Cambridge University Press, Cambridge. [13]

Charlesworth, D. and B. Charlesworth. 1979. The evolution and breakdown of S-allele systems. Heredity 43:41-55. [13]

Charlesworth, D. and B. Charlesworth. 1979a. Selection on recombination in a multi-locus system. Genetics 91:575-580. [6]

Charlesworth, D. and B. Charlesworth. 1979b. Selection on recombination in clines. Genetics 91:581-589. [6]

Charlesworth, D., B. Charlesworth and C. Strobeck. 1979. Selection for recombination in partially self-fertilizing populations. Genetics 93:237-244. [6]

Charnov, E. L. 1979. Simultaneous hermaphroditism and sexual selection. Proc. Natl. Acad. Sci. USA 76:2480-2484. [13, 14]

Charnov, E. L. 1980. Sex allocation and local mate competition in barnacles. Mar. Biol. Letters 1:269-272. [14]

Charnov, E. L. 1982. *The Theory of Sex Allocation*. Princeton University Press, Princeton. [1, 14]

Charnov, E. L. and J. J. Bull. 1986. Sex allocation, pollinator attraction and fruit dispersal in cosexual plants. J. Theor. Biol. 118:321-325. [14]

Charnov, E. L., J. Maynard Smith and J. J. Bull. 1976. Why be an hermaphrodite? Nature 263:125-126. [14]

Chaudhury, A. M. and G. R. Smith. 1984. A new class of *Escherichia coli recBC* mutants: Implications for the role of RecBC enzyme in homologous recombination. Proc. Natl. Acad. Sci. USA 81:7850-7854. [2]

Chaudhury, A. M. and G. R. Smith. 1985. Role of *Escherichia coli* RecBC enzyme in SOS induction. Molec. Gen. Genet. 201:525-528. [2]

Cheng, K. C. and G. R. Smith. 1984. Recombinational hotspot activity of chi-like sequences. J. Mol. Biol. 180:371-377. [2]

Chepko-Sade, B. D. and W. M. Shields, with J. Berger, Z. T. Halpin, W. T. Jones, L. D. Mech, M. E. Nelson, L. L. Rogers, J. Rood and A. Smith. 1987. The effects of dispersal and social structure on effective population size. In *Mammalian Dispersal Patterns: The Effects of Social Structure on Population Genetics*, B. D. Chepko-Sade and Z. T. Halpin (eds.). University of Chicago Press. [15]

Chinnici, J. P. 1971a. Modification of recombination frequency in *Drosophila*. I. Selection for increased and decreased crossing over. Genetics 69:71-83. [6]

Chinnici, J. P. 1971b. Modification of recombination frequency in *Drosophila*. II. The polygenic control of crossing over. Genetics 69:85-96. [6]

Chomet, P. S., S. Wessler and S. L. Dellaporta. 1987. Inactivation of the maize transposable element activator (AC) is associated with its DNA modification. EMBO J. 6:295-302. [3]

Chovnick, A., G. H. Ballantyne, D. L. Baillie and D. G. Holm. 1970. Gene conversion in higher organisms: Half-tetrad analysis of recombination within the rosy cistron of *Drosophila melanogaster*. Genetics 66:315-329. [9]

Christensen, B. 1961. Studies on cyto-taxonomy and reproduction in the Enchytraeidae. Hereditas 47:387-450. [16]

Churchill, F. B. 1979. Sex and the single organism: Biological theories of sexuality in mid-nineteenth century. Stud. Hist. Biol. 3:139-177. [1]

Churchill, F. B. 1985. Weismann's continuity of the germ-plasm in historical perspective. Freiburger Universitaetsblaetter 87/88:107-124. [1]

Clark, A. J. 1973. Recombination deficient mutants of *E. coli* and other bacteria. Annu. Rev. Genet. 7:67-86. [2]

Clark, A. J. 1980. A view of the RecBC and RecF pathways of *E. coli* recombination. In *ICN-UCLA Symposium on RecF pathways of E. coli* recombination. In *ICN-UCLA Symposium on Molecular and Cellular Biology*, B. Alberts and C. F. Fox (eds.). Academic Press, New York. [2]

Clark, A. J. 1985. Conjugation and its aftereffects in *E. coli*. In *The Origin and Evolution of Sex*, H. O. Halvorson and A. Monroy (eds.). Alan R. Liss, New York. [10, 12]

Clark, A. J. and A. D. Margulies. 1965. Isolation and characterization of recombination deficient mutants of *E. coli* K12. Proc. Natl. Acad. Sci. USA 53:451-459. [2]

Clark, W. C. 1973. The ecological implications of parthenogenesis. Bull. Ent. Soc. New Zeal. 2:103-113. [1]

Clarke, A. G. 1971. The effects of maternal pre-immunization on pregnancy in the mouse. J. Reprod. Fert. 24:369-375. [13]

Clarke, B. 1976. The ecological genetics of host-parasite relationships. In *Genetic Aspects of Host-Parasite Relationships*, A. E. R. Taylor and R. Muller (eds.). Blackwell Scientific, Oxford. [1, 11]

Clegg, M. T., C. R. Horch and J. F. Kidwell. 1979. Dynamics of correlated genetic systems. VI. Variation in recombination rates in experimental populations of *Drosophila melanogaster*. J. Hered. 70:297-300. [6]

Clough, D. W., K. M. Kunkel and R. L. Davidson. 1982. 5-azacytidine induced reactivation of a *Herpes simplex* thymidine kinase gene. Science 216:70-73. [3]

Cockerham, C. C. and B. S. Weir. 1968. Sib mating with two linked loci. Genetics 60:629-640. [13]

Cohen, S. N. 1976. Transposable genetic elements and plasmid evolution. Nature 263:731-738. [12]

Cole, C. J. 1984. Unisexual lizards. Sci. Amer. 250:94-100. [9]

Cook, R. E. 1981. Plant parenthood. Nat. Hist. 90:30-35. [13]

Cooke, M. and E. Meynell. 1969. Chromosomal transfer mediated by de-repressed R factors in F⁻ *Escherichia coli* K12. Genet. Res., Camb. 14:79-87. [12]

Cooper, D. W., P. G. Johnston, G. B. Sherman and J. L. VandeBerg. 1977. The control of gene activity on eutherian and metatherian X chromosomes: A comparison. In *Reproduction and*

Evolution, J. H. Calaby and C. H. Tyndale-Biscoe (eds.). Austral. Acad. Sci., Canberra. [16]

Cosmides, L. M. and J. Tooby. 1981. Cytoplasmic inheritance and C intragenomic conflict. J. Theor. Biol. 89:83-129. [17]

Couzin, D. A. and D. P. Fox. 1974. Variation in chiasma frequency during tulip anther development. Chromosoma 46:173-179. [16]

Coyne, J. A. 1974. The evolutionary origin of hybrid inviability. Evolution 28:505-506. [13]

Craig, N. L. and J. W. Roberts. 1980. *E. coli* RecA protein-directed cleavage of phage lambda repressor requires polynucleotide. Nature 283:26-30. [2]

Craig, N. L. and J. W. Roberts. 1981. Function of nucleoside triphosphate and polynucleotide in *Escherichia coli recA* protein-directed cleavage of phage lambda repressor. J. Biol. Chem. 256:8039-8044. [2]

Craig-Holmes, A. P., F. B. Moore and M. W. Shaw. 1973. Polymorphism of human C-band heterochromatin. I. Frequency of variants. Amer. J. Hum. Genet. 25:181-182. [6]

Crick, F. 1979. Split genes and RNA splicing. Science 204:264-271. [10]

Crow, J. F. 1958. Some possibilities for measuring selection intensities in man. Hum. Biol. 30:1-13. [4]

Crow, J. F. 1970. Genetic loads and the cost of natural selection. Biomathematics 1:128-177. [4]

Crow, J. F. 1979. Genes that violate Mendel's rules. Sci. Amer. 240(2):134-146. [4, 16]

Crow, J. F. 1984. The P-factor: A transposable element in *Drosophila*. In *Mutation, Cancer and Malformation*, Chu and Generoso (eds.). Plenum, New York. [4]

Crow, J. F. and M. Kimura. 1965. Evolution in sexual and asexual populations. Amer. Natur. 99:439-450. [1, 4, 6, 10]

Crow, J. F. and M. Kimura. 1969. Evolution in sexual and asexual populations: A reply. Amer. Natur. 103:89-91. [1, 4, 10]

Crow, J. F. and M. Kimura. 1970. *An Introduction to Population Genetics Theory*. Harper & Row, New York. [15]

Crow, J. F. and M. Kimura. 1979. Efficiency of truncation selection. Proc. Natl. Acad. Sci. USA 76:396-399. [4]

Crow, J. F. and T. Nagylaki. 1976. The rate of change of a character correlated with fitness. Amer. Natur. 110:207-213. [13]

Crowe, L. K. 1971. The polygenic control of outbreeding in *Borago officinalis*. Heredity 27:111-118. [13]

Cruden, R. W. 1977. Pollen-ovule ratios: A conservative indicator of breeding systems in flowering plants. Evolution 31:32-46. [14]

Cruden, R. W. and D. L. Lyon. 1985. Patterns of biomass allocation to male and female functions in plants with different mating systems. Oecologia 66:299-306. [14]

Cuellar, O. 1971. J. Morphol. 133:139-165. [9]

Cuellar, O. 1977. Animal parthenogenesis. Science 197:837-843. [1]

Cuellar, O. 1979. On the ecology of coexistence in parthenogenetic and bisexual lizards of the genus *Cnemidophorus*. Amer. Zool. 19:733-786. [1]

Cullis, C. A. 1977. Molecular aspects of the environmental induction of heritable changes in flax. Heredity 38:129-154. [3]

D'Ari, R., J. George and O. Huisman. 1979. Suppression of *tif*-mediated induction of SOS functions in *Escherichia coli* by an altered *dna*B protein. J. Bacteriol. 140:381-387. [2]

Darlington, C. D. 1939. *The Evolution of Genetic Systems*. Cambridge University Press, Cambridge. [4]

Darwin, C. 1839. *Journal of Researches into the Geology and Natural History of the Various Countries Visited by the H. M. S. Beagle, Under the Command of Captain Fitzroy, R. N. from 1832 to 1836*. Henry Colburn, London. [1]

Darwin, C. 1859. *On the Origin of Species by Means of Natural Selection, or the Preservation of Favoured Races in the Struggle for Life*. John Murray, London. [1, 15]

Darwin, C. 1868. *The Variation of Animals and Plants Under Domestication*, 2 Volumes. John Murray, London. [1]

Darwin, C. 1876. *The Effects of Cross and Self Fertilization in the Vegetable Kingdom*. John Murray, London. [1]

Darwin, C. 1877. *The Different Forms of Flowers on Plants of the Same Species*. John Murray, London. [14]

Darwin, E. 1794. *Zoonomia; or, The Laws of Organic Life*, Vol. 1. J. Johnson, London. [1]

Dawkins, R. 1976. *The Selfish Gene.* Oxford University Press, Oxford. [1]

Dawkins, R. 1982. *The Extended Phenotype.* Oxford University Press, Oxford. [1, 4]

Dawson, P. S. and K. L. Berends. 1985. Linkage of the *reindeer* and *alate* prothorax loci and sex differences in recombination group IX of *Tribolium castaneum.* Can. J. Genet. Cytol. 27:276-278. [16]

Day, P. R. 1974. *The Genetics of Host-Parasite Interactions.* W. H. Freeman, San Francisco. [11]

de Boer, L. E. M. 1980. Do the chromosomes of the kiwi provide evidence for a monophyletic origin of the ratites? Nature 287:84-85. [16]

De Boer, P. and F. A. van der Hoeven. 1977. Son-sire regression based heritability estimates of chiasma frequency, using T70H mouse translocation heterozygotes and the relation between univalence, chiasma frequency and sperm production. Heredity 39:335-343. [6]

DeFlora, S., P. Zanacchi, A. Camoirano, C. Bennicelli and B. S. Badolati. 1984. Genotoxic activity and potency of 135 compounds in the Ames reversion test and in a bacterial DNA-repair test. Mutat. Res. 133:161-198. [9]

Detlefsen, J. A. and E. Roberts. 1921. Studies on crossing over. I. The effect of selection on crossover values. J. Exp. Zool. 32: 333-354. [6]

Devoret, R., M. Blanco, J. George and M. Radman. 1975. Recovery of phage lambda from ultraviolet damage. In *Molecular Mechanisms for Repair of DNA,* Part A, P. C. Hanawalt and R. B. Setlow (eds.). Plenum, New York. [2]

Devoret, R., M. Pierre and P. L. Moreau. 1983. Prophage O/80 is induced in *Escherichia coli* K12 *rec*A430. Molec. Gen. Genet. 189:199-206. [2]

Devoret, R. 1981. Inducible error-prone repair and induction of prophage lambda in *Escherichia coli.* Prog. Nucl. Acid. Res. 26:251-263. [2]

Dewees, A. A. 1975. Genetic modification of recombination rate in *Tribolium castaneum.* Genetics 81:537-552. [6]

Dobzhansky, Th., F. J. Ayala, G. L. Stebbins and J. W. Valentine. 1977. *Evolution.* W. H. Freeman, San Francisco. [15]

Doerfler, W. 1983. DNA methylation and gene activity. Annu. Rev. Biochem. 52:93-124. [3]

Doly, J., D. Le Roscouet and C. Anagnostopoulos. 1981. Substrate specificity and adenosine triphosphate activity of the ATP-dependent deoxyribonuclease of *Bacillus subtilis.* Eur. J. Biochem. 114:493-499. [2]

Doolittle, W. F. and C. Sapienza. 1980. Selfish genes, the phenotype paradigm and genome evolution. Nature 284:601-603. [4, 10]

Dougherty, E. C. 1955. Comparative evolution and the origin of sexuality. Syst. Zool. 4:145-169, 190. [1, 4, 10, 15]

Drake, J. W. 1974. The role of mutation in bacterial evolution. Symp. Soc. Gen. Microbiol. 24:41-58. [9]

Dressler, D. and H. Potter. 1982. Molecular mechanisms in genetic recombination. Annu. Rev. Biochem. 51:727-761. [9]

Drlica, K. 1984. Biology of bacterial deoxyribonucleic acid topoisomerases. Microbiol. Rev. 48:273-289 [2]

Dubnau, D. A. 1982. Genetic transformation in *Bacillus subtilis.* In *The Molecular Biology of the Bacilli,* D. A. Dubnau (ed.). Academic Press, New York. [12]

Dutreix, M., P. L. Moreau, A. Bailone, F. Galibert and R. Devoret. In preparation. New *rec*A mutations that discriminate repressors. [2]

East, E. M. 1918. The role of reproduction in evolution. Amer. Natur. 52:273-289. [4, 5, 10]

Eberhard, W. 1980. Evolutionary consequences of intracellular organelle competition. Quart. Rev. Biol. 55:231-49. [17]

Ebinuma, H. and N. Yoshitake. 1981. The genetic system controlling recombination in the silkworm. Genetics 99:231-245. [6]

Edmunds, G. F. and D. N. Alstad. 1978. Coevolution in insect herbivores and conifers. Science 199:941-945. [11]

Edmunds, G. F. and D. N. Alstad. 1981. Responses of black pine leaf scales to host plant variability. In *Insect Life History Patterns: Habitat and Geographic Variation,* R. F. Denno and H. Dingle (eds.). Springer-Verlag, New York. [11]

Egelman, E. H. and A. Stasiak. 1986. Structure of helical RecA-DNA complexes. Complexes formed in the presence of ATP-γ-S or ATP. J. Mol. Biol. 191:677-697. [2]

Ehrlich, P. R. and P. H. Raven. 1969. Differentiation of populations. Science 165:1128-1232. [13]

Eitner, G., A. S. Solonin and V. I. Tanyashin. 1981. Cloning of a recA-like gene of *Proteus mirabilis*. Gene 14:301-308. [2]

Eldredge, N. 1971. The allopatric model and phylogeny in Paleozoic invertebrates. Evolution 25:156-167. [1]

Eldredge, N. 1985. *Unfinished Synthesis: Biological Hierarchies and Modern Evolutionary Thought*. Oxford University Press, Oxford. [1]

Eldredge, N. and S. J. Gould. 1972. Punctuated equilibria: An alternative to phyletic gradualism. In *Models in Paleobiology*, T. J. M. Schopf (ed.). Freeman and Cooper, San Francisco. [1]

Ellstrand, N. C. and J. Antonovics. 1984. Experimental studies of the evolutionary significance of sexual reproduction. II. A test of the density-dependent hypothesis. Evolution 39:657-666. [1]

Emmerson, P. T. and P. Howard-Flanders. 1967. Cotransduction with thy of a gene required for genetic recombination in *E. coli*. J. Bacteriol. 93:1729-1731. [2]

Engels, W. R. 1983. The P family of transposable elements in *Drosophila*. Annu. Rev. Genet. 17:315-344. [4]

Eshel, I. 1985. Evolutionary genetic stability of Mendelian segregation and the role of free recombination in the chromosomal system. Amer. Natur. 125:412-420. [4]

Eshel, I. and E. Akin. 1983. Coevolutionary instability of mixed Nash solutions. J. Math. Biol. 18:123-133. [11]

Eshel, I. and M. W. Feldman. 1970. On the evolutionary effect of recombination. Theor. Pop. Biol. 1:88-100. [4, 6, 7, 10, 17]

Eshel, I. and W. D. Hamilton. 1984. Parent-offspring correlation in fitness under fluctuating selection. Proc. Roy. Soc. London B 222:1-14. [11]

Ettinger, L. 1986. Meiosis: A selection stage preserving the genome's pattern of organization. Evol. Theor. 8:17-26. [17]

Evans, R. 1986. Niche expansion in bacteria: Can infectious gene exchange affect the rate of evolution? Genetics 113:775-795. [12]

Fairweather, D. S., M. Fox and P. Margison. 1987. The in vitro life span of MRC-5 cells is shortened by 5 azacytidine-induced demethylation. Exp. Cell Res. 168:153-159. [3]

Falconer, D. S. 1966. Genetic consequences of selection pressure. In *Genetic and Environmental Factors in Human Ability*, J. S. Meade and A. S. Parkes (eds.). Oliver and Boyd, Edinburgh. [13]

Falkow, S. 1975. *Infectious Multiple Drug Resistance*. Pion, London. [12]

Farley, J. 1982. *Gametes and Spores: Ideas About Sexual Reproduction*. Johns Hopkins University Press, Baltimore. [1]

Faulds, D., N. Dower, M. Stahl and F. Stahl. 1979. Orientation-dependent recombination hotspot activity in phage lambda. J. Mol. Biol. 131:681-695. [2]

Faulk, W. P., A. Temple, R. E. Lovins and N. Smith. 1978. Antigens of human trophoblasts: A working hypothesis for their role in normal and abnormal pregnancies. Proc. Natl. Acad. Sci. USA 75:1947-1951. [13]

Feinstein, S. I. and K. B. Low. 1986. Hyper-recombining recipient strains in bacterial conjugation. Genetics 113:13-33. [9]

Feldman, M. 1972. Selection for linkage modification. I. Random mating populations. Theor. Pop. Biol. 3:324-346. [5, 11]

Feldman, M. W. and B. Balkau. 1972. Some results in the theory of three gene loci. In *Population Dynamics*, T.N.E. Greville (ed.). Academic Press, New York. [6]

Feldman, M. W., F. B. Christiansen and L. D. Brooks. 1980. Evolution of recombination in a constant environment. Proc. Natl. Acad. Sci. USA 77:4838-4841. [6, 7]

Feldman, M. W. and U. Libermann. 1986. An evolutionary reduction principle for genetic modifiers. Proc. Natl. Acad. Sci. USA 83:4824-4827. [5, 11]

Felsenstein, J. 1965. The effect of linkage on directional selection. Genetics 52:349-363. [5, 6]

Felsenstein, J. 1974. The evolutionary advantage of recombination. Genetics 78:737-756. [1, 4, 5, 6, 8, 10, 15]

Felsenstein, J. 1985. Recombination and sex: Is Maynard Smith necessary? In *Evolution: Essays in Honour of John Maynard Smith*, P. J. Greenwood, P. H. Harvey and M. Slatkin (eds.). Cambridge University Press, Cambridge. [1, 5, 7, 11]

Felsenstein, J. and S. Yokoyama. 1976. The evolutionary advantage of recombination. II. Individual selection for recombination. Genetics 83:845-859. [1, 4, 5, 7, 15]

Festing, M. 1973. A multivariate analysis of subline divergence in the shape of the mandible in C57BL/Gr mice. Genet. Res., Camb. 21:121-132. [3]

Finch, P. W., P. Chambers and P. T. Emmerson. 1985. Identification of the Escherichia coli recN gene products as a major SOS protein. J. Bacteriol. 164:653-658. [2]

Finch, P. W., C. Brough and P. T. Emmerson. 1986a. Molecular cloning of a recA-like gene of Methylophilus methylotrophus and identification of its product. Gene 44:47-53. [2]

Finch, P. W., R. E. Wilson, K. Brown, I. D. Hickson, A. E. Tomkinson and P. T. Emmerson. 1986b. Complete nucleotide sequence of the Escherichia coli recC gene of the thyA-recC intergenic region. Nuc. A. Res. 14:4437-4451. [2]

Finch, P. W., A. Storey, K. E. Chapman, K. Brown, I. D. Hickson and P. T. Emmerson. 1986c. Complete nucleotide sequence of the Escherichia coli recB gene. Nuc. A. Res. 14:8573-8582. [2]

Finch, P. W., A. Storey, K. Brown, I. D. Hickson and P. T. Emmerson. 1986d. Complete nucleotide sequence of recD, the structural gene for the subunit α of Exonuclease V of Escherichia coli. Nuc. A. Res. 14:8583-8594. [2]

Finney, D. J. 1952. The equilibrium of a self-incompatible polymorphic species. Genetica 26:33-64. [13]

Fisher, R. A. 1930. The Genetical Theory of Natural Selection. Clarendon Press, Oxford. [1, 4, 5, 6, 10, 14, 15]

Fisher, R. A. 1935. The sheltering of lethals. Amer. Natur. 69:446-445. [13]

Fisher, R. A. 1941. Average excess and average effect of a gene substitution. Ann. Eugen. 11:53-63. [13]

Fisher, R. A. 1958. The Genetical Theory of Natural Selection, 2nd Ed. Dover, New York. [12]

Fisher, R. A. 1960. The Design of Experiments, 7th Ed. Hafner, New York. [4]

Fisher, R. A. 1965. The Theory of Inbreeding, 2nd Ed. Academic Press, New York. [13]

Fitch, W. M. and W. R. Atchley. 1985. Evolution in inbred strains of mice appears rapid. Science 228:1169-1176. [3]

Flateau, E., F. A. Gonzales, L. A. Michelowski and P. A. Jones. 1984. DNA methylation in 5 aza-2'-deoxycytidine resistant variants of C3H 10T 1/2 C18 cells. Mol. Cell. Biol. 4:2098-2012. [3]

Flor, H. H. 1956. The complementary genic systems in flax and flax rust. Adv. Genet. 8:29-54. [8, 11]

Forejt, J. 1973. Centromeric heterochromatin polymorphism in the house mouse. Chromosoma 43:187-201. [6]

Formosa, T. and B. M. Alberts. 1986. DNA synthesis dependent on genetic recombination: Characterization of a reaction catalyzed by purified bacteriophage T4 proteins. Cell 47:793-806. [2]

Franklin, I. and R. C. Lewontin. 1970. Is the gene the unit of selection? Genetics 65:707-734. [6, 11]

Futcher, A. B. and B. S. Cox. 1983. Maintenance of the 2 fm circle plasmid in populations of Saccharomyces cerevisia. J. Bacteriol. 154:612-622. [9]

Gale, M. D. and H. Rees. 1970. Genes controlling chiasma frequency in Hordeum. Heredity 25:393-410. [6]

Gasson, J. C., R. Ryder and S. Bourgeous. 1983. Role of de novo DNA methylation in the glucocorticoid resistence of a T lymphoid cell line. Nature 302:621-623. [3]

Geddes, P. and J. A. Thompson. 1901. The Evolution of Sex, 2nd Ed. Scott, New York. [1]

Geddes, P. and J. A. Thompson. 1914. Sex. Henry Holt, New York. [15]

Gellert, M., J. W. Little, C. K. Oshinsky and S. B. Zimmerman. 1968. Joining of DNA strands by DNA ligase of E. coli. Cold Spring Harbor Symp. Quant. Biol. 21-26. [2]

Gellert, M., K. Mizuuchi, M. H. O'Dea and H. A. Nash. 1976. DNA gyrase: An enzyme that introduces superhelical turns into DNA. Proc. Natl. Acad. Sci. USA 73:3872-3876. [2]

Gellert, M. 1981. DNA topoisomerases. Annu. Rev. Biochem. 50:879. [2]

Gensler, H. L. and H. Bernstein. 1981. DNA damage as the primary cause of ageing. Quart. Rev. Biol. 56:279-303. [1]

Gerritson, J. 1980. Sex and parthenogenesis in sparse populations. Amer. Natur. 115:718-742. [1]

Ghiselin, M. T. 1969a. *The Triumph of the Darwinian Method*. University of California Press, Berkeley. [1]

Ghiselin, M. T. 1969b. The evolution of hermaphroditism amoung animals. Quart. Rev. Biol. 44:189-208. [1]

Ghiselin, M. T. 1974. *The Economy of Nature and the Evolution of Sex*. University of California Press, Berkeley. [1, 5, 6, 8, 10, 11, 14, 15]

Ghiselin, M. T. 1974. A radical solution to the species problem. Syst. Zool. 23:536-554. [1]

Ghiselin, M. T. 1981. Categories, life and thinking. Behav. Brain Sci. 4:269-313 (with commentary). [1]

Ghiselin, M. T. In press. The economy of the intellect. [1]

Ghiselin, M. T. In press. Bioeconomics and the metaphysics of selection. J. Soc. Biol. Struct. [1]

Ghiselin, M. T. In press. Evolutionary aspects of marine invertebrate reproduction. In *Reproduction of Marine Invertebrates*, A. C. Giese and J. S. Pearse, (eds.). [1]

Ghosh, R. K., K. A. I. Siddiqui, G. Mukhopadhyay and A. Ghosh. 1985. Evidence that a system similar to the *recA* system of *Escherichia coli* exists in *Vibrio cholerae*. Molec. Gen. Genet. 200:439-441. [2]

Gill, T. J. 1983. Immunogenetics of spontaneous abortions in humans. Transplantation 35:1-6. [13]

Gillen, J. R. and A. J. Clark. 1974. The RecE pathway of bacterial recombination. In *Mechanisms in Recombination*, R. F. Grell (ed.). Plenum, New York. [2]

Gillen, J. R., D. K. Willis and A. J. Clark. 1981. Genetic analysis of the RecE pathway of genetic recombination in *Escherichia coli* K12. J. Bacteriol. 145:521-532. [2]

Gillespie, J. H. 1975. Natural selection for resistance to epidemics. Ecology 56:493-495. [11]

Gilpin, M. E. 1975. Limit cycles in competition communities. Amer. Natur. 109:51-60. [11]

Ginsburg, L. R., P. M. Bingham and S. Yoo. 1984. On the theory of speciation induced by transposable elements. Genetics 107:331-341. [9]

Glassberg, J., R. R. Meyer and A. Kornberg. 1979. Mutant single-strand binding protein of *Escherichia coli*: Genetic and physiological characterization. J. Bacteriol. 140:14-19. [2]

Glesener, R. R. 1979. Recombination in a simulated predator-prey interaction. Amer. Zool. 19:763-771. [1, 5]

Glesener, R. R. and D. Tilman. 1978. Sexuality and the components of environmental uncertainty: Clues from geographic parthenogenesis in terrestrial animals. Amer. Natur. 112:659-673. [1, 11]

Goldberg, I. and J. J. Mekalanos. 1986. Cloning of the V. *cholerae recA* gene and construction of V. *cholerae* mutant. J. Bacteriol. 165:715-722. [2]

Good, A. and D. A. Hickey. 1986. The spread of transposable P elements in mixed P-M populations of *Drosophila melanogaster*. Genetics 113:72. [9]

Gottesman, M. M., M. L. Hicks and M. Gellert. 1973. Genetics and functions of DNA ligase in *Escherichia coli*. J. Mol. Biol. 77:531-547. [2]

Gould, S. J. and R. C. Lewontin. 1979. The spandrels of San Marco and the Panglossian paradigm: A critique of the adaptationist program. Proc. Roy. Soc. London B 205:581-98. [17]

Graham, J. B. and C. A. Istock. 1979. Gene exchange and natural selection cause *Bacillus subtilis* to evolve in soil culture. Science 204:637-639. [12]

Grant, V. 1958. The regulation of recombination in plants. Cold Spring Harbor Symp. Quant. Biol. 23:337-363. [15]

Grant, V. 1971. *Plant Speciation*. Columbia University Press, New York. [15]

Green, M. M. 1959. Effects of different wild-type isoalleles on crossing-over in *Drosophila melanogaster*. Nature 184:294. [6]

Green, M. R. 1986. Pre-mRNA splicing. Annu. Rev. Genet. 20:671. [2]

Greenwood, J., P. H. Harvey and M. Slatkin. 1985. *Evolution: Essays in Honor of John Maynard Smith*. Cambridge University Press, Cambridge. [5]

Griffith, M. H. 1928. Significance of pneumococcal types. J. Hyg., Camb. 27:113-159. [12]

Gruneberg, H. 1970. Is there a viral component in the genetic background? Nature 225:39-41. [3]

Gross, K. L. and J. D. Soule. 1981. Differences in biomass allocation to reproductive and vegetative structures of male and female plants of a dioecious perennial herb, *Silene alba* (Miller) Krause. Amer. J. Bot. 68:801-807. [14]

Gudas, L. J. and A. B. Pardee. 1976. DNA synthesis inhibition and the induction of protein X in *Escherichia coli*. J. Mol. Biol. 101:459-477. [2]

Gustafsson, A. 1946-1947. Apomixis in higher plants, I-III. Lunds Univ. Arsskrift 42:1-67, 43:69-179, 181-371. [14]

Haeckel, E. 1866. *Generelle Morphologie der Organismen*, 2 Vols. Reimer, Berlin. [1]

Haigh, J. 1978. The accumulation of deleterious genes in a population: Muller's ratchet. Theor. Pop. Biol. 14:251-267. [4, 5, 8]

Haldane, J. B. S. 1922. Sex ratio and unisexual sterility in hybrid animals. J. Genet. 12:101-109. [16]

Haldane, J. B. S. 1937. The effect of variation on fitness. Amer. Natur. 71:337-349. [4]

Haldane, J. B. S. 1942. Selection against heterozygosis in man. Ann. Eugen. 11:333-340. [13]

Haldane, J. B. S. 1949. Disease and evolution. La Ricerca Scientifica (Suppl.) 19:68-76. [11]

Halvorson, H. O. 1985. Beginnings of sexuality in prokaryotes. In *The Origins and Evolution of Sex*, H. O. Halvorson and A. Monroy (eds.). Alan R. Liss, New York. [10, 12]

Hamilton, M. S. and I. Hellstrom. 1978. Selection for histoincompatible progeny in mice. Biol. Reprod. 19:267-270. [13]

Hamilton, W. D. 1964. The genetical evolution of social behavior. J. Theor. Biol. 7:1-15, 17-52. [1]

Hamilton, W. D. 1966. The moulding of senescence by natural selection. J. Theor. Biol. 12:12-45. [1, 13]

Hamilton, W. D. 1967. Extraordinary sex ratios. Science 156:477-488. [14, 16]

Hamilton, W. D. 1980. Sex versus non-sex versus parasite. Oikos 35:282-290. [1, 4, 5, 6, 8, 11]

Hamilton, W. D. 1982. Pathogens as causes of genetic diversity in their host populations. In *Population Biology of Infectious Diseases*, R. M. Anderson and R. M. May (eds.). Springer-Verlag, New York. [1, 11]

Hamilton, W. D. 1986. Instability and cycling of two competing hosts with two parasites. In *Evolutionary Processes and Theory*, S. Karlin and E. Nevo (eds.). Academic Press, Orlando, Florida. [11]

Hamilton, W. D. 1987. Kinship, recognition, disease and intelligence: Constraints of social evolution. In *Biological Aspects of Optimal Strategy and Social Structure*, T. Ito (ed.). Japan Scientific Series Press, Tokyo. [11]

Hamilton, W. D., P. A. Henderson and N. A. Moran. 1981. Fluctuation of environment and coevolved antagonist polymorphisms as factors in the maintenance of sex. In *Natural Selection and Social Behavior*, R. D. Alexander and D. W. Tinkle (eds.). Chiron Press, New York. [11, 16]

Hamilton, W. D. and R. M. May. 1977. Dispersal in stable habitats. Nature 269:578-581. [1]

Hamilton, W. D. and M. Zuk. 1982. Heritable true fitness and bright birds: A role for parasites? Science 218:384-387. [11, 16]

Hamood, A. N., G. S. Pettis, C. D. Parker and M. A. McIntosh. 1986. Isolation and characterization of the *Vibrio cholerae recA* gene. J. Bacteriol. 167:375-378. [2]

Hanawalt, P. C., P. K. Cooper, A. K. Ganeson and C. A. Smith. 1979. DNA repair in bacteria and mammalian cells. Annu. Rev. Biochem. 48:783-836. [9]

Hannah-Alvah, A. 1965. The premeiotic stages of spermatogeneisis. Adv. Genet. 13:157-226. [7]

Harper, A. B. 1982. The selective significance of partial apomixis. Heredity 48:107-116. [5]

Harper, J. L., B. R. Rosen and J. White. 1986. The growth and form of modular organisms. Phil. Trans. Roy. Soc. London B. 313:250. [17]

Harrington, R. W., Jr. 1975. Sex determination and differentiation among uniparental homozygotes of the hermaphroditic fish *Rivulus marmoratus* (Cyprinodontidae: Atheriniformes). In *Intersexuality in the Animal Kingdom*, R. Reinboth (ed.). Springer-Verlag, New York. [17]

Hayes, W. 1953. Observations on a transmissible element determining sexual differentiation in *Bacterium coli*. J. Gen. Microbiol. 8:72-88. [9]

Hays, J. B. and S. Boehmer. 1978. Antagonists of DNA gyrase inhibit repair and recombination of UV-irradiated phage lambda. Proc. Natl. Acad. Sci. USA 75:4125-4129. [2]

Heath, D. J. 1977. Simultaneous hermaphroditism: Cost and benefit. J. Theor. Biol. 64:363-373. [14]

Hedrick, P. W., G. Thomson and W. Klitz. 1986. Evolutionary genetics: HLA as an exemplary system. In *Evolutionary Processes and Theory*, S. Karlin and E. Nevo (eds.). Academic Press, Orlando, Florida. [11]

Heller, R. and J. Maynard Smith. 1978. Does Muller's ratchet work with selfing? Genet. Res., Camb. 32:289-293. [5, 7, 8, 15]

Herriot, R. M., E. M. Meyer and M. Vogt. 1970. Redefined nongrowth medium for stage II development of competence in *Haemophilus influenzae*. J. Bacteriol. 101:517-524. [12]

Heslop-Harrison, J. 1972. Sexuality of angiosperms. In *Plant Physiology: A Treatise*, Vol. 6C, F. C. Steward (ed.). Academic Press, New York. [14]

Hickey, D. A. 1982. Selfish DNA: A sexually-transmitted nuclear parasite. Genetics 101:519-531. [1, 4, 10]

Hickey, D. A. 1984. DNA can be a selfish parasite. Nature 311:417-418. [9]

Hickey, D. A. and B. F. Benkel. 1985. Splicing and the evolution of introns. Nature 316:582. [9]

Hickey, D. A. and B. F. Benkel. 1986. Introns as relict retro-transposons: Implications for the evolutionary origin of eukaryotic mRNA splicing mechanisms. J. Theor. Biol. 121:283-291. [9]

Hickey, D. A., A. Loverre and G. C. Carmody. 1986. Is the segregation distortion phenomenon in Drosophila due to active recurrent genetic transposition? Genetics 114:665-668. [9]

Hill, W. G. and A. Robertson. 1966. The effect of linkage on limits to artificial selection. Genet. Res., Camb. 8:269-294. [4, 5, 6]

Hill, W. G. and A. Robertson. 1968. Linkage disequilibrium in finite populations. Theor. Appl. Genet. 38:226-231. [4]

Hiraizumi, Y., L. Sandler and J. F. Crow. 1960. Meiotic drive in natural populations of Drosophila melanogaster. III. Population implications of the segregation distorter locus. Evolution 14:433-444. [9]

Holden, L. R. 1979. New properties of the two-locus partial selfing model with selection. Genetics 93:217-236. [6]

Holliday, R. 1964. A mechanism for gene conversion in fungi. Genet. Res., Camb. 5:282-304. [2, 3]

Holliday, R. 1968. Genetic recombination in fungi. In Replication and Recombination of Genetic Material, W. J. Peacock and R. D. Brock (eds.). Austral. Acad. Sci., Canberra. [3]

Holliday, R. 1979. A new theory of carcinogenisis. Brit. J. Cancer. 40:513-522. [3]

Holliday, R. 1984. The biological significance of meiosis. In Controlling Events in Meiosis, C. E. Evans and H. G. Dickenson (eds.). S. E. B. Symposia 38, Cambridge University Press, Cambridge. [3, 7]

Holliday, R. 1985. The significance of DNA methylation in cellular ageing. In Molecular Biology of Ageing, A. D. Woodhead, A. D. Blackett and A. Hollaender (eds.). Plenum, New York. [3]

Holliday, R. 1986a. Gene conversion. In Evolutionary Perspectives and the New Genetics, H. Gershovitz, D. L. Rucknagel and R. E. Tashian (eds.). Alan R. Liss, New York. [3]

Holliday, R. 1986b. Strong effects of 5-azacytidine on the in vitro lifespan of human diploid fibrolasts. Exp. Cell Res. 166:543-552. [3]

Holliday, R., R. E. M. Halliwell and V. Rowell. 1976. Genetic characterization of rec1, a mutant of Ustilago maydis defective in repair and recombination. Genet. Res., Camb. 27:413-453. [2]

Holliday, R. and P. A. Jeggo. 1985. Mechanisms for changing gene expression and their possible relationship to carcinogenesis. Cancer Surveys 4:557-581. [3]

Holliday, R. and J. E. Pugh. 1975. DNA modification mechanisms and gene activity during development. Science 187:226-232. [3]

Holloman, W. K., R. Wiegand, C. Hoessli and C. M. Radding. 1975. Uptake of homologous single-stranded fragments by superhelical DNA: A possible mechanism for initiation of genetic recombination. Proc. Natl. Acad. Sci. USA 72:2394-2398. [2]

Hollstein, M. and J. McCann. 1979. Short-term tests for carcinogens and mutagens. Mutat. Res. 65:133-226. [9]

Holmes, J. C. 1983. Evolutionary relationships between parasitic helminths and their hosts. In Coevolution, D. J. Futuyma and M. Slatkin (eds.). Sinauer Associates, Sunderland, Massachusetts. [11]

Holsinger, K. E. and M. W. Feldman. 1981. A single locus model of selection in permanent translocation heterozygotes. Theor. Pop. Biol. 20:218-240. [13]

Holsinger, K. E. and M. W. Feldman. 1983. Linkage modification with mixed random mating and selfing: A numerical study. Genetics 103:323-333. [6]

Honigberg, S. M., B. J. Rao and C. M. Radding. 1986. Ability of RecA protein to promote a search for rare sequences in duplex DNA. Proc. Natl. Acad. Sci. USA 83:9586-9590. [2]

Hopf, R., R. E. Michod and M. Sanderson. In press. On the effect of reproductive system on mutation load and the number of deleterious mutations. Theor. Pop. Biol. [9]

Horii, Z. I. and A. J. Clark. 1973. Genetic analysis of the recF pathway to genetic recombination in Escherichia coli: Isolation and characterization of mutants. J. Mol. Biol. 80:327-344. [2]

Horii, T., T. Ogawa and H. Ogawa. 1980. Organization of the recA gene of E. coli. Proc. Natl. Acad. Sci. USA 77:313-317. [2]

Howard-Flanders, P., S. C. West, J. R. Rusche and E. H. Egelman. 1984a. Molecular mechanisms of general genetic recombination: The DNA binding sites of RecA protein. Cold Spring Harbor Symp. Quant. Biol. 571-580. [2]

Howard-Flanders, P., S. C. West and A. Stasiak. 1984b. Role of RecA protein spiral filaments in genetic recombination. Nature 309:215-220. [2]

Howard-Flanders, P., S. C. West, J. R. Rusche and E. H. Egelman. 1984b. Molecular mechanisms of general genetic recombination: The DNA binding sites of RecA protein. Cold Spring Harbor Symp. Quant. Biol., Cold Spring Harbor Laboratory, New York. [2]

Hsieh, P., S. Meyn and D. Camerini-Otero. 1986. Partial purification and characterization of a recombinase from human cells. Cell 44:885-894. [2]

Hull, P. 1969. Maternal-foetal incompatibility associated with the H-3 locus in the mouse. Heredity 24:203-209. [13]

Hutson, V. and R. Law. 1981. Evolution of recombination in populations experiencing frequency-dependent selection with time delay. Proc. Roy. Soc. London B 213:345-359. [1, 11]

Huxley, T. H. 1854. Upon animal individuality. Proc. Roy. Inst. 1:184-189. [1]

Irino, N., K. Nakayama and H. Nakayama. 1986. The recQ gene of Escherichia coli K12: Primary structure and evidence for SOS regulation. Molec. Gen. Genet. 205:298-304. [2]

Jackson, J. B. C. 1985. Distribution and ecology of clonal and aclonal benthic invertebrates. In Population Biology and Evolution of Clonal Organisms, J. B. C. Jackson, L. W. Buss and R. E. Cook (eds.). Yale University Press, New Haven. [15]

Jacob, F. and E. L. Wollman. 1961. Sexuality and Genetics of Bacteria. Academic Press, New York [12]

Jaenike, J. 1978. An hypothesis to account for the maintenance of sex within populations. Evol. Theor. 3:191-194. [1, 6, 7, 8, 11]

Jaenike, J. and R. K. Selander. 1979. Evolution and ecology of parthenogenesis in earthworms. Amer. Zool. 19:729-737. [1]

Jagiello, G., M. Ducayen, J. S. Fang and J. Graffeo. 1976. Cytological observations in mammalian oocytes. Chrom. Today 5:43-64. [9]

Jain, S. K. and A. D. Bradshaw. 1966. Evolutionary divergence amoung adjacent plant populations. I. The evidence and its theoretical analysis. Heredity 21:407-441. [13]

James, D. A. 1965. Effects of antigenic dissimilarity between mother and foetus on placental size in mice. Nature 205:613-614. [13]

James, D. A. 1967. Some effects of immunological factors on gestation in mice. J. Reprod. Fert. 14:265-275. [13]

Janzen, Daniel H. 1977. What are dandelions and aphids? Amer. Natur. 111:586-9. [17]

Jayakar, S. D. 1970. A mathematical model for interaction of gene frequencies in a parasite and its host. Theor. Pop. Biol. 1:140-164. [11]

Jeggo, P. A. and R. Holliday. 1986. Azacytidine reactivation of a DNA repair gene in Chinese hamster ovary cells. Mol. Cell. Biol. 6:2944-2949. [3]

John, B. 1973. The cytogenetic systems of grasshoppers and locusts. II. The origin and evolution of supernumerary segments. Chromosoma 44:123-146. [6]

Johnston, S. A., T. P. M. den Nijs, S. J. Peloquin and R. E. Hanneman, Jr. 1980. The significance of genic balance to endosperm development in interspecific crosses. Theor. Appl. Genet. 57:5-9. [13]

Jones, A. P. 1985. Altering gene expression with 5-azacytidine. Cell 40:485-486. [3]

Jones, G. H. 1967. The control of chiasma distribution in rye. Chromosoma 22:69-90. [6]

Jones, K. W. and L. Singh. 1985. Snakes and the evolution of sex chromosomes. Trends in Genet. 55-61. [16]

Jones, P. A. 1986. DNA methylation and cancer. Cancer Res. 46:461-466. [3]

Kanda, N. 1982. Spontaneous sister chromatid exchange in vivo. In Sister Chromatid Exchange, A. A. Sandberg (ed.). Alan R. Liss, New York. [9]

Karlin, S. 1973. Sex and infinity: A mathematical analysis of the advantages and disadvantages of genetic recombination. In The Mathematical Theory of the Dynamics of Biological Populations, M. Bartlett and R. Hiorns (eds.). Academic Press, New York. [6]

Karlin, S. 1975. General two-locus selection models: Some objectives, results and interpretations. Theor. Pop. Biol. 7:364-398. [6]

Karlin, S. and D. Carmelli. 1975. Numerical studies on two-loci selection models with general viabilities. Theor. Pop. Biol. 7:399-421. [6]

Keener, S. L., K. P. McNamee and K. McEntee. 1984. Cloning and characterization of recA genes from *Proteus vulgaris*, *Erwinia caratovora*, *Shigella flexneri* and *E. coli* B/r. J. Bacteriol. 160:153-160. [2]

Kidwell, M. G. 1972a. Genetic change of recombination value in *Drosophila melanogaster*. I. Artificial selection for high and low recombination and some properties of recombination-modifying genes. Genetics 70:419-432. [6]

Kidwell, M. G. 1972b. Genetic change of recombination value in *Drosophila melanogaster*. II. Simulated natural selection. Genetics 70:433-443. [6]

Kidwell, M. G. 1983. Evolution of hybrid dysgenesis determinants in *Drosophila melanogaster*. Proc. Natl. Acad. Sci. USA 80:1655-1659. [9]

Kidwell, M. G., J. F. Kidwell and J. A. Sved. 1977. Hybrid disgenesis in *Drosophila melanogaster*: A syndrome of aberrant traits including mutation, sterility and male recombination. Genetics 86:813-833. [4]

Kimura, M. 1956. A model of a genetic system which leads to closer linkage by natural selection. Evolution 10:278-287. [4, 6]

Kimura, M. 1959. Conflict between self-fertilization and outbreeding in plants. Annu. Report Nat. Inst. Genet., Japan 9:87-88. [13]

Kimura, M. 1962. On the probability of fixation of mutant genes in a population. Genetics 47:713-719. [5]

Kimura, M. 1983. *The Neutral Theory of Molecular Evolution*. Cambridge University Press, Cambridge. [4]

Kimura, M. and J. F. Crow. 1978. Effect of overall phenotypic selection on genetic change at individual loci. Proc. Natl. Acad. Sci. USA 75:6168-6171. [4]

Kimura, M. and T. Maruyama. 1966. The mutation load with epistatic gene interactions in fitness. Genetics 54:1337-1351. [4]

King, C. E. 1972. Adaptation of rotifers to seasonal variation. Ecology 53:408-418. [1]

King, J. L. 1966. The gene interaction component of the genetic load. Genetics 53:403-413. [4]

Kirkpatrick, M. 1985. Sex and cycling parasites: A simulation study of Hamilton's hypothesis. J. Theor. Biol. 119:263-271. [11]

Kirkpatrick, M. 1986. The handicap mechanism of sexual selection does not work. Amer. Natur. 127:222-40. [17]

Kirkwood, T. B. L. 1977. Evolution of ageing. Nature 270:301-304. [3]

Kirkwood, T. B. L. 1981. Repair and its evolution: Survival versus reproduction. In *Physiological Ecology: An Evolutionary Approach to Resource Use*, C. R. Townsend and P. Calow (eds.). Sinauer Associates, Sunderland, Massachusetts. [3]

Kirkwood, T. B. L. and T. Cremer. 1982. Cytogerontology since 1881: A reappraisal of August Weismann and a review of modern progress. Hum. Genet. 60:101-121. [3]

Kirkwood, T. B. L. and R. Holliday. 1979. The evolution of ageing and longevity. Proc. Roy. Soc. London B 205:531-546. [1, 3]

Kirkwood, T. B. L. and R. Holliday. 1986. Ageing as a consequence of natural selection. In *The Biology of Human Ageing*, A. H. Bittles and K. J. Collins (eds.). Cambridge University Press, Cambridge. [3]

Kiyasu, P. K. and M. G. Kidwell. 1984. Hybrid dysgenesis in *Drosophila melanogaster*: The evolution of mixed P and M populations maintained at high temperature. Genet. Res., Camb. 44:251-259. [9]

Klar, A. J. S., J. N. Strathern, J. R. Broach and J. B. Hicks. 1981. Regulation of transcription in expressed and unexpressed mating type cassettes of yeast. Nature 289:239-244. [9]

Kmiec, E. and W. Holloman. 1982. Homologous pairing of DNA molecules promoted by a protein from *Ustilago*. Cell 29:367-374. [2]

Kmiec, E. and W. Holloman. 1983. Heteroduplex formation and polarity during strand transfer promoted by *Ustilago rec*1 protein. Cell 33:857-864. [2]

Kmiec, E. and W. Holloman. 1984. Synapsis promoted by *Ustilago rec*1 protein. Cell 36:593-598. [2]

Kobayashi, I., M. M. Stahl, F. R. Fairfield and F. W. Stahl. 1984. Coupling with packaging explains apparent nonreciprocality of chi-stimulated recombination of bacteriophage lambda by RecA and RecBC functions. Genetics 108:773-794. [2]

Kobori, J. A., E. Strauss, K. Minard and L. Hood. 1986. Molecular analysis of the hotspot of recombination in the murine major histocompatability complex. Science 234:173-179. [3]

Kokjohn, T. A. and R. V. Miller. 1985. Molecular cloning and characterization of the recA gene of *Pseudomonas aeruginosa* PAO. J. Bacteriol. 163:568-572. [2]

Kolmos, L., R. Zamir, H. Joshua and I. Halbrecht. 1977. Common HLA antigens in couples with repeated abortions. Clin. Immunol. Immunopathol. 7:330-335. [13]

Kolodner, R., R. A. Fishel and M. Howard. 1985. Genetic recombination of bacterial plasmid DNA: Effect of recE mutations on plasmid recombination in *Escherichia coli*. J. Bacteriol. 163:1060-1066. [2]

Koltin, Y., J. R. Raper and G. Simchen. 1967. The genetic structure of the incompatibility factors of *Schizophyllum commune*: The B. factor. Proc. Natl. Acad. Sci. USA 57:55-62. [6]

Kondrashov, A. S. 1982. Selection against harmful mutations in large sexual and asexual populations. Genet. Res., Camb. 40:325-332. [4, 7, 15]

Kondrashov, A. S. 1984a. Deleterious mutations as an evolutionary factor. I. The advantage of recombination. Genet. Res., Camb. 44:199-217. [4, 12, 15]

Kondrashov, A. S. 1984b. A possible explanation of cyclical parthenogenesis. Heredity 52:307-308. [15]

Konrad, B. E. 1977. Method for the isolation of *Escherichia coli* mutants with enhanced recombination between chromosomal duplications. J. Bacteriol. 130:167-172. [2, 9]

Konrad, B. E. and I. R. Lehman. 1975. Novel mutants of *E. coli* that accumulate very small DNA replicative intermediates. Proc. Natl. Acad. Sci. USA 72:2150-2154. [2]

Kornberg, A. 1980. *DNA Replication*. W. H. Freeman, San Francisco. [2]

Kowalczykowski, S. C. 1987. Mechanistic aspects of the DNA strand exchange activity of *Escherichia coli* RecA protein. Trends in Biochem. Sci. 12:141-145. [2]

Kress, W. J. 1981. Sibling competition and evolution of pollen unit, ovule number and pollen vector in angiosperms. Syst. Bot. 6:101-112. [13]

Krieber, M. and M. R. Rose. 1986a. Molecular aspects of the species barrier. Annu. Rev. Ecol. Syst. 17:465-485. [9]

Krieber, M. and M. R. Rose. 1986b. Males, parthenogenesis and the maintenance of anisogamous sex. J. Theoret. Biol. 122:421-440. [9]

Kushner, S. R., H. Nagaishi, A. Templin and A. J. Clark. 1971. Genetic recombination in *E. coli*: The role of exonuclease I. Proc. Natl. Acad. Sci. USA 68:824-827. [2]

Kushner, S. R., H. Nagaishi and A. J. Clark. 1974. Isolation of exonuclease VIII: The enzyme associated with the sbcA indirect suppressor. Proc. Natl. Acad. Sci. USA 71:3593-3597. [2]

Labov, J. B. 1981. Pregnanacy blocking in rodents: Adaptive advantages for females. Amer. Natur. 118:361-371. [13]

Lafuse, W. P., N. Berg, S. Savarirayan and C. S. David. 1986. Mapping of a second recombination hot spot within the I-E region of the mouse H-2 gene complex. J. Exp. Med. 163:1518-1528. [3]

Lam, S. T., M. M. Stahl, K. D. McMilim and F. W. Stahl. 1974. Rec-mediated recombinational hotspot activity in bacteriophage. II. A mutation which causes hot spot activity. Genetics 77:425-433. [2]

Lamb, B. C. and M. R. T. Wickramaratne. 1973. Corresponding-site interference, synaptonemal complex structure and 8+:0m and 7+:1m octads from wild-type × mutant crosses of *Ascobolus immersus*. Genet. Res., Camb. 22:113-124. [9]

Lamb, R. Y. and R. B. Willey. 1979. Are parthenogenic and related bisexual insects equal in fertility? Evolution 33:774-775. [1]

Lande, R. and D. W. Schemske. 1985. The evolution of self-fertilization and inbreeding depression in plants. I. Genetic models. Evolution 39:24-40. [13]

Laski, F. A., D .C. Rio and G. M. Rubin. 1986. Tissue specificity of *Drosophila* P element is regulated at the level of mRNA splicing. Cell 44:7-19. [4]

Latter, B. D. H. and A. Robertson. 1962. The effects of inbreeding and artificial selection on reproductive fitness. Genet. Res., Camb. 3:110-138. [13]

Law, C. N. 1961. Recombination in the X-chromosome of *Drosophila melanogaster*. Nature 191:1180-1181. [6]

Lawrence, M. J. 1958. Genotypic control of crossing-over on the first chromosome of *Drosophila melanogaster*. Nature 182:889-890. [6]

Lawrence, M. J. 1963. The control of crossing-over in the X-chromosome of *Drosophila melanogaster*. Heredity 18:27-46. [6]

Lawrence, M. J., D. F. Marshall, V. E. Curtis and C. H. Fearon. 1985. Gametophytic self-incompatibility re-examined: A reply. Heredity 54:131-138. [13]

316 LITERATURE CITED

LeClerc, J. E. and J. K. Setlow. 1974. Transformation in *Haemophilus influenzae*. In *Mechanisms in Recombination*, R. F. Grell (ed.). Plenum, New York. [12]

Lederberg, J. 1951. Prevalence of *Escherichia coli* strains exhibiting genetic recombination. Science 114:68-69. [12]

Lederberg, J., E. M. Lederberg, N. D. Zinder and E. R. Lively. 1951. Recombination analysis of bacterial heredity. Cold Spring Harbor Symp. Quant. Biol. 16:413-440. [12]

Lederberg, J. and E. L. Tatum. 1946. Novel genotypes in mixed cultures of biochemical mutants of bacteria. In *Hereditary Variation in Microorganisms*, Cold Spring Harbor Symp. Quant. Biol. 11:113-114. [12]

Lederberg, J. and E. L. Tatum. 1946. Gene recombination in *Escherichia coli*. Nature 158:558. [2, 12]

Levene, H. 1953. Genetic equilibria when more than one ecological niche is available. Amer. Natur. 87:331-333. [8]

Levin, B. R. 1981. Periodic selection, infectious gene exchange and the genetic structure of *Escherichia coli* populations. Genetics 99:1-23. [12]

Levin, B. R. 1986. The maintenance of plasmids and transposons in natural populations of bacteria: A review, recantation and speculative progress report. In *Proceedings of Conference on Evolution and Environmental Spread of Antibiotic Resistance Genes*, S. Levy and R. Novick (eds.). Cold Spring Harbor Press, New York. [12]

Levin, B. R., A. C. Allison, H. J. Bremermann, L. L. Cavalli-Sforza, B. C. Clarke, R. Frentzel-Beyme, W. D. Hamilton, S. A. Levin, R. M. May and H. R. Thieme. 1982. Evolution of parasites and hosts group report. In *Population Biology of Infectious Diseases*, R. M. Anderson and R. M. May (eds.). Dahlem Konferenzen 1982. Springer-Verlag, Berlin. [11]

Levin, B. R. and R. E. Lenski. 1983. Coevolution in bacteria and their viruses and plasmids. In *Coevolution*, D.J. Futuyma and M. Slatkin (eds.). Sinauer Associates, Sunderland, Massachusetts. [2, 7, 10, 11, 12]

Levin, B. R. and R. E. Lenski. 1985. Bacteria and phage: A model system for the study of the ecology and coevolution of hosts and parasites. In *Ecology and Genetics of Host-Parasite Interactions*, D. Rollinson and R. M. Anderson (eds.). Academic Press, London. [11]

Levin, B. R., F. M. Stewart and V. Rice. 1979. The kinetics of conjugative plasmid transmission: Fit of a simple mass action model. Plasmid 2:247-260. [12]

Levin, D. A. 1975. Pest pressure and recombination systems in plants. Amer. Natur. 109:437-451. [1, 11]

Levin, D. A. and H. Kerster. 1974. Gene flow in seed plants. Evol. Biol. 7:139-220. [13]

Levin, S. A. 1983. Some approaches to the modelling of coevolutionary interactions. In *Coevolution*, M. Nitecki (ed.). University of Chicago Press, Chicago. [11]

Levine, A., P. L. Moreau, S. G. Sedgwick, R. Devoret, S. Adhya, M. Gottesman and A. Das. 1978. Expression of a bacterial gene turned on by a potent carcinogen. Mutat. Res. 50:29-35. [2]

Levine, R. P. and E. E. Levine. 1954. The genotypic control of crossing over in *Drosophila pseudoobscura*. Genetics 39:677-691. [6]

Levine, R. P. and E. E. Levine. 1955. Variable crossing over arising in different strains of *Drosophila pseudoobscura*. Genetics 40:399-405. [6]

Levins, R. 1965. Theory of fitness in a heterogeneous environment. V. Optimal genetic systems. Genetics 52:891-904. [6]

Lewin, B. 1985. *Genes II*. Wiley, New York. [12]

Lewis, D. 1941. Male sterility in natural populations of hermaphrodite plants: The equilibrium between females and hermaphrodites to be expected with different types of inheritance. New Phytol. 40:56-63. [14]

Lewis, D. 1979. Genetic versatility of incompatibility in plants. New Zeal. J. Bot. 17:637-644. [13]

Lewis, J. W. 1981a. On the coevolution of pathogen and host. I. General theory of discrete time coevolution. J. Theor. Biol. 93:927-951. [11]

Lewis, J. W. 1981b. On the coevolution of pathogen and host. II. Selfing hosts and haploid pathogens. J. Theor. Biol. 93:953-995. [11]

Lewis, W. M., Jr. 1983. Interruption of synthesis as a cost of sex in small organisms. Amer. Natur. 121:825-834. [1]

Lewontin, R. C. 1964a. The interaction of selection and linkage. I. General considerations; heterotic models. Genetics 49:49-67. [6]

Lewontin, R. C. 1964b. The interaction of selection and linkage. II. Optimum models. Genetics 50:757-782. [6, 11]

Lewontin, R. C. 1971. The effect of genetic linkage on the mean fitness of a population. Proc. Natl. Acad. Sci. USA 68:984-986. [5, 6]

Lewontin, R. C. 1974. *The Genetic Basis of Evolutionary Change*. Harvard University Press, Cambridge. [1]

Lewontin, R. C. 1980. Models of natural selection. In *Vito Volterra Symposium on Mathematical Models in Biology*, Lecture Notes in Biomathematics 39, C. Barigozzi (ed.). Springer-Verlag, Berlin. [11]

Lewontin, R. C. and P. Hull. 1967. The interaction of selection and linkage. III. Synergistic effects of blocks of genes. Der Zuchter 37:93-98. [6]

Lewontin, R. C. and K. Kojima. 1960. The evolutionary dynamics of complex polymorphisms. Evolution 14:458-472. [6]

Li, C. C. 1967. Fundamental theorem of natural selection. Nature 214:505-506. [13]

Li, C. C. 1976. *First Course in Population Genetics*. Boxwood Press, Pacific Grove, California.

Lieb, M. 1983. Specific mismatch correction in bacteriophage lambda crosses by very short patch repair. Molec. Gen. Genet. 191:118-125. [2]

Lieb, M. 1985. Recombination in the lambda repressor gene: Evidence that very short patch (VSP) mismatch correction restores a specific sequence. Molec. Gen. Genet. 199:465-470. [2]

Lieberman, R. P. and M. Oishi. 1974. The *recBC* deoxyribonuclease of *Escherichia coli*: Isolation and characterization of the subunit proteins and reconstitution of the enzyme. Proc. Natl. Acad. Sci. USA 71:4816-4820. [2]

Lifschytz, E. and D. L. Lindsley. 1974. Sex chromosome activation during spermatogenesis. Genetics 78:323-331. [16]

Lilley, D. M. and B. Kemper. 1984. Cruciform-resolvase interactions in supercoiled DNA. Cell 36:413-422. [2]

Lillis, M. and M. Freeling. 1986. Mu transposons in maize. Trends in Genet. 2:183-188. [3]

Lindsley, D. L. and L. Sandler. 1977. The genetic analysis of meiosis in female *Drosophila melanogaster*. Phil. Trans. Roy. Soc. London B 277:295-312. [6]

Little, J. W. and J. E. Harper. 1979. Identification of the *lex*A gene product of *E. coli* K12. Proc. Natl. Acad. Sci. USA 76:6147-6151. [2]

Little, J. W. and D. W. Mount. 1982. The SOS regulatory system of *E. coli*. Cell 29:11-22. [2]

Livak, K. J. 1984. Organization and mapping of a sequence on the *Drosophila melanogaster* X and Y chromosomes that is transcribed during spermatogenesis. Genetics 107:611-634. [16]

Lloyd, D. G. 1979. Some reproductive factors affecting the selection of self-fertilization in plants. Amer. Natur. 113:67-79. [14]

Lloyd, D. G. 1980a. Benefits and handicaps of sexual reproduction. Evol. Biol. 13:69-111. [1, 14]

Lloyd, D. G. 1980b. Sexual strategies in plants. III. A quantitative method for describing the gender of plants. New Zeal. J. Bot. 18:103-108. [14]

Lloyd, D. G. 1980c. Sexual strategies in plants. I. An hypothesis of serial adjustment of maternal investment during one reproductive session. New Phytol. 68:69-70. [13]

Lloyd, D. G. 1984. Gender allocations in outcrossing cosexual plants. In *Perspectives on Plant Population Ecology*, R. Dirzo and J. Sarukhan (eds.). Sinauer Associates, Sunderland, Massachusetts. [14]

Lloyd, D. G. 1985. Parallels between sexual strategies and other allocation strategies. Experientia 41:1277-1285. [14]

Lloyd, D. G. 1987. Allocations to pollen, seeds and pollination mechanisms in self-fertilizing plants. Funct. Ecol. 1:83-89. [14]

Lloyd, D. G. and K. S. Bawa. 1984. Modification of the gender of seed plants in varying conditions. Evol. Biol. 17:255-338. [14]

Lloyd, R. G., A. Thomas. 1984. A molecular model for conjugational recombination in *Escherichia coli* K12. Molec. Gen. Genet. 197:328-336. [2]

Loaring, J. M. and P. D. N. Herbert. 1981. Ecological differences among clones of *Daphnia pulex* Leydig. Oecologia 51:162-168. [1]

Lord, E. M. 1981. Cleistogamy: A tool for the study of floral morphogenesis, function and evolution. Bot. Rev. 47:421-449. [14]

Love, P. E. and R. E. Yasbin. 1986. Induction of the *Bacillus subtilis* SOS-like response by *E. coli* RecA protein. Proc. Natl. Acad. Sci. USA 83:5204-5208. [2]

Lovett, C. M. and J. W. Roberts. 1985. Purification of a RecA protein analogue from *Bacillus subtilis*. J. Biol. Chem. 260:3305-3313. [2]

Lovett, S. T. and A. J. Clark. 1983. Genetic analysis of regulation of the RecF pathway of recombination in *Escherichia coli*. J. Bacteriol. 153:1471-1478. [2]

Lovett, S. T. and A. J. Clark. 1984. Genetic analysis of the *recJ* gene of *Escherichia coli* K12. J. Bacteriol. 157:190-196. [2]

Lovett Doust, J. and P. B. Cavers. 1982a. Biomass allocation in hermaphrodite flowers. Can. J. Bot. 60:2530-2534. [14]

Lovett Doust, J. and P. B. Cavers. 1982b. Resource allocation and gender in the Green Dragon *Arisaema dracontium* (Araceae) Amer. Midl. Natur. 108:144-148. [14]

Lovett Doust, J. and J. L. Harper. 1980. The resource costs of gender and maternal support in andromonoecious umbellifer, *Smyrnium olusatrum* L. New Phytol. 85:251-264. [14]

Low, B. 1968. Formation of merodiploids in matings with a class of *rec*-recipient strains of *E. coli* K12. Proc. Natl. Acad. Sci. USA 60:160-167. [2]

Lucchesi, J. C. 1976. Interchromosomal effects. In *The Genetics and Biology of Drosophila*, Vol. 1A, M. Ashburner and E. Novitski (eds.). Academic Press, London. [6]

Lundquist, P. D. and B. R. Levin. 1986. Transitory derepression and the maintenance of conjugative plasmids. Genetics 113:483-497. [12]

Luria, S. E. and R. Dulbecco. 1948. Genetic recombination leading to production of active bacteriophage from ultraviolet inactivated bacteriophage particles. Genetics 34:93-125. [2]

Luykx, P. and R. M. Syren. 1979. The cytogenesis of *Incistermes schwarzi* and other Florida termites. Sociobiology 4(2):191-209. [16]

Lynch, M. 1984. Destabilizing hybridization, general-purpose genotypes and geographic parthenogenesis. Quart. Rev. Biol. 59:257-290. [1, 10, 11, 17]

Lynch, M. and W. Gabriel. 1983. Phenotypic evolution and parthenogenesis. Amer. Natur. 122:745-764. [1]

Malmberg, R. 1977. The evolution of epistasis and the advantage of recombination in populations of bacteriophage T4. Genetics 86:607-621. [4]

Mann, T. 1984. *Spermatophores*. Springer-Verlag, Berlin. [16]

Manning, J. T. 1976. Gamete dimorphism and the cost of sexual reproduction: Are they separate phenomena? J. Theor. Biol. 55:393-395. [1]

Manning, J. T. 1976. Is sex maintained to facilitate or minimize mutational advance? Heredity 36:351-357. [15]

Manning, J. T. 1983. The consequences of mutation in multi-clonal asexual species. Heredity 50:15-19. [5]

Marcou, D. 1961. Notion de longevitie et nature cytoplasmique due determinant de la senescence chez quelqeus champignons. Ann. Sci. Nat. Bot. 12:653-764. [3]

Margulis, L. and D. Sagan. 1986. *Origins of Sex: Three Billion Years of Recombination*. Yale University Press, New Haven. [1, 4, 10, 12, 15]

Margulis, L., D. Sagan and L. Olendzenski. 1985. What is sex? In *The Origin and Evolution of Sex*, H. O. Halvorson and A. Monroy (eds.). Alan R. Liss, New York. [9]

Marshall, D. L. and N. C. Ellstrand. 1986. Sexual selection in *Raphanus sativus*. Experimental data on nonrandom fertilization, maternal choice and consequences of multiple paternity. Amer. Natur. 127:446-461. [16]

Martin, F. G. and C. C. Cockerham. 1960. High speed selection studies. In *Biometrical Genetics*, O. Kempthorne (ed.). Pergamon, London. [6]

Martin, R. 1977. A possible genetic mechanism of aging, rejuvenation and recombination in germinal cells. In *Human Cytogenetics*, R. S. Sparks, D. E. Comings and C. F. Fox (eds.). Academic Press, New York. [15]

Maruyama, T. and M. Kimura. 1980. Genetic variability and effective population size when local extinction and recolonization of subpopulations are frequent. Proc. Natl. Acad. Sci. USA 77:6710-6714. [12]

Masters, M. 1985. Generalized transduction. In *Genetics of Bacteria*, J. Scaife, D. Leach and A. Galizzi (eds.). Academic Press, New York. [12]

Mather, K. 1943. Specific differences in *Petunia*. J. Genet. 45:215-235. [13]

Maupas, E. 1889. La rejeunissement chez les cilies. Arch. Zool. Exp. Gen. (2)7:149-517. [1]

Maupas, E. 1900. Modes et formes de reproeuction chez des Nematodes. Arch. Zool. Exp. Gen. (3)8:463-624. [1]

May, R. M. 1979. When to be incestuous. Nature 279:192-194. [13]

May, R. M. 1983a. Nonlinear problems in ecology and resource management. In *Chaotic Behaviour of Deterministic Systems*, G. Iooss, R. H. G. Helleman and R. Stora (eds.). North-Holland, Amsterdam. [11]

May, R. M. 1983b. Parasitic infections as regulators of animal populations. Amer. Sci. 71:36-44. [11]

May, R. M. 1985. Host-parasite associations: Their population biology and population genetics. In *Ecology and Genetics of Host-Parasite Interactions*, D. Rollinson and R. M. Anderson (eds.). Academic Press, London. [11]

May, R. M. and R. Anderson. 1983. Epidemiology and genetics in the coevolution of parasites and hosts. Proc. Roy. Soc. London B 219:281-31. [6, 11]

May, R. M. and R. M. Anderson. 1983a. Coevolution of parasites and hosts. In *Coevolution*, D. J. Futuyma and M. Slatkin (eds.). Sinauer Associates, Sunderland, Massachusetts. [11]

May, R. M. and W. J. Leonard. 1975. Nonlinear aspects of competition between three species. SIAM J. Appl. Math. 29:243-253. [11]

Maynard Smith, J. 1959. A theory of ageing. Nature 184:956-958. [1]

Maynard Smith, J. 1962. The causes of ageing. Proc. Roy. Soc. London B 157:115-127. [1]

Maynard Smith, J. 1966. *The Theory of Evolution*, 2nd Ed. Penguin Books, Harmondsworth. [1]

Maynard Smith, J. 1968. Evolution in sexual and asexual populations. Amer. Natur. 102:469-473. [1, 4, 5]

Maynard Smith, J. 1971. The origin and maintenance of sex. In *Group Selection*, G. C. Williams (ed.). Aldine Atherton, Chicago. [5, 11, 14]

Maynard Smith, J. 1971. What use is sex? J. Theor. Biol. 30:319-335. [1, 6, 10]

Maynard Smith, J. 1974. The theory of games and the evolution of animal conflicts. J. Theor. Biol. 47:209-221. [11]

Maynard Smith, J. 1975. Evolution of sex. Nature 254. [1]

Maynard Smith, J. 1976. A short term advantage for sex and recombination through sib-competition. J. Theor. Biol. 63:245-258. [1, 7, 10]

Maynard Smith, J. 1977. The sex habit in plants and animals. In *Measuring Selection in Natural Populations*, F. B. Christiansen and T. M. Fenchel (eds.). Springer-Verlag, Heidelberg. [13]

Maynard Smith, J. 1977. Why the genome does not congeal. Nature 268:693-696. [6, 10]

Maynard Smith, J. 1978. *The Evolution of Sex*. Cambridge University Press, Cambridge. [1, 4, 5, 6, 10, 11, 12, 15, 17]

Maynard Smith, J. 1979. The effects of normalizing and disruptive selection on genes for recombination. Genet. Res., Camb. 33:121-128. [8]

Maynard Smith, J. 1980. Selection for recombination in a polygenic model. Genet. Res., Camb. 35:269-277. [5, 6, 7]

Maynard Smith, J. 1982. *Evolution and the Theory of Games*. Cambridge University Press, Cambridge. [8, 11, 14]

Maynard Smith, J. 1986. Contemplating life without sex. Nature 324:300-301. [3, 4, 7]

Maynard Smith, J. and R. W. L. Brown. 1986. Competition and body size. Theor. Pop. Biol. 30:166-179. [11]

Maynard Smith, J. and R. Hoekstra. 1980. Polymorphism in a varied environment: How robust are the models? Genet. Res., Camb. 35:260-277. [8]

Maynard Smith, J. and G. C. Williams. 1976. Reply to Barash. Amer. Natur. 110:897. [5]

Mayo, O. 1974. Effect of age on chiasma number in man. Hum. Hered. 24:144-150. [16]

Mayr, E. 1963. *Animal Species and Evolution*. Harvard University Press, Cambridge. [1, 16]

Mayr, E. 1982. *The Growth of Biological Thought: Diversity, Evolution and Inheritance*. Belknap, Harvard University Press, Cambridge. [16]

Mayr, E. 1985. August Weismann und die Evolution der Organismen. Freiburger Universitaetsblaetter 87/77:61-82. [1]

Mays Hoopes, L. L., A. Brown and R. C. C. Huang. 1983. Methylation and rearrangement of mouse intracisternal particle gene during development, ageing and myeloma. Mol. Cell. Biol. 3:1371-1380. [3]

McCauley, D. E. 1983. A unique approach to the evolution of sex. Evolution 37:1323-1324. [15]

McDevitt, H. O. 1977. Conclusions and prospects. In *HLA and Disease*, J. Dausset and A. Svejgaard (eds.). Munksgaard, Copenhagen. [13]

McDevitt, H. O. and W. F. Bodmer. 1972. Histocompatibility antigens, immune responsiveness and susceptibility to disease. Amer. J. Med. 52:1-8. [13]

McDevitt, H. O. and W. F. Bodmer. 1974. HL-A, immune response genes and disease. Lancet i:1269-1275. [13]

McEntee, K. 1977. Protein X is the product of the recA gene of E. coli. Proc. Natl. Acad. Sci. USA 74:5275-5279. [2]

McEntee, K., G. M. Weinstock and I. R. Lehman. 1980. RecA protein-catalyzed strand assimilation: Stimulation by E. coli single-stranded DNA-binding protein. Proc. Natl. Acad. Sci. USA 77:857-861. [2]

McEntee. K. and G. M. Weinstock. 1981. The RecA enzyme of Escherichia coli and recombination assays. In The Enzymes, Academic Press. [2]

McIntyre, J. A. and W. P. Faulk. 1979a. Maternal blocking factors in human pregnancy are found in plasma not serum. Lancet ii:821-823. [13]

McIntyre, J. A. and W. P. Faulk. 1979b. Trophoblast modulation of maternal allogenic recognition. Proc. Natl. Acad. Sci. USA 76:4029-4032. [13]

Medvedev, Zh. A. 1981. On the immortality of the germ line: Genetic and biochemical mechanisms. Mech. Age. Devel. 17:331-359. [3]

Meselson, M. S. and C. M. Radding. 1975. A general model for genetic recombination. Proc. Natl. Acad. Sci. USA 72:358-361. [2, 3, 9]

Meyers, D. A. and T. H. Beaty. 1986. Genetic Analysis Workshop IV: Summary of two-point and multipoint mapping of 11p. Genet. Epid. 3 (Suppl. 1): 91-111. [6]

Michod, R. E. 1986. On fitness and adaptedness and their role in evolutionary explanation. J. Hist. Biol. 19:289-302. [9]

Michod, R. E. and W. D. Hamilton. 1980. Coefficents of relatedness in sociobiology. Nature 288:694-697. [13]

Miklos, G. L. G. and R. N. Nankivell. 1976. Telomeric satellite DNA functions in regulating recombination. Chromosoma 56:143-167. [6]

Mizuuchi, K., M. Gellert and H. A. Nash. 1978a. Involvement of supertwisted DNA in integrative recombination of bacteriophage lambda. J. Mol. Biol. 121:375-392. [2]

Mizuuchi, K., M. H. O'Dea and M. Gellert. 1978b. DNA gyrase: Subunit structure and ATPase activity of the purified enzyme. Proc. Natl. Acad. Sci. USA 75:5960-5963 [2]

Mizuuchi, K., B. Kemper, J. Hays and R. Weisberg. 1982. T4 endonuclease VII cleaves Holliday structures. Cell 29:857 [2]

Mode, C. J. 1958. A mathematical model for the co-evolution of obligate parasites and their hosts. Evolution 12:158-165. [11]

Monk, M., M. Boubelik and S. Lenhart. 1987. Temporal and regional changes in DNA methylation in the embryonic, extraembryonic, and germ cell lineages during mouse embryo development. Development 99:371-382. [3]

Moore, W. S. 1984. Evolutionary ecology of unisexual fishes. In Evolutionary Genetics of Fishes, B. J. Turner (ed.). Plenum, New York. [17]

Moran, G. F., J. C. Bell and A. J. Hilliker. 1983. Greater meiotic recombination in male vs. female gametes in Pinus radiata. J. Hered. 74:62. [16]

Moran, P. A. P. 1962. The Statistical Processes of Evolutionary Theory. Clarendon Press, Oxford. [5]

Moreau, P. L. 1987. Effects of overproduction of single-stranded DNA binding protein on RecA-protein-dependent processes in Escherichia coli. J. Mol. Biol. 194:621-634. [2]

Moreau, P. L. and J. W. Roberts. 1984. RecA protein-promoted lambda repressor cleavage: Complementation between RecA441 and RecA430 proteins in vitro. Molec. Gen. Genet. 198:25-34. [2]

Morton, N. E., J. F. Crow and H. J. Muller. 1956. An estimate of the mutational damage in man from data on consanguineous marriages. Proc. Natl. Acad. Sci. USA 42:855-863. [13]

Mukai, T. 1964. The genetic structure of natural populations of Drosophila melanogaster. I. Spontaneous mutation rate of polygenes controlling viability. Genetics 50:1-19. [8]

Mukai, T. 1969. The genetic structure of natural populations of Drosophila melanogaster. VII. Synergistic interaction of spontaneous mutant polygenes controlling viability. Genetics 61:749-761. [4, 7]

Mulcahy, D. L. 1974. Correlation between speed of pollen tube growth and seedling height in Zea mays L. Nature 249:491-493. [13]

Mulcahy, D. L. 1979. The rise of the angiosperms: A genecological factor. Science 206:20-23. [13]

Mulcahy, D. L. 1983. Models of pollen tube competition in Geranium maculatum. In Pollination Biology, L. Real (ed.). Academic Press, New York. [16]

Mulcahy, D. L. and G. B. Mulcahy. 1975. The influence of gametophytic competition on sporophytic quality in *Dianthus chinensis*. Theor. Appl. Genet. 46:277-280. [13]

Mulcahy, D. L. and G. B. Mulcahy. 1983. Gametophytic self-incompatibility re-examined. Science 220:1247-1251. [13]

Mulcahy, D. L. and G. B. Mulcahy. 1985. Gametophytic self-incompatibility, or, the more things change.... Heredity 54:139-144. [13]

Mulcahy, D. L. and G. B. Mulcahy. 1987. The effects of pollen competition. Amer. Sci. 75:44-50. [16]

Mulcahy, D. L., G. B. Mulcahy and D. MacMillan. 1986a. The heterosis model: A progress report. In *Biotechnology and Ecology of Pollen*, D. L. Mulcahy, G. B. Mulcahy and E. Ottaviano (eds.). Springer-Verlag, New York. [13]

Mulcahy, D. L., G. B. Mulcahy and E. Ottaviano (eds.). 1986b. *Biotechnology and Ecology of Pollen*. Springer-Verlag, New York. [13]

Muller, H. 1883. *The Fertilisation of Flowers*. Macmillan, London. [14]

Muller, H. J. 1932. Some genetic aspects of sex. Amer. Natur. 66:118-138. [1, 4, 5, 6, 7, 10, 17]

Muller, H. J. 1950. Our load of mutations. Amer. J. Hum. Genet. 2:111-176. [4]

Muller, H. J. 1958. Evolution by mutation. Bull. Amer. Math. Soc. 64:137-160. [4]

Muller, H. J. 1964. The relation of recombination to mutational advance. Mutat. Res. 1:2-9. [1, 4, 5, 6, 7, 8, 10, 15]

Murtagh, C. E. and G. B. Sharman. 1977. Chromosomal sex determination in monotremes. In *Reproduction and Evolution*, J. H. Calaby and C. H. Tyndale-Biscoe (eds.). Austral. Acad. Sci., Canberra. [16]

Musser, J. M., S. K. Barenkamp, D. M. Granoff and R. K. Selander. 1986. Genetic relationship of serologically nontypable and serotype b strains of *Haemophilus influenzae*. Infec. and Immun. 52:183-191. [12]

Musser, J. M., D. M. Granoff, P. Pattison and R. K. Selander. 1985. A population genetic framework for the study of invasive diseases caused by serotype b strains of *Haemophilus influenzae*. Proc. Natl. Acad. Sci. USA 82:5078-5982. [12]

Nagylaki, T. 1976. A model for the evolution of self-fertilization and vegetative reproduction. J. Theor. Biol. 58:55-58. [14]

Nakayama, H., K. Nakayama, N. Nakayama, N. Irino, Y. Nakayama and P. C. Hanawalt. 1984. Isolation and genetic characterization of a thymineless death-resistant of *Escherichia coli* K12: Identification of a new mutation (recQ1) that blocks the RecF recombination pathway. Mol. Gen. Genet. 195:474-480. [2]

Nasrallah, M. E. 1974. Genetic control of quantitative variation in self-incompatibility proteins detected by immunodiffusion. Genetics 76:45-50. [13]

Nei, M. 1967. Modification of linkage intensity by natural selection. Genetics 57:625-641. [5, 6, 11]

Nei, M. 1969. Linkage modification and sex difference in recombination. Genetics 63:681-699. [6]

Nei, M. 1970. Accumulation of nonfunctional genes on sheltered chromosomes. Amer. Natur. 104:311-322. [13]

Nettancourt, D. de. 1977. *Incompatibility in Angiosperms*. Springer-Verlag, Berlin. [13]

Nokkala, S. and C. Nokkala. 1983. Achiasmatic male meiosis in two species of *Saldula* (Saldidae, Hemiptera). Hereditas 99:131-134. [16]

Nokkala, S. and C. Nokkala. 1984. Achiasmatic male meiosis in the heteropteran genus *Nabis* (Nabidae, Hemiptera). Hereditas 101:31-35. [16]

Nomura, T. 1982. Parental exposure to X rays and chemicals induces heritable tumours and anomalies in mice. Nature 296:575-577. [3]

Ober, C. L., A. O. Martin, J. L. Simpson, W. W. Hauck, D. B. Amos, D. D. Kostyu, M. Fotino and F. H. Allen, Jr. 1983. Shared HLA antigens and reproductive performance among Hutterites. Amer. J. Hum. Genet. 35:994-1004. [13]

Ochman, H. and R. K. Selander. 1984. Evidence for clonal population structure in *Escherichia coli*. Proc. Natl. Acad. Sci. USA 81:198-201. [12]

Ogawa, T., H. Waboko, T. Tsurimoto, T. Horii, H. Masukata and H. Ogawa. 1978. Characteristics of purified RecA protein and the regulation of its synthesis in vivo. Cold Spring Harbor Symp. Quant. Biol. 43. [2]

Ohno, S. 1967. *Sex Chromosomes and Sex-Linked Genes*. Springer-Verlag, Berlin.

Ohta, T. 1971. Associative overdominance caused by linked detrimental mutations. Genet. Res., Camb. 18:277-286. [13]

Ohta, T. 1973. Effect of linkage on behavior of mutant genes in finite populations. Theor. Pop. Biol. 4:145-162. [13]

Ohta, T. and C. C. Cockerham. 1974. Detrimental genes with partial selfing and effects on a neutral locus. Genet. Res., Camb. 23:191-200. [13]

Ohta, T. and M. Kimura. 1970. Development of associative overdominance through linkage disequilibrium in finite populations. Genet. Res., Camb. 16:165-177. [13]

Orgel, L. E. and F. H. C. Crick. 1980. Selfish DNA: The ultimate parasite. Nature 284:604-607. [4, 10]

Orlove, M. J. and C. L. Wood. 1978. Coefficients of relationship and coefficients of relatedness in kin selection: A covariance form for the rho formula. J. Theor. Biol. 73:679-686. [13]

Ornduff, R. 1969. Reproductive biology in relation to systematics. Taxon. 18:121-133. [14]

Orr-Weaver, T. L. and J. W. Szostak. 1985. Fungal recombination. Microbiol. Rev. 49:33-58. [2, 9]

Orskov, F. and I. Orskov. 1961. The fertility of *Escherichia coli* antigen test strains in crosses with K12. Acta. Path. et. Microbiologica Scand. 51:280-290. [12]

Orskov, F. and I. Orskov. 1983. Summary of a workshop on the clone concept in epidemiology, taxonomy and evolution of the Enteriobacteriacae and other bacteria. J. Infect. Dis. 148:346-357. [12]

Owen, R. 1849. *On Parthenogenesis, or the Successive Production of Procreating Individuals From a Single Ovum*. John van Voorst, London. [1]

Oyama, S. 1985. *The Ontogeny of Information*. Cambridge University Press, Cambridge. [15]

Parker, E. D. Jr. 1979. Ecological implications of clonal diversity in parthenogenetic morphospecies. Amer. Zool. 19:753-762. [1]

Parker, G. A., R. R. Baker and V. G. F. Smith. 1972. The origin and evolution of gamete dimorphism and the male-female phenomenon. J. Theor. Biol. 36:529-553. [5]

Parsons, P. A. 1958. Selection for increased recombination in *Drosophila melanogaster*. Amer. Natur. 92:255-256. [6]

Partridge, L. 1980. Mate choice increases a component of offspring fitness in fruit flies. Nature 283:290-291. [16]

Pastor, J. B. and H. G. Callan. 1952. Chiasma formation in spermatocytes and oocytes of the turbullarian *Dendrocoelum lacteum*. J. Genet. 50:449-454. [16]

Pawl, G., R. Taylor, K. Minton and E. C. Friedberg. 1976. Enzymes involved in thymine dimer excision in bacteriophage T4-infected *Escherichia coli*. J. Mol. Biol. 108:99-109. [9]

Peacock, W. J. 1970. Replication, recombination and chiasmata in *Goniaea australasiae* [Orthopetera: Acrididae]. Genetics 65:593-617. [9]

Pearl, R. J. and J. R. Miner. 1935. Experimental studies on the duration of life. IX. The comparative mortality of certain lower organisms. Quart. Rev. Biol. 10:60-79. [1]

Person, C. 1966. Genetic polymorphism in parasitic systems. Nature 212:266-267. [11]

Phizicky, E. M. and J. W. Roberts. 1981. Induction of SOS functions: Regulation of proteolytic activity of *E. coli* RecA protein by interaction with DNA and nucleoside triphosphate. Cell 25:259-267. [2]

Picksley, S. M., P. V. Attfield and R. G. Lloyd. 1984. Repair of DNA double-strand breaks in *Escherichia coli* K12 requires a functional recN product. Molec. Gen. Genet. 195:267-274. [2]

Picksley, S. M., S. J. Morton and R. G. Lloyd. 1985. The recN locus of *Escherichia coli* K12: Molecular analysis and identification of the gene product. Molec. Gen. Genet. 201:301-307. [2]

Pittendrigh, C. 1958. Adaptation, natural selection and behavior. In *Behavior and Evolution*. A. Roe and G. G. Simpson (eds.). Yale University Press, New Haven. [15]

Plack, A. 1957. Sexual dimorphism in Labiatae. Nature 180:1218-1219. [14]

Plack, A. 1959. Effect of gibberellic acid on corolla size. Nature 182:610. [14]

Plotkin, H. C. and F. J. Odling-Smee. 1981. A multiple-level model of evolution and its implications for sociobiology. Behav. Brain Sci. 4:225-268. [15]

Ponticelli, A. S., D. W. Schultz, A. F. Taylor and G. R. Smith. 1985. Chi-dependent DNA strand cleavage by RecBC enzyme. Cell 41:145-151. [2]

Porras, O., D. A. Caugant, B. Gray, T. Lagerard, B. R. Levin and C. Svanborg Eden. 1986. Difference in structure between type b and nontypable *Haemophilus influenzae* populations. Infect. and Immun. 53:79-89. [12]

Porter, R. D., T. McLaughlin and B. Low. 1979. Transduction versus "conjuduction": Evidence for multiple roles for exonuclease V in genetic recombination in *Escherichia coli*. Cold Spring Harbor Symp. Quant. Biol. 1043-1047. [2]

Pressing, J and D. C. Reanney. 1984. Divided genomes and intrinsic noise. J. Mol. Evol. 20:135-146. [4]

Price, G. R. 1970. Selection and covariance. Nature 227:520-521. [13]

Price, G. R. 1972. Fisher's "fundamental theorem" made clear. Ann. Hum. Genet. 36:126-140. [13]

Price, M. V. and N. M. Waser. 1979. Pollen dispersal and optimal outcrossing in *Delphinium nelsoni*. Nature 277:294-297. [13]

Price, M. V. and N. M. Waser. 1982. Population structure, frequency-dependent selection and the maintenance of sexual reproduction. Evolution 36:35-43. [5, 11]

Prout, T. 1953. Some effects of variations in the segregation ratio and of selection on the frequency of alleles under random mating. Acta. Genetica 4:148-151. [9]

Prudhommeau, C. and J. Proust. 1974. UV irradiation of polar cells of *Drosophila melanogaster* embryos. V. A study of the meiotic recombination in females with chromosomes of a different structure. Mutat. Res. 23:63-66. [9]

Queller, D. C. 1983. Kin selection and conflict in seed maturation. J. Theor. Biol. 100:153-172. [13]

Queller, D. C. 1984. Models of kin selection on seed provisioning. Heredity 53:151-165. [13]

Quillardet, P., P. L. Moreau, H. Ginsburg, D. W. Mount and R. Devoret. 1982. Cell survival UV-reactivation and induction of prophage lambda in *Escherichia coli* K12 overproducing RecA protein. Molec. Gen. Genet. 188:37-43. [2]

Radding, C. M. 1978. Genetic recombination: Strand transfer and mismatch repair. Annu. Rev. Biochem. 47:847-880. [2]

Radding, C. M. 1982. Homologous pairing and strand exchange in genetic recombination. Annu. Rev. Genet. 405-437. [2]

Radding, C. M. 1983. General recombination. In *Lambda II*, R. W. Hendrix, J. W. Roberts, F. W. Stahl, R. A. Weisberg (eds.). Cold Spring Harbor Press, New York [2]

Radding, C. M. 1985. The molecular and enzymatic basis of homologous recombination. In *Genetics of Bacteria*, J. Scaife, D. Leach and A. Galizzi (eds.). Academic Press, New York. [12]

Radding, C. M., J. Flory, A. Wu, R. Kahn, C. DasGupta, D. Gonda, M. Bianchi and S. S. Tsang. 1983a. Three phases in homologous pairing: polymerization of RecA protein on single-stranded DNA, synapsis and polar strand exchange. Cold Spring Harbor Symp. Quant. Biol. 76. [2]

Radding, C. M., C. DasGupta, A. M. Wu, R. Kahn and J. Flory. 1983b. Recombination activities of *Escherichia coli* RecA protein: Synapsis and strand exchange. Nuc. A. Res. [2]

Radman, M. 1975. SOS repair hypothesis: Phenomenology of an inducible DNA repair which is accompanied by mutagenesis. In *Molecular Mechanisms for Repair of DNA*, P. C. Hanawalt, R. B. Setlow (eds.). Plenum, New York. [2]

Radman, M. and R. Wagner. 1986. Mismatch repair in *Escherichia coli*. Annu. Rev. Genet. 20:523-538. [4]

Ralls, K., P. H. Harvey and A. M. Lyles. 1986. Inbreeding in natural populations of birds and mammals. In *Conservation Biology: The Science of Scarcity and Diversity*, M. E. Soule (ed.). Sinauer Associates, Sunderland, Massachussets. [15]

Raper, J. R., M. G. Baxter and A. H. Ellingboe. 1960. The genetic structure of the incompatibility factors of *Schizophyllum commune*: The A-factor. Proc. Natl. Acad. Sci. USA 46:833-842. [6]

Rauth, S., K. Y. Song, D. Ayares, L. Wallace, P. D. Moore and R. Kucherlapati. 1986. Transfection and homologous recombination involving single-stranded DNA substrates in mammalian cells and nuclear extracts. Proc. Natl. Acad. Sci. USA 83:5587-5591. [2]

Razin, A. and H. Cedar. 1984. DNA methylation in eukaryotic cells. Int. Rev. Cytol. 92: 159-186. [3]

Razin, A., H. Cedar and A. D. Riggs. 1984. DNA *Methylation: Biochemistry and Biological Significance.* Springer-Verlag, New York. [3]

Read, A. F. 1987. Comparative evidence supports the Hamilton and Zuk hypothesis on parasites and sexual selection. Nature 328:68-70. [11]

Reanney, D. 1976. Extrachromosomal elements as possible agents of adaptation and development. Microbiol. Rev. 40:552-590. [12]

Redfield, R. 1984. The evolutionary role of recombination in bacteria and phage. Genetics 107:S87. [9]

Reiss, Michael J. 1987. Evolutionary conflict over the control of offspring sex ratio. J. Theor. Biol. 125:25-39. [17]

Resnick, J. and R. Sussman. 1982. *Escherichia coli* single strand DNA binding protein from wild type and *lex*C113 mutant affect in vitro proteolytic cleavage of phage lambda repressor. Proc. Natl. Acad. Sci. USA 79:2832-2835. [2]

Resnick, M. A., T. Chow, J. Nitiss and J. Game. 1984. Changes in the chromosomal DNA of yeast during meiosis in repair mutants and the possible role of deoxyribonuclease. Cold Spring Harbor Symp. Quant. Biol. 49:639-649. [9]

Rice, W. R. 1983. Parent-offspring pathogen transmission: A selective agent promoting sexual reproduction. Amer. Natur. 121:187-203. [11]

Riggs, A. D. 1975. X chromosome inactivation, differentiation and DNA methylation. Cyt. Cell Genet. 14:9-25. [3]

Riggs, A. D. and P. A. Jones. 1983. 5-methyl cytosine, gene regulation and cancer. Adv. Cancer Res. 40:1-30. [3]

Roberts, J. W. and R. Devoret. 1983. Lysogenic induction. In *Lambda II*, R. W. Hendrix, J. W. Roberts, F. W. Stahl, and R. A. Weisberg (eds.). Cold Spring Harbor Press, New York. [2]

Roberts, J. W., C. W. Roberts, N. L. Craig and E. M. Phizicky. 1979. Activity of the *Escherichia coli rec*A gene product. Cold Spring Harbor Symp. Quant. Biol. 43:917-920. [2]

Robertson, A. 1966. A mathematical model of the culling process in dairy cattle. Animal Prod. 8:95-108. [13]

Rocklin, R. E., J. L. Kitzmiller, C. B. Carpenter, M. R. Garovoy and J. R. David. 1976. Absence of an immunologic blocking factor from the serum of women with chronic abortions. New Eng. J. Med. 295:1209-1213. [13]

Rocklin, S. and G. Oster. 1976. Competition between phenotypes. J. Math. Biol. 3:225-261. [11]

Rose, A. M. and D. L. Baillie. 1979. A mutation in *Caenorhabditis elegans* that increases recombination frequency more than threefold. Nature 281:599-600. [6]

Rose, M. R. 1982. A physiological barrier for the maintenance of anisogamous sex. J. Theor. Biol. 94:801-813. [9]

Rose, M. R. 1983. The contagion mechanism for the origin of sex. J. Theor. Biol. 101:137-146. [10, 1]

Rose, M. R. and W. F. Doolittle. 1983. Molecular mechanisms of speciation. Science 220:157-162. [9]

Rose, M. R. and R. J. Redfield. In press. Is sex an adaptation? Evol. Theory. [9]

Rupp, W. D. and P. Howard-Flanders. 1968. Discontinuities in DNA synthesized in an excision defective strain of *Escherichia coli* following ultraviolet irradiation. J. Mol. Biol. 31:291-304. [9]

Rupp, W. D., C. E. Wilde, D. L. Reno and P. Howard-Flanders. 1971. Exchanges between DNA strands in ultraviolet-irradiated *Escherichia coli.* J. Mol. Biol. 61:25-44. [2]

Ryder, L. P., A. Svejgaard and J. Dausset. 1981. Genetics of HLA disease association. Annu. Rev. Genet. 15:169-187. [11]

Saluz, H. P., J. Jiricny and J. P. Jost. 1986. Genomic sequencing reveals a positive correlation between the kinetics of strand-specific DNA methylation and the overlapping estradiol/gluco-corticord receptor binding sites and the rate of avian vitellogenin mRNA synthesis. Proc. Natl. Acad. Sci. USA 83:7167-7177. [3]

Sancar, A., C. Stachelek, W. Konigsberg and W. D. Rupp. 1980. Sequences of the recA gene and protein. Proc. Natl. Acad. Sci. USA 77:2611-2615. [2]

Sandler, L., D. L. Lindsley, B. Nicoletti and G. Trippa. 1968. Mutants affecting meiosis in natural populations of *Drosophila melanogaster.* Genetics 60:525-558. [6]

Sari-Gorla, M., E. Ottaviano and D. Faini. 1975. Genetic variability of gametophytic growth in maize. Theor. Appl. Genet. 46:289-294. [13]

Sasaki, A. and Y. Iwasa. 1987. Optimal recombination rate in fluctuating environments. Genetics 115:377-388. [4]

Schacter, B., L. R. Weitkamp and W. E. Johnson. 1984. Parental HLA compatibility, fetal wastage and neural tube defects: Evidence for a T/t-like locus in humans. Amer. J. Hum. Genet. 36:1082-1091. [13]

Schemske, D. W. 1978. Evolution of reproductive characteristics in *Impatiens* (Balsaminacae): The significance of cleistogamy and chasmogamy. Ecology 59:596-613. [14]

Schewe, M. J., D. T. Suzuki and U. Erasmus. 1971. The genetic effects of mitomycin C in *Drosophila melanogaster*. II. Induced meiotic recombination. Mutat. Res. 12:269-279. [9]

Schoen, D. J. 1982. Male reproductive effort and breeding systems in an hermaphroditic plant. Oecologia 53:255-257. [14]

Schoen, D. J. and M. T. Clegg. 1985. The influence of flower color on outcrossing rate and male reproductive success in *Ipomoea purpurea*. Evolution 39:1242-1249. [16]

Schoen, D. J. and D. G. Lloyd. 1984. The selection of cleistogamy and heteromorphic diaspores. Biol. J. Linn. Soc. 23:303-322. [14]

Schultz, D. W. and G. R. Smith. 1986. Conservation of chi cutting activity in terrestrial and marine enteric bacteria. J. Mol. Biol. 189:585-595. [2]

Schultz, D. W., J. Swindle and G. R. Smith. 1981. Clustering of mutations inactivating a chi recombinational hot spot. J. Mol. Biol. 146:275-286. [2]

Schultz, J. and H. Redfield. 1951. Interchromosomal effects on crossing over in *Drosophila*. Cold Spring Harbor Symp. Quant. Biol. 16:175-197. [6]

Schultz, R. J. 1961. Reproductive mechanism of unisexual and bisexual strains of the viviparous fish *Poeciliopsis*. Evolution 15:302-325. [9]

Schwann, T. 1839. *Mikroskopische Untersuchungen ueber die Uebereinstimmung in der Struktur und dem Wachstum der Tiere und Pflanzen*. Berlin. [1]

Schwartz, D. and E. Dennis. 1986. Transposase activity of the Ac controlling element in maize is regulated by its degree of methylation. Mol. Gen. Genet. 205:476-482. [3]

Seavey, S. R. and K. S. Bawa. 1986. Late-acting self-incompatibility in angiosperms. Bot. Rev. 52:195-219. [13]

Sedgwick, S. G. and P. A. Goodwin. 1985. Differences in mutagenic and recombinational DNA repair in enterobacteria. Proc. Natl. Acad. Sci. USA 82:4172-4176. [2]

Seger, J. 1983. Conditional relatedness, recombination and the chromosome numbers of insects. In *Advances in Herpetology and Evolutionary Biology: Essays in Honor of Ernest E. Williams*, A. J. G. Rhodin and K. Miyata (eds.). Museum of Comparative Zoology, Cambridge, Massachusetts. [11]

Seger, J. and R. Trivers. 1986. Asymmetry in the evolution of female mating preferences. Nature 319:771-773. [16]

Seifert, H. S. and R. D. Porter. 1984a. Enhanced recombination between lambda plac5 and F42lac: Identification of cis- and trans-acting factors. Proc. Natl. Acad. Sci. USA 81:7500-7504. [2]

Seifert, H. S. and R. D. Porter. 1984b. Enhanced recombination between lambda-plac5 and mini-F-lac: The tra regulon is required for recombination enhancement. Molec. Gen. Genet. 193:269-274. [2]

Selander, R. K. and B. R. Levin. 1980. Genetic diversity and structure in populations of *Escherichia coli*. Science 210:545-547. [12]

Selander, R. K., R. M. NcKinneym, T. S. Whittam, W. F. Bibb, D. J. Brenner, F. S. Nolte and P. Patterson. 1985. Genetic structure of populations of *Legionella pneumophila*. J. Bact. 163:1021-1037. [12]

Selander, R. K. and T. S. Whittam. 1983. Protein polymorphism and the genetic structure of populations. In *Evolution of Genes and Proteins*, M. Nei and R. K. Koehn (eds.). Sinauer Associates, Sunderland, Massachusetts. [7]

Serrano, J. 1981. Male achiasmatic meiosis in *Caraboidea* [Coleoptera, Adephaga]. Genetica 57:131-137. [16]

Shapiro, J. A., (ed.). 1983. *Mobile Genetic Elements*. Academic Press, New York. [9]

Shapiro, J. A., S. L. Adhya and A. I. Bukhari. 1977. Introduction: New pathways in the evolution of chromosome structure. In *DNA Insertion Elements, Plasmids and Episomes*, A. I. Bukhari, J. A. Shapiro and S. L. Adhya (eds.). Cold Spring Harbor Press, New York. [2]

Shaw, D. D. 1972. Genetic and environmental components of chiasma control. II. The response to selection in *Schistocerca*. Chromosoma 37:297-308. [6]

Sher, A., R. Correa-Oliveira, P. Brindley and S. L. James. 1986. Selection of the host for resistance: Genetic control of protective immunity to schistosomes. In *Parasitology—Quo Vadit?*, Proceedings of the Sixth International Congress of Parasitology, M. J. Howell (ed.). Austral. Acad. Science, Canberra. [11]

Sherman, P. W. 1979. Insect chromosome numbers and eusociality. Amer. Natur. 113:925-935. [11]

Sherman, P. W., T. D. Seeley and H. K. Reeve. In press. Parasites, pathogens and polyandry in social Hymenoptera. Amer. Natur. [11]

Shields, W. M. 1979. Philopatry, inbreeding and the adaptive advantages of sex. Ph.D. dissertation, Ohio State University, Columbus. [15]

Shields, W. M. 1982a. *Philopatry, Inbreeding and the Evolution of Sex.* State University of New York Press, Albany. [1, 9, 13, 15]

Shields, W. M. 1982b. Inbreeding and the paradox of sex: A resolution. Evol. Theor. 5:245-279. [1, 15]

Shields, W. M. 1983. Optimal inbreeding and the evolution of philopatry. In *The Ecology of Animal Movement*, I.R. Swingland and P.J. Greenwood (eds.). Clarendon Press, Oxford. [15]

Shields, W. M. 1987. Dispersal and mating systems: Investigating their causal connections. In *Mammalian Dispersal Patterns: The Effects of Social Structure on Population Genetics*, B. D. Chepko-Sade and Z. T. Halpin (eds.). University of Chicago Press, Chicago. [15]

von Siebold, C. T. E. 1857. *On a True Parthenogenesis in Moths and Bees: A Contribution to the History of Reproduction in Animals.* John van Voorst, London. [1]

Siegel, R. W. 1967. Genetics of ageing and the life cycle of ciliates. In *Aspects of the Biology of Ageing*, H. W. Woolhouse (ed.). Soc. Exp. Biol. Symp. 21, Cambridge University Press, Cambridge. [3]

Simchen, G. and J. Stamberg. 1969. Genetic control of recombination in *Schizophyllum commune*: Specific and independent regulation of adjacent and nonadjacent chromosomal regions. Heredity 24:369-381. [6]

Simmons, G. M. 1986. Gonadal dysgenesis determinants in a natural population of *Drosophila melanogaster*. Genetics 114:897-918. [16]

Simpson, B. B. and J. L. Neff. 1983. Evolution and diversity of floral rewards. In *Handbook of Experimental Pollination Biology*, C. E. Jones and R. J. Little (eds.). Scientific and Academic Editions, New York. [14]

Slatkin, M. 1975. Gene flow and selection in a two-locus system. Genetics 81:787-802. [6]

Slilaty, S. N. and J. W. Little. 1987. Lysine-156 and serine-119 are required for LexA repressor cleavage: A possible mechanism. Proc. Natl. Acad. Sci. USA 84:3987-3991. [2]

Slobodchikoff, C. N. 1982. Why asexual reproduction?: Variation in populations of the parthenogenetic wasp, *Venturia canescens* (Hymenoptera: Ichneumonidae). Ann. Entomol. Soc. 76:23-29. [15]

Slobodkin, L. B. and A. Rapoport. 1974. An optimal strategy of evolution. Quart. Rev. Biol. 49:181-200. [15]

Smith, A. 1776. *An Inquiry Into the Nature and Causes of the Wealth of Nations* (2 Vols.). Strahan and Cadell, London. [1]

Smith, C. A. and W. E. Evenson. 1978. Energy distribution in reproductive structure of *Amaryllis*. Amer. J. Bot. 65:714-716. [14]

Smith, G. R. 1983a. Chi hot spots of generalized recombination. Cell 34:709-710. [2]

Smith, G. R. 1983b. General recombination. In *Lambda II*, R. W. Hendrix, J. W. Roberts, F. W. Stahl and R. A. Weisberg (eds.). Cold Spring Harbor Press, New York. [2, 3]

Smith, G. R. 1985. Site specific recombination. In *Genetics of Bacteria*, J. Scaife, D. Leach and A. Galizzi (eds.). Academic Press, New York. [12]

Smith, G. R., D. W. Schultz, A. F. Taylor and K. Triman. 1981. Chi sites RecBC enzyme and generalized recombination. Stadler Genet. Symp. 25-37. [2]

Smith, G. R., S. K. Amundsen, A. M. Chaudhury, K. C. Cheng, A. S. Ponticelli, C. M. Roberts, D. W. Schultz and A. F. Taylor. 1984. Roles of RecBC enzyme and chi sites in homologous recombination. Cold Spring Harbor Symp. Quant. Biol. 485-495. [2]

Smith, H. O., D. B. Danner and R. A. Deich. 1981. Genetic transformation. Annu. Rev. Biochem. 50:41-68. [12]

Snell, T. W. 1979. Intraspecific competition and population structure in rotifers. Ecology 60:494-502. [1]

Southwick, E. E. 1984. Photosynthate allocation to floral nectar: A neglected energy investment. Ecology 65:1775-1779. [14]

Spofford, J. B. 1969. Heterosis and the evolution of duplications. Amer. Natur. 103:407-432. [4]

Stahl, F. W. 1979. Special sites in generalized recombination. Annu. Rev. Genet. 13:7-24. [2, 3]

Stahl, F. W. and M. M. Stahl. 1977. Recombination pathway specificity of Chi. Genetics 86:715-725. [2]

Stahl, F. W., M. M. Stahl, R. E. Malone and J. M. Craseman. 1980. Directionality and nonreciprocicality of chi-mediated recombination in phage lambda. Genetics 94:235-248. [2]

Stanley, S. M. 1975. A theory of evolution above the species level. Proc. Natl. Acad. Sci. USA 72:646-650. [1]

Stanley, S. M. 1976. Clades verses clones in evolution: Why we have sex. Science 190:282-283. [1]

Stanley, S. M. 1978. Chronospecies' longevities, the origin of genera and the punctuational model of evolution. Paleobiology 4:26-40. [1]

Stasiak, A., A. Z. Stasiak and T. Koller. 1984. Visualization of RecA-DNA complexes involved in consecutive stages of an in vitro strand exchange reaction. Cold Spring Harbor Symp. Quant. Biol. 560-571. [2]

Stearns, S. C. 1985. The evolution of sex and the role of sex in evolution. Experientia 41:1231-1235. [1, 15]

Stebbins, G. L. 1950. *Variation and Evolution in Plants*. Columbia University Press, New York. [4]

Stebbins, G. L. 1960. The comparative evolution of genetic systems. In *Evolution After Darwin*, Vol. 1, S. Tax (ed.). University of Chicago Press, Chicago. [1]

Steenstrup, J. J. S. 1845. On the alternation of generations; or, the propagation and development of animals through alternate generations; a peculiar form of fostering the young in the lower classes of animals. Proc. Roy. Soc. London. [1]

Steinmetz, M., K. Minard, S. Horvath, J. McNichols, C. Wake, E. Long, B. Mach and L. Hood. 1982. A molecular map of the immune response region of the major histocompatibility complex of the mouse. Nature 300:35-42. [3]

Steinmetz, M., D. Stephen and K. Fischer-Lindahl. 1986. Gene organization and recombinational hot spots in the murine major histocompatibility complex. Cell 44:895-904. [3]

Stent, G. S. and R. Calendar. 1979. *Molecular Genetics: An Introductory Narrative*, 2nd Ed. W. H. Freeman, San Francisco. [12]

Stephenson, A. G. 1981. Flower and fruit abortion: Proximate causes and ultimate functions. Annu. Rev. Ecol. Syst. 12:253-279. [13]

Stephenson, A. G. and R. I. Bertin. 1983. Male competition, female choice and sexual selection in plants. In *Pollination Biology*, L. Real (ed.). Academic Press, New York. [13, 16]

Stephenson, A. G. and J. A. Winsor. 1986. *Lotus corniculatus* regulates offspring quality through selective fruit abortion. Evolution 40:453-458. [16]

Stewart, F. M. and B. R. Levin. 1977. The population biology of bacterial plasmids: A priori conditions for the existence of conjugationally trasmitted factors. Genetics 87:209-228. [9]

Stewart, F. M. and B. R. Levin. 1984. The population biology of bacterial viruses: Why be temperate? Theor. Pop. Biol. 26:93-117. [9]

Stewart, G. J. and C. A. Carlson. 1986. The biology of natural transformation. Annu. Rev. Microbiol. 40:211-235. [12]

Stimson, W. H., A. F. Strachan and A. Shepherd. 1979. Studies on the maternal immune response to placental antigens: Absence of a blocking factor from the blood of abortion-prone women. Brit. J. Obstet. Gynecol. 86:41-45. [13]

Strathmann, Richard. 1974. The spread of sibling larvae of sedentary invertebrates. Amer. Natur. 108:29-44. [17]

Strobeck, C. 1980. Heterozygosity of a neutral locus linked to a self-incompatibility locus or a balanced lethal. Evolution 34:779-788. [13]

Strobeck, C., J. Maynard Smith and B. Charlesworth. 1976. The effects of hitchhiking on a gene for recombination. Genetics 82:547-558. [1, 5, 6, 7, 10]

Sturgeon, K. B. 1979. Monoterpene variation in ponderosa pine xylem resin related to western pine beetle predation. Evolution 33:803-814. [11]

Sturtevant, A. H. 1915. No crossing over in the female of the silkworm moth. Amer. Natur. 49:42-44. [9]

Sturtevant, A. H. and K. Mather. 1938. The interrelations of inversions, heterosis and recombination. Amer. Natur. 72:447-452. [4, 5, 6, 7]

Suomalainen, E. 1966. Achiasmatische oogenese bei trichopteren. Chromosoma 18:201-207. [16]

Suomalainen, E., L. M. Cook and J. R. G. Turner. 1973. Achiasmatic oogenesis in the Heliconiine butterflies. Hereditas 74:302-304. [16]

Suomalainen, E., A. Saura and J. Lokki. 1976. Evolution of parthenogenetic insects. Evol. Biol. 9:209-257. [1]

Sutherland, G. 1985. The enigma of the fragile X chromosome. Trends in Genet. 1:108-112. [3]

Sved, J. A. 1968. The stability of linked systems of loci with a small population size. Genetics 59:543-563. [13]

Symington, L. S. and R. Kolodner. 1985. Partial purification of an enzyme from *Saccharomyces cerevisae* that cleaves Holliday junctions. Proc. Natl. Acad. Sci. USA 82:7247-7251. [2]

Szauter, P. 1984. An analysis of regional constraints on exchange in *Drosophila melanogaster* using recombination-defective meiotic mutants. Genetics 106:45-71. [6]

Szostak, J. W., T. L. Orr-Weaver, R. J. Rothstein and F. W. Stahl. 1983. The double-strand-break repair model for recombination. Cell 33:25-35. [2, 3, 4, 9]

Tanksley, S. D., D. Zamir and C. M. Rick. 1981. Evidence for extensive overlap of sporophytic and gametophytic gene expression in *Lycopersicon esculentum*. Science 213:453-455. [13, 16]

Taylor, A. and G. R. Smith. 1980. Unwinding and rewinding of DNA by the RecBC enzyme. Cell 22:447-457. [2]

Taylor, A. F., D. W. Schultz, A. S. Ponticelli and G. R. Smith. 1985. RecBC enzyme nicking at chi sites during DNA unwinding: Location and orientation-dependence of the cutting. Cell 41:153-163. [2]

Taylor, C. and W. P. Faulk. 1981. Prevention of recurrent abortion with leucocyte transfusions. Lancet ii:68-70. [13]

Taylor, P. D. and G. C. Williams. 1982. The lek paradox is not resolved. Theor. Pop. Biol. 22:392-409. [17]

Tazima, Y. 1964. *The Genetics of the Silkworm*. Prentice-Hall, Englewood Cliffs, N.J. [9]

Teague, R. 1976. A result on the selection of recombination altering mechanisms. J. Theor. Biol. 59:25-32. [6]

Telander-Muskavitch, K. M. and S. Linn. 1981. RecBC-like enzymes: Exonuclease V deoxyribonucleases. In *The Enzymes*, P. D. Boyer (ed.). Academic Press, New York. [2]

Temme, D. H. 1986. Seed size variability: A consequence of variable genetic quality among offspring? Evolution 40:414-417. [13]

Templeton, A. R. 1983. Natural and experimental parthenogenesis. In *The Genetics and Biology of Drosophila*, Vol. 3C, M. Ashburner, H. L. Carson and J. M. Thompson (eds.). Academic Press, New York. [7]

Templeton, A. R., H. Hemmer, G. Mace, U. S. Seal, W. M. Shields and D. S. Woodruff. 1986. Local adaptation, coadaptation and population boundaries. Zoo Biology 5:115-125. [15]

Ter-Avanesian, D. V. 1978. The effect of varying the number of pollen grains used in fertilization. Theor. Appl. Genet. 52:77-79. [13]

Tessman, E. S. and P. K. Peterson. 1985. Isolation of protease-proficient, recombinase-deficient *recA* mutants of *Escherichia coli* K12. J. Bacteriol. 163:688-695. [2]

Thompson, V. 1976. Does sex accelerate evolution? Evol. Theor. 1:131-156. [4]

Thomson, G. 1981. A review of theoretical aspects of HLA and disease associations. Theor. Pop. Biol. 20:168-208. [11, 13]

Thomson, G., W. Klitz, E. J. Louis, S. K. Lo, J. Bertrams, M. Baur and M. Neugbauer. In press. HLA and IDDM predisposition: New aspects. Genet. Epid. [13]

Thuriaux, P. 1977. Is recombination confined to structural genes of the eukaryotic chromosome? Nature 268:460-462. [7, 3]

Tilman, D. 1982. *Resource Competition and Community Structure*. Princeton University Press, Princeton. [8]

Tiwari, J. L. and P.I. Terasaki. 1985. *HLA and Disease Associations*. Springer-Verlag, New York. [13]

Tooby, J. 1982. Pathogens, polymorphism, and the evolution of sex. J. Theor. Biol. 97:557-576. [11]

Toussaint, A. 1985. Bacteriophage Mu and its use as a genetic tool. In *Genetics of Bacteria*. J. Scaife, D. Leach and A. Galizzi (eds.). Academic Press, New York. [12]

Tracey, M. L. and B. Dempsey. 1981. Recombination rate variability in *Drosophila melanogaster* females subjected to temperature stress. J. Hered. 72:427-428. [6]

Treco, D., Thomas, B. and N. Arnheim. 1985. Recombination hot spot in the human β globin gene cluster: Meiotic recombination of human DNA fragments in *Saccharomyces cerevisiae*. Mol. Cell. Biol. 5:2029-2038. [3]

Treisman, M. 1976. The evolution of sexual reproduction: A model which assumes individual selection. J. Theor. Biol. 60:421-431. [11]

Treisman, M. and R. Dawkins. 1976. The "cost of meiosis": Is there any? J. Theor. Biol. 63:479-484. [1, 14, 17]

Tremblay, C. and M. R. Rose. 1985. Population dynamics of gene transfer. Theor. Pop. Biol. 28:359-381. [9]

Trivers, R. L. 1972. Parental investment and sexual selection. In *Sexual Selection and the Descent of Man 1871-1971*, B. Campbell (ed.). Aldine Atherton, Chicago. [16]

Trivers, R. L. 1985. *Social Evolution*. Benjamin/Cummings, Menlo Park, California. [16]

Tucic, N., F. J. Ayala and D. Marinkovic. 1981. Correlation between recombination frequency and fitness in *Drosophila melanogaster*. Genetica 56:61-69. [16]

Turner, J. R. G. 1967a. On supergenes. I. The evolution of supergenes. Amer. Natur. 101:195-221. [6]

Turner, J. R. 1967b. Why does the genotype not congeal? Evolution 21:645-656. [1, 6, 10]

Turner, J. R. G. 1979. Genetic control of recombination in the silkworm. I. Multigenic control of chromosome 2. Heredity 43:273-293. [6]

Turner, J. R. G. and P. M. Shappard. 1975. Absence of crossing-over in female butterflies (*Heliconius*). Heredity 34(2):265-269. [16]

Uyenoyama, M. K. 1984. On the evolution of parthenogenesis: A genetic representation of "the cost of meiosis." Evolution 38:87-102. [1, 10, 11, 13, 15, 17]

Uyenoyama, M. K. 1985. On the evolution of parthenogenesis. II. Inbreeding and the "cost of meiosis." Evolution 39:1194-1206. [1, 13, 15]

Uyenoyama, M. K. 1986. Inbreeding and the "cost of meiosis:" The evolution of selfing in populations practicing biparental inbreeding. Evolution 20:388-404. [1, 13]

Uyenoyama, M. K. In press. Genetic transmission and the evolution of reproduction: The significance of parent-offspring relatedness to the "cost of meiosis." In *Meiosis*, P. B. Moens (ed.). Academic Press, New York. [1]

Uyenoyama, M. K. and J. Antonovics. 1986. The evolutionary dynamics of mixed mating systems: On the adaptive value of selfing and biparental inbreeding. In *Perspectives in Ethology*, Vol. 7, P. H. Klopfer and P. Bateson (eds.). Plenum, New York. [13]

Uyenoyama, M. K. and B. O. Bengtsson. 1982. Towards a genetic theory for the evolution of the sex ratio. III. Parental and sibling control of brood investment ratio under partial sib-mating. Theor. Pop. Biol. 22:43-68. [13]

Valentin, J. 1972. Effect of maternal age on recombination in X in *D. melanogaster*. Drosophila Info. Serv. 48-49. [16]

Valentin, J. 1973. Selection for altered recombination frequency in *Drosophila melanogaster*. Hereditas 74:295-297. [6]

Van Loenhoud, P. J. and H. Duyts. 1981. A comparative study of the germination ecology of some microspecies of *Taraxacum* Wigg. Acta Bot. Neerl. 30:161-182. [7]

Van Valen, Leigh. 1975. Group selection, sex, and fossils. Evolution 29:87-98. [17]

Ved Brat, S. V. 1966. Genetic systems in *Allium*. II. Sex differences in meiosis. Chrom. Today. 1:31-40. [16]

Vrijenhoek, R. C. 1979. Genetics of a sexually reproducing fish in a highly fluctuating environment. Amer. Natur. 113:17-29. [1]

Vrijenhoek, R. C. 1984. Ecological differentiation amoung clones: the frozen niche hypothesis. In *Population Biology and Evolution*, K. Woehrmann and V. Loschcke (eds.). Springer-Verlag, Heidelberg. [1]

Waddington, K. E. 1983. Pollen flow and optimal outcrossing distance. Amer. Natur. 122:147-151. [13]

Wakelin, D. 1985a. Genetic control of immunity to helminth infections. Parasitology Today 1:17-23. [11]

Wakelin, D. 1985b. Genetics, immunity and parasite survival. In *Ecology and Genetics of Host-Parasite Interactions*, D. Rollinson and R. M. Anderson (eds.). Academic Press, London. [11]

Walker, G. C. 1985. Inducible DNA repair systems. Annu. Rev. Biochem. 54:425-457. [2]

Walker, I. 1978. The evolution of sexual reproduction as a repair mechanism. I. A model for self-repair and its biological implications. Acta Biotheoretica 27:133-158. [15]

Walker, I. and R. M. Williams. 1976. The evolution of the cooperative group. Acta Biotheoretica 25:1-43. [15]

Wang, W. B. and E. S. Tessman. 1986. Location of functional regions of the *Escherichia coli* RecA protein by DNA sequence analysis of RecA protease-constitutive mutants. J. Bacteriol. 168:901-910. [2]

Warren, D. C. 1940. Crossing over and sex in the fowl. Amer. Natur. 74:93-95. [16]

Waser, N. M. and M. V. Price. 1983. Optimal and actual outcrossing in plants and the nature of plant-pollinator interaction. In *Handbook of Experimental Pollination Biology*, C. E. Jones and R. J. Little (eds.). Van Nostrand Reinhold, New York. [13]

Waser, N. M. and M. V. Price. 1985. Reciprocal transplant experiments with *Delphinium nelsoni* (Ranunculacae): Evidence for local adaptation. Amer. J. Bot. 72:1726-1732. [13]

Wassom, D. L. 1985. Genetic control of the host response to parasitic helminth infections. In *Genetic Control of Host Resistance to Infection and Malignancy*, E. Skamene (ed.). Alan R. Liss, New York. [11]

Watanabe, T. 1963. Episome-mediated transfer of drug resistance in Enterobacteriacae. VI. High frequency transfer system in *Escherichia coli*. J. Bacteriol. 85:788-749. [12]

Watson, I. D. and H. G. Callan. 1963. The form of bivalent chromosomes in newt oocytes at first metaphase of meiosis. Quart. J. Micros. 104:281-294. [16]

Watt, V. M., C. J. Ingels, M. S. Urdea and W. J. Rutter. 1985. Homology requirements for recombination in *Escherichia coli*. Proc. Natl. Acad. Sci. USA 82:4768-4772. [12]

Weinshall, D. 1986. Why is a two-environment system not rich enough to explain the evolution of sex? Amer. Natur. 128:736-750. [4, 11, 17]

Weir, B. S. and C. C. Cockerham. 1973. Mixed self and random mating at two loci. Genet. Res., Camb. 21:247-262. [13]

Weisberg, R. A. and A. Landy. 1983. Site-specific recombination in phage lambda. In *Lambda II*, R. W. Hendrix, J. W. Roberts, F. W. Stahl and R. A. Weisberg (eds.). Cold Spring Harbor Press, New York. [2]

Weismann, A. 1889. *Essays upon Heredity and Kindred Biological Problems*, translated by E. B. Poulton, S. Schonland and A. E. Shipley. Clarendon Press, Oxford. [8]

Weismann, A. 1891. *Essays Upon Heredity and Kindred Biological Problems*, 2nd Ed., Vols. I and II. Clarendon Press, Oxford. [1]

West, S. C., E. Cassuto and P. Howard-Flanders. 1982. Role of SSB protein in RecA promoted branch migration reactions. Molec. Gen. Genet. 186:333-338. [2]

West, S. C., E. Cassuto and P. Howard-Flanders. 1982. Postreplication repair in *E. coli*: Strand exchange reactions of gapped DNA by RecA protein. Molec. Gen. Genet. 187:209-217. [9]

West, S. C. and A. Korner. 1985. Cleavage of cruciform DNA structures by an activity from *Saccharomyces cerevisae*. Proc. Natl. Acad. Sci. USA 82:6445-6449. [2]

West, S. C. and J. W. Little. 1984. *P. mirabilis* RecA protein catalyses cleavage of *Escherichia coli* LexA protein and the lambda repressor in vitro. Molec. Gen. Genet. 194:111-113. [2]

Westergaard, M. 1958. The mechanism of sex determination in dioecious flowering plants. Adv. Genet. 9:217-281. [16]

Westoby, M. and B. Rice. 1982. Evolution of seed plants and inclusive fitness of plant tissues. Evolution 36:713-724. [13]

White, M. J. D. 1938. A new and anomalous type of meiosis in a mantid, *Callimantis antillarum* Saussure. Proc. Roy. Soc. London B 125[841]:517-523. [16]

White, M. J. D. 1945. *Animal Cytology and Evolution*. Cambridge University Press, Cambridge. [9, 16]

White, M. J. D. 1965. Chiasmatic and achismatic meiosis in African eumastacid grasshoppers. Chromosoma 16:271-307. [16]

White, M. J. D. 1973. *Animal Cytology and Evolution*, 3rd Ed. Cambridge University Press, New York. [4, 6, 9]

Whitehouse, H. L. K. 1982. *Genetic Recombination: Understanding the Mechanisms*. Wiley, New York. [2, 6, 9]

Whitehouse, H. L. K. and P. J. Hastings. 1965. The analysis of genetic recombination on the polaron hybrid DNA model. Genet. Res. 6:27-92. [3]

Whittaker, R. H. 1969. Evolution of diversity in plant communities. Brookhaven Symp. Biol. 22:178-196. [11]

Wiens, D. and B. A. Barlow. 1979. Translocation heterozygosity and the origin of dioecy in *Viscum.* Heredity 42:201-222. [16]

Willetts, N. S. 1985. Plasmids. In *Genetics of Bacteria,* J. Scaife, D. Leach and A. Galizzi (eds.). Academic Press, New York. [12]

Willetts, N. S., A. J. Clark and K. B. Low. 1969. Genetic location of certain mutations conferring recombination deficiency in *E. coli.* J. Bacteriol. 97:244-249. [2]

Willetts, N. S. and D. W. Mount. 1969. Genetic analysis of recombination deficient in *Escherichia coli* K12 carrying *rec* mutations cotransducible with thyA. J. Bacteriol. 100:923-934. [2]

Willetts, N. S. and R. Skurray. 1980. The conjugation system of F-like plasmids. Annu. Rev. Genet. 14:41-76. [9]

Willetts, N. and R. Skurray. 1986. Structure and function of the F factor and mechanism of conjugation.

Willetts, N. S. and B. M. Wilkins. 1984. Processing of plasmid DNA during bacterial conjugation. Microbiol. Revs. 48:24-41. [12]

Williams, G. C. 1957. Pleiotropy, natural selection and the evolution of senescence. Evolution 11:398-411. [1, 8]

Williams, G. C. 1966. *Adaptation and Natural Selection: A Critique of Some Current Evolutionary Thought.* Princeton University Press, Princeton. [1, 17]

Williams, G. C. 1971. Introduction. In *Group Selection,* G. C. Williams (ed.). Aldine Atherton, Chicago. [14]

Williams, G. C. 1975. Sex and evolution. In *Monographs in Population Biology,* Princeton University Press, Princeton. [1, 5, 6, 7, 10, 11, 15]

Williams, G. C. 1980. Kin selection and the paradox of sexuality. In *Sociobiology: Beyond Nature/ Nurture?,* G. W. Barlow and J. Silverberg (eds.). Westview, Boulder. [1, 15, 17]

Williams, G. C. 1985. A defense of reductionism in evolutionary biology. Oxford Surv. in Evol. Biol. 2:1-27. [17]

Williams, G. C. and J. B. Mitton. 1973. Why reproduce sexually? J. Theor. Biol. 39:545-554. [1, 5, 17]

Williams, R. M. and I. Walker. 1978. The evolution of sexual reproduction as a repair mechanism. II. Mathematical treatment of the wheel model and its significance for real systems. Acta Biotheoretica 27:159-184. [15]

Willing, R. P. and J. P. Mascarenhas. 1984. Analysis of the complexity and diversity of mRNAs from pollen and shoots of *Tradescantia.* Plant Physiol. 75:865-868. [13]

Willson, M. F. 1979. Sexual selection in plants. Amer. Natur. 113:777-790. [13]

Willson, M. F. 1983. *Plant Reproductive Ecology.* Wiley, New York. [13]

Willson, M. F. and N. Burley. 1983. *Mate Choice in Plants: Tactics, Mechanisms and Consequences.* Princeton University Press, Princeton. [13, 16]

Willson, M. F. and P. W. Price. 1977. The evolution of inflorescence size in *Asclepias* (Asclepiadacae). Evolution 31:495-511. [14]

Willson, M. F., L. J. Miller and B. J. Rathcke. 1979. Floral display in *Phlox* and *Geranium:* Adaptive aspects. Evolution 33:52-63. [14]

Wilson, D. S. 1980. *The Natural Selection of Populations and Communities.* Benjamin/Cummings, Menlo Park, California. [17]

Wilson, V. L. and P. A. Jones. 1983. DNA methylation decreases in ageing but not in immortal cells. Science 220:1055-1057. [3]

Winsor, J. A., L. E. Davis and A. G. Stephenson. In press. The relationship between pollen load and fruit maturation and its effect on offspring vigor in *Cucurbita pepo.* Amer. Natur. [16]

Witkin, E. M. 1976. Ultraviolet mutagenesis and inducible DNA repair in *Escherichia coli.* Bacteriol. Rev. 40:869-907. [2]

Wolfe, M. S. and J. A. Barrett. 1980. Can we lead the pathogen astray? Pl. Dis. 64:148-155. [11]

Wolfe, M. S., J. A. Barrett and J. E. E. Jenkins. 1981. The use of cultivar mixtures for disease control. In *Strategies for the Control of Cereal Disease,* J. F. Jenkyn and R. T. Plumb (eds.). Blackwell Scientific Publications, Oxford. [11]

Wright, M., G. Buttin and J. Hurwitz. 1971. The isolation and characterization from *Escherichia coli* of an adenosine triphosphate-dependent deoxyribonuclease directed by *rec*B, C genes. J. Biol. Chem. 246:6543-6555. [2]

Wright, S. 1921. Systems of mating. II. The effects of inbreeding on the genetic composition of a population. Genetics 6:124-143. [13]

Wright, S. 1931. *Evolution in Mendelian Populations*. Genetics 16:97-159. [7, 15]

Wright, S. 1932. The roles of mutation, inbreeding, crossbreeding and selection in evolution. Proc. 6th Inter. Cong. Genet. 1:356-366. [4]

Wright, S. 1935. The analysis of variance and the correlations between relatives with respect to deviations from an optimum. J. Genet. 30:243-256. [6]

Wright, S. 1968-1978. *Evolution and the Genetics of Populations*, 4 Vols. University of Chicago Press, Chicago. [1, 15]

Wright, S. 1982. The shifting balance theory and macroevolution. Annu. Rev. Genet. 16:1-19. [1, 4]

Wynne-Edwards, V. C. 1962. *Animal Dispersion in Relation to Social Behavior*. Oliver and Boyd, London. [1]

Yagi, Y. and D. B. Clewell. 1980. Recombination-deficient mutant of *Streptococcus faecalis*. J. Bacteriol. 143:966-970. [2]

Yamamoto, M. 1979. Interchromosomal effects of heterochromatic deletions on recombination in *Drosophila melanogaster*. Genetics 93:437-448. [6]

Yamamoto, M. and G. L. G. Miklos. 1978. Genetic studies on heterochromatin in *Drosophila melanogaster* and their implications for the functions of satellite DNA. Chromosoma 66:71-98. [6]

Yamamoto, T. 1961. Progenies of sex-reversal females mated with sex-reversal males in the Medeka, *Oryzias latipes*. J. Exp. Zool. 146:163-179. [16]

Yisraeli, J., R. S. Adelstein, D. Melloul, V. Nudel, D. Yaffe and H. Cedar. 1986. Muscle specific activation of a methylated chimeric actin gene. Cell 46:409-416. [3]

Yonesaki, T., Y. Ryo, T. Minagawa and H. Takahashi. 1985. Purification and some of the functions of the products of bacteriophage T4 recombination genes, *uvs*X and *uvs*Y. Eur. J. Biochem. 148:127-134. [2]

Young, J. P. W. 1981. Sib competition can favor sex in two ways. J. Theor. Biol. 88:755-756. [1]

Yu, P. 1972. Some host parasite genetic interaction models. Theor. Pop. Biol. 3:347-357. [11]

Zinder, N. 1985. The origin of sex: An argument. In *The Origin and Evolution of Sex*, H. O. Halvorson and A. Monroy (eds.). Alan R. Liss, New York. [10, 12]

Zinder, N. D. and J. Lederberg. 1952. Genetic exchange in *Salmonella*. J. Bact. 64:679-699. [12]

Zink, R. T., J. K. Engwall, J. L. McEvoy and A. K. Chatterjee. 1985. RecA is required in the induction of pectin lyase and carotovoricin in *Erwinia caratovora* (ssp. caratovora). J. Bacteriol. 164:390-396. [2]

Zinkernagel, R. M. and P. C. Doherty. 1977. Possible mechanisms of disease-susceptibility associated with major transplantation antigens. In *HLA and Disease*, J. Dausset and A. Svejgaard (eds.). Munksgaard, Copenhagen. [13]

Zuk, M. In press. The effects of gregarine parasites on spermatophore production in field crickets. Behav. Ecol. Sociobiol. [11]

Index